Loach on Loach

in the same series

WOODY ALLEN ON WOODY ALLEN edited by Stig Björkman
ALMODÓVAR ON ALMODÓVAR edited by Frédéric Strauss
ALTMAN ON ALTMAN edited by David Thompson
DANNY BOYLE in conversation with Amy Raphael
BURTON ON BURTON edited by Mark Salisbury
CASSAVETES ON CASSAVETES edited by Ray Carney
CRONENBERG ON CRONENBERG edited by Chris Rodley
DE TOTH ON DE TOTH edited by Anthony Slide
FELLINI ON FELLINI edited by Costanzo Costantini
GILLIAM ON GILLIAM edited by Ian Christie
HAWKS ON HAWKS edited by Joseph McBride
HERZOG ON HERZOG edited by Paul Cronin
HITCHCOCK ON HITCHCOCK edited by Sidney Gottlieb
KIEŚLOWSKI ON KIEŚLOWSKI edited by Danusia Stok
MIKE LEIGH ON MIKE LEIGH edited by Amy Raphael
LYNCH ON LYNCH edited by Chris Rodley
MALLE ON MALLE edited by Philip French
MINGHELLA ON MINGHELLA edited by Timothy Bricknell
POTTER ON POTTER edited by Graham Fuller
SAYLES ON SAYLES edited by Gavin Smith
SCHRADER ON SCHRADER edited by Kevin Jackson
SCORSESE ON SCORSESE edited by David Thompson and Ian Christie
SIRK ON SIRK conversations with Jon Halliday
TRIER ON VON TRIER edited by Stig Björkman

Loach on Loach

Edited by Graham Fuller

faber

This revised and updated edition first published in 2025
by Faber & Faber Limited
The Bindery, 51 Hatton Garden
London EC1N 8HN

Typeset by Ian Bahrami
Printed and bound by CPI Group (UK) Ltd, Croydon, CR0 4YY

All rights reserved
© Ken Loach, 1998, 2025
Commentary and Introductions © Graham Fuller, 1998, 2025
Photographs on pages 8, 17, 19, 30, 33, 41, 42, 45, 49, 51, 55, 59, 60, 62, 65, 67, 69, 93, 95, 102 (top), courtesy of BFI; on pages 25 and 29, courtesy of the BBC Photograph Library; on pages 102 (bottom), 103, 106, 109 (by Paul Chedlow), 115, 118, 122, 124 (top by Joss Barratt; bottom by Brennan Linsley), 125, 126, 127, 157, 160 (by Joss Barratt), courtesy of Parallax Pictures; on pages 164–385 (by Joss Barratt, except for page 209 by Merrick Morton), courtesy of Sixteen Films

The right of Ken Loach and Graham Fuller to be identified as authors of this work has been asserted in accordance with Section 77 of the Copyright, Designs and Patents Act 1988

A CIP record for this book
is available from the British Library

ISBN 978–0–571–38606–2

Printed and bound in the UK on FSC® certified paper in line with our continuing commitment to ethical business practices, sustainability and the environment.
For further information see faber.co.uk/environmental-policy

Our authorised representative in the EU for product safety is
Easy Access System Europe, Mustamäe tee 50, 10621 Tallinn, Estonia
gpsr.requests@easproject.com

2 4 6 8 10 9 7 5 3 1

Contents

Acknowledgements vii
Introduction by Graham Fuller ix

1 FIRST SHOTS 1
Oxford, the West End, *Z Cars*, *Diary of a Young Man*

2 PLAYS OF HOPE 10
Up the Junction, *The Coming Out Party*, *Cathy Come Home*,
In Two Minds, *The Golden Vision*, *The Big Flame*,
The Rank and File, and others

3 STRUGGLE 37
Poor Cow, *Kes*, *Family Life*, *Days of Hope*, *The Price of Coal*,
Black Jack, *The Gamekeeper*, *Looks and Smiles*, *Fatherland*

4 BLOCKADE 72
In Black and White, *A Question of Leadership*, *Which Side
Are You On?*, *Perdition*, *The Flickering Flame*

5 REJUVENATION 89
Hidden Agenda, *Riff-Raff*, *Raining Stones*, *Ladybird, Ladybird*,
Land and Freedom, *Carla's Song*, *My Name Is Joe*

6 SOME REFLECTIONS 129

7 LESSONS 133
More on *Perdition*; a new era

8 LOOKING TO SCOTLAND 144
*My Name Is Joe, Sweet Sixteen, Ae Fond Kiss,
Tickets, The Angels' Share*

9 IN THE AMERICAS 195
Bread and Roses, 11'09"01 – September 11

10 IRELAND'S MANACLES 216
The Wind That Shakes the Barley, Jimmy's Hall

11 PERFIDIOUS ALBION 251
The Navigators, It's a Free World . . ., Route Irish

12 THE PEOPLE'S GAME 278
*Looking for Eric, Another City: A Week in the Life
of Bath's Football Club*

13 LABOUR GAINS AND PAINS 297
The Spirit of '45, Clement Attlee, Aneurin Bevan,
Tony Benn, Jeremy Corbyn, Keir Starmer

14 THE NORTH-EASTERN TRILOGY 311
I, Daniel Blake, Sorry We Missed You, The Old Oak

15 REBECCA O'BRIEN 360
Interview with Loach's producer partner at Sixteen Films

16 PAUL LAVERTY 378
Interview with Loach's long-time screenwriter

17 CONCLUSION 401

Filmography 405
Bibliography 443
A Note on the Editor 448
Index 449

Acknowledgements

Loach on Loach presents interviews with Ken Loach that were conducted over a period of thirty-one years. Those published in the 1998 edition took place on 18 January 1993 (when Ken was in Los Angeles); 27 February 1996 (New York); 22 and 23 August 1996 (Liverpool and London); and 25 November 1997 (London). We did the first and last interviews on the phone, the rest in person. The interviews added for this second edition occurred on 11, 12 and 18 May and 6 September 2023, and on 3 March and 3 April 2024. The May talks in London were marathon in-person sessions; we did the others via Zoom. Sincere thanks to Ken for these illuminating (and, frankly, unforgettable) conversations and for his participation in this project over the years.

The excerpted interview with Jim Allen was done at his Manchester home on 25 August 1997; Jim, who died in 1999, leaves a vivid memory. The Zoom interviews with Rebecca O'Brien (who was in London) took place on 20 September and 3 October 2023; the Zoom interview with Paul Laverty (who was shivering in Edinburgh) was on 23 April 2024. My gratitude to Rebecca and Paul for sharing their stories, insights and reflections, and for their email correspondence. Emma Lawson, Ken's assistant at Sixteen Films, proved an invaluable ally. Thanks to her for her help, and to her colleague Naomi Smith for locating a screener of *Another City*. Anne Gartside at StudioCanal kindly arranged a screening of *The Old Oak*.

Walter Donohoe at Faber commissioned the first edition; Mattia Visani of Cue Press in Bologna initiated and commissioned the second. I am indebted to both for their unwavering support, passion for the films and saint-like patience. Thanks also to Faber's Louise

Brice, Jennifer Shelton and Anne Owen, to Ian Bahrami for his suggestions and impeccable copy-editing, and to Mark Bolland for his eagle-eyed proofreading. Melanie Gee meticulously compiled the index.

The commentaries on *Sorry We Missed You* and *The Old Oak* in Chapter 14 originated in reviews that I wrote for *Cineaste*; I am grateful to the magazine's editor-in-chief, Gary Crowdus, and reviews editor, Cindy Lucia, for letting me adapt those pieces here. The spring 2024 Ken Loach retrospective at Manhattan's Film Forum couldn't have been timelier: thank you, Bruce Goldstein, Mike Maggiore, Andrea Torres, Adam Walker and Stephanie Gross. I received research help from the staff in the reference section of the New York Public Library at 42nd Street in Manhattan, Einde O'Callaghan, Aaron Nolan of Connolly Books (connollybooks.org) in Dublin, and the labour historian Conor McCabe, editor of *The Lost & Early Writings of James Connolly 1889–1898* (Iskra Books, 2024).

The Old Oak shows us that it takes a village. This book's villagers are Graham Rickson, Claire Millar, Annette Kennerley, Ray Fuller (1929–2008), Mary Smith, Nigel and Sarah Strongitharm – and, above all, Katrina and Victoria Fuller, who enabled the writing and editing of it.

Introduction

'If we had succeeded here – and we could have done –
we would have changed the world.'
David Carr in *Land and Freedom*

When Ken Loach was persuaded to become involved in this project in 1996, he said, 'It's a bit egotistical, isn't it? I can't imagine anyone wants to hear me waffling on.' In its self-effacement, it was a characteristically Loachian comment, and the one, above all others, that I most vehemently disagreed with during the several meetings that enabled *Loach on Loach* to come into being. For there were pressing reasons why a personal account by Loach of his career should become a matter of record. First of all, there is no biography of Loach and only one book of commentary on his work as a film-maker in the English language.* Second, the social imperatives of Loach's work mean it is in danger of becoming the intellectual property of a particular branch of film studies, which has a tendency to obfuscate the spirit in which his TV plays and films were made; Loach's accessible conversation in the following pages reminds us that his prime concern is people, not rhetoric or ideology, no matter that his work is rooted in political struggle. Third, Loach has been scandalously neglected in terms of his craft as a director, on which, of course, the ideas in his films depend for their lucidity. How Loach and his collaborators made their early television plays and how, thirty years later, they make their feature films are central to this book.

Loach is a naturally modest man. Indeed, he is a walking oxymoron: a film director apparently without ego. Cinematographer Chris Menges may have had Loach's unusual combination of

---

* Since this was written in 1998, five English-language and many European-language books about Loach and his films have been published. See Bibliography, pp. 444–5.

gentleness, steel and purpose in mind when he said, 'Ken is the man I admire most.'* Of the legions of directors who have addressed my tape-recorder over the years, Loach has been the least directorly in manner, the one least interested in attaching cosmic significance to the profession. The point would not be worth making except that it's germane both to Loach's approach to making his films and their dogged insistence on a democratic, egalitarian way of life. Says Loach, 'We are all equally important, and drama is not the preserve of the middle class.' His TV dramas and documentaries and his feature films cling to that thread through thick and thin, seeking to draw attention to situations where people routinely undercut or actually destroy the equality, liberty and livelihoods of others – in the workplace, in the home and in society at large.

It may, then, be heretical to suggest it, but Loach is the single most important – by which I mean urgent – voice in British film and TV of the last third of the century. That's not to slight his crucial collaborators, who include writers Nell Dunn, Jeremy Sandford, Neville Smith, Jim Allen, Barry Hines, Bill Jesse, Rona Munro and Paul Laverty; producers Tony Garnett, Rebecca O'Brien and Sally Hibbin; script editor Roger Smith; cinematographers Tony Imi, Chris Menges and Barry Ackroyd; and such diverse and inspired actors as Carol White, Bill Dean, Peter Kerrigan, Ken Jones, David Bradley, Sandy Ratcliff, Grace Cave, Robert Carlyle, Ricky Tomlinson and Crissy Rock. But Loach, of course, is the common denominator in the works he has signed and his is the unifying vision we are concerned with here.

Loach's work is exemplary on several fronts: as a thorn in the side of those opposed to political and social change, as a repository of humanism, as the spirit of independent cinema in a country that doesn't really have one, and simply in terms of evolving, innovatory technique. He is really the only contemporary world-class filmmaker spanning cinema and television, fiction and documentary, who prioritizes polemics over commercial needs every time out. And of the angry young men of the Left who emerged from the BBC in the 1960s, Loach is the one who has most consistently stuck to the task of using film as a means of dissent in a world in which it's axiomatic that people in power will exploit and betray those who aren't.

* Quoted in David Chell, *Moviemakers at Work* (Microsoft Press, 1987).

Perhaps the most alarming revelation to have emerged from his films over the years, though, is the recognition that the betrayal and disenfranchisement of working-class people come, invariably, at the hands of those who are supposed to protect and support their interests: the social services who take Cathy's children away from her in *Cathy Come Home* and Maggie's from her in *Ladybird, Ladybird*; the mothers who batter away at their daughters' self-esteem in *In Two Minds* and *Family Life*; the mother who neglects Billy and the brother who kills his kestrel in *Kes*; the trade union officials who sell out their members in *The Big Flame*, *The Rank and File* and the banned documentary series *Questions of Leadership*; the steelworker turned gamekeeper who breeds birds for the idle rich to kill in *The Gamekeeper*; the British forces of law and order who harass the Irish or Northern Irish population or shoot to kill in *Days of Hope*, the documentary short *Time to Go* and *Hidden Agenda*; the communists who doom the efforts of the POUM militia group in the Spanish Civil War in *Land and Freedom*; and so on. Screenwriting theory holds that the greatest opponent is the most intimate opponent: time and again, Loach's dramas, whether true or fictional, bear out that notion in its full, tragic complexity.

Loach's career falls into four distinct phases, each of which roughly corresponds to the four decades in which he has been active: the fruitful *Wednesday Play* era (the 1960s); the foray into feature films and longer television dramas (the 1970s); the documentary period when Loach's attempts to tackle Thatcherism were throttled by censorship (the 1980s); and the mature feature film era (the 1990s). After some experiments in Brechtian non-naturalism in the mid-1960s, Loach gravitated towards a naturalistic, observational style that seeks to replicate life as it actually is. The *cinéma vérité* quality of his films is crucial to their explication of political and social dynamics. It is as if he recognized that, stylistically as well as morally, 'the truth will set you free'. In a filmic tradition that enfolds the British kitchen sink school and the Czech New Wave, the French youth cinema of the late 1990s and Zhang Yimou's *The Story of Qiu Ju*, Loach is the master of what Deborah Knight describes as 'critical realism'* – experimental naturalism in the service of social

---

* George McKnight (ed.), *Agent of Challenge and Defiance: The Films of Ken Loach* (Flicks Books, 1997), p. 68.

criticism, as derived from Emile Zola's manifesto of literary naturalism. In Loach's work, this is illustrated by a downbeat *mise-en-scène* with images of social decay and malaise, and unsentimental stories about ordinary, unheroic working-class people doing what little they can to make ends meet and make life tolerable in the face of faceless institutional and capitalistic oppression: the uncaring society of Thatcher and post-Thatcher Britain in *Looks and Smiles*, *Riff-Raff*, *Raining Stones* and *Ladybird, Ladybird*, which extends back to First World War England and Ireland in *Days of Hope*, forward to the inner-city Glasgow of Tony Blair's Britain of the late 1990s in *My Name Is Joe*, and beyond to the Popular Army shooting a Spanish militiawoman in the back in *Land and Freedom* and Contra atrocities in Nicaragua in *Carla's Song*.

Given Loach's ethical decision to paint life as it is and to refuse the seductions of stylization or the placebos and panaceas of happy endings, the world his films describe is not a pretty one or one that offers much hope of resolution; this has cost them wider commercial acceptance. It is a world in which the struggle goes on. Yet the idea that Loach's films are depressive or ultimately forlorn is a fundamental misconception. Although hope is also betrayed in them with familiar regularity, hope has a habit of resurfacing, for Loach is, quietly, a psychological realist, too. *Poor Cow's* Joy will drift along having affairs, watching her son grow until he's old enough to go on the dole. Bob finally gets his daughter a communion dress in *Raining Stones*. *Ladybird, Ladybird*'s Maggie and Jorge will keep trying to put a family together. David's granddaughter carries the torch lit in pre-Franco Spain in modern Liverpool in *Land and Freedom*; the dockers of the same city in *The Big Flame* continue to fight casualization in *The Flickering Flame*. (One only despairs for the offspring of the Everton supporters of *The Golden Vision*.)

Sometimes, if hope evaporates for Loach's protagonists – Billy in *Kes*, Janice in *Family Life* – the point is made during the course of the film that society must begin to take responsibility for its ills and inequalities. And if the struggles in Loach's films seem endless, there is, as in life, alleviation in the shape of communal rituals and moments of self-actualization: the flirty, energized pub life and camaraderie of women factory workers in *Up the Junction*; Joy and her lover Dave escaping the slums for a few days in the country; Janice and her boyfriend going for a spin around town;

Billy gaining the respect of his class by describing how he trains his kestrel; Maggie singing in a pub – and Susan trying to in *Riff-Raff*; Bob and his mate Tommy chasing a sheep on a Lancashire moor and stealing turf from the Conservative Party bowling green in *Raining Stones*. The zest of people striving to change their lives for the better is captured in the to-and-fro debates of the mobilized workers in *The Big Flame* and *The Rank and File* and those of the collectivizing villagers of *Land and Freedom* and *Carla's Song*. As much as Loach's films are about the particular problems of the disenfranchised, they are also a celebration of the business of living, wherein lies their great, abiding humanism.

Although *Land and Freedom* and *Carla's Song* broadened the international range of Loach's work, its greatest legacy may be as a mirror to Britain between 1965 and the end of the century – although this is a premature judgement since Loach is still out there in the field. Certainly, no other film-maker has documented the period so rigorously, passionately and prolifically. Whether his films have been widely seen or censored, they have drawn attention to a spectrum of social evils: anti-abortionism, homelessness, unsafe working conditions, unemployment, unfair wages, the inadequacy of social services and mental healthcare. Political evils, too: imperialism, fascism (the police brutality towards striking miners in *Which Side Are You On?* echoes the suppression of the POUM in *Land and Freedom*) and the erosion of democracy in all its forms.

Loach has, additionally, been influential as a film-maker. In 1997 alone, the diaspora of Loach's cinema included *Brassed Off*, *Under the Skin*, *Nil by Mouth*, *TwentyFourSeven* and *The Full Monty* – the latter social-realist comedy hugely indebted to *Riff-Raff*. Among directors working exclusively on low budgets, only John Cassavetes and Eric Rohmer have achieved as much. I will go further and say that if British cinema has ever produced a Renoir it is Ken Loach. It should feel lucky it has him, as should we all, for true voices of dissent are seldom heard these days.

Graham Fuller, June 1998

INTRODUCTION TO THE SECOND EDITION

Loach had recently completed *My Name Is Joe* (1998) when the first set of interviews for this book took place. Though I subsequently interviewed him about *Bread and Roses* (2000), *The Wind That Shakes the Barley* (2006) and *The Angels' Share* (2012) for newspaper articles, twenty-five years passed before we sat down in May 2023 to begin the interviews comprising Chapter 7 onwards.

Since *My Name Is Joe*, Loach has directed thirteen full-length fiction films, three short fiction films for inclusion in anthology projects and three documentaries, including the full-length *The Spirit of '45* (2013). With the exception of *The Navigators* (2001), written by Rob Dawber, all the fiction films and both shorts were written by Paul Laverty. That their seventeen collaborations, beginning with *Carla's Song* (1996), were released in cinemas in the space of twenty-seven years is a modern film-making phenomenon, not least because Britain is inhospitable ground for films that are so critical of its institutions. It was made possible by the endlessly resourceful Rebecca O'Brien, who – having co-produced *Hidden Agenda* (1990) – produced all of Loach's films, excepting *Carla's Song*, from *Land and Freedom* (1995) onwards. In this edition, interviews with Laverty and O'Brien supplement the interviews with Loach that (adding to the originals) parse the making and intentions of each film he directed between 1998 and 2023, analyse the social and political developments that prompted them, and examine the creative methods that make them such distinct works of social realism. If aspiring directors are prepared to sift through the pages, they will find among them an informal manual on how to make films that replicate real life.

Critical assessments of Loach's cinema have proliferated since the 1998 edition was published. British film scholars Jacob Leigh, John Hill, David Archibald and David Forrest have written books on it, and many articles have appeared in academic journals. David Hayward authored an accessible biographical study. In-depth features and reviews have appeared in such leading English-language film magazines as *Cineaste* and *Sight and Sound*. Though the academic work is rigorous, its limited audience means it scarcely buffers the noisy and often vicious (at best, damning-with-faint-praise) critiques written by the reviewers of right-leaning newspapers, who are invariably in attack mode before they enter the screening rooms. Some establishment commentators have been known to savage the films, or Loach personally, without seeing them, as was the case with *The Wind That Shakes the Barley*.

There has also emerged a tendency, among even liberally minded critics, to fault Loach's films because they are 'didactic' (more accurately, they are illustrative) and don't conform to journalistic standards of so-called objectivity – as if film reviewing itself is an activity devoid of personal biases and tastes. Except when portraying malefactors like gangsters and fascists, Loach and Laverty have, in fact, scrupulously represented the cases of all the main characters in their films. The otherwise self-sacrificing Rosa betrays the Justice for Janitors movement in *Bread and Roses* (2000) because losing her cleaning job would prevent her from paying her sick husband's medical bills, which she can meet only by also working as a prostitute. Father Sheridan, the puritanical priest who supports the landed gentry over the poor farming families they've evicted in *Jimmy's Hall* (2014), gets a fair hearing and comes across as a shrewd and intelligent, if wrong-headed, antagonist of Jimmy Gralton, whose integrity he respects. The contract-hungry delivery company's boss Maloney in *Sorry We Missed You* (2019) and the embittered men who resent the locating of Syrian refugees in their ailing former pit village in *The Old Oak* (2023) get to justify their positions, if not their actions. Time and again in my conversations with Loach, we arrived at Jean Renoir's dictum (sometimes phrased differently) that 'unfortunately, everyone has their reasons'; Loach, Laverty and the films' other writers let everyone explain those reasons.

In *The Wind That Shakes the Barley*, the Black and Tans' brutal treatment of Irish civilians, which so incensed those conservative reviewers who did see the film, is explained by a rattled English lieutenant as the inevitable psychological reaction of soldiers dehumanized by their experiences on the Western Front. 'What do you fucking well expect?' he snaps at the captured IRA rebel Damien O'Donovan. 'These men fought at the Somme, up to their necks in vomit, in filthy trenches, while their friends got blown apart in front of their eyes!' Loach has said that 'balance' is irrelevant to the film because, as Damien reminds the officer, the British are maintaining their imperial presence in Ireland despite the mandate of the democratically elected Sinn Féin party 'for an Irish Republic separate from Great Britain'.

Yet *The Wind That Shakes the Barley* doesn't flinch from depicting Damien's self-brutalizing execution of a young friend he's known all his life for betraying the IRA, or the IRA flying column's slaughter of occupying soldiers, as in the recreation of an ambush like that of 28 November 1920, when seventeen British Auxiliaries were killed at Kilmichael, which was a reprisal for the Croke Park massacre on Bloody Sunday (itself a reprisal) a week before. It's true that Loach does not show the IRA volunteers finishing off wounded Auxiliaries, as the real volunteers were apparently ordered to by their leader, Tom Barry, in case the wounded had falsely surrendered with the intention of shooting their captors.* Instead of point-blank shootings, Loach, averse to graphic violence and its effects, shows how traumatized some of the volunteers are by their actions. The Irish historian John Dorney has observed: 'We will never know exactly what happened at Kilmichael. But because of its symbolic importance, and because it can be used to show that the IRA were either brave and skilful soldiers, or according to taste, cowardly and bloody terrorists, we may expect it will be argued about for many years to come.'†

The interviews in the first edition of *Loach on Loach* touched on how the films – in the name of protecting ordinary people and enabling them to work for a decent standard of living – integrate and reflect the Marxist analysis Loach made in the 1960s in response to the failure of Harold Wilson's Labour government to support its working-class constituency. Hopefully, the second edition's longer interviews and more detailed descriptions of the films, beginning with *My Name Is Joe*, strengthen that interpretation. Yet they should also remind us that the wellspring of the films, and of Loach's politics, is their galvanizing empathy for workers who have been profited from, endangered, eliminated, robbed of their livelihoods, unhoused, colonized, exiled and (as shown by the films set in deindustrialized Scotland and the English north-east)

---

* One Auxiliary who escaped the ambush was caught by the volunteers and executed.
† 'Today in Irish History, November 28 1920 – The Kilmichael Ambush', theirishstory.com, 28 November 2014.

programmatically marginalized and impoverished. There are also the films that express outrage on behalf of people who have been tortured and murdered by right-wing counter-revolutionary or imperial forces: *Hidden Agenda*, *Land and Freedom*, *Carla's Song*, the devastating Loach–Laverty short that forms part of *11'09"01 – September 11* (2002), *The Wind That Shakes the Barley*, *Route Irish* (2010).

Through gutsy debates and arguments, the films champion common ownership and explain the necessity for workers to organize and engage in the political struggle to overturn exploitation by bosses whose profits depend on underpaying them, denying them sickness and holiday pay, or 'rationalizing' them – precisely the strategy that bred casualization and the gig economy. The potential for revolutionary change is glimpsed (even as its supporters are being sold out) in *Days of Hope* (1975), *Land and Freedom*, *Carla's Song* and *The Wind That Shakes the Barley*.

'Marxist' is a loaded term in Western political discourse, thanks to the threat it poses to amassing private wealth and its corruption by Stalinism, which Loach and Jim Allen demonstrate in *Land and Freedom*. The same goes for 'militant' and 'radical', descriptors that are typically hauled out whenever a Loach film needs reviewing. Such labelling conveniently sidesteps the passionate humanism behind the films' politics. Their bones are solidarity, community spirit, collective action, teamwork; kindness, compassion, helping, sharing; the resistance to ruling-class oppression; and not forgetting warmth, decency and humour. The paranoid message that Loach's opponents try to propagate is that the films are nothing but hardline socialist tracts. In truth, they show, more than the work of any other major film-maker, how we should live in the world if people are to endure without fear, hunger and despair.

Graham Fuller, May 2025

CHAPTER 1

First Shots

Oxford, the West End, *Z Cars*, *Diary of a Young Man*

Kenneth Loach was born in Nuneaton, Warwickshire, on 17 June 1936. He attended King Edward VI Grammar School in Nuneaton and, following two years of National Service, entered St Peter's Hall, Oxford, as a law student. While at university, he served as president of the Oxford University Dramatic Society and secretary of the Experimental Theatre Club. He acted in repertory and briefly in the West End, and in 1961 joined Northampton Repertory Theatre as an assistant director on a sponsorship from ABC TV. In 1963, when the BBC was gearing up to launch its second channel, Loach was recruited as a trainee television director.

He made his debut on a half-hour domestic drama called *Catherine* (1964), written by Roger Smith and featuring Loach's future producer, Tony Garnett, in a leading role. Loach next directed three fifty-minute episodes of *Z Cars*, the famously 'gritty', Merseyside-based police series about the detectives, desk officers and patrol car men of Newtown CID, which had been airing since January 1962. Loach was then entrusted to direct three of the six parts of *Diary of a Young Man* (1964). Written by *Z Cars* creators Troy Kennedy Martin and John McGrath, this was the modish saga of two naïve young northern men adrift in London on the cusp of the swinging sixties. Mixing stills, voice-overs, direct address to the camera, and location and studio footage with 'live' studio material, the series was groundbreaking in its day as an abrasive progenitor of non-naturalism in studio-based television plays. Loach was inspired by the experience and incorporated some of Martin and McGrath's methods into his early *Wednesday Plays*, although non-naturalism was not, for him, the way ahead.

GRAHAM FULLER: *You would have been three when the Second World War broke out, nine when it ended. Do you have specific memories of it?*

KEN LOACH: Yes. Thinking about it now brings back the air raids to me very vividly. Where I lived, Nuneaton, isn't far from Coventry, and so we got some of the fallout when Coventry was bombed. We spent a lot of nights in the Anderson shelter next door. There'd be cups of tea and the air-raid wardens would call around every now and then and bring me bits of shrapnel, which, of course, I collected. It was all very exciting for a small child.

Eventually, when the raids got bad, my mother and I – I was an only child – went to stay with an aunt in Devonshire. But the street in Exeter where we stayed was heavily bombed and several people were killed. We were lucky to escape; the windows of our house blew in and there was terrible damage. There was obviously no point staying in Devon so we went home after a week or two. I remember we took a night-time trip from Devon to Somerset to get away, and that was thrilling for a six-year-old.

Did you have any inklings in your teen years that you would become interested in cinema?

No, but I was fanatical about the theatre from as early as I can remember. I was especially excited by Shakespeare. I'm sure I didn't understand it particularly well, but I loved the language. My other passion was reading history, admittedly at a fairly anecdotal level. I just enjoyed the sense of the past: I would visit old churches and photograph monuments and collect mementoes. It was an intense source of interest and delight. We lived only thirty miles from Stratford-upon-Avon, and when I was in my middle teens we would cycle over to Stratford to see an afternoon performance of Shakespeare, or even an evening performance, getting home at two o'clock in the morning. By then I was desperate to be an actor.

Do you remember your first movie-going experiences?

Not specifically. Nuneaton was a very ordinary industrial town of about 60,000 or 70,000 people. It had four cinemas; one of them, the Hippodrome, showed Continental, usually X-rated films, and I used to go to see those. I don't remember much about them, except that Italian and French films were generally more interesting than American films. I don't recall any of the British films I saw.

In the past, one of the things that you've said was significant to your development was that your father was a wage-earner. Can you explain what you meant by that?

My father was like everybody else's father, like our house was like everybody else's house and our family was like everybody else's family. He was an electrician who became the foreman in charge of maintenance at the factory where he worked, the Alfred Herbert Machine Tool Factory in Coventry; in its heyday I think it was the biggest in the country. He was always quite determined not to be on the staff, as they called it, and I never quite knew why that was. I think he felt he was better off getting his wage weekly and, I guess, managing his money that way. But I don't think I meant more than that when I said he was a wage-earner.

Were your parents political at all?

No. I think my father might have voted Conservative if he had been, although maybe not towards the end of his life. He died twenty years ago; my mother's still alive and very active and tires me out. I think I probably reacted against my father's being non-political and a *Daily Express* reader when I was a student. It was then that I developed an interest in seeing things from another point of view.

You did your National Service in the Royal Air Force before you went up to Oxford. How did that affect you?

I didn't mind it much at the time. In retrospect, I think it killed off any lingering possibility of my having an academic career because two years in the RAF just destroyed my capacity for solitary work. I was a typist in the office of the equipment section. I volunteered to go anywhere abroad. There was another lad I worked with who was a bit older than me and was married and had a child. He asked if he could stay in England, but they sent him to Hong Kong and me to Nottingham. It was sheer perversity. I was in Nottingham for two years, but there was nothing in the RAF that excited my interest so I started doing amateur theatre. That's when the bug really bit. I lived out of the camp illegally for three months at one point and would get the first bus every morning; reveille would be at six. It was a daft time really. Once I got to Oxford to read law, it took me a long time to get into the idea of studying because of that two-year break.

Did you study law with the intention of eventually practising it?

I had a fanciful idea of what the law was, really. It was all about becoming one of the luminaries of the bar like Marshall Hall. It soon became clear that I wasn't going to be a lawyer of any kind, so it wasn't long before I got sidetracked by theatre.

I just had a ball, an absolutely glorious time at Oxford. I spent all my time acting in plays and directing them, too many of them. I was threatened with being sent down at one stage – quite rightly. After two years of National Service, it was like being let out of school. Suddenly you're in this magnificent city with all these opportunities. But National Service also taught me to realize that, as a student at Oxford, I was extremely privileged. To be in that place at that time was unbelievable good fortune, so I made the most of it.

Have you ever regretted not becoming a lawyer?

There was a period about ten years ago when I got that feeling you get every now and then that the business you're in is not really a fit one for a grown-up. As a film-maker, you're forever involved in things that constantly inflate their own importance. I felt I would have had a far more satisfactory life if I'd been a lawyer because at least then I'd have had some relationship with people that would have made a difference to their lives. By comparison, film-making is an indulgent activity.

I'd say that's true of most commercial film-making, but virtually all of the plays and films you've made have had social or political content.

Maybe. It's just that every now and then you get a sense of dissatisfaction with what you've done with your allotted span and you think you'd have been better off doing something else.

Going back to Oxford and the 1950s, do you consider that you were part of the meritocracy of that time?

Yes. There were a lot of public-school boys there, of course, and it wasn't that remarkable to them that they'd be going to Oxford or Cambridge. But most of the people at my college were the first people from their families ever to go to any university, especially those of us from working families.

Was it at Oxford that you discovered the writings of the Angry Young Men?

Only John Osborne at that point. I didn't get to know most of the novelists until after I'd left university; in fact, I didn't read much at all at Oxford. It's often the case that you don't start reading until it's no longer expected. Brecht was fashionable, however, and I got to know his work a bit.

Did you discover cinema at Oxford?

No. That was still to come. I saw some European films in the one cinema in Oxford that would show them. I didn't really start to enjoy cinema until I was working in television, and I certainly didn't relate to it or imagine that I would be a part of it or have anything to do with it. It was still just a way to fill two hours.

What did you do immediately after graduation?

I did various jobs. I tried to start a theatre group in Bedford with a friend called Bill Hays, who later became a television director. We had some crazy idea that it would work, but it didn't and we ended up teaching at a junior school for a term. Then, hard as it is to believe, I got a job as an understudy in a West End revue called *One Over the Eight*. It was written by Peter Cook, whom I didn't know at all. Funnily enough, I'd been in a revue at Oxford with his future partner, Dudley Moore, who wrote the music for some of the shows we put on.

One Over the Eight had a very talented West End company. It starred Kenneth Williams, Lance Percival, Sheila Hancock and Jill Gascoine, who was a dancer and has since become a well-known actress. The producer had seen me in a show at Oxford and offered me this job, which I was totally unfit to do. On my first day, I opened the door into the rehearsal room very gingerly, hoping that nobody would notice me, and sidled along to the nearest bench I could find. Sheila Hancock came up to me and said, 'Who are you?' And I said, 'I'm the understudy.' And she said, 'Have they measured you for my frocks?' I said, 'What do you mean?' She said, 'They're terribly mean, you know. They only have one understudy for all the parts.' And for a moment I had a flicker of uncertainty. Actually, I was understudying Lance, who was the second lead.

Did you go on?

Not to do that part, mercifully, but I was in one of the sketches every night. We'd have an understudy rehearsal every Thursday morning. The worst part of it was that I was supposed to dance, which was obviously out of the question. Jill, who was slightly bigger than she is now, would gallop across the stage at me, and I was supposed to grab her round the waist, turn her 360 degrees, and lift her into the air and put her down feet first in front of me. I had no chance of ever accomplishing this. Every Thursday morning, her head would end up on the floor with her legs flailing around in front of my face. It was a disaster. Fortunately, I never had to do it in front of an audience.

In 1961, you found your way to Northampton Repertory Theatre, where you directed murder mysteries.

Yes, it was a training course for six assistant directors sponsored by ABC. At Northampton Rep, most of the plays were directed by Lionel Hamilton, but he wasn't particularly fond of doing murder mysteries so I got to do those. It was very valuable because I was in the company of professional actors for a year. I saw how actors worked well and how they worked badly and their fears and their anxieties. I learned a lot about their process and what makes it work and how to facilitate it, and about the good and bad things that actors can do to each other. A good actor lives off the people he's acting with; a bad actor acts in a vacuum. A good actor gives support to the other people in the scene; a bad actor gives nothing. That generosity is vital. That's why you should never audition an actor in isolation and say, 'Read this,' because it denies the very first principle of acting, which is response. I wouldn't dream of having an actor try out for something by having them act or read on their own. Virtually everything we say is subject to what other people say.

Did you ever edit or rework the texts of the plays you directed at Northampton?

No. Repertory theatres in those days did West End successes or classics, and the idea of new writing was virtually unheard of at that level; it was largely restricted to the Royal Court. Once or twice a new play was sent in. Jeremy Seabrook – now a very good and well-known writer on mainly sociological issues – came from Northampton, and he wrote a play in the local dialect. It was a really interesting piece, nothing like the rep had ever put on before. It wasn't Lionel's cup of tea, so I worked on that, but it was a very rare occurrence. The subtitle said it was a 'threnode', so that put Lionel right off. Usually the plays came in, you did them, and that was it.

In 1963, you joined the BBC. Tell me about your initial experience there.

I applied to join the BBC as an assistant floor manager and was turned down, but I then applied as a director and got in – strange logic. I was put on a six-week training course, which wasn't really about anything except how the BBC worked, what the BBC ethos was and what form you had to fill in to get the wardrobe department to deliver the costumes on time. There was one class called 'What to Do with Your Cameras', and that was the extent of the technical training.

After that, I was given a half-hour television studio job to do, *Catherine* (1964), in which, as it happened, I cast an actor called Tony Garnett. We met later on, quite by chance, when he was a story editor.

I knew nothing about television or films, and at first it was a question of not making too much of a fool of myself, which was quite difficult. I cut my teeth on *Z Cars*, which had a good reputation. At the core of it, it had very good actors who all knew each other well and had built up a strong working relationship. So when

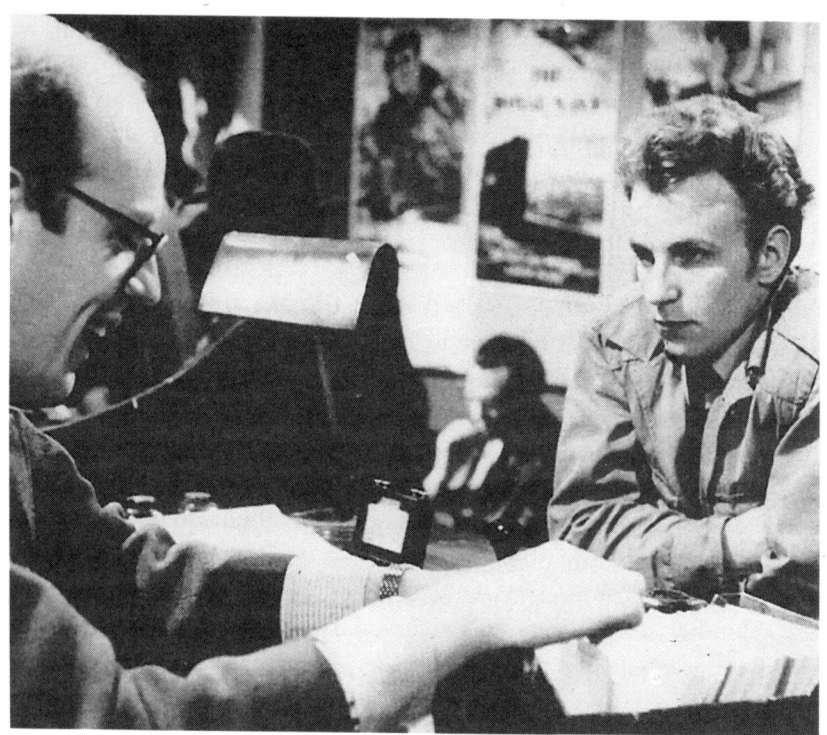

Diary of a Young Man: up in the Smoke.

a young director came in who really knew nothing about the business – well, you were really there to be consumed. By and large, they were very generous, but for me it was just a question of getting through each show.

I didn't direct my episodes of Z Cars very well; if you look at them now, they look pretty crappy. They went out live, and that was a frightening experience – nerve-racking. At the time Z Cars was regarded as a mould-breaking police series, which it probably was. The police were shown as ordinary, fallible mortals. But, without question, it was different from what we'd had before.

To take one example, The Whole Truth *(1964) – which was about the problems of a punch-drunk boxer – combined studio work, including back projection for the patrol-car scenes, with bits of film. The studio scenes are admittedly theatrical, but there's an undeniable flavour of authenticity.*

Yes, but I wouldn't dare to see it now. It's better that it lives on as a memory.

But were you starting to see television's potential as a writer's or director's medium at this time?

That came two or three years later. When I arrived, television drama was very studio-bound. It wasn't cinematic at all but more like a theatre set in a studio, with sets with three sides and cameras pointing in from each end. Often it was done live, and everybody built up to this great moment of the performance, so you performed a bit here, performed a bit there, then dashed across the studio floor and performed somewhere else. If the director kept the boom out of the shots, that was a major triumph.

I didn't start to think about television as a medium until I began working with John McGrath and Troy Kennedy Martin, who had begun *Z Cars* – they were the inspiration and imagination behind it. I did a series with them, *Diary of a Young Man*, directing three of the six episodes. I didn't do very well, but their ideas were stimulating. They wanted to take television drama by the scruff of its neck and deconstruct it by playing with a new, non-naturalistic language. Troy was against that kind of very encrusted, mannered, studio-bound realism, and he wanted to dismantle it. The famous article he wrote in *Encore** was obviously very influenced by what he knew of Brecht. It threw up ideas like divorcing sound from picture and using non-naturalistic editing devices. In *Diary of a Young Man* we cut to music, used sequences of stills, and voice-overs – all the things that, rather curiously, were taken up by commercials more than anything else. That series was mostly a laboratory to see how you could disturb that very formal, traditional way of making and shooting TV drama in a studio.

Did you feel you started to pick up some directorial technique working on Diary of a Young Man?

Not really. I was still rigid with fear.

---

* 'Nats Go Home: First Statement of a New Drama for Television', *Encore* 48 (March–April 1964).

CHAPTER 2

Plays of Hope

Up the Junction, The Coming Out Party, Cathy Come Home, In Two Minds, The Golden Vision, The Big Flame, The Rank and File, and others

The election of Harold Wilson's Labour government in Britain in 1964, following the thirteen 'lost' years of Tory rule, coincided with a sense of ferment among the young, primarily socialist writers and directors gathering at the BBC under the leadership of the ebullient Canadian Sydney Newman. Having spearheaded ITV's successful *Armchair Theatre*, Newman had been appointed head of BBC drama in 1963 with an apparent mandate to clear away the prevailing proscenium-arch aesthetic. It was in 1964 that Newman launched the *Wednesday Play*, which, in its six-year run, would redefine the parameters of the British television play both in terms of political content and dramatic potential.

Loach would direct ten *Wednesday Plays*, and the experience would enable him to discover both his eye (as a *metteur en scène* of rigorous naturalism) and his voice (as a socialist-humanist) – particularly after he threw in his lot with script editor Roger Smith and Smith's assistant Tony Garnett on *Up the Junction* (1965). The influence of Troy Kennedy Martin would be briefly felt in Loach's direction of Nell Dunn's script, specifically in the way Loach cut the images to the music and in the collaged narrative. This boisterous slab of working-class south London life additionally showed the influence of Godard and such recent British kitchen-sink dramas as *A Taste of Honey* (1961) and *A Kind of Loving* (1962). Over the course of Loach and Garnett's collaboration, however, it was their practical Marxist analysis that provided their work with its abiding theme: class betrayal.

The tentative marriage of drama and documentary in *Up the Junction* was full blown by the time of the Garnett-produced *Cathy Come Home* (1966), which was not only filmed *plein air* on real locations, but interrupted its hugely controversial story of a young mother and her family's decline into homelessness with vox pop interviews and housing statistics. These were watershed days at the BBC. *Cathy* liberated the *Wednesday Play* from the electronic studio, and its switching between fact and fiction inaugurated a politically heated debate about the very nature of TV drama that made the arguments about naturalism and non-naturalism seem like schoolboy stuff. For Loach, the point was to 'get the best of both worlds – to get the insights into personal relationships and experiences that you can get through fiction, and yet to set them in a firm, concrete context. The shock you get by cutting back and forth between the private world and the public world was just what we wanted.'*

Loach and Garnett's next *Wednesday Play* was David Mercer's *In Two Minds* (1967), a mock-documentary about the effects of unenlightened mental healthcare on a young woman driven into schizophrenia by her bullying mother; they would remake it in 1971 as the feature film *Family Life*. Then came Neville Smith's *The Golden Vision* (1968), a pleasingly upbeat docudrama about real players and fictional supporters of Everton Football Club.

The last pair of Loach–Garnett single plays for the BBC allied Loach to one of his fiercest and most loyal collaborators. Written by Jim Allen, *The Big Flame* (1969), Loach's final *Wednesday Play*, and *The Rank and File* (1971), commissioned for *Play for Today*, respectively examined an occupation by Liverpool dockers threatened by casual labour and a strike by glassworkers in St Helens from the perspective of rank-and-file union members in the process of being sold down the river by their leaders. Terse, sclerotic *vérité* dramas that do not flinch or waver from the language, debate and violence of collective industrial action and its systematic oppression, yet never hysterical in their denunciations, these two films elicited a full-blooded naturalistic style from Loach that would serve him well as, with the *Wednesday Play* era coming to an end in 1970, he began to explore the possibilities of cinema.

---

* Paul Kerr, 'The Complete Ken Loach', *Stills Magazine*, May/June 1986.

GRAHAM FULLER: *Before we talk about the* Wednesday Play *era, perhaps you could set the record straight on your politics. You've been described as an orthodox Marxist, a Trotskyist and several other things, but I know that you're not very fond of any of those labels.*

KEN LOACH: They're just used to beat you. Where to start? In the early 1960s, we were all very anxious to see the Labour Party in power again, after a very long period of Conservative rule. Harold Wilson was quite a charismatic figure. He had a provincial accent and seemed to be speaking the language of the working people. There was an excitement about his campaign for the 1964 general election, much more so than there was about Tony Blair in 1997. But, of course, it very quickly became apparent that, as prime minister, Wilson wasn't going to change the world or change anything much at all, not even as much as Clement Attlee in 1945.

People's hopes about what a Labour government could do in Britain were very quickly shattered. So I was certainly ready to have an alternate analysis presented that would show why Wilson just wasn't reaching out to what might have been expected. And that analysis was a Marxist analysis. I started to read history in a way I hadn't read it before – all the books you would expect, by people like Christopher Hill and Eric Hobsbawm – to see how political developments happened. And Tony Garnett introduced me to writers like Jim Allen, who had a much longer political history than I did. The idea of a class analysis was the one we identified with. What we realized was that social democrats and Labour politicians were simply acting on behalf of the ruling class, protecting the interests of capital. Once you make that kind of analysis, then everything fits into place and continues to do so.

The other important thing was that the political people I met and listened to were anti-Stalinist. From the outset, that made sense to me because if you wanted to defend the idea of socialism, you didn't have to defend Russian communism under Stalin, who destroyed the left-wing opposition and murdered the people who were opposed to him, and whose regime was clearly an atrocious dictatorship responsible for the most appalling horrors. Once you understood that, you wouldn't have Stalin's crimes hanging around your neck every time you suggested socialism as an alternative in Britain. That was vital.

There's still that dividing line if you look at the British left of the 1990s. There are those who trace their socialist lineage back to the left opposition to Stalin, and I would say that they are still basically socialists. And there are those who emerged from some Stalinist group or party who have made a set of compromises and thrown their lot in with Tony Blair or joined the social democrats.

I would be surprised if, as a socialist, you hadn't become disillusioned by the events of the last thirty years.

Certainly, the unlikelihood of a strong socialist government taking power – one which would prioritize the workers and working-class people – was disappointing. But it's not disillusioning in the sense that the political analysis I accepted doesn't give you any kind of illusions about Labour politicians. *Their* analysis is that capitalism is still progressive, which is why they never take on the City or endorse common ownership, and the bottom line is that they will defend employers' rights to make a profit before they will defend job security and decent wages. As competition gets harsher and harsher, so workers are increasingly on the defensive. And, of course, you have no illusions at all about any so-called socialist government.

It's clear where your sympathies lie in any political discussion, so do you think it's possible to see your films as true dialectics?

I think they're films about a process that is dialectical: that is, the struggle between opposing forces to push events forward. But they're more a description of one side of that process, which is the working-class side. They're often about people's attempts to be articulate or to come to some understanding of their situation; their attempts to develop a class consciousness, and the attempts of the people who try to lead them away from a class consciousness towards collaboration and accepting their lot or towards fighting and struggling. But they're films that show or describe that dialectical struggle rather than embody it.

You had directed Tony Garnett* in your first play, Catherine *(1964). You re-encountered him again as a script editor when you began working on the BBC* Wednesday Plays *and he became your producing partner.*

I owe Tony a great deal. I think we were quite a good team. We had a lot in common in terms of our ideas and our approach to what was important, but Tony had skills and talents that I certainly didn't have, and he was able to make space for the films to happen at the BBC. He was very good at meeting with writers, bringing them along and being both enthusiastic and constructive about what they wrote. I also worked with (writer/story editor) Roger Smith, and he, too, was very strong in getting writers to bring the best out of their scripts. I learned a lot from them both. And the friendships we established have lasted. Certainly they have sustained me in the dark times!

Did you and Garnett speak the same political language?

I think Tony was more political than I was in those days. He'd grappled with ideas that until we met I hadn't considered.

---

* Tony Garnett was born on 3 April 1936 in Birmingham, the son of a toolmaker. He won a scholarship to Birmingham Central Drama School, acted in provincial repertory theatre for eighteen months, and in 1957 began studying experimental psychology at London University. He continued to act in repertory and appeared on television in Troy Kennedy Martin's *Incident at Echo Six* (1958), in the BBC Shakespeare series *Age of Kings* (1960), and in two plays by David Mercer, as well as the Loach-directed *Catherine*.

Garnett subsequently became a prolific BBC story editor and producer. The collaborations with Loach are as follows: *Up the Junction* (1965, story editor), *Cathy Come Home* (1966), *In Two Minds* (1967), *The Golden Vision* (1968), *The Big Flame* (1969), *Kes* (1969), *Family Life* (1971), *After a Lifetime* (1971), *Days of Hope* (1975), *The Price of Coal* (1977), *Black Jack* (1979).

Garnett's non-Loach TV work includes Jim Allen's *The Lump* (1967) and *The Spongers* (1978), as well as *Law and Order* (1978) and *Between the Lines* (1993). His films include *Prostitute* (1980), *Handgun* (1982), *Earth Girls Are Easy* (1988) and *Shadow Makers* (1989 – US: *Fat Man and Little Boy*).

In 1965, you and Garnett made Up the Junction, *which gives an impression of working-class life in Clapham. It does tell a story, but not with the conventionally linear narrative structure of film and TV drama.*

No, it was meant as a kaleidoscope of fragmented images. The idea of a story that is complete and resolved and too well worked never feels right to me because it doesn't have any loose ends. It's just phony; life is full of loose ends. And when you put together incidents and anecdotes and images from people's lives, they do add up to a set of experiences that indicate the way they live and why they live that way, and that raises all sorts of questions. So that fragmentation was deliberate. It's something I've tried to do at different times; with *Riff-Raff* I tried to capture the same sort of feeling.

I had read Nell Dunn's book *Up the Junction*. It was made up of little vignettes, like newspaper pieces or descriptions, and there are these three young women characters who run through them. The script was pieced together more or less directly from the book, which is very visual and quite cinematic. I scribbled down what I wanted and then talked it through with Nell.

Can you describe how the play was filmed?

The whole thing is a curious kind of hodge-podge. It arose in the form it did in a very bizarre way. There was a gap in the BBC schedule, and so we had six weeks to get something together. In those days there was less supervision from above at the BBC; we could just decide in the office what we were going to do. It was agreed that I would knock a script out of this little book and make a collage of events and mood pieces.

The theory back then was that you were making TV plays, not films, so you had to make them electronically in the studio. But the BBC did allow you two or three days to do location shooting, like shots of people getting in a car, driving somewhere, then getting out of the car, whereupon you'd cut back to the studio. So we said, 'OK, we'll take those two or three days,' but we actually managed to nick four days of location shooting altogether. And in those four days we filmed half of what would end up in the final seventy-two-minute piece. I had a young cameraman, Tony Imi, who just put the camera on his shoulder and ran for four days.

At that point we knew that after we'd done the studio scenes we'd end up with something that looked like two different pieces. One piece was racy and hand-held and followed the action; the other piece would be very staid studio interiors. So when the day of the studio shoot came, I didn't plan the shots like you'd normally plan them. The technicians were in an uproar, because they didn't know what was going to happen. But we got the cameramen all together and said, 'Look, this isn't like a normal TV drama; sometimes you're going to be on your own, you've got to find the shots. The action will happen, and I'll tell you roughly where it is, but you've got to find it, and that's how it will be.' We did record it like that, and we ended up with all these random studio shots to play with.

You were meant to vision mix on the spot, in the studio, to eliminate editing, but we shot it more like a film so that it would have to be cut. In those days, you were only allowed about two or three edits, because cutting tape in 1965 was like building Stonehenge; it was a very cumbersome, slow business, and in this case it would take a much longer time than we'd been allocated. At that point there was a crisis meeting. The people above said, 'You can't work like this. We can't cut the tape. You wasted two whole days in the studio. What are you going to do?'

The only solution was to cut it on the 16mm back-up print that the BBC used at that time as a safety measure. This was greeted with absolute horror because they said it wasn't up to broadcast quality – it was very grey and misty – except in an emergency. But they let us cut on 16mm in the end because it was the only way they could salvage the material. Now we'd known of this possibility beforehand, which meant we could, in effect, make a film. But it was totally breaking the rules.

Up the Junction is a bit chaotic in many ways. But it showed there was a way of subverting the conventional, stolid, 'man-walks-through-door, cut-into-centre-of-room, cut-to-close-up' style of TV drama of the time. Our whole intention, at that stage, was to make films – not studio-based theatre.

There are sequences in the Clapham pub where the actors are speaking to the camera as if they are being interviewed by somebody doing a TV documentary. Similarly, when the tally man (played by George Sewell) is driving his car through the streets of

Clapham and bragging about how he exploits his women customers, he addresses the camera in the back seat of his car. Were you consciously trying to replicate documentary-style interviews?

Yes. When she was writing the novel Nell had recorded people's conversations as they talked to her, or as *though* they had talked to her and that, in a way, matched our feeling for documentary, our wish to include documentary elements in the films. We interviewed and filmed a number of the actors as if they were talking to a documentary film-maker and then absorbed it into that overall jigsaw.

It was very much to do with our programming slot. For about forty weeks a year, the *Wednesday Play* aired every Wednesday at 9 p.m., after the late-evening news. We were very anxious for our plays not to be considered dramas but as continuations of the news. The big investigative documentary programme at the time was *World in Action* – it still is, really – and we tried to copy its

Up the Junction: Vickery Turner, Carol White, Geraldine Sherman (front).

techniques and cut with a rough, raw, edgy quality, which enabled us to deal with issues head on.

At the time, in the mid-1960s, there was a big debate about abortion going on in Britain, and in *Up the Junction* one of the girls has an abortion. We got a doctor to give us an interview, and he talked about the need for abortion to be legal and available and the consequences of it not being available. It was typical of the little factual pieces we cut into the drama.

Did it have any effect on the abortion issue?

I don't know. When you're young, though, causing shock and outrage is always very satisfactory. I suppose the film tapped into the liberal climate of the time and contributed something in a tiny way, but I don't want to make any extensive claims for it.

You cut the film in rhythm to pop songs in several places. What prompted that?

I didn't think too much about it at the time, but it was a hangover from Troy Kennedy Martin's ideas about breaking up the cutting so that you're constantly giving the film a shot in the arm. We were trying to get the excitement pop music has for a lot of people and to make it part of the fabric of the film so it became another current, or voice inside it. We enjoyed cutting it that way. Cutting to music is old hat now, but it was quite new then. The mid-1960s was a time, of course, when there was a big surge in British pop and when youth culture was burgeoning. The music conveyed the excitement a lot of people felt about that invigorated, anti-establishment mood. There was a feeling around that things were changing, and we wanted to be part of that and give it a push. Not very political – that came later.

But do you think Up the Junction *is political in that it shows working people living their communal lives and coping with economic hardships with little hope of advancement?*

I think that, like Nell's writing, it's more of a celebration, an enjoyment, of people's company – sharing their disasters, sharing their humour, and just the fun of being with them. That's something I've

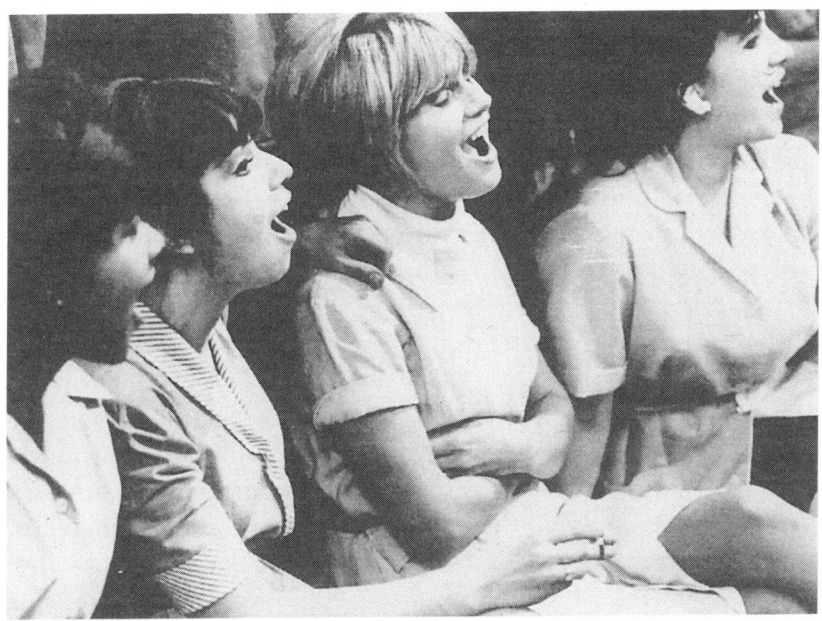

Up the Junction: working women.

tried to do in pieces by different writers on a number of occasions, because out of it comes a sense of solidarity and also a sense that people are important. It shows that people have a value, which is political, I suppose, because, by and large, working-class people are not given that value and that dignity and that respect. We are all equally important, and drama is not the preserve of the middle class.

There's actually a lot of working-class drama, but you often sense – and that was certainly the case at the time we're talking about – that the people in them are being patronized, although perhaps not intentionally. It happens particularly when you have actors imitating the way they think working-class people speak, which leads to caricature. That was something we were very determined not to do, out of respect.

Identifying ordinary people as the proper subjects for drama is a way of saying these people have political importance. If there is ever to be change, then it will come through working people. It won't come because somebody who is elected thinks they're going to do a little bit of good. It comes through people like those in *Up the Junction* getting organized and motivated to change things.

To what extent did you work with non-actors during the Wednesday Play *era?*

Not at all, really. I actually think the distinction between actors and non-actors is a false one because the whole process of meeting actors and auditioning them is about finding people who are believable, who can make something that is fictional true, and make a film live. So they have to be able to act; the only question is whether they've acted before or not. Sometimes it's a good idea if they have, and sometimes it's not necessary. But, basically, it's a question of finding the best person for a part. I tend to work with them all the same way.

Up the Junction aired on 3 November 1965. The same week, Keith Dewhurst's English Civil War play, The Siege of Manchester, *directed on film by Herbert Wise, and a* Z Cars *episode written by Elwyn Jones and set entirely inside the police station were also broadcast by the BBC. At the end of that week, you participated in a BBC2* Line Up *studio discussion with both Wise and Jones. What was interesting was that although* Z Cars *had a reputation for being authentic and gritty, Jones was extremely critical of your attempts to take your camera out on the streets. As a writer, his particular gripe was that he suspected you were abandoning Nell Dunn's script and letting the actors ad lib. Which was not quite the case, was it?*

No, and it was rather foolish of him to say it was, really. That wasn't the point at all. There was this heresy that a script was a separate entity and that the film or the programme was the next best thing, an adequate or inadequate representation of this thing that existed before. But a script isn't a separate thing. It's only a means to an end – which is the film.

I have enormous respect for writers and I don't subscribe to the *auteur* theory of film-making. When I direct a film, I don't try to be the author. It's self-evident to me that a film is a collaboration, in which, if anyone is the most important contributor, it's the writer. Still, what the writer has provided is only a stage in the process. What matters is that what is actually on the celluloid is a valuable experience and that there's a sense of authenticity about what you've created. If you stick slavishly to the exact words of a script, and the hyphens and dashes and pauses – everything that's on the page – you're making it very difficult to achieve that authenticity. The page doesn't exist when you see the film, so why adhere to this mannered, formalized thing when simply by rephrasing something you can provoke a response in your actors that is absolutely instinctive and, therefore, true?

That kind of worship of the dots and commas in a script just seems misguided to me. It comes, of course, from the theatre tradition of not changing a word of the play. You interpret it, but that's a whole other discipline, which has nothing to do with film-making. The grammar of television is film grammar – wide shot, medium shot, close-up, cuts, dissolve, fade, mix. It's film. That whole theatrical legacy is something that Elwyn Jones was a very good exponent of. But the trouble with filming drama like theatre is that you can see the hesitation in the actors' eyes, their thought processes, their struggle to be articulate, their quandaries about where to move next, and even the fact that they've rehearsed what they're saying – just what's going on in their heads. That's not to say it hasn't been expertly done on occasions, but as a basic technique it's a dead end.

What did you think of Peter Collinson's 1967 feature film version of Up the Junction?

It was scripted by Roger Smith, a very good friend of mine. They didn't try to remake what we'd made. Roger took Nell's story of a middle-class girl who goes to live with working people in Battersea and other elements of Nell's personal situation and wove them in. It was a very different film.

Following your Up the Junction, *the BBC aired another* Wednesday Play *you'd directed, a musical called* The End of Arthur's Marriage.

Yes, I was guilty of that. (It was nearly the end of my marriage, too!) Christopher Logue, who's a fine poet, had written a very funny, imaginative script, a surreal fantasy with songs by Stanley Myers about a man who is given some money to pay a deposit on a house and goes off and buys an elephant with his daughter. There were scenes involving the elephant going down a canal on a barge. There was no way I could achieve that. I could see it in my head, but I didn't have the technique or experience to bring it off. I was the wrong person for the job, unfortunately. It was the first time I had shot anything on film, too, and it was a total cock-up.

Your next Wednesday Play *was* The Coming Out Party, *which was shown just before Christmas 1965. You'd worked previously with the writer, James O'Connor, on a* Wednesday Play *called* Three Clear Sundays, *a Cockney crime drama that now looks very primitive. But* The Coming Out Party *was much better, largely because you worked with some of the* Up the Junction *ensemble – including Carol White, George Sewell, Rita Webb and Hilda Barry – and caught the same spirit with the camera running around the actors in a London pub and letting them talk to it. It also anticipates* Kes *in its matter-of-factness and in its empathy for its protagonist, a young boy neglected by his family. It's a play that hasn't been discussed very much, presumably because it didn't have the stylistic surprises or the political shock of* Up the Junction, *but it stands the test of time. Do you remember it?*

Just about. Working with Jimmy was very valuable. He was a terrific writer – amusing, perceptive, full of raw energy and wit – and he wrote about experiences I knew nothing of. His writing had the same kind of vitality that Joan Littlewood's stage productions had, and a lot of the actors that I worked with had worked with Joan. I admired and enjoyed her work enormously and tried to emulate it – the way you often emulate someone when you're starting out. I was trying to get the same sense of randomness that she got in live theatre. It was a way of telling a story where the images appeared arbitrary but none the less a story emerged. It still seems to me that a lot of films and television dramas just show you the main actors, as though they live in a vacuum. If you take a look round where you and I are talking now [a café in a converted warehouse in Liverpool's Albert Dock], there are people everywhere doing things, and everybody's got their own projects that they're working on and walking to and going from and talking about. And everyone's involved in relationships. That sense of a story emerging almost at random from all that to become a communicable experience is an idea I like because it suggests the richness of everything that's going on. It's much more real than it would be if you just gave life to one person moving in isolation through this same landscape. It's a way of giving dramatic life to the way we are.

What had brought you to the realization that you wanted to create the strongest sense of actuality in the plays and films you direct?

I think it came from trying to be critical of the way actors worked and what was generally accepted as good acting. In the case of *The Coming Out Party*, it was about trying to do justice to Jimmy's script, because he was the writer I was working with at that time. A writer like Jimmy breathed a reality that the actors who would be the accepted casting for a BBC play just couldn't bring. So we looked at the fringes of the acting profession and tried to get, say, a comedy actor to play a serious part. We wanted to shake up the process a bit and try to find ways of catching people off guard and doing things they weren't aware they were going to do. What was exciting was wondering where the actors would go in a given moment and trying to catch that unexpected response. To be honest, I've always preferred watching documentaries rather than television dramas, which I've always disliked. I find them very hard to watch because of the machine-like way they grind down the spontaneity of the actors' performances. So, where possible, I've tried to find ways of knocking television acting off balance, by putting people in shadows, for example, so that they become enigmatic and obscure and you're not certain what's there. The point is to make everything a little less obvious, to hint at things, suggest things, not explain them until they're fully exposed. I suppose all this grew out of a dissatisfaction with the predictability of what I'd seen.

Do non-naturalistic forms of drama offend you?

It's important to be clear what's meant by terms like non-naturalism. What I've always disliked is when what's in front of the camera – the performances – are grotesque, over the top, or parodies or caricatures. I believe it's possible to film something that is quite real. If you then cut it in such a way that you consciously put one event or moment against another so it goes against the normal narrative line that you'd expect, the result will be jolting. You're saying to the audience, 'Here's a few frames of this and here's a few frames of that, and here's a sequence of this and a sequence of that.' You can cut the thing together so it breaks the naturalism of the storyline and makes the audience critical of what they're seeing, aware that they're watching a piece of film come together. So in that sense it's not natural, but from the point of view of what is in front of the camera, that should still be very real. I like disjointed cutting, and even using an inappropriate soundtrack on occasions, but I've never liked overacting or saturated performances.

Frequently in these early plays, we see groups of two, three or four people comparing their experiences and sharing their opinions. That kind of dialogue became a staple of your films and plays, especially in those written by Jim Allen, from The Big Flame *(1969) onwards, and also in your documentaries: I'm thinking of the round-table discussion that concludes* Questions of Leadership *and the free-for-all about land reform in* Land and Freedom. *One might even say it's the very essence of your work. Were you conscious of it evolving as a means of political discourse?*

I think those early conversations were a precursor to what came later. I find the loose exchange of opinions in group conversations – with people pushing in all the time and jousting with their ideas – to be very energetic and revealing, and I enjoy them very much. I think people are often at their best and at their most eloquent when they do that. Working-class people have an eloquence that's very seldom recognized. I noticed that again doing the research for the film we're making about the dockers up in Liverpool [*The Flickering Flame*, 1996]: everybody we've spoken to is articulate, sharp, to the point and has well-formed ideas. It's a quality that's never represented in the way politics is treated on television, where everything is mediated through politicians, who have tired voices and use tired phrases. There's a cliché that goes, 'Everybody is fed up with politics.' Well, they're fed up with politics as presented to them, so they leave it to the politicians. But the crispness and the imaginative use of language by people who are really involved in a struggle – like the Liverpool dockers are – is very impressive and inspiring. It's clear that there's a reality that exists quite separate from the way politics is treated, and that there's a way of presenting politics that isn't just someone droning on.

Cathy Come Home: Ray Brooks and Carol White.

Those arguments always look haphazard but, of course, they're very carefully selected, pruned and guided, particularly in the cutting room. It's particularly energizing and entertaining in Jim's work, where you see the cut and thrust of argument, ideas fighting for space and, as you say, a political discourse being followed.

Was Cathy Come Home *the first opportunity you had to make a film that dealt head on with a social or political issue?*

Yes. Tony and I were getting increasingly interested in films about social issues and subjects at that time. After *Up the Junction*, which had the abortion story in it, it was quite a lateral progression to go on to examine the destruction of a family that had become homeless. It came about quite by chance. Nell Dunn was married to the writer Jeremy Sandford. I met him through her, and he showed me a two-page outline of *Cathy Come Home*. I remember reading it and being absolutely bowled over by it. Tony and I were very eager to tell the story.

Cathy *has even more of a documentary flavour than* Up the Junction, *particularly in the use of statistics about homelessness.*

Yes. I found that collision exciting. The complementing of a fictional story with a factual context places a responsibility on the fiction to be as well researched as any piece of journalism, or any book. The characters that you're filming in the fiction have got to be as credible as the people they're passing in the street. So in a way, it's a kind of test for what you set up: the fictional elements you put in the film have to be as authentic as any bit of actuality you happen to catch.

Did you feel you pulled that off in Cathy Come Home?

I can't tell, really. I'd say that sometimes we did, and sometimes we didn't.

You filmed the climactic sequence at the railway station, when Cathy is finally separated from her children by the police, in long shot. It has the effect of saying she's completely on her own and no one's going to protect her, and it's harrowing to watch. Do you recall shooting it?

Yes. It was all done very quickly, obviously with a hidden camera. The key thing was to find a camera position that would give us good coverage of what was happening and wouldn't be seen by the people passing by. We gave Carol White [who played Cathy] a position with the two kids on the station seats and then let her sit there for a bit and found a way to cue the actors playing the social workers and the police to come over and take the children. I remember we had to allow enough time to elapse after my going up and talking to her so that the passers-by would just be walking past normally. It was before the days of walkie-talkies, so we had to use hand signals. We only had one shot at it really because you don't want to put the kids through that sort of thing more than once. It was upsetting to do it, although we were running around with a camera so fast and juggling so many elements that we didn't have time to dwell upon that while we were doing it. Those feelings hit you more in retrospect. We shot *Cathy* in three weeks. It was quite an extraordinary chase around.

One of the direct results of Cathy Come Home *was the founding of Shelter, a charity that has done a lot to combat homelessness in Britain. But I believe that as far as you and Tony Garnett were concerned, this was an inadequate response to the film.*

Shelter's done some terrific work. It's been an excellent resource for research and has obviously helped a lot of families find homes, and that's a very positive thing. What's inadequate is the idea that homelessness is a problem that should be solved by a charity. It boils down to a structural problem within society: Who owns the land? Who owns the building industry? How does housing relate to employment? How do we decide what we produce, where we produce it, under what conditions? And housing fits into that. You can't abstract housing from the economic pattern. So it is a political issue; the film just didn't examine it at that level.

I think *Cathy*'s a film about a social situation; it's not a political film because it doesn't deal with structure at all – the structure of what makes people homeless. It accepts the fact of homelessness without analysis, and it's the story of a family caught in that grip and how it's shattered by it. But it doesn't try to explain the cause, and therefore it doesn't deal with politics; it deals with personal tragedy. Of course, everyone says they're against homelessness, in the same way they say they're against sin. Politicians of various shades and hues spoke up and claimed *Cathy* as their own. They said, 'What a powerful film. Yes, *we're* against homelessness, and our remedy for it is this-that-and-the-other.' I remember that Anthony Greenwood, who was then minister of housing, asked to see us and told us how much he appreciated *Cathy*. We said, 'Fine. But what are your plans to deal with homelessness?' And he ummed and ahhed and talked around it and obviously . . . nothing. I also heard – I don't know if it was true – that Edward Heath had commented favourably on it. Well, if somebody like that could accept it favourably rather than be challenged by it, then it certainly couldn't have been very political. As a result, we said to ourselves that if we were to do a film like that again, we'd somehow have to tackle the ownership of land, the building industry and the financing behind it. Otherwise you're not really challenging anything.

What appealed to you specifically about the Laingian* ideas expressed in In Two Minds?

They seemed to fit in with the rest of what we were doing. Laing was an interest of the writer, David Mercer, and Tony, who had studied psychology. *In Two Minds* was very much Tony's project. He certainly introduced me to R. D. Laing's books, to Laing himself and to others who'd worked with Laing. What I felt most confident in dealing with in *In Two Minds*, and again in *Family Life* [Loach and Garnett's 1971 feature version], were the family relationships. I tended to take the medical aspects on trust, because the premise seemed to make sense.

Can you elaborate?

Growing up implies that you will become separate from your parents. You are an independent other person. But it's common, natural even, for parents to see themselves in their children. When this becomes extreme, the parent may see the child as an extension of themselves. Then the child's sense of self is shaken. Who am I? Do I exist at all? And – in the way Janice expresses it metaphorically in the film – my mother is killing me. It was the process of family life that I responded to in the story. We tried to push these ideas further with the feature film.

---

* R. D. Laing (1927–89), radical British psychiatrist whose clinical interests were directed towards psychosis and what he described as 'ontological insecurity'. Laing contended that schizophrenia was a response to malignant family situations and advocated nurture of patients instead of physical treatments like insulin coma and electroshock therapy.

We'll come back to that. Now you'd directed Neville Smith as an actor in a Wednesday Play *called* Wear a Very Big Hat *(1965), and then he and the newsreader Gordon Honeycombe collaborated on a drama–documentary called* The Golden Vision. *It's an atmospheric piece about a group of Everton Football Club supporters and includes footage of some games and interviews with such Everton players as Alex Young, the 'Golden Vision' himself. And Neville Smith played an Everton fan who makes a football widow of his pregnant wife.*

Neville had been the lead in *Wear a Very Big Hat*. He was very good and very funny. As we got to know each other, he talked about wanting to write a script about Everton, and in particular about the centre forward, Alex Young. He wrote a very good piece, and it was a nice idea to make the main story element the group of fans; the factual stuff was the team. There was a dream-like element to it, as well, in the scene at the end when [actor] Ken Jones imagines himself playing and scoring for Everton. That dream idea was unusual at the time, but it's commonplace now.

The Golden Vision: Everton supporters delayed by wedding.

It's exactly the same fantasy lived out by Brian Glover's games master, who imagines he's Bobby Charlton in Kes. *We know we're watching one of your films when, in* The Golden Vision, *we hear the old Evertonian, Mr Paisley, reminiscing about the General Strike. Were you trying to contextualize football as a proletarian sport?*

I wouldn't want to make that claim for it. I think it's just about these supporters' enjoyment of football – their incredible passion for it. It's something that brings them alive and brings out humour and other qualities in them. It's also very much about a place – Liverpool – where all that happens.

One of Neville's strengths as a writer was the way he conceived roles for a whole group of actors and comics and singers and welcomed them into the experience. They included people like Ken Jones and Bill Dean, who really carried the film; I greatly enjoyed their company and I've worked with a lot of them since.

Later on, you directed a Neville Smith play called After a Lifetime *(1971). The lifetime in question – the man who has died – was*

After a Lifetime: carrying the legacy of the General Strike.

another veteran of the General Strike. Again, do you consider this a political piece?

Well, I guess so. It's about the man's legacy – political and personal. But it's largely a comedy, not so much about the old fellow as about his sons – one played by Neville, the other by Jimmy Coleman – the uncles and nephews and the relationships that emerge between them. Some of it is quite touching and thoughtful, but I think the comedy sequences work better than anything else.

In 1969, you began your long collaboration with Jim Allen* on his play The Big Flame. *Did you meet and talk about the ideas in the piece first, or was it presented as a script?*

It was pretty much presented as a script. It was a very good script, too, but I think it could have been a better film if I'd been more experienced. All the ideas that Jim has been consistently interested in – the conflicts between employers and the workforce, the nature of the rank and file, the roles played by trade unions and the press – were well expressed in *The Big Flame*. I think, in a way, it's Jim's

---

* Born in Manchester on 7 October 1926, Allen is a former building worker, miner, docker, iron foundry worker, hospital cleaner and blacklisted labour organizer. He began writing on the long-running Granada Television soap opera *Coronation Street* in January 1965 and completed an eighteen-month stint before resigning: 'I wrote an episode in which everyone from the Rover's Return goes on a mystery tour and the bus goes over the cliff, killing every member of the cast. It was the best episode I wrote but it made me very unpopular and, of course, it was never made. I was never fired – I think I was one of the few writers who actually walked out.' (Interview with editor, September 1996.)

Allen's first television drama, *The Lump*, directed by Jack Gold and produced by Tony Garnett for the *Wednesday Play* series in 1967, examined the exploitation of casual labour in the building trade – the same theme examined by Loach and writer Bill Jesse in *Riff-Raff* (1991).

Allen is the writer of the following Loach-directed plays and films: *The Big Flame* (1969), *The Rank and File* (1971), *Days of Hope* (1975), *Hidden Agenda* (1990), *Raining Stones* (1993), *Land and Freedom* (1995). Allen's play *Perdition* (1987), directed by Loach, was withdrawn from the Royal Court Theatre (see Chapter 4). Allen's other TV plays include *United Kingdom* and the Garnett-produced *The Spongers* (1978), both directed by Roland Joffe.

definitive script. I wish I'd had the chance to do it, say, twenty years later, because the bones of it were terrific.

Like all strikes, the strike shown in that film was about power and who holds it. Specifically, it shows an occupation by Liverpool dockers and how that occupation was dealt with. Jim wrote the play in '67, before the '68 occupations, so what he wrote about actually happened the next year. It should have been a film of epic proportions with a cast of thousands constantly on the move, but we didn't have the resources to make a film on that scale. In fact, there's just a handful of people in it, so I don't think it does the script justice.

Jim Allen's next play, The Rank and File *(1971), was also about workers organizing and the political leverage of strike action. Specifically, it recreates the struggles at the Pilkington Glassworks in St Helens in 1970. Your direction was markedly more urgent than on* The Big Flame.

Yes. I think my work was a bit better, although it had the same sort of elements in it. But I think the script of *The Big Flame* was stronger.

Can you set out, from your personal perspective, what The Rank and File *is about thematically?*

Once again it's a play about where power lies, and how the various elements in society will behave in an industrial situation and what the different imperatives are. Specifically, it shows the clash of interests between the employer, who must have an efficient, docile labour force to produce competitively, and the workforce, which is concerned with job security, good conditions, good pay and the right to organize collectively. In the end, of course, those two are incompatible – the fundamental premise is that they can't co-exist – so there has to be a struggle, and then it's a question of who is the stronger. The whole system is based on conflict.

The prevailing propaganda, of course, maintains that the class system no longer exists, that we're all the same class and we all have the same interests. Therefore it's better that industry does well, because then we all benefit from the wealth it generates. But I think that idea is basically flawed. It isn't like that. There *are*

The Rank and File: Neville Smith and Bill Dean.

conflicting interests. And conflict will continue until there is a fundamental change.

Do you think there's a validity in keeping industries alive because they supply jobs, even if those industries are deemed not economically viable – the closure of British coal mines in the 1980s and '90s being the most suggestive example?

Well, 'not economically viable' is a loaded term that really only applies to one model of society. An industry that's not productive in the context of a market economy may not be economically viable, although it may be an essential service. However, an economy organized for everyone's mutual benefit would properly determine what is environmentally sound and socially useful to produce – things that we all enjoy and need. Then people would work in those industries in a way that was good for them and for society in general. People would share the pleasant work and the unpleasant work. And as technology developed, the benefits would spread to everybody. But that's not the way it is now. New technology is used by the employers to maximize profits at the expense of the workforce. It doesn't mean shared work; it means unemployment.

Isn't that a Luddite view, though?

I don't want to defend old ways of doing things that are labour-intensive and neglect new developments. It's not about that in the end, although people often will fight to defend what they have. And understandably, because the alternative is the dole. In the long term, the real concern here is about who owns the technology, how it's used and for whose benefit it's used.

Was the BBC opposed to The Rank and File?

They made us shoot it in Stoke-on-Trent because they said it would be too easily identifiable as the Pilkington's strike if we actually shot it in St Helens – which was silly. I think we were a bit out on a limb and needed the protection of someone like Sydney Newman [the ebullient, progressive head of BBC drama].

Tony was very skilful at keeping our space on the *Wednesday Play*, and I think there was a period when the BBC was happy to have these left-wing film-makers doing their thing, because it showed how diverse and tolerant the BBC could be. But there were always battles on the margins. I remember we had a particular struggle on *The Rank and File* – which was actually a *Play for Today* – to get in this quotation from Trotsky. It was a provocative idea, but actually quite a bland quotation. It wasn't the words the BBC objected to – it was the very fact that Trotsky had said them.

You've occasionally stepped away from your turf to direct different kinds of television films or documentaries. In 1973, you wrote and directed a play based on Chekhov's A Misfortune. *Why did you do that?*

For personal reasons I hadn't worked for a year. This was quite a way back. It was one in a little series of plays from short stories – James Joyce and Chekhov – that Melvyn Bragg was producing for the *Full House* series. I did it because it was different from what I had been doing.

Later on, I did *Auditions* (1980), which is a little documentary about three dancers trying to make a go of it – basically they're these stage-struck kids who end up dancing at the end of a pier. I always find the unglamorous end of theatre interesting and funny; it makes you smile. It's something that I can identify with, and I guess I've always been a little stage-struck myself.

Then, much later, I did *The View from the Woodpile*. After doing a series of documentaries, I had a very thin period in the mid-1980s. I wanted to work in fiction again, but I couldn't raise anything beyond some money for this small documentary for Central Television. It was a quiet little piece, but it was a happy experience. I worked with a group of kids from the Black Country, and in the film we tried to explore their experiences by getting them to dramatize themselves – so it is part drama, part documentary. I feel some affection for the film because the kids were very genuine and very warm and it's the only time I've worked in the industrial Midlands, despite coming from there myself. We shot it in about ten days. I enjoyed it.

How would you assess the Wednesday Play *period in terms of what you learned as a film-maker?*

I know I personally made several howlers, but I think it was a time when a group of us collectively made a few pushes forward. We tried lots of different things, and sometimes they came off and sometimes they didn't. It was very productive from that point of view. There were all kinds of ideas about what television drama could be and what the possible forms were for the medium. To reassess it briefly, at one end of the spectrum there were writers like Troy Kennedy Martin and John McGrath attempting to break up the naturalistic form. At the other end there were attempts to find a new kind of realism by using documentary techniques and documentary strands. So we tried to push the medium out in all kinds of different ways, and I'd say some of them were successful and some failed.

There remained, of course, a literary tradition practised by writers like David Mercer, and that needed a type of direction that I'm not very good at. But the tension between that kind of work and the kind that I and others were trying to do meant that the form was always being pushed to the edge in one way or another. It was a lively time.

How would you rate the social effectiveness of the plays and films you and your collaborators made?

It's difficult to say whether they were successful or not. Some of them – such as *Cathy Come Home* – made rather a splash at the time. I think that in the long term their success in prompting any political change was obviously minimal, because we've ended up with Tony Blair as prime minister. I suppose some of them might have encouraged or given support to people who were struggling on other fronts, but I think there's a danger of over-estimating the effect they had.

CHAPTER 3

Struggle

Poor Cow, Kes, Family Life, Days of Hope, The Price of Coal, Black Jack, The Gamekeeper, Looks and Smiles, Fatherland

Increasingly frustrated by the bureaucratic procedures of the BBC, Loach made his initial foray into feature films with *Poor Cow* (1967), adapted by Loach and Nell Dunn from one of her novels and produced by Joseph Janni. It gave Carol White (who had played one of the Clapham girls in the Loach/Dunn play *Up the Junction* and Cathy in *Cathy Come Home*) the part of Joy, a free-spirited young London woman married to a small-time crook who is sent to prison, whereupon she takes up with one of his mates. With its slum backdrop and pre-feminist consciousness (particularly well evinced through White's first-person narration), and its resigned acceptance that women like Joy are circumscribed by their situation, *Poor Cow* retains its sympathetic social message.

Loach was discouraged by his first brush with the British film industry, however, and in 1969 he and his television producer Tony Garnett duly set up Kestrel Films to realize their own modest independent projects. Working for the first time with a script by the Barnsley schoolteacher and novelist Barry Hines, they began with *Kes* (1969). Loach and cinematographer Chris Menges had studied the recent crop of sharp-edged humanist films from Czechoslovakia, and they duly brought to *Kes* a cool, crisp perspective on the blighted prospects of a working-class lad – briefly alleviated by his training of a kestrel – in a Yorkshire mining community.

Although the distributor nearly botched the release of the film, it was successful at the British box office (its regional accents were dubbed for the American release print). But the next Kestrel production, *Family Life* (1971), a superb feature version of David Mercer's *In Two Minds* (1967), the Loach–Garnett *Wednesday*

Play about Laingian solutions to family-induced schizophrenia, was a commercial failure and dented the outfit's bankability.

In 1970, Edward Heath's Conservative government was elected. In 1974, Labour returned to power following Heath's defeat at the hands of the obdurate miners' union, but Loach, Garnett and their writers had no illusions about what Labour and the trade unions were about to do for the workers. In attempting a radical historical reassessment of the left's betrayal of the left, Loach and Garnett embarked on their most ambitious BBC film, the epic Jim Allen-scripted four-parter *Days of Hope* (1975), which traced the upheavals of the British Labour movement between 1916 and 1926 through the experiences of three characters. Although one of the TV events of the era, the serial was marred by its overarching didacticism. *The Price of Coal* (1977), written by Barry Hines in two parts for the BBC's *Play for Today*, championed the miners as the heroes of the working-class movement, but its message fell largely on deaf ears in Jubilee year.

Working with Garnett for the last time, Loach wrote and directed *Black Jack* (1979), an eighteenth-century children's adventure story developed by the fledgling Goldcrest company and financed by the National Film Finance Corporation and a French company that insisted on a French protagonist before it went bankrupt. The film is little more than a diversion, and it seemed that Loach was beginning to drift. However, the election of Margaret Thatcher in 1979 would eventually refocus his political agenda and steer him towards documentary. First came *The Gamekeeper* (1980), made for ATV's short-lived film wing Black Lion and the second Loach–Hines–Menges masterpiece – this one a docudrama about class exploitation on a rural estate. Also for Black Lion, the same team made *Looks and Smiles* (1981), a drama about unemployment in the early Thatcher years that looked altogether too slick.

This chapter also includes discussion of Loach's *Fatherland* (1986), his first film for Channel 4 and his sole collaboration with writer Trevor Griffiths. A dour portrait of a dissident East German folk singer, who finds himself no freer in the West than in the East after he defects, the film spirals awkwardly into a Cold War thriller in its final act. In its use of genre conventions, it prefigures *Hidden Agenda* (1990), the film that would reinvigorate Loach as a feature director, but it otherwise belongs to the brave but inconsistent middle period of his career.

GRAHAM FULLER: *In 1967, you made your first feature film,* Poor Cow, *which you and Nell Dunn adapted from another of her novels. Looked at today, it's striking for the way it allows the Carol White character, Joy, to enjoy her sexuality – it was almost feminist in that respect. Like* Up the Junction, *it's a celebration of a certain kind of working-class woman, and that was unusual in the British cinema of the time.*

KEN LOACH: There was something very attractive in the way Nell's writing captured this sense of the irrepressible. The life force just keeps pounding through, and that always makes you optimistic. I think Joy is well named. There's a kind of energy about her. Despite her circumstances, you can't put her down totally. You know she'll ride through the tragedies and care for her child and always come bouncing back, and that's what we tried to make the film about.

It's also a film about inner-city slum life. You folded in a series of shots of the Victorian tenements where Joy and her son live, and there's an episode in which Joy's small son gets trapped in a fridge on a bomb site – and this is only twenty years after the war. The social commentary is implicit in the cutting together of these kinds of images.

I think that's true. Those old places had all the vices and virtues that you'd expect. They had a sense of neighbourliness and mutual support and collective identity – all those good things. But they also had bad sanitation and overcrowding. The late 1960s was a transitional period when there were still a lot of those communities in being; they've pretty much all been smashed down since. So, yes, all that was an important element.

Shortly after making *Poor Cow*, I felt that it was very flawed, because it had influences that were too obviously stuck on; they weren't absorbed enough into the film. I think we were still very high on the French New Wave at the time, with ideas like only cutting if you're jumping to a different time period in the film. Consequently, I held some of the shots far too long. Also, the interviews to camera probably seem a little mannered now. All that was a hangover from earlier things I'd done that had worked more successfully. In both *Cathy* and *Poor Cow* they just look too self-conscious. I think *Poor*

Cow is quite an immature film. There's a modishness about it, I think, which I tried to rise above afterwards.

Tell me about working with the late Carol White,* whom you directed four times. In a way, because of the downbeat context in which you placed her, she was the anti-Julie Christie – Christie being the pre-eminent filmic symbol of the swinging sixties.

Like the best actors, Carol worked on instinct. There were two sides to her. One was the Hammersmith kid who knew working-class life in London and could be true to it. And the other was the girl who'd been in films when she was a teenager and had been taught to be glamorous, and that was the side she was in love with. The two elements pulled her in different directions. Obviously, when she was working with us, we weren't interested in the glamorous side, and Carol responded in a very truthful way to Cathy's situation. She'd been close enough to hard times to understand it – not intellectually, but just in her gut, and she was very strong in that film. I think *Cathy* was her best work. By the time we got to *Poor Cow*, she was getting offers for other kinds of films again. She was cast in a Michael Winner film [*I'll Never Forget What's'isname*, 1967] and was desperate to do it, so we agreed she could do it at the same time we were filming. It wasn't a good idea because she would come to our film with a glamorous hairdo and having been carted about in a limousine all day. I believe Carol wanted to move away from being an ordinary woman, but I don't think she was a very good performer when she tried to be glamorous, even by the standards of those kinds of films. It was a shame because she could have gone on and done good work. Eventually, of course, she went to the United States, which was a disastrous move, because she was miscast and all the qualities that made her good – particularly her vulnerability – were taken advantage of. The best actors are always vulnerable. They should be open and they should bruise easily – that's what people respond to. If, when you're making a film, you can protect that quality, it's a strength. But it's a weakness if you

---

* Born in London in 1942, White worked in television and films as a child, becoming a leading lady in British cinema in the mid-1960s. Loach directed her in *Up the Junction, The Coming Out Party, Cathy Come Home* and *Poor Cow*. She died in 1991.

Poor Cow: Ken Loach, Nell Dunn, Carol White, Jeremy Sandford.

Poor Cow: Terence Stamp and Carol White.

Poor Cow: John Bindon and Carol White.

expose that vulnerability in a film and can't protect yourself or don't get any protection from anyone else.

I think in the best moments Carol could melt you. She was one of the main reasons *Cathy Come Home* worked – if it worked – because people responded to her and remembered her. So she was one of the many people that I certainly owe a lot to, because after that the doors opened.

Like The Coming Out Party *and some of your earlier plays,* Poor Cow *has a crime element. In keeping with your policy of casting from life, as it were, you cast John Bindon as Joy's husband, who's a robber. Bindon himself was actually a villain, wasn't he?*

He had a colourful past. He was a great character, and we saw the attractive side of his personality: he was very funny and told us all these tales, so I relied on him a lot for the verisimilitude of some of the scenes. He was actually very strong in the original version; unfortunately, I think the print that goes around now was post-synched by John and Carol, and I don't think it was done very well.

I'd never be involved in anything like post-synching because you lose all the authenticity.

From that initial experience of making a feature, did you get a sense that working in the film industry was difficult and that raising money would always be a struggle?

It was a fairly nightmarish experience, probably the worst experience of filming that I've had. I think I was very naïve about the film industry. The actual genesis of *Poor Cow* was unfortunate. With *Up the Junction* and *Cathy Come Home* and the other films we'd made at the BBC, the team was Tony and me and the writer, Nell or Jeremy, for example. We should have made *Poor Cow* in that way, but a producer, Joe Janni,* came along who said he could raise the money and get proper distribution and take care of everything. In the end, that meant there wasn't a place for Tony, and I think the film suffered because of that. I think Tony would have been far more stringent about how it was made and what the content was. I missed his sharpness of mind. Also, Joe brought in people from the film industry and I brought in people I knew from television, and the two didn't blend. We had more or less two crews working side by side and not mixing. Then the shoot overran by five or six weeks, mainly because I didn't really know what I was doing. So it wasn't a very happy experience, and I think it shows in the film.

You mentioned the French New Wave. Was Jean-Luc Godard a particular influence on you?

I think we'd found him very challenging, and his example gave us a lot of energy and desire to get in there with a camera. I don't think he was a particularly long-term influence.

What about Italian neo-realism?

That influenced me more. Those classic post-war Italian films just

---

* Joseph Janni, an independent producer working with Anglo-Amalgamated, put up £270,000 to make *Poor Cow*. Born in Milan in 1916, he had a legendary success with *The Glass Mountain*, and went on to produce many John Schlesinger films, beginning with *A Kind of Loving* (1962) and *Billy Liar* (1963).

seem to have an immense respect for people. They give people space and they're concerned with their concerns. I think they make Godard seem a little flashy.

And the Czech New Wave?

Very important. There is always a danger of misreading a foreign film because you're not getting all the nuances of language, but the work of directors like Miloš Forman* and Jiří Menzel† and others who worked in the 1960s still came across to us as very humanist, compassionate films. They weren't soft in any way, but had a very sharp, wry wit. At times, they were quite savage but still with that strong humanist streak. That's what we took from them, anyway. They made us feel that they were the kinds of films we wanted to make.

Your next feature film was Kes, *which clearly marked a shift in style. It had much sharper, cleaner images than your previous films and the camera is placed much more in the position of observer. The tone and pacing is also more relaxed. Were these conscious changes?*

Yes, very conscious. They were a reaction to some of the work in *Poor Cow*, which, as I said earlier, had become mannered. They also relate to what we've just been talking about, because the style of *Kes* was a consequence of seeing Czech cinema, which made me feel that some of the stuff we'd been working on was a little shallow.

Kes was photographed by Chris Menges. Chris had been the camera operator on *Poor Cow* and subsequently worked with the Czech cameraman Miroslav Ondříček on Lindsay Anderson's *If* (1968). That was a very positive experience for Chris in that it confirmed what he himself was thinking about in terms of how light should be photographed, about which lenses were sympathetic and which weren't, and about how to contain the action. We talked a lot about that and decided that the effort shouldn't be to make the

---

* Notably *A Blonde in Love* (1965) and *The Fireman's Ball* (1967).
† Notably *Closely Observed Trains* (1966) and *Capricious Summer* (1968).

Kes: David Bradley as Billy with his kestrel.

camera do all the work, but should be to make what is in front of the camera as authentic and truthful as possible. The camera's job was to record it in a sympathetic way and to be unobtrusive, not to be slick. So when we came to do *Kes*, there was a conscious move away from a newsreely, chasing kind of photography to a more reflective, observed, sympathetically lit style of photography.

Can you be more specific?

The idea was to light the scenes in such a way that the space we were shooting would be lit rather than the shot itself. That was very important because it meant we could dispense with the idea of actors having to hit their marks, and that liberated them to move about at will. We also wouldn't be concerned about bathing them in a pool of light or catching a light in their eyes, which is the traditional way of shooting someone. We wanted to light the space so that the light fell democratically but unostentatiously on everyone. Not only is it more pleasing that way, but the lighting isn't then saying, 'This is the leading actor in the scene or the film and these other actors aren't so important.' This is what we did on *Kes*, and it became a central tenet of how we worked.

Would you say that it's generally harder to make a scene or an image look real than it is to make it look fake or stylized, which is what most films do, particularly Hollywood films?

Making things look fake is the easy way. A technical demand like getting actors to hit their marks may not seem very important, but it can be a distraction, because no matter how skilled they are, it creates another level of consciousness in their minds, and I think that must crucially detract from their capacity to be totally involved with the other person in the scene.

To what extent do you block scenes?

It's very straightforward. We'll work out roughly how the scene is going to play up to perhaps halfway through the scene to see where the actors feel comfortable standing or sitting or whatever. Normally I will say, 'OK, you're starting the scene with the intention of doing a certain thing. How does it fall naturally?' We'll then try to arrange the furniture in the room so that it makes a pleasing frame. I try to lay the traps, as it were. If, when the actors come in and instinctively start to move or position themselves somewhere else, then the cameraman and I will try to redo the shot in such a way that we can accommodate the actors and still make a pleasing picture. The actors will feel that they've rearranged the frame, even though I'll have perhaps manipulated it in such a way that they'll have followed a course that I've predetermined. But they shouldn't be aware of that; they should feel that what they've done is entirely of their own volition.

On some of your early TV plays, you did a lot of takes. But you've said that actors usually only have the energy for one or two good takes and after that they start to run out of steam. I'm curious to know if your shot ratio has gone down over the years.

Probably not. It depends what you're trying to get. You might do quite a lot of takes of a scene from one angle – maybe seven or eight – because you might be looking to use the early parts of that shot with the later parts of the scene shot from a different angle. The early parts of the early takes will usually be good. I tend to let them run on because the actors might hit the high point of the later part of the scene, although sometimes, obviously, they'll hit the high point in a later take. It's also important to run the whole scene each time if you can, so that it has a flow and because you're usually playing the later part of a scene off the emotion of the early part. If you break it down into separate shots, it can get very bitty, so long takes are important. If you do break it down, you might just do four takes to start with so as not to deplete the emotion at the end of a scene.

What will dictate the length of a shot, in terms of time?

Depends on the scene. Action shots tend to be shorter, but if there's a dialogue scene, the shot's as long as the scene is.

You tend to keep the camera at a respectful distance.

Again, a lot of this came out of my admiration of Czech film-makers and the fixed lenses they used. My memory is that they didn't use the zoom at all. I didn't want to use it myself on films because I'd used it a lot in the past in the same way that documentaries used it, and I found that quite irritating after a bit. I like the placidity of a fixed lens and the fact that it doesn't jolt the audience. Once you're accustomed to what the lens's vision is, then you can stay with that and the audience isn't constantly being pulled in and out. I don't like using a wide-angle lens because it will also tend to push up from below the actors and distort their features and turn them into objects; it's not sympathetic in that way. I'd rather not crowd the actors or be so intrusive. If you give people space, it gives them a dignity. A slightly narrow lens – but not a telephoto lens – just seems more respectful.

What about camera placement?

What's important is that you place the camera in such a way that it doesn't inhibit the actor. It mustn't be in too close or in the actor's eyeline all the time so he or she can relate to the other people in the scene without the camera pushing in or intruding. That means standing back a little way, which is another argument for having a slightly longer lens. But it's no use being unobtrusive if you can't get a good shot, so it's a question of finding a place that allows you to find a nice frame, even if the actors are doing things that you haven't planned. That usually means taking up a fixed position that nevertheless allows you mobility so you can follow the actors and cover what they're doing. The frame will often be moving, but the camera actually isn't moving physically; in other words, you're panning rather than tracking. Another reason not to track is that the take you end up using isn't usually the best: one, because the actors you're following have got to hit their marks, and, as I've said, it's better if they don't have that restriction in their minds; two, the focus is much more variable on a tracking shot. If the camera is fixed, then it's much easier for the focus puller.

When you say 'a nice frame', does that mean it's authentic, or do you actually compose shots for their pictorial value?

Both. I think you should feel subconsciously that the objects in the frame are balanced, but if you come out of a shot and say, 'Ah, yes, isn't that a stunning frame?' then you've lost the point of it. It should just seem right, although in an implicit rather than a predictable way. It shouldn't strike you as a self-consciously beautiful shot; that's showing off.

In films like Kes, Black Jack, Days of Hope, *to some extent, and* The Gamekeeper, *you have partly or wholly rural settings that lend themselves to landscapes and images of nature. Most film-makers would take advantage of the inherent beauty in the countryside, but I sense you would consider it decadent to go for a shot that was beauty for beauty's sake.*

Yes. I think you need to communicate the sense of landscape, but it's the landscape that should be beautiful, not the shot. It's important that you link the audience to the landscape as unselfconsciously as you can.

Kes was based on Barry Hines's novel Kestrel for a Knave, *and Hines himself wrote the screenplay. Will you talk about your collaboration?*

It was Tony who found the book and introduced me to Barry. I thought it was a terrific piece of writing – it had a very good balance, it was neat and well shaped, and everything about it had a rightness. (The script was a collaboration, but I don't want to make anything of that. The film is so close to the book anyway.)

Working with Barry is a joy. He and I – like Tony and I – were a similar age and from a similar background, and we see things in a similar way – the same kind of things make us smile. We filmed at the school [in Barnsley, Yorkshire] he taught at, and that was where we found David Bradley, who played Billy. He was just one of the kids in the class who was the right age. The kestrel, or kestrels, actually – which were called Freeman, Hardy and Willis – were trained by Barry's brother, Richard, who showed David how to work with the birds himself. Everything had an appropriate size about it, and it was helpful to shoot on such a modest scale. For the first time, we felt we were able to achieve a situation where the film crew was there to serve the actors in the film. It wasn't a case of just telling people what to do. I think that's always been very important: as film-makers, we're not there to order people around; we're there to listen, to absorb and to try to draw people out and

Kes: David Bradley and producer Tony Garnett on location.

serve them. And, as far as we could, that's what we did on *Kes*. I think Barry enjoyed the elements that the people in the film were willing to bring to it. For example, he enjoyed Brian Glover's and Colin Welland's performances; as did we all. It was a very happy experience.

Barry Hines's book opens with a quotation which states that the kestrel was the one animal in medieval society that the lower echelons could freely own. It's a symbol of egalitarianism.

Exactly. It's the bird for the riff-raff of the world.

There's a sadness at the end of the film in that, rather like the women in Up the Junction *and Cathy in* Cathy Come Home, *Billy is trapped in his world with no real hope of improvement.*

He's absolutely trapped. In the film, through the story, you see a whole side to life that the world cannot afford to see, that it can't afford to acknowledge. At the time, in the north of England, boys like Billy were needed for unskilled labour. People who saw the film said to us, 'Couldn't he get a job in a zoo?' which misses the entire point, because if it's not Billy who's going to be exploited as unskilled labour, it's going to be someone else who's in that predicament; the world requires him and people like him to fill that role. The world just isn't prepared to take on board the fact that he has this talent and imagination, because he's expected to work down the pit all his life, like his brother, and that's if he's lucky. Something that we didn't get quite right in the film is that Jud, Billy's brother, is provoked to kill the bird because Billy's failure to place Jud's bet meant that Jud lost the equivalent of a week's wages. He could have had a week off work. A week in the sun and the open air, not underground with the coal dust in his lungs. It was important that Jud didn't come off as just a villain, because he's entitled to be angry, but, as I say, we didn't quite pull that off.

You said when we were discussing In Two Minds *that you pushed the Laingian ideas further in the feature film version,* Family Life.

In the television film, the Laingian therapist was an unseen presence. You just heard his voice. I thought that was a bit mannered, a

Family Life: Ken Loach with Sandy Ratcliff and Grace Cave.

bit artificial. So in the film, he's there on the screen. He was played by a real doctor, Mike Riddall, who took to the idea of the film very well. Obviously, the family in the film is a fictional family, but Mike was very subtle and clever at exploring the real personalities of the people we brought in to play the other characters. In a way, what emerged was almost a documentary about the people in the film – particularly the mother, who was played by Grace Cave, an extraordinary woman representative of so much of what we now call family values. I'd wondered where on earth I'd find somebody to play this part because the key was to cast an actress who would not pass judgement on or distance herself from the character. Clearly, in the story, that character has a very claustrophobic relationship with her daughter and embodies traditional values which, if they're carried too far or are overstated, can be very repressive.

Where did you find her?

I went to the Conservative Association in Walthamstow and met with the ladies' committee. I remember going to meet them – it was a formidable encounter, and one woman, Grace, was far more formidable than the rest. I tried out some short scenes with her, and she was very powerful; she just spoke her mind without any inhibition. So I gave her the part and, in a way, I think she became the driving force of the film. I frequently directed her through Bill Dean, who played the father and whom I'd worked with before, or through Mike. Bill's character, too, was dominated by Grace's, and was defeated, but he'd sort of come to terms with it.

In a situation where there might be off-screen tension between actors, would you encourage or manipulate that tension to serve the film, or do you simply rely on the script?

It's a conjunction between the two. I don't think it's healthy to manipulate an off-screen relationship, but if the right actors have been cast, the on-screen relationship will be right, too. For example, there was no way that the relationship between Grace and Sandy Ratcliff, who played the daughter in *Family Life,* was going to be anything other than what it was because Sandy was a free spirit, true to the 1960s, and yet thoroughly able to understand what it was like to be dominated by a woman like Grace. I relied a lot on Bill, who understood the relationship that we wanted to create and, of the three main actors, was the most conscious of what it should be like. Sandy understood the relationship, too, but Grace went her own way. So I didn't need to manipulate them off-screen. The casting took care of the relationships that evolved between the actors in front of the camera.

But was Grace aware that the woman she was playing was clearly a destructive force?

No, not at all. In her mind the mother was being as good a parent as she could be under the circumstances. She didn't believe that it was the mother's fault that the daughter was ill, because there were outside influences at work on her. She believed in the traditional values of respect and obligation and a sense of hierarchy and children doing what they're told. She believed that the mother, above all, would know what her child was like and had a very stern sense of discipline that was intolerant of youthful indiscretions or excesses. At the end, when Grace saw the film, she said rather revealingly that we'd given her a fair crack of the whip.

Which implied that she also understood something about the damaging nature of the relationship?

No, I don't think so. But it was important she didn't understand that. I don't think an actor should see the totality. An actor should see the world through the eyes of the character. That's why I don't like actors to see the entire script of the film they're working on. I don't want them to take a bird's-eye view. I just want them to go through the events at the level of their character.

Is that something you've always insisted on?

Pretty much – perhaps sometimes more rigorously than others. But I think it's a good idea.

After Family Life *there was a hiatus in your career.*

Yes – a long hiatus.

The Wednesday Play *era had come to an end. And then, in 1971, you had a family tragedy.**

Yes. I didn't work for about a year or two after that. Obviously, the family had to pull itself together the best way it could. The trouble with film-making is it means you have to go away quite a lot, and I felt I couldn't go away for that period. But then you move on.

You next embarked on Days of Hope, *written by Jim Allen. Will you describe how you and he work together?*

I guess we'll have a sense of what a project might be and we'll talk around it for a bit. If there's possibly a story there, then Jim will write down a few pages and stick them in the post to me – he doesn't travel to London much if he can avoid it. I'll scribble my notes on his pages and send them back. Then, after we've done this for a bit, I'll go up and see him, and we'll sit around his kitchen table and try to thrash something out. When we've done that, he'll start writing the thing.

Even though all his characters speak as if they're from Manchester, Jim writes a certain kind of muscular, powerful dialogue

---

* On 2 May of that year, Loach and his wife, Lesley, were seriously injured in a car accident, in which Mrs Loach's mother and their five-year-old son were killed.

very well; he's unique in the way he captures the rhythms of working-class speech.

How much of his original dialogue will make it through to the finished film?

A lot, but it varies. Where there's an emotional exchange or the cut and thrust of argument, then we'll take Jim's script and let the actors fight it out using his language but extemporizing around it. Actors tend to feel they've done more than they have, because when you get to the editing you often cut back to the script.

What about story structure?

That's the hardest part. I think we've got more demanding about it as we've gone on.

How did Days of Hope *evolve?*

It was something that just grew. The original plan was for Jim, Tony and me to do a film on Northern Ireland, and then it turned into a story about a guy who deserted from the British Army at the time of the First World War because he didn't want to fight the Irish and who was eventually drafted into a mining area. Then it spread into a two-parter and, by the time it became the story of three young people from the First World War up to the General Strike, it had turned into four parts. One of the characters is a lad, completely apolitical, who volunteers for the army and, because of what happens to him, becomes militant in the Labour movement. The other two characters are his sister and her husband, a conscientious objector who is apparently very left-wing. He becomes a trade union official, but by the time of the General Strike, he's a Labour MP who wants to end the strike as soon as possible. The marriage founders because his wife, like her brother, has become militant. I think the whole project is a bit uneven because it started life in one way and then turned into something else.

The characters have very solid arcs in the way they each develop. But there's a sense that you and Jim Allen were interested in dramatizing their political positions more than realizing them

Ken Loach directing *Days of Hope*.

as people; by the fourth episode, the human story has all but evaporated.

I think that's a fair criticism. It's certainly patchy. Sometimes it comes alive and sometimes you can feel the wheels grinding around a bit. It's a little didactic in the way we twist what happens to the characters to fit an idea. The problem was we just didn't keep control of the structure well enough. It was evolving as we were doing it, and we needed to have worked more tightly on the script before we started to shoot it. It was very instructive from that point of view.

The scenes you're referring to are about the debacle that followed the General Strike, where there was a big conflict with the union leaders. Jim wrote this long scene where everybody was putting their point of view. It was still being written the day before we did the scene, and more and more pages of dialogue were coming in. I said, 'Jim, Jim, we can't shoot this. Not only is it undramatic, but we've run out of time.' But Jim is a very political animal, and he said, 'Yes, but we've got to cover ourselves against the Stalinists.' I said, 'Jim, in the end, it's only a film.' I think I just about lost that argument.

There's a sequence at the beginning of the second episode when the Tommies billet themselves in a house in Northern Ireland. There's a local girl there. They abuse her and then ask her to sing, and she sings a very plaintive Republican song. It's a brief but powerful metaphor for the relationship between England and Northern Ireland.

Yes. The soldiers have imposed themselves on the family, and they're drinking and taking the piss and being crude with the girl and just making fools of themselves. They prod her up to start singing, and she sings. And as she sings, they have a sense of shame. The sense of shame is stronger than the drink. And, in a way, she reminds them of who they are and where they come from and their own families. It was important there to break the stereotype of soldiers as brutes.

In a later sequence, a deputation of miners goes to meet with the mine owner, who sits down and listens to their grievances, but in his attempt to empathize with them he comes across as patronizing. It's not an impartial characterization.

I've always tried to cast people who are intelligent and sympathetic and are not caricatures in any way. But it's very hard for them not to appear like that because the audience is judging them like that. The guy who played that role is actually a very nice man, and we certainly didn't want him to appear overbearing.

It's interesting: when we came to do *The Gamekeeper*, the upper-class people who come and shoot the birds out of the sky are people who really go shooting – they are very well off financially and quite well known among the aristocracy. And I guess they're more like caricatures than any actors I've ever cast, which is really strange.

One could argue that upper-class people do tend to caricature themselves. Without attaching any value judgement to them, they are a recognizable type.

Yes. But the great danger is that, in a film, everybody's expecting them to be overplayed, and the danger is that people who make casting decisions often cast actors who do overplay those parts. Then the film loses its seriousness because the target's too soft. It's much more interesting if those parts are played by people who are intelligent, shrewd and skilful.

It's not that the mine owner in Days of Hope *is a caricature – it's more complex than that. He's kindly in his demeanour, and says he believes that he and the miners should work together. It's all very well for him to say that, of course, given his relative position, but the more understanding he tries to be, the less he is, somehow.*

Well, he's got the miners on his own ground. He was pretty well protected. The army moved into the coal fields in that period, in order to be ready if there was serious trouble. I don't think we would do a scene like that now. I think it was too corny. There's the velvet glove and there's the iron fist in the next field. The scene is too obvious. I think we'd try to be a bit more subtle now.

Days of Hope *came out in 1975. There had been a miners' strike in Britain in 1972 and then another in early 1974, which brought down Edward Heath's Conservative government. Looking at the film retrospectively, do you see it as a direct allegory for 1970s Britain, and was it intended as one at the time?*

I don't think we were aware of that. I think it was a story that was worth telling – the story of the struggles of the 1920s, when the revolution in Russia was a few years old and when there were big disturbances in Britain, leading to the biggest disturbance of all, the General Strike of 1926. When you're fifty years away from something like that, as we were when we made the film, the kinds of roles that people play become much clearer. We were really trying to reawaken the memory of that time and to rescue that history. That's something Jim and I have been particularly concerned with in the work we've done together. When people experience political upheaval in the present, it always seems like it comes out of nowhere, but there's always a long struggle that's gone on before it, and if we know what happened in the past, we can better understand what's going on now.

In a sense, Days of Hope *is about history itself.*

Yes. Who creates history and who it belongs to.

But it's been criticized for showing an oversimplified version of events.

Well, people always say that. Some said the different political positions were outlined too clearly; other people said it was all too complicated. But it couldn't have been both. I don't think it was oversimplified. It's not like you're writing a book when you make a film or TV series. You just have to try to take the essence and be true to that.

Days of Hope was very darkly lit.

Yes. That was probably a misjudgement, certainly in some parts of it.

I wondered if it was your way of visually describing history. Black Jack was similarly dark.

I think it's better if you don't light every corner if you do things that are set in the past. You can't recreate the past – all you can do is indicate it. And the more you expose what you've set up to a blinding light, the more false it is. I think the past should be kind of murky and enigmatic and opaque and that was particularly the case with *Black Jack*. If a costume drama is brightly lit, it's plainly false. But if it's a little shrouded in smoke or dirt or darkness, then your imagination can fill in the details. And that's more evocative.

How do you go about getting that rough, grainy look?

You stand in the room and say, 'Where's the light coming from?' And once you've found it you amplify it just a little, which means you're shooting on a fairly low light level, and that makes the image less hard-edged. You then shoot it like you're a sympathetic observer in the corner.

To sum up, what was the value of Days of Hope?

I suppose – like a lot of things we've worked on – it was just another shoulder to the wheel, an attempt to give support to those who are actively in the front line. Films are some way back from the front line. If you're making a film, you're not actually in the political dispute. You're nicely paid, thank you very much, and you're somewhere safe. From that privileged position, you try to give support to those who have got their lives on the line – or their livelihoods, I should say.

Days of Hope: 1916.

What were your feelings about the new Labour government elected under Harold Wilson in 1974?

I think I knew what the Labour Party was when it was elected in 1964, but I was much clearer about that when it was re-elected. It is – or it was at the time – the enemy in another guise, but accountable in different ways than the Conservative Party. Labour obviously has a different constituency, and it's an area in which you can struggle politically. But as far as leadership goes, it's still the enemy.

You and Tony Garnett and Barry Hines next collaborated on The Price of Coal. *What were you trying to achieve there?*

It was a way of describing a mining community with two complementary stories. The idea of work is something I always find interesting to try to film, because people – if they're not unemployed – spend most of their lives at work, and their personalities, their behaviour, their relationships are formed and determined by what they do. Miners exemplify that, because a mining community is dominated by and shaped by one kind of work. There's a richness in that content that's very special. The location, too, is very

The Price of Coal: lives at risk.

special, because miners are like urban workers, but the pits are usually in the countryside. That was something that Barry wrote very strongly about. Most of my father's family were miners and the area I came from was a mining area, so I've always felt a connection to it myself. Then, historically, miners have always played such a strong part and been in the vanguard of the struggle. So those are the reasons why we did it.

The Price of Coal wasn't as militant as it would have been if it had been written by, say, Jim Allen.

No. But then you can't go on making the same film every other day. It did raise political questions. But you try to raise them in a more subterranean way sometimes.

Your next film was Black Jack, *a children's adventure film set during the eighteenth century. It seems like an odd choice for you. Why did you make it?*

Family Life had become a bit of a cult in France, Italy, Sweden and various other places, but in England it did very badly because distributors didn't know what to make of it. After that, it became near impossible for us to raise money for a feature film for a long time. But Tony was always looking for finance and he discovered that if we made a film that was aimed at the children's market, and could make it a French co-production, we could get backing from the National Film Finance Corporation. Our kids had read Leon Garfield's books, and I looked at them again and found *Black Jack*. We had to change the main adult character to a Frenchman, which was stupid really because although the actor [Jean Franval] who played him was very good, it changed the story.

It was about a lad who's good-natured but very innocent, and he has an adventure with two very strange companions. One is the Frenchman, who escapes being hanged through a trick of being able to keep his windpipe open, the other is a girl who is thought to be mad. The boy ends up saving them, not through any grand design but just through his ordinariness and innate common sense. As you say, it's an adventure story, a romance. The book had a special atmosphere, and it was interesting to attempt to make a film of it that was evocative and imaginative rather than something that was laid out in front of you.

Do you think it lent itself to a social or political theme?

Everything has a social context. We tried to enjoy the exotic quality and the atmosphere of it – the England of two hundred years ago was another country – without being heavy-handed about any social content. Whatever story you tell, you just try to make it true to the characters – who they are, where they're from and what they're doing.

The most striking images are of the fairground people moving around the countryside. They're outsiders, riff-raff – the eighteenth-century underclass.

Yes, that idea was there. Travelling with those people is part of the healing process for the girl. She comes from a very constrained bourgeois family that had kept her on a very tight rein. Just being out among people who don't care how she talks or how she dresses

Black Jack: Jean Franval.

Black Jack: Stephen Hirst and Louise Cooper.

or whether she washes is very liberating for her. Martin's* work brought the fairground to life!

Black Jack is downbeat for a children's film. Do you think it perhaps required a more heightened cinematic style?

That could well be the case. My memory of it is that there are moments in it that are quite nice, but as a whole it just wasn't strong enough. It all ended more or less in tears because we didn't have enough money to dub it properly, and so it was dubbed in one weekend – and I guess it sounds like that. I wish I could have recut it, but it was one that got away.

Why did you and Tony Garnett dissolve your partnership after Black Jack?

I think Tony felt he'd gone as far as he could in England. He wanted to try to work outside the British film and television system, so he went to America. I think we had been very lucky. We'd had a long collaboration – longer than you'd normally expect in this business, and it had been a very good time for us. The sad thing was that during the 1970s we couldn't raise the money to do more cinema work because we didn't fit in with the pattern of cinema investment – people didn't want to put money into the kinds of films we wanted to make. So our main focus had been television, and that was fine. But the problem was that a film for television is shown once, or twice if you're lucky, and then that's it. It was a pity because we'd struck an interesting vein and we just weren't able to mine it.

Before we leave the 1970s, I have to ask you why the BBC's 'McCarthyist' blacklist led to Tony Garnett being investigated by the security forces, while you were left alone?

Well, *as far as I know* they left me alone. I didn't know whether to be put out by that or not really [*laughs*], but I can't account for it. I guess I have to apologize for not being on the blacklist.

---

* Martin Johnson, designer and long-time colleague.

Phil Askham had a small role as the executioner in Black Jack, *and then, of course, the lead in your next film,* The Gamekeeper, *adapted by Barry Hines from another of his novels. You made it for ATV. Was it helpful to get away from the bureaucracy of the BBC at that time?*

Yes, although the ITV companies have their own layers of bureaucracy. It was Charles Denton who had asked me to go to ATV in the first place. He was very hospitable in making space, so I worked there on and off for quite a few years.

The Gamekeeper was great fun to make – as far as any film can be fun. Phil wasn't a gamekeeper in reality. He was a former miner who was selling cash registers at the time, but he was very good at performing the gamekeeper's tasks and, in a way, the film is partly a documentary about his skills and his personality.

The film depicts a man who's basically unaware that he is being exploited by the class system.

Yes. The subtleties of class are exposed by the gamekeeper's work and who he is and where he lives. Like all of Barry's work, the essence of it is very neat and simple and precise. The image of the gamekeeper as someone who protects land and the game birds by keeping out people like himself – other ordinary people – and maintaining it as a preserve for aristocrats to visit briefly once or a few times during the year when they destroy the birds he has raised is very powerful. The question the film asks is: whose land is it and who gets the benefit from it? Of all the fictional films we made around that time, I think this was the one that worked the best. That's my hunch, anyway. I think it's no coincidence that it was the shortest of those films and the most clearly defined.

The Gamekeeper *is an emphatically English film, both in its acknowledgement of residual feudalism and in its immersion in the rural scene. Although it shows the changing of the seasons and appreciates the landscape, it doesn't romanticize it or sentimentalize the country. It's not at all bucolic. It makes me wonder what your perspective is on literature or art that celebrates rural England, particularly that of the Romantics, some of whom – Blake, Shelley – were socialists, of course.*

The Gamekeeper: Phil Askham confronting trespassers.

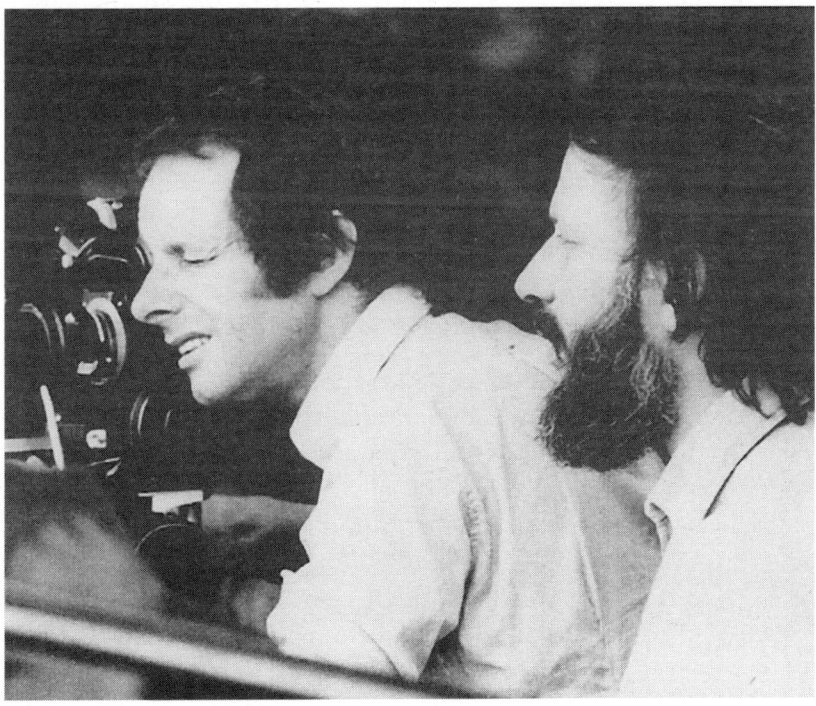

Ken Loach and cinematographer Chris Menges (right).

I was brought up on Wordsworth. I read the Romantics at school a lot and carried on reading them for pleasure and found great delight in their work. I think there's always been a link, or a tension, between the sense of freedom that you feel when you're walking through the fields or woods – and it's just you and the sky and the trees – and the knowledge that that land invariably belongs to someone else, who either just tolerates your presence or considers you a trespasser. That sense of private ownership interferes with your sense of freedom, and I think that's what's interesting from the point of view of the work we've tried to do. It seems you can look at a lot of the countryside from a train or a car, but if you try to set foot on it, you're usually told to keep off. And that becomes more poignant the more you enjoy it or the memory of it, and the more you read poets, playwrights and novelists who celebrate the pastoral.

My grandfather, who was a miner, had only a small terraced house, but he always managed to keep a pig or some hens. There'd be one pig at the bottom of the garden and another hanging up in the kitchen being smoked. So even though he was living in a little town in the Midlands, there was always a sense of rural life going on. That's something we've absolutely lost now in Britain, except in the heart of the countryside. If a town-dweller kept a pig at the bottom of their garden now, the environmental health authorities would put an end to it. So that sense of immediacy with animals and with nature is something one feels the loss of.

Your next film, Looks and Smiles, *was from another Barry Hines script. To what extent was it consciously predicated on the need to address the escalating unemployment of the early Thatcher years?*

Originally, it was going to be much more about this boy and his girlfriend. Barry had found a quotation from Chekhov where a girl asks an old relative, 'How did girls attract boys when you were young?' and she replies, 'In the usual way – with looks and smiles.'

It had been ten years since Barry and I had done *Kes* when we started to think about *Looks and Smiles*. The thing about the boy in *Kes* was that he was a lad with all kinds of possibilities, and yet society had planned that he would be a manual worker, and that's all he was ever going to be, whoever he was. The interesting thing, a decade later, was that the problem facing a lad like him wouldn't be that he was going to do a job that he wasn't suitable for – but that he wouldn't have a job at all. That just seemed like an interesting thing to explore.

We see the main character, Mick, trying to fix up his motorcycle in the shed. Was the motorcycle intended as a symbol, like Billy's kestrel in Kes?

Not as crude as that. It was just something that he would do to pass the time. To tell you the truth, we never thought of the kestrel as a symbol. I don't think we ever once discussed the symbolic resonance of it – again, tending and training the bird was just what Billy did.

In the second half of Looks and Smiles, *Mick's girlfriend's story takes over. She comes from a broken home, and eventually he drives her on his motorbike from Sheffield to Bristol, where her dad lives. This adventure throws the narrative into a completely different direction.*

An idea that we had – and it's an idea that, I guess, I've come back to on various occasions – is that there's something quite satisfying about

Looks and Smiles: Graham Green (right) as the unemployed lad.

a story that has an arbitrary quality. When you add it all together what is apparently arbitrary actually complements the whole story. It's like creating a mosaic or a collage from different fragments.

Looks and Smiles is really just a story about three kids. The boy we're with most of the time, Mick, is constantly failing. His girlfriend is much more together, but she's unhappy and wants to be with her father. The third kid has avoided the unemployment issue by joining the army, but when he comes back on leave he gets taught some real violence.

Why weren't you happy with the film?

I was aware that we'd got a bit self-indulgent momentarily. It should have been a funnier film than it was. I think I just wasn't tough enough in the shooting and in the cutting, and I think it should have just been a bit sharper and tighter and a quarter of an hour quicker. It's too lethargic and gently paced, and when I think about it now I want to give it a kick up the arse.

As a feature film-maker, did you feel that you'd had enough for a while?

Cinema films seemed a dead end from where I was standing. It took us *years* to raise money. The films would then be made and they'd be seen by nobody, and it seemed that we were hitting our heads against a brick wall. Also, I think I'd lost my way a bit – and lost touch with the kind of raw energy of the things we'd done in the mid-1960s and with *Kes*. The films I was making weren't incisive enough. I wasn't getting the right projects and I wasn't getting the right ideas. And so that's why I tried documentaries not long after the big political change occurred in Britain.

Your only other feature in the 1980s was Fatherland. *You and Trevor Griffiths have the same political sympathies, but his script for the film was unlike anything you'd worked on before: it was more European than English and less obviously social-realist than most of your work.*

Again, I don't think I did a very good job. It's an uneasy film, and I think a different director would have made a better one. Trevor's writing is not the kind I do justice to. It's much more literary than I'm used to and it doesn't allow space for the people in the film to move around in the same way that they do in our other films; also, I don't think my way of working with actors was suitable for it. It's not better or worse; it's just different. I think it needed to be steered more than I was able to steer it. In other words, I think it shouldn't have been so observed.

It needed to be more plot-driven?

I think so. The movement in it needed to be more sharply delineated. Frankly, I don't think I was very competent at film-making in that period. I see, in retrospect, that I'd lost any sense of clarity in the work I was doing. I tried to do the film that Trevor and I had talked about, but it wasn't there really, and I think I have to take responsibility for that because the director's first duty is to the script. I think he had written one kind of film and I tried to make

Fatherland: Gerulf Pannach as the dissident folk singer.

another kind, not through wilfulness but just because that's the way my working methods led me. That was interesting, though, and I learned more from it because of that.

Do you think the film worked thematically?

The whole idea of making a film about a songwriter who rejects and is rejected by the East because he's critical of their regimes and who is welcomed by the West as a hero, but who rejects the West as well, got lost. The reason was that we had this whole other strand about the singer's and the journalist's search for the singer's father and his father's involvement in the Spanish Civil War. That in itself was an interesting story but perhaps not altogether central to the one we'd started with.

Hidden Agenda also deals with an investigation in which a mystery is unravelled, but I found it a lot easier to work with and I hope it's a good deal crisper. I think I felt on much more secure territory with that. For one thing, it was a lot easier to work in Northern Ireland because I understood the nuances of the language much better than I did working in Germany, and the exploration of the dirty war in Northern Ireland – what the British state has done to the Irish over the years – was like home territory to me.

Did you feel that the revelations about the singer's father seemed tacked on in Fatherland?

Yes. It was a very difficult scene to shoot, and tended to draw the film out too long, whereas in *Hidden Agenda* the underlying story emerges in dribs and drabs throughout the film. It's a better structure.

Fatherland *comments on the continuing presence of the Nazis in Germany today. I believe you had problems with the German backers of the film over that.*

Yes. There was one scene in the film that worked quite well. It showed a press conference where the singer is welcomed rather grossly to West Germany by a Christian Democrat politician who says that in the West he will find freedom, he'll be able to work, and the more controversial he is, the more he'll get paid. So the singer stands up and says he doesn't need any lessons in freedom from somebody who owes his position to the Fascist tradition, and generally has a go at him. ZDF had paid for the film, and when they saw that scene they cut it for the television broadcast. It was ironic they should cut the only decent scene in the film.

CHAPTER 4

Blockade

In Black and White, A Question of Leadership, Which Side Are You On?, Perdition, The Flickering Flame

Ken Loach might have been expected to hit his prime as a director of feature films during the 1980s. At the start of the decade he was not yet fifty, and the launch of Channel 4 with its alternative agenda and aggressive Film on Four wing would surely have afforded him the opportunity to make low-budget polemical films; as it did, say, Mike Leigh (*Meantime*, 1983). But Loach was now without the counsel of Tony Garnett, who had been his producer between 1966 and 1979. Loach was, in any case, convinced that the only way to confront the crisis in the British trade union movement that greeted the Thatcher government's draconian policies was to make not fiction films but documentaries.

The result was the most blighted period of Loach's career, as he met with political censorship – no less pernicious for being unofficial – at every turn. His four-part Channel 4 documentary *Questions of Leadership* was blocked by the Independent Broadcasting Authority (and forces working behind the scenes). His film about miners' art during the 1984–5 strike was kicked off London Weekend Television's *South Bank Show*. And the Jim Allen play, *Perdition*, which Loach was directing at London's Royal Court Theatre, was pulled just before opening night.

In this chapter, Loach talks about the process of censorship in each instance and gives his opinions about how and why the programmes and the play were banned. The content of the miners film, *Which Side Are You On?*, and *Perdition* is discussed in the interview. It is useful here to describe the content of *A Question of Leadership* and *Questions of Leadership*. In 1980, Thatcher had routed the steel strikers. Working with Barry Hines, Loach compiled *A Question of Leadership*, in which steelworkers, miners and union members from other industries coherently and rationally discuss long-term Conservative plans to create unemployment and undermine trade union solidarity on one hand, and the complicity of union leadership on the other, with the goal of restructuring the British economy. ATV, which financed the film, decided it contravened IBA guidelines and kept this first Loachian salvo against the silent conspiracy of government, management and trade union leaders off the air for over a year. When it was eventually broadcast (by ATV alone instead of on the ITV network), it had been cut and a 'balancing' coda featuring a defensive union official had been appended.

Nothing if not obdurate, Loach embarked on *Questions of Leadership* (1983), which was commissioned by Channel 4. It consisted of four fifty-minute films – flat, essential documentaries, which, in their accumulation of detail about the trade union leaders' betrayal of the rank and file, reinforced the idea of a historical pattern and prophesied the eventual emasculation of the unions during the Thatcher years. The first film dealt with the Lawrence Scott and Electromotors closure, the steel strike, industrial disputes at British Rail (over flexible rostering) and British Leyland, and the National Health Service pay dispute. The second film examined democracy – or the lack of it – in the electricians' union, several of whose members appear in silhouette for fear of reprisals, and whose leader, Frank Chapple, walks out during an interview. The third film is about the shop-steward movement and the sacking of British Leyland shop steward Derek ('Red Robbo') Robinson, and links between British trade unionists and American interests. The fourth film is an edited round-table discussion at Warwick University, in which shop stewards and convenors voice rank-and-file criticisms of union leaders' accountability and are answered in kind by such apologists for the union line as the embattled Ken Cure of the engineering workers' union, John Golding MP and Kate Losinka of the Civil and Public Services Association.

GRAHAM FULLER: *You've described your disillusionment with making movies at the beginning of the 1980s. Notwithstanding that, how come you didn't go to Channel 4 for feature money when it was launched in 1982?*

KEN LOACH: I should have done. I should have talked to Jim [Allen] or Barry [Hines] or Nell [Dunn] or Neville [Smith] – one of the people I had worked well with before – and said, 'Now's our chance.' But I didn't because, as I say, I'd lost direction as regards feature films. But I also wanted to try to make a contribution, however minimal, to the political struggle that was going on. As you know, by the early 1980s working people were getting hammered right, left and centre. Margaret Thatcher had embarked on her catastrophic project of revitalizing the economy in the way she saw fit – restoring the profit margins by attacking the working class. Unemployment went from half a million to over three million in a year or so. Factories were closing. Families were being destroyed. With that in mind, the idea of making a feature film which took three years to finance and another year to come out and then got shown in an art house to ten people and a dog just seemed a crazy thing for me to be doing.

You felt you could address Thatcherism more rapidly and effectively through non-fiction?

Yes. And the group I was affiliated with at ATV [later Central Television] was the documentary department, so my access to a television slot was through documentary.

This was a period in which your work was to be very heavily censored. Before we talk about it, I'd like to jump back to 1970, when you made a documentary called In Black and White *for the Save the Children Fund that LWT refused to broadcast. What happened there?*

That was curious. The Save the Children Fund wanted a film that would explain their work in both England and Africa – Kenya and Uganda. It seemed an interesting project, so I went ahead and filmed it, working with Jeremy Seabrook. We shot the British stuff in Blackburn and then went to Kenya. What we found there was that the people who were supporting Save the Children were the leaders of the business community, and that what they were really concerned with was developing a middle class that was favourable to the West. Their main project was a school called Starehe. It seemed to us that the kids who'd been brought there – who were orphans or kids from poor areas – were being given a Western education, wore Western clothes and got up every morning and saluted the British flag. The libraries were full of cast-off books from the public schools, so you'd find *Biggles* and P. G. Wodehouse in a library for African kids. The headmaster was a guy who had the record for shooting more Mau Mau than anyone else. There was a black American teacher there who was outraged by all this, and he'd had a row with the headmaster because he wasn't allowed to wear a colourful African shirt he'd bought in a market there; the kids weren't allowed to wear indigenous clothing either. We interviewed this teacher, and he put into words what we were feeling: that this school was an exercise in neo-colonialism and it was about developing middle-class people who would become civil servants who would look to the West. So we included all this in the film, and when we got back we showed it, in our innocence, to the Save the Children Fund. It immediately attempted to take the film away from us and would have destroyed it. In the end, I think the negative was preserved in a vault somewhere, but the film was never shown. We thought that LWT would support us and say, 'We've invested most of the money in this film and we're going to show it.' But not at all. One of the gentlemen who ran Save the Children phoned up one of his mates at LWT and said, 'Don't have anything to do with this.' And so LWT wrote off their investment.

Was this the first time you'd experienced censorship?

Yes. We'd been accustomed to battles at the BBC, but this was the first example of ruthless suppression we encountered.

In 1980, you made A Question of Leadership, *a one-off film that was finally shown a year and a week after its original air date and with a certain amount of finessing. Despite that setback, you were able to expand the idea into the four-part* Questions of Leadership. *What was the process?*

A Question of Leadership was a discussion about the steel strike shortly after it had finished. It was made for ATV with the understanding that it would have a national slot, but in the end they just broadcast it in the Midlands area after a lot of arguing and cutting. But when Channel 4 started up, Paul Madden, the commissioning editor for documentaries, told me he could have shown it and invited us to make a more elaborate documentary on the issue of how effectively the trade union leadership was representing the interests of its members.

What was your strategy?

The premise was to try to explore the relationship between leadership and the interests of ordinary working people through the main industrial disputes there had been in the previous few years. There was a lot of information and a lot of arguments to present, so I did it in the simplest, most direct, most traditional way I could, which was through people telling their stories. They were people who were articulate and eloquent, but probably wouldn't be if we just did straight one-on-one interviews with them. I tried instead to gather little groups of them together, to get the spontaneous back and forth of a real story being told. We illustrated it with whatever material we could get, mainly stills, and decided to keep voice-over to a minimum. At the end, there was a discussion in which the participants thrashed it out among themselves.

The story the programmes told was that in the first three years of the Thatcher government there had been a whole series of major strikes and the possibilities of more by an organized workforce that was basically militant, undefeated, and prepared to fight closures, prepared to fight wage cuts, prepared to fight all the things that we now take for granted as an act of God. The response of the union leaders to this militancy was to make certain that each strike happened on its own; not to call out other sections of the union in support; to do a deal before the goal was achieved so that the people out on strike were constantly confused; not to challenge the employers or the government in the way the workers who were prepared to take action wanted. As a result, all the strikes were defeated. So that's what the films said, and we criticized the union leaders for their political programmes, for the lack of democracy within the unions, for the way they worked in a bureaucratic way to suppress opposition.

The overriding idea that emerges is that trade union leaders habitually betray their members. Intellectually, this is a difficult concept to grasp: why would men who came out of the rank and file do that?

That's the history of social democracy. If your idea of a progressive economic model is that privately owned companies produce goods for profit and it is the trade unions' job to get the best wages and conditions they can for their members, then you will fight the employer as hard as you can over wage cuts and redundancies, but in the end you'll accept them. Although they'd never admit it, that's the analysis accepted by the trade unions, who are dependent on the employers making profits and will support their ability to do so. Ultimately, you can only defend jobs and conditions and wages and all the rest if you can say, 'Move out, we own the factory. We'll have a planned economy.'

There was a moment we referred to in *Days of Hope* when there was a possibility of a general strike in 1921, and the trade union leaders were confronted by Lloyd George, who said, 'Yes, you can bring this country to a standstill. Yes, you can ruin the economy if you go on strike. Yes, you can topple the government. But have you considered an alternative – what will you do?' But trade union leaders have never had an alternative. They have nothing to replace an employer with if they bring one down, so when it comes to the crunch they will always back down. They will only defend wages and jobs up to a point. The essence of trade union leadership is you push things as far you can and then you do a deal. That's why someone like Arthur Scargill,* who's the only decent trade union leader there's been in Britain for years, was anathema to other trade union leaders in the 1980s because he *wouldn't* do a deal. Arthur was saying, 'The employers have one set of interests, and we have another, and they're incompatible.' For most trade union leaders, it's enough just to vote Labour every five years.

The question of betrayal, to use an emotive word, is something we see time and time again, and that's what we tried to show in the films. It's the classic pattern of every strike. The workers come out to defend wages or jobs. The trade union says, 'OK, it's an official strike.' The employer makes an offer. The trade union leadership makes a few concessions and tells the workers, 'You've got

---

* President of the National Union of Mineworkers.

to accept it.' The workers don't want to accept it. The trade union says, 'OK, you're on your own and the strike's not official.' The trade union leadership then becomes the enemy. The only big strike that never happened in this way was the miners' strike.

Can you describe the mechanism of censorship – as you see it – that caused Questions of Leadership *to be banned? There must have come a point when you knew that the so-called Labour Party mafia was going to weigh in against these films.*

Yes. We knew when we did the interview with Frank Chapple, the EETPU* official, that we had to handle it carefully, and so we had Keith Harper, the *Guardian*'s very well-respected industrial correspondent, ask the questions. But Chapple still walked out, and we knew we were in dangerous territory. Then, in the discussion that followed the first three programmes, the AUEW† senior official, Ken Cure, had obviously got the wind up, and he was soundly trounced by Bernard Connolly, a shop steward from the Sheffield steel industry, on the Lawrence Scott [closures] issue. It was very funny, and it had the kind of crackle that politics on television ought to have: real confrontation and argument and passion that's not mediated by some bloody TV anchorman.

Of course, Cure was humiliated, and rightly so because he was in the wrong. But then the word got out and the four programmes, which were scheduled to be transmitted to coincide with the TUC conference in September 1983, were pulled by Channel 4 after representations by the IBA. I gather they had received complaints from Frank Chapple and Terry Duffy.‡ We were told that they'd got to be cut down from four programmes to three. It didn't matter which one we dropped; there were just too many. Now nobody explained to me what information was duplicated in the programmes and nobody said, 'Oh, this bit's boring and it's got to go.' It wasn't argued editorially – it was argued politically. The initial suggestion was that every programme would be followed by another half-hour programme of somebody offering an alternative viewpoint, which

---

* Electrical, Electronics, Telecommunications and Plumbing Union.
† Amalgamated Union of Engineering Workers.
‡ President of the AUEW.

was plainly nonsense. To our minds, the alternative view was put every night of the week on the news, or on *Panorama* or *This Week* or any of the other political programmes. Then I was told that other trade union leaders, including those who were hostile to us, had to be asked to appear in these other programmes, which Liz Forgan of Channel 4 was going to commission from the independent production company Blackrod. I phoned up Blackrod and was informed they'd been told *not* to make the balancing programmes. Then I phoned up Liz Forgan and said, 'What's going on?' She said, 'Well, I'm pursuing it and I'm asking the trade union leaders to appear and we need a positive response. But so far they've not agreed and I can't get hold of them.' That, in fact, was the week of the TUC conference, and the union leaders were all in one place and appearing on television left, right and centre. So the idea that they couldn't be contacted was rubbish, but Channel 4 not getting 'a positive response' meant none of our shows could go on. This became a central issue, because it appeared some people had the right to veto programmes being transmitted and others didn't, although I was told by [Channel 4 chief executive] Jeremy Isaacs's office that people could not censor programmes by choosing not to appear. That was being said on the one hand, yet on the other hand, the principle was being contravened because Channel 4 was, in effect, allowing the right of veto.

You have to remember the political complexion of the people involved, the ones who had the power to decide these things. The chairman of Channel 4 was Edmund Dell, an ex-Labour minister, a right-winger, a founder member of the Social Democratic Party – a signatory of the Limehouse Declaration.* The head of the IBA was Lord [George] Thomson of Monifieth, ex-Labour minister, a right-winger, signatory of the Limehouse Declaration. The people making the complaints were Frank Chapple, Labour right-winger, signatory of the Limehouse Declaration. The producing company was Central

---

* The Limehouse Declaration of January 1981 occasioned a crucial split in the Parliamentary Labour Party. Non-socialists and right-wing Labour MPs (and former MPs like Roy Jenkins and Shirley Williams), believing the Labour cause to be hopeless, deserted to the Social Democratic Party. The SDP's subsequent alliance with the Liberal Party severely damaged Labour's performance at the 1983 general election.

Television, and on its board was Robert Maxwell. And the people he nominated to discuss this issue included Sam Silkin, ex-Labour minister and right-winger. So the people the programmes were criticizing were the very people who had the power to stop them being broadcast. You don't need to suggest a conspiracy – they all had the same political interest. And so the programmes rattled between these various parties, each one delaying them, saying, 'You must cut them down.' And that process went on for a year. As I said, they'd been cut from four programmes to three. Then they were cut from three to two, and I was told that a third programme had to be made to balance these two. So that third programme was made, and then I heard nothing for some months. Finally, one day, I picked up a press release in the office at Central – it hadn't been sent to me – that said they'd decided to drop the programmes and not to resubmit them to the IBA or to Channel 4 because they'd had legal advice that they were defamatory.

I went back to Central and said, 'By chance I saw this press release. In the first place, the legal advice which you have paid for was given by Peter Carter-Ruck, a legal firm specializing in defamation, who advised that the programmes were not defamatory and could be defended.' And I said that whatever suggestions Carter-Ruck and your own lawyers had made, I'd agreed to abide by, and that whatever they wanted to cut, I would cut. And, of course, I never got a reply. So it was a fraud.

Do you know who finally pulled the plug?

I understand that Robert Maxwell sent along Sam Silkin when the board of Central discussed the programmes, and that Silkin, without having seen them, simply said, 'These are not the kind of programmes we should be involved in.' That's what I heard. I'd be happy to have it refuted if somebody can come up with facts.

What is your opinion about Channel 4's failure to see the whole thing through?

I think that Channel 4 acted with utmost hypocrisy. Jeremy Isaacs, in particular, emerged with very little credit. By and large he had his subordinates deal with us, but on the occasions I discussed it with him, he made no defence of the programmes' right to be heard.

The people in the programmes had never been on television before, with one small exception, and they had never been allowed to put their points of view before, yet Channel 4 had the remit to allow views different from the mainstream to be expressed. He offered no defence for that, and I thought he was quite unprincipled throughout. What made it all the more galling was that in his book* about his time at Channel 4, he said that I'd been in Turkey – which I had, for a film festival – and claimed that I'd said the political censorship in Britain was just as bad as they had there and that I was a victim of it. Of course, I never said that. It was a misquote; he never checked what I said. If we'd applied the same standards of journalism to our films that he applied to his own book, he would have had grounds for complaint. But, of course, we were a bit more rigorous than he was. When I taxed him with it and said, 'Would you please correct this? It doesn't represent my position,' he chose to ignore it.

Do you feel there's any kind of redress against this kind of political censorship in Britain?

Political censorship is very subtle. It's very rare that the system breaks down to such an extent that a programme is made which won't be shown, because the checks and balances in the making of programmes ensure that those that would be banned never get made. Northern Ireland is a case in point, because the outright ban that existed on the Republicans speaking was not effectively challenged by the broadcasters; they just accepted it. Even before the ban, you never heard of Republicans getting a chance to explain why Ireland should be one country or why Northern Ireland should be independent of Britain. The only question that ever got asked of the Republicans was, 'When are you going to stop bombing innocent civilians?' The question of political censorship in broadcasting really never arises because the people who are appointed to the critical positions are political appointees, therefore the whole gatekeeping mechanism ensures that ideas that they don't want broadcast never get into the studios.

* Jeremy Isaacs, *Storm Over 4: A Personal Account* (Weidenfeld & Nicolson, 1989).

Was it possible for you to show Questions of Leadership *theatrically?*

No. It had been banned because of the spurious reason it was defamatory. Central was technically the producer of the programmes. If they'd agreed that they were defamatory and somebody had sued, it would have been very difficult for me as an individual to defend that. Certainly it would have gone to court, and I'm sure we would have won, but I just didn't have the resources for that. I'm sure there were umpteen pirate copies of the film floating about, but I couldn't publicly show it because the people involved were very litigious.

There was an ironic situation a few years ago when the National Film Theatre ran a series of banned programmes. It showed *Which Side Are You On?*, a film I made about the miners' strike, which had been made for and then rejected by the *South Bank Show* but was finally shown on Channel 4. I said to the NFT, 'I can't claim this programme was banned, but *Questions of Leadership* definitely was, so why don't you show that?' They said, 'Oh, no, we can't do that. We depend on the goodwill of the ITV companies and the BBC to supply the material, so we can't show anything they've banned outright.' So this festival was exactly the opposite of what it said it was. It was a festival of programmes that had *not* been banned. I actually went over to the NFT with the *Questions of Leadership* cassettes and stood there and said, 'OK, I've got them here if you want to see them.' And everybody said they did, but the poor person running the show said, 'No, no – I can't put them in the machine.'

In the end did you just accept that Questions of Leadership *wasn't going to be seen?*

You can fight something like this as long as there's juice in the argument and as long as people will listen to you. The difficulty is that it becomes obsessive, and if you're just one individual film-maker fighting the battle, the other side is winning twice, because not only are you being stopped from showing one programme, you're too tied up with it to make anything else. I spent a year getting *Questions of Leadership* made and another trying to get it on. That was all I did, and I eventually ran into debt. But as long as someone would print a newspaper article about it, it was worth just hammering on, because it was an embarrassment to the people who blocked us.

Did you face resistance to Which Side Are You On? *from the outset?*

In class terms, the miners' strike was probably the most important political event since the war. I tried everywhere to get a documentary made, rang up every kind of person who has commissioned documentaries. They all said, 'No, we know what you're going to do.'

Finally, I approached Melvyn Bragg and said, 'What about doing a documentary about the songs and the poems of the miners' strike on the *South Bank Show*?' There had been a fantastic outpouring of creative work about the strike in the miners' communities, particularly from the women. Melvyn agreed to do it, and Chris Menges and I shot the thing in four days, just running around in a van, with Chris carrying the camera on his shoulder – it was like a return to the old days. It's no great shakes as a film, but the content is extraordinary.

Much of what the miners and their families were writing about was the fact that the police were kicking three kinds of shit out of them every time they went on the picket line. In the last part of the film they sing the songs and read the poems that dealt with the police violence, and we used footage of the police beating people up with their truncheons. I was pleased with that section; I thought it was quite powerful. None of this, of course, was being reported on television. It just wasn't spoken about, and even the most liberal reporters were constantly attacking the miners for *their* picket-line violence.

We showed the film to the *South Bank Show* people, and they looked very serious and said, 'We can't show this.' I said, 'Why not?' They said it wasn't artistic enough. And then, after much negotiation, they said they'd show it provided we cut the last part, and, of course, we said, 'No way.' But they wouldn't relent, and it was never shown by LWT. Channel 4 aired it about three months later.

Did the directive to cut the offending sequences come from Melvyn Bragg or from someone higher up at London Weekend Television?

It seemed that the power behind the throne was Nick Elliott [LWT's controller of Drama and Arts]. He was the person who said they wouldn't show the film. If a similar programme had been made about police brutality in Chile, say, and it showed the folk art or simple verses that people in Chile had written about the thugs who kicked Allende out of power, it would have obviously been shown. But because it was the British bobby who was putting the boot in, it was considered unacceptable. We had a lot of censorship in the 1980s, but this was one of the most disgraceful episodes.

It wasn't the last. In 1987, the Jim Allen play Perdition, *which you were directing at the Royal Court Theatre, was cancelled. Before we talk about that fiasco, I'd like to know what had drawn you to the theatre in the first place?*

Jim had talked to me on and off about the stage play he was writing. It was about events that took place in Budapest in the last year of the war, and the mechanism that had enabled the Nazis to put half a million Jews on trains to the concentration camps in a very short space of time when they were losing the war and had very little strength left. The Royal Court had commissioned it. It was good, meaty writing, it was an exciting story about a subject I didn't know much about but which fascinated me, and it was by Jim, so I agreed to direct it when he asked. It was for practically no money, but he said it would only take a few weeks.

The charge made against the play was that it was anti-Semitic.

The essence of the story is that Zionist leaders in Hungary did a deal with the Nazis that allowed for certain people selected by the Zionists to go free and leave the country, provided instructions were given to the vast majority of Jews to board the trains going to the camps. That deal was actually struck and accepted. It's a matter of record, and it all came out in the trial in Israel after the war. I don't think the structure of Jim's play was ideal, but in a way that didn't matter because the story was so strong. We got a very good, committed cast for it, and we were well into rehearsals when Max Stafford-Clark, director of the Royal Court, showed the script – in his naïveté, I think – to some people from a Zionist organization. They, of course, hit the roof, because implicit in the story was a criticism of Zionism and of the idea of Israel as a state based on race. I had a meeting with a man who was presented to me as a concentration camp survivor. I met him on that understanding, but in a very short space of time it became clear that he was there not because of his own experience but because of his implacable opposition to anything that discussed the origins of Zionism or what these events in Budapest would have indicated about Zionism. And within days, every national newspaper carried a long feature attacking the play, and Jim and me – mainly Jim, me a little – as being anti-Semitic. Bernard Levin wrote a shoddy piece in *The Times* that indicated he hadn't read the play. Lord Goodman wrote an equally squalid article in the *Evening Standard* accusing us of peddling anti-Semitic lies and suggesting we were trying to deny the Holocaust had ever happened. At no point did anybody examine the arguments in the play, and the central thesis of the piece was not denied. The accusations of anti-Semitism were a smokescreen that was blatant nonsense because you would only have to read one line of the play to see it's based on the fact of the murder of six million Jews and the horror of that crime and the horror of racism. But the newspapers didn't let that stand in the way of a good polemic. The way they steamrollered over what we were trying to do was just amazing.

Did you not also get drawn into a debate about the distinction between attacking Zionism and being anti-Semitic?

Yes. It's been well documented that the classic technique of Zionists is to identify Jews with Zionism, so that if you attack the political ideology, you attack the Jews. There were many examples of that given in the course of the play, and it was a tactic used against us.

How were you told that the play was not going to open?

It was scandalous. We were due to open within a day or two, when Max Stafford-Clark told me one evening he was going to withdraw the play after this pressure from Zionists, including some who were on the board of the Royal Court. I said, 'Will you at least keep the decision open until you've spoken to Jim in the morning?' He agreed to that, but in fact gave the news to the press first. We had a shouting match at that point, and I said, 'Now you must go and tell the cast because I shan't.' The cast was getting ready for the technical run-through in the morning, and he came and sat on the stage in the theatre upstairs and announced he was going to withdraw the play. It was a most extraordinary scene, because as he sat there one member after another of the cast cut him to ribbons for the lack of principle. It's not as if he could say the play was untrue or shake any of its basic tenets. The actors asked if they could at least perform it for their agents and their friends so that they could see it wasn't anti-Semitic. But we were told we couldn't even do that, and would we leave the theatre immediately? Of all the contemptible exhibitions I've seen in my life, that was the most disgusting. It was very odd because he just sat there and took all their anger and then walked off. It was as if he had to suffer this abuse to purge himself of the sin.

Given all these experiences, did you feel that you were in the midst of a climate of censorship?

Yes, it was a bizarre period – one of the darker moments. Professionally, it was very bad for me because it seemed everything I touched couldn't be seen. In terms of documentaries, it was difficult to get work because people thought, 'Whatever this guy does it's going to be untransmittable.' And in terms of feature films, the feeling was, 'Whatever he does, it will be in an impenetrable accent and nobody will understand it, and we shall have to subtitle it wherever it goes – and it will be about a miserable subject and rather boring anyway.' So the possibilities of work were declining rapidly.

You made a few other, mostly short, documentaries in the late 1980s and early '90s, but have concentrated on feature films since Hidden Agenda *(1990). The main exception has been* The Flickering Flame *(1996), a film about the continuing industrial dispute on the Liverpool docks, which had been the subject of* The Big Flame, *the Jim Allen* Wednesday Play *you'd directed in 1969. You resume the story in September 1995, when eighty dockers working for a private contractor, Torside, were sacked for protesting at having to work overtime for an unfair wage. The 329 dockers employed by the Mersey Docks and Harbour Company were then sacked for refusing to cross the picket line. Do you think the Torside dockers were set up so that Mersey Docks could get back to casualization?*

Yes. I think that when the opportunity arose, management seized upon it and got rid of these 409 dockers who weren't already casualized. How conscious the trap was and how far back it was laid, it's difficult for me to say because the management wouldn't speak to us when we were making the film. The management must have known a picket line would be set up and that the dockers would refuse to cross it, so it's difficult to resist the conclusion that they were set up.

In the film you include the phone call in which your researcher requests an interview with the management at Mersey Docks but is denied. Ethically speaking, had you not attempted to contact the company, would that have made the film unbalanced as a piece of journalism?

I don't think of it like that. It's just part of the story. I think the whole notion of balance is complicated because it all depends on where you put the point of balance. So 'I don't know' is the honest answer to that.

Two weeks after the Guardian *weekend section published John Pilger's sympathetic article on the dockers' plight, the* Independent's Sunday Review *published a spoiler for the film: a location report from Liverpool in which the writer [Decca Aitkenhead] suggested that the dockers' strike and, indeed, the documentary itself were the last bastions of a lost cause.*

That was a despicable piece. Before the reporter came up to Liverpool, we asked her what her position was. She said she was all for the dockers, so we gave her complete access. We made friends with her, and she was invited into dockers' homes. The article totally ignored the politics of the situation and suggested that making the film was part of some personal crusade of my own, based on a struggle that no longer had any relevance. In fact, the management offensive to move from permanent employment to casual labour and the workers' struggle to resist that couldn't be more contemporary. It's a struggle that will carry on in the twenty-first century. It's entirely the management line to suggest that this issue is out of date and that these workers are dinosaurs. For the reporter to swallow that shows her inability to see through the management propaganda.

But certainly the goalposts have shifted on the front lines since you began making films. Do you think a mythology has arisen around the notion of a global economy that obscures the fact that working people are even worse off now than they were back in the days of The Rank and File *and* The Big Flame?

They're certainly worse off, because the economic system has moved on. In the 1960s, there was a good shop stewards' movement, which meant that the trade union bureaucracies had to respond to the rank and file and their representation. Back then, knowing that you had a job, the struggle was to get good wages and conditions. Then it became a struggle to defend factories against closure. Now it's a struggle to stop all work from becoming casual, de-unionized and hire-and-fire-at-a-moment's-notice, with *no* job security.

So the site of the battle has certainly shifted and organized labour has been losing steadily. As that's happened the economy gets more and more unstable, so that now the collapse of some finance house in Japan can mean that foreign investment in Britain may be threatened. Globalization inevitably increases the instability, which is what the Marxists have been saying all along. Far from being out of date, as most observers insist, the original Marxist analysis is just beginning to bear fruit.

It's very hard to watch the dockers' wives describing on camera how they've barely got enough to live on. However, the film is sparing with those images; nor do you dwell upon the black-and-white vintage footage of casual labour, or shots of the recent mass marches, all of which tend to be emotive. Does a documentary like this require that kind of restraint, because of the risk of sentimentalizing the struggle?

Yes. Those protest march images are the kind everyone's familiar with, and I thought to myself, 'We've seen all that and there's nothing new in it.' You can reinforce the clichés if you're not careful. And I didn't want to go too far back into the past because the inference is, 'Oh, this is a struggle of the past.' And, as I've said, it's very much of now.

CHAPTER 5

Rejuvenation

Hidden Agenda, Riff-Raff, Raining Stones, Ladybird, Ladybird, Land and Freedom, Carla's Song, My Name Is Joe

Because Loach was largely silenced by censorship during the 1980s, it was a demoralizing decade for him, both in terms of his evolution as a film-maker and, what is undoubtedly more important to the man himself, as a voice of outraged dissent against Thatcherism's onslaught on the trade unions and the impoverishment of the working class. The brash so-called British film renaissance of 1985–6, propelled by Goldcrest, Palace Pictures and Channel 4, did not incorporate Loach (although he made the poorly received *Fatherland* during that time), and he would retrospectively characterize himself during this period as an outcast walking up and down Wardour Street, briefcase in hand, in a futile search for finance.

The 1990s, however, would re-establish Loach as a world-class feature film-maker, a master craftsman not only committed to representing the struggles of the socially and politically disenfranchised, but newly inspired as a storyteller. There are three key factors in this not unextraordinary renaissance. First, Loach was especially invigorated by his partnership with Jim Allen. Following the critically acclaimed and appropriately controversial *Hidden Agenda* (1990), their initial film collaboration, they went on to make *Raining Stones* (1993) and *Land and Freedom* (1995). Simultaneously, Loach began to develop productive relationships with other polemically driven writers – Bill Jesse (*Riff-Raff*, 1991), Rona Munro (*Ladybird, Ladybird*, 1994), Paul Laverty (*Carla's Song*, 1996; *My Name Is Joe*, 1998) – in the way that he had previously with Allen, Nell Dunn, Neville Smith and Barry Hines. Second, Loach found a pair of producers, Rebecca O'Brien and Sally Hibbin of Parallax Pictures, who were sympathetic to his ideas and working methods and have been able to raise financing for his projects, usually from Channel 4 and foreign co-production sources.*

The third factor was the teaming of Loach and Barry Ackroyd, who has photographed all of Loach's features since *Riff-Raff* and has brought to them the kind of uncompromising visual rawness that had been lacking from Loach's films in the *Looks and Smiles* era. Ackroyd's cinematography restored to Loach's and his writers' world its aesthetic integrity.† No longer affiliated to a television company, Loach was also seemingly liberated by the necessity of working within what passes as a British independent film movement with its limited commercial imperatives. In other words, for the first time he began to make 'movies' in the same spirit that he made *Kes*: low-budget, trenchant in their sociological critiques, and yet impelled by conventional narrative techniques. The shift suited Loach immediately. *Hidden Agenda*, a fictional version of the Stalker Affair, is a tense, galvanizing, fact-based conspiracy-theory thriller about a mainland police detective's investigation of the Royal Ulster Constabulary's 'shoot-to-kill' policy and the historical ramifications of British 'dirty tricks' in Northern Ireland. It was a marked advance on Loach's previous thriller, *Fatherland*, with which it shared structural similarities.

Loach's next three films were powerful social morality tales about people who, down but not out in the late- and post-Thatcher years, are forced to muster all their reserves of humour and warmth to survive. *Riff-Raff* is the story of a love affair between a Scottish labourer, newly released from prison, and an Irish girl who dreams of being a singer. Its backdrop is an unsafe London building site, where the non-unionized brickies, hod-carriers and roofers strive to get through each day without injuring or killing themselves; the attempt of one of them to organize the workforce leads to his dismissal. *Raining Stones*, set on a Manchester housing estate, is about

---

* The budgets of Loach's features since the mid-1980s are as follows: *Fatherland* £800,000, *Hidden Agenda* £2 million, *Riff-Raff* £750,000, *Raining Stones* £950,000, *Ladybird, Ladybird* £850,000, *Land and Freedom* £2.75 million, *Carla's Song* £3 million, *My Name Is Joe* £2.7 million.
† Other key members of the team are Martin Johnson (production designer), Jonathan Morris (editor) and Ray Beckett (sound).

an unemployed Catholic man's efforts to make some money to pay for his daughter's communion dress; the film is shot through with the desperation of a community whose pride has been ripped away from them, along with their jobs. *Ladybird, Ladybird* wrenchingly examines the plight of a Liverpudlian woman in London whose children are taken into care by the social services following a house fire that took place while she was absent. Quick to condemn, the social workers have little interest in the fact that the woman was abused as a child and battered by her common-law husband, but is now forging a stable relationship with a responsible man. This unflinching domestic 'case history'* parallels *Cathy Come Home* in its analysis of the authoritarianism of the welfare state and *Family Life* in its probing of systematic psychological oppression on the domestic front.

Subsequently, Loach has turned to historical canvases. *Land and Freedom*, his and Allen's Spanish Civil War film, returns to the theme of the left's betrayal of the left in its story of a young British communist who fights alongside and forges relationships with members of a Marxist militia group that is eventually put down by Stalinist apparatchiks following the Barcelona May Days. Epic in scale, *Land and Freedom* riskily locates the political in the personal in the brief love affair between the Liverpudlian hero and the doomed anarchist heroine. The film is on surer ground in its daring recreation of a Spanish village's public debate about agrarian collectivization: one of the purest socialist-realist sequences in all of Loach's work. *Land and Freedom* was followed by *Carla's Song*. Written by civil rights lawyer Paul Laverty, it is a kind of political mystery story about a Glaswegian bus driver who falls in love with a beautiful, war-scarred Nicaraguan refugee and travels with her to Managua and beyond to help her find her Sandinista boyfriend, a torture victim of the Contras. The political revelations in this film are not especially

---

* The docudrama debate that had surrounded earlier Loach films like *Cathy Come Home* was reignited by Carol Sarler's article about the apparent distortion of facts in *Ladybird, Ladybird* in the *Sunday Times Magazine* on 14 August 1994. The article admits that the film 'was based on a real case', but fails to grasp that it is still a work of fiction. See George McKnight (ed.), *Agent of Challenge and Defiance: The Films of Ken Loach* (London, Flicks Books, 1997), pp. 44–5.

revelatory – a former CIA operative (the equivalent of Harris in *Hidden Agenda*) tells how he jumped ship when faced with the nature and extent of Pentagon-sponsored Contra atrocities – nor does it fully engage with the complexities of the revolution at either a historical or grass-roots level. For all that, it is a well-intentioned piece that captures the brief moment of possibility and ferment that followed the overthrow of the fascist Somoza regime.

The Glasgow sequences were the best in *Carla's Song*. Felicitously, Loach returned to Glasgow to make *My Name Is Joe*, from another Paul Laverty script, when the first edition of this book was being compiled.

GRAHAM FULLER: *During the late 1980s, you directed a number of television commercials – for the* Guardian, *for Tetley's Bitter, among others. Was that for financial reasons?*

KEN LOACH: Yes. I was lucky in that I had a friend who was involved with a commercials company. In that business you need someone to promote you, and for that reason once you start directing commercials, it's difficult to just do two or three and then walk away from them. I felt obliged to the people who had got me out of my financial mess.

Did it feel like a compromise?

It was indefensible, really. The people I worked with were very good professionals. The difficulty for me was, having being publicly identified with a socialist point of view, I shouldn't sell my services to advertisers. You can't be in both camps. So I didn't feel very comfortable doing it. But whether or not anybody bothered to take any notice, it enabled me to be seen as somebody who doesn't always make untransmittable work and who has a bit of basic professional craft alongside whatever daft ideas I also seem to have.

Hidden Agenda *certainly reinvigorated your career as a film-maker. How did the project come to you?*

At a time when the possibility of my making a feature film seemed quite remote, I got a call, oddly enough, from David Puttnam, asking

Hidden Agenda: Brian Cox and Frances McDormand.

if I would fancy doing a film about the Stalker Affair.* This was when he was at Columbia. Obviously, Puttnam has a very good reputation as somebody who gets films made, so it wasn't an idle invitation and that was good for my self-confidence. Jim and I started to work on the script and then, of course, Puttnam left Columbia and we were left with it. But at least we had a project and we were alive again, and after a couple of years trying to raise about £2 million to make it, we finally got it made. We couldn't get any money from Britain, of course, and it was an American company, Hemdale, that financed it.

Had you and Jim Allen been considering a film about the Irish Troubles since you addressed them in Days of Hope?

Oh, yes. Jim's family is from Ireland, so it's a subject he feels very close to. In fact, Tony [Garnett] had tried to do a contemporary drama on Northern Ireland when he was at the BBC, but he'd been turned down.

The film's scope extends beyond the Stalker Affair, of course. The British politician whom Kerrigan visits towards the end of the film

---

* In 1985, John Stalker, Deputy Chief Constable of the Greater Manchester Police, investigated the 'shoot to kill' policy of the RUC in Northern Ireland. His investigation was obstructed and no prosecutions resulted from his findings.

is a thinly veiled Airey Neave, and Harris, the renegade Special Branch man who informs Kerrigan of British 'dirty tricks', is based on Colin Wallace* and Fred Holroyd, the whistleblowing former army intelligence officers. Through the politician, Kerrigan learns of the plot to destabilize Wilson's government.

Yes. We wanted the film to be more than about the 'shoot to kill' policy. Harris is closer to Wallace than Holroyd, although Holroyd was an adviser on the film. Wallace had been involved in supplying disinformation about the IRA, and he'd been asked to disseminate black propaganda against British politicians, but he'd refused. His revelations that a faction within the British intelligence services were out to discredit Harold Wilson and members of his cabinet are things that everybody now accepts happened, but nobody has ever been made accountable for them. What we tried to do in *Hidden Agenda* was say very clearly to people, 'Look, the British have death squads in Northern Ireland. They have behaved like terrorists and they've used terrorists to carry out killings. They've been involved in the torture of political suspects. And some elements of British intelligence have used the same black propaganda techniques against British politicians that they've used against the IRA. Now what are we going to do about it?' But none of the film critics who wrote about it chose to deal with the content. They danced around the film and said whether they thought it was good or bad, but nobody took on board the essence of what it's about. Nobody ever took us on and said, 'No, the British didn't do this,' or even came out and said, 'OK, we've got a secret service which is acting against the democratically expressed wishes of the people. What do we do about it?' You hope some of these notions linger with people in the audience, but in terms of public debate it's very difficult to get anything started. One of the ongoing frustrations of film-making is that you try to put out a set of ideas or a piece of evidence in front of an audience, while being as gripping and as entertaining as you can, but critics never deal with the substance or follow up on the questions you're asking in a film.

* Wallace claimed that in the early 1970s he was employed by MI5 to wage smear campaigns against Labour politicians, including Prime Minister Harold Wilson. He alleged that Conservative MP Airey Neave was encouraging propaganda against the Wilson government.

Is this why you regard most film criticism as decadent?

I think so, yes. The critics will examine the brush strokes, but they won't stand back and see the content of the painting. I don't know why that is.

Certainly, in Britain there's a lack of a serious critical tradition beyond Sight and Sound. *The vast majority of film reviews are strictly consumer-oriented.*

Sight and Sound has been too elitist – at least it was in the 1970s and '80s. I don't mind a film being deconstructed if it appears to say one thing but actually says something else if you examine the images it presents. I think that's a good and valid point. But it's a dereliction of duty to construct an argument about a film in cinematic language but not deal with it politically as well.

Hidden Agenda: 'Fiction inspired by fact.'

Given the way you've described Hidden Agenda *as a film about events that happened but which are presented in a fiction, how does one sift historical truth from it?*

I guess it's best described as fiction inspired by fact. It's very close in its depiction of the murders that were carried out by the RUC and in the corrupting effect of the British presence in Northern Ireland, but the whole issue of fact or fiction gets quite tricky at this point, and I'm not sure we solved it altogether satisfactorily – or the attempt to weave together the Stalker elements with the conspiracy against Wilson.

Were you comfortable embracing the thriller elements of Hidden Agenda*?*

I never felt we had to make it in any particular way, as long as we told the story incisively – that alone should work.

Did you work with Sinn Féin at all?

We didn't work *with* them. Obviously, I talked to them. But I also talked to the Ulster Unionist, Ken Maginnis. We met people from both sides.

Why did the RUC interview you?

They came to see me right at the end of the shoot and said that they were usually misrepresented and that they hoped our film gave them a fair hearing. But *Hidden Agenda* wasn't really about the RUC – it was about British dirty tricks.

The film was called 'the IRA entry at Cannes' by some right-wing politician* when we took it to the festival, and it was generally attacked when it came out as an IRA film and as a film that supported terrorists. A number of cinemas refused to show it because they didn't want to show anything that put British soldiers in a bad light. It did moderately well, I think, and just about made its money back.

Rebecca O'Brien worked as co-producer on Hidden Agenda*, beginning your long collaboration with her and, soon afterwards,*

---

* Conservative MP Ivor Stanbrook.

with Sally Hibbin at Parallax Pictures. Had you been looking for a producing partner since you and Tony Garnett parted?

I'd been looking for a base since I left the BBC. Central had been very hospitable to me while I was there, but I spent a lot of the 1980s blundering around Soho with a briefcase, wondering where to make the next phone call from. That wasn't really solved until I got together with Sally at Parallax. I'd met Rebecca on a little film that I was due to make with her in Ireland and from which I was released. She then came on board *Hidden Agenda* and stayed with it for two years, producing budgets, doing feasibility studies, setting it up first in Belfast, then in Liverpool, and finally in London. It was a long process, and she was immensely loyal throughout it. And, yes, you're right, a director does need a good producer.

Riff-Raff was your first film at Parallax and the film on which you began working with new writers again, in this case Bill Jesse. How did you meet him?

I met him through a mutual friend when I was working out of Columbia and getting *Hidden Agenda* ready. He was a writer from Scotland who was working on a building site at the time; he'd had a play produced but hadn't written anything for the cinema. I read some of his stuff and I liked his dialogue very much. He'd got a sharp eye for characters and for anecdotes. I used to meet him in the evenings after he'd finished work, along with some of the people he was working with, and I'd listen to them talk. We thought there was a film in what they were saying about the building trade. It would revolve around a Scot working on a London building site, like Bill himself. So we got a few hundred quid together for a treatment. Then Channel 4 agreed to pay to develop a script, which Bill wrote while I was making *Hidden Agenda*.

Did he turn in a tightly written piece? The film has a spontaneous, improvised feel.

There certainly was a script, but we allowed scope for people to chip in and say things and take everybody by surprise as much as possible. As usual, we didn't show the script to the performers until we actually had to, so it had that open-ended feel about it when we were doing it.

Had many of the actors actually had experience working on building sites?

Pretty much all of them. Robert Carlyle had been a painter and decorator for five years before he became an actor. Jimmy Coleman, who plays the Liverpool lad who throws the cordless phone off the building, is a roofer. Ricky Tomlinson had been a plasterer and was one of the 'Shrewsbury Three', who were building workers imprisoned for organizing a strike in the early 1970s. A fair bit of that comes out in the film, and Ricky added a lot to his own dialogue.

In the scenes in the pub in Up the Junction, *a young builder describes being caught taking a bath by a woman estate agent, and then tells how he nearly fell and killed himself because of unsafe conditions on a building site. Both those dialogue scenes are actualized in* Riff-Raff. *One is a comedy scene; the other has much more serious ramifications.*

You're right! I'd forgotten the connection with *Up the Junction*. The scenes in *Riff-Raff* came out of talking to Bill. He knew people who had been injured on building sites. The danger is worse on smaller sites where a lot of the work is subcontracted and there's no union representation protecting people against hazardous working conditions. It's not uncommon on these sites for men to work under aliases.

The defeat of the unions in the 1980s had opened the door for the return of the old days of the Lump, where building workers had no protection from danger, exploitation or instant dismissal. I remember talking to a group of building workers shortly after we did *Riff-Raff*, and they were saying there had been eleven deaths of building workers in the previous two months in London. But nobody knew what their real names were. That's just Dickensian, isn't it?

There are two stories intertwined in the film. One is about the Ricky Tomlinson character, Larry, and his thwarted attempts to organize; the other is the love story involving Stevie [Robert Carlyle] and Susan [Emer McCourt]. They meet when he finds and returns her handbag; eventually they move in together. It ends when he finds her shooting up. There was a heroin epidemic in London and the north of England in the late 1980s. Was this a comment on that?

In a way, I think that after making a very carefully structured film like *Hidden Agenda* I wanted to do something that appeared random but actually had a coherence. We tried to build a relationship that was based on anecdotes and real people. Susan was based on a couple of girls that Bill had known, and the incident with the handbag was something that had happened to him. As the character of Stevie developed, it was a question of working out who'd be at the other end of the handbag. We wanted a relationship between Stevie and Susan that was deeply felt and mutually dependent, but which was transient. So we had to find a mechanism that could split them up and that was true to the girl – that would explain her, in a way – and that was true to the time, which heroin certainly was at that moment.

On the whole, though, Riff-Raff *was a lighter film than you'd made for years.*

It was a relief. I think I'd got far too po-faced and heavy-handed and that I needed to make films with a lighter touch. It was a pleasure to work with Bill, who was a very funny man. Unfortunately, he died just before we'd finished cutting the film, which was very sad. I think we would have done another one together if he'd lived.

Has your method of working with actors who are semi-professionals or people who have a little bit of performance experience changed over the years?

It's always a matter of judgement on the day: what you tell them, how you prepare the ground, how you set it up. I think I've tried to refine the methods and, in the end, take more chances. In a way, the more reckless you are, the more extraordinary the results you get, provided you assess the risks. The more you try to go for safety first, the less successful you are. I've been very lucky with the people we've cast, but I think what has become clearer over the years is that you have to direct for them. You not only have to guide their performances by talking to them, you actually have to create events for them to respond to. A lot of effort has to go into the circumstances in which they can work, and you find that most of your directing goes into creating something off-camera. You never tell the person in front of the camera that you want them to look happy, sad, surprised, whatever. You leave them alone to concentrate on what is happening off-camera. It could be street activity, an argument, anything. It may be something to which they're not directly related, but it provides the context in which they can perform and it takes the pressure and responsibility off them while you're filming them and makes it easier for them just to be. That way they don't have to do something to be interesting.

Presumably you think it's a more organic way of working compared with the technique used in Up the Junction *and as late as* Kes, *where you would have characters standing at a bar giving an anecdote about themselves in response to a direct question from you standing behind the camera?*

That was something different. I haven't done that for a long time and I'm not sure I would want to do it again. I think it was a way of working that belonged to then. It was true then, but now I find it a bit false.

We talked earlier about how you became dissatisfied with your stylistic choices in the period from Kes *to* Looks and Smiles. *Do you feel that you made a shift with* Riff-Raff? *Certainly that film and the two which followed it,* Raining Stones *and* Ladybird, Ladybird, *have a vitality and spontaneity about them; a sense, in fact, of being less* directed.

Doing *Hidden Agenda*, in particular, gave me and the team we'd gathered around us a surge of energy again for making films, which was then given another push by *Riff-Raff*. The energy comes from working with people like Ricky Tomlinson and Bobby Carlyle and some of the actors I'd met in Liverpool. It was like an affirmation that, yes, if you give people their heads, they will produce something that's interesting and worth hearing about and worth seeing and just extraordinary, really. So I think there was a shift, and it was a shift away from the predetermined surface of the films we were working on. Obviously, the core of each film was very well thought out, but what we started getting, I believe, was a kind of zest and the whiff and taste of real experience. If there was a change of tack, it was to say, 'To hell with it. I don't know how many years I've got left to make films, so let's just go for broke. Do it without a safety net.' I think perhaps on *Looks and Smiles* I'd tried to do it *with* a safety net, and that got rather boring. It's much more exciting to walk the wire without one.

Do you think your documentary period in the 1980s sharpened your storytelling instincts because of the economy of style that documentary requires?

No, it was just the feeling that I'd got a second chance – perhaps a last chance – at doing films again, and I'd better not piss it away. I think some of the work I'd done had been a little bit indulgent, so it was back to first principles. The energy in *Riff-Raff* owed nothing to the documentaries, but rather to the idea of going back to the things that worked well when we were doing films like *Up the Junction*: that sense of vitality and movement and not hanging about for people to bare their souls, but just cutting to the core of what was happening. The fact that we shot *Riff-Raff* in 16mm and that there wasn't much money helped, because we couldn't sit around thinking, 'Where can we put in the production values? Where can we trick it out with pretty shots?' We had to get to the essence of what was happening between the people. And since we had to shoot it in five weeks, that meant people had to move fast, and when they do that there's a lot of energy around, which makes the performances better.

Did this new energy also affect where you placed the camera or how often you moved it?

No, it didn't affect that. It just concentrated the mind not wasting time setting up things that weren't central to the story. We had to be ruthless with the script and cut out anything that was indulgent.

What about editing?

We didn't necessarily cut faster, but said to ourselves, 'What's the point of this scene?' and tried to get it quicker. Anything the film could live without, we'd cut.

Do you apply that same economy to the use of music in your films? Should music be used to heighten emotion, or is that a lazy option?

Jim Allen and Ken Loach.

Riff-Raff: Robert Carlyle and Emer McCourt.

Riff-Raff: Ricky Tomlinson.

I think it's too easy to view a film as an opera, where the music underscores the emotions. I find it glib and I think it coarsens whatever is happening between the actors. Music will tend to generalize the feelings you're striving for by turning the mood into sadness or pathos or whatever. It will never achieve the complexity that the emotions – the relationships – should have. Also I find it just too soupy, really, and I don't care for it. But I think music can sometimes steer the audience into a way of looking at a scene, as a kind of signpost along the road, so that it's not winding up the emotion but is nevertheless saying, 'Try looking at this scene this way.' So music that is laid on a film in post-production should be very sparing. The moment you feel that it's manipulating the emotions, you should cut it out, otherwise it cheapens what the actors have done, if they've got it right. The music should be there, just very subtly underneath, to give you a moment to think or pause or consider.

Sometimes, if the music is an active part of the film, then that can be deeply emotional. In *Land and Freedom*, the members of the militia who bury the people who have been killed in the raid on the village sing 'The Internationale'. Certainly, when we shot that, it was very emotional, and the significance of the song is very emotional. It's part of the present tense of the film and it's very important. We hoped some of the music in *Carla's Song* would have the same resonance.

Your next film, Raining Stones, *was, I assume, very personal to Jim Allen?*

In some ways. After *Hidden Agenda* and, particularly, *Riff-Raff*, I felt I wanted to work with Jim on the subject that I think he knows best – the people of the area where he lives in Manchester. We'd done *Days of Hope*, we'd done *Hidden Agenda*. We'd also worked on scripts that hadn't got made, including his play *Perdition*. Of all the writers I know, he's the one most rooted in his own experience, and I felt he would be strongest writing a contemporary story from a little anecdote dispatched, as it were, from the front line and which revealed how ordinary people were coping in that part of the north at that time: it would show the state of play. So Jim hit on this central idea of a Catholic couple faced by their seven-year-old daughter's first communion and the need to buy her a dress. They haven't got a pot to piss in, so how does the husband, Bob, who's unemployed, go about paying for the dress? It's about how he tries to raise the money and the trouble that he gets in. It's a comedy about debt really, but it's got a sharp edge.

More than anything you'd previously done, Raining Stones *is a ray of light.*

Yes. It has quite a tender feeling, which is what I think you get when you meet people like Bob and his wife. But there's a hard edge underneath it. The attraction was to tell what was apparently a simple story, but in which we'd just draw the curtain back on a whole way of life – people scrambling just to stay afloat.

Isn't it also about maintaining a vestige of dignity when you're beaten down?

Absolutely. It's about people who are beaten down but are not broken. The important thing about Bob is that he's not destroyed and he's desperately trying to keep his self-respect intact. It's also about different kinds of morality. There's nothing wrong with nicking a sheep off the moor to sell to a butcher or nicking the turf off the Conservative Party bowling green. That's fair game. But you don't prey on your own kind, as the loan shark does – that's unacceptable.

The loan shark struck me as being a more pernicious version of the tally man who preys on housewives by getting them to buy goods on hire purchase in Up the Junction.

But the loan shark didn't come out of any cinematic memory of mine. Loan-sharking is a common occurrence in that community and in many other communities. It was a very natural part of the story and not exceptional in that time or place, but obviously it has horrific consequences.

Was there a danger that Bob's killing of the loan shark could have turned the film into a melodrama?

It was a danger, and one we were very aware of. But I think it was the kind of situation that's occurred once or twice in films we've done: people get to such a pitch of desperation that they're just

Raining Stones: 'A contemporary story from a little anecdote dispatched from the front line.'

going to strike out, which is what Bob does when he finds the loan shark in the car park. The trickier scene was the one with the priest, when Bob confesses to him what he's done, and the priest says, 'Fuck the loan shark.' People usually laugh or smile when they see that, because it's not what you expect from a priest. We thought it would prick the bubble of Bob's guilt, but there had to be a fine line. We may have tiptoed over to the wrong side of it. I don't know, really. I think it's all right.

Certainly one has no moral qualms about the death of the loan shark.

No.

Your next film, Ladybird, Ladybird, *was based on an actual case history of a woman who keeps losing custody of her children. What, for you, was the kernel of the story?*

We received a letter from a woman who had worked as a social worker with the real 'Maggie'. What was interesting to me about it was not the idea of a shock-horror exposé of a woman whose children were taken away from her by the social services, which would be better done as a documentary, but the damage that was done to someone as a child and how that leads to a cycle of abuse. Maggie has been left with a kind of residual anger, which leads to her accepting violent behaviour as an adult and carrying it out herself, which in turn leads to her losing her children, which leads to more grief and more rage. How that cycle perpetuates itself is not something you can show in a documentary; it needs to be written as a piece of fiction.

I was looking around for a writer. Sally [Hibbin] alerted me to Rona Munro's work as a playwright, which I immediately liked. I met Rona and liked her very much, and we went to see the real couple together and talked about what the sense of the film should be. We knew we couldn't tell the story in a linear form because it would just seem like a catalogue of disasters that ends tragically. It seemed to us that the developing relationship between Maggie and Jorge would best determine the shape of the film, and that that would also make it optimistic because, despite what happens, they stay together. Despite Maggie kicking the shit out of Jorge at every opportunity, she desperately needs him and he needs her, and the grief and everything else Maggie experiences would then become a part of that relationship.

What were your and Rona's uppermost thoughts about Maggie's personality during the writing process?

I think the whole point was to show, as far as we could, the full complexity of Maggie, and to try to understand why the social workers come to the decisions they do. She's obviously a very difficult woman, but there's a reason for that – the abuse she's gone through. Ultimately, we felt it was a film about grief and loss and how, if those feelings are suppressed, they turn into a terrifying rage. Maggie is deeply damaged. Nevertheless, she's got enormous guts and courage and such determination to be a mother that nobody's going to stop her being one. To us, she was like a heroine of tragic proportions because she had this fatal flaw. But there was an explanation for it; it didn't come out of thin air.

I feel very warmly towards *Ladybird, Ladybird*. I can see it's quite a tough film for people to take. But there's a quality in Crissy [Rock]'s and Vladimir [Vega]'s acting that you only get once or twice in a lifetime as a director. Crissy was phenomenal. She revealed things about the depth of people's feelings that were just extraordinary at the time. I feel quite privileged to have worked with her, and Vladimir, too, because he was also essential to us in that way.

We auditioned lots and lots of people to play Maggie, but there was something about Crissy that struck a chord and seemed right for that part. She's a performer from Liverpool – mainly a comic – who plays the clubs, and she'd been through the mill a bit herself, as she told us when we first met. She was terrific to work with – amazing energy.

What kind of direction did she require of you?

I was telling you earlier about directing off-camera, and *Ladybird, Ladybird* was a case in point. It was never a question of directing Crissy directly or telling her what to do, but of making things happen for her to respond to, arranging things for her to tackle – for example, the seizing of her children by the social services people. It was all about creating the context.

Ladybird, Ladybird: Crissy Rock.

Presumably she never saw the whole script?

No. When something was going to come as a shock to Maggie in the story, then I'd want it to come as a shock to Crissy, so obviously she wouldn't see the script beforehand. Where she'd be reacting to something that wasn't a surprise, where it was a question of some development, then she'd perhaps get the script a day or two before. I wouldn't rehearse it with the other actors so that she'd always hear the lines spoken to her freshly. It's a commonplace to say it, but acting is about *reacting*, isn't it? The first time you hear something, you respond to it in a way that you never would if you were to hear it again.

Did you allow Crissy to improvise?

Yes. But after the first take, I'd try to steer the subsequent takes a certain way and suggest some different lines. Then she'd usually incorporate them in the improvisation. It's actually a very pragmatic way of working.

Is there a risk that a scene can get out of control if it isn't rehearsed and nailed down?

It should get out of control, really. If it's always under control, it can often turn out dry and predictable. The main thing is to work out with the cameraman where it's best to put the camera so he can cope. I know we became a little unstuck on that once or twice when we were shooting *Land and Freedom* in Spain.

Generally, will you describe to actors what you want of them before you shoot a scene?

No, not before it. I'll tell them bits and pieces as we go along. But it depends on the scene. If there's going to be a lot of information passed, then you need to stick to the script pretty closely. *Hidden Agenda* was different from most things we'd done because a lot of it consisted of police interrogations, which are obviously highly informational. The big showdown between Kerrigan and Brodie [the RUC chief] was an example of something that came almost entirely from the script. You could never improvise a scene that was as tightly and economically written as that. I don't worship the idea of improvisation for its own sake. It's just something to use when it's appropriate. All that matters is what you get on the screen.

Would you describe your way of film-making as filming the process of the actors as they work their way through the story?

The idea is that they start at the beginning of the story and they experience it, and that's what you film, as far as you can, given all the compromises that film-making involves. The scene they do one day is the rehearsal for the scene they're going to do the next day.

Ladybird, Ladybird is a harrowing journey, and the scenes where Maggie is battered by Simon [Ray Winstone] are among the most brutal you've ever filmed. You've already talked about the story having an optimistic quality, but as a film-maker who needs to make a story palatable to the general public, are you conscious during the scripting and shooting stages of the need to leaven such grimness with moments of humour and tenderness, or do they work their way in naturally?

I think if you just observe how people are and how people get by, you'll notice funny things or tender moments happening anyway. In a way, it would be unrealistic to exclude them, because you'd be excluding a huge part of life. There aren't enough of those moments in *Ladybird, Ladybird*, unfortunately. We should have captured more moments where Maggie's wry humour enabled you to smile a bit more. She is, in fact, very witty and uses language in a very sharp way, but there are so many desperately sad situations in the film that it's hard to smile.

Was it difficult shooting the violent scene I just referred to with the child actors present?

They didn't see the full thing that we see when they gave their reaction shots. Crissy and Ray only acted a toned-down version of that in front of them, and the little girl's mother was present throughout. It was still a nightmare having to put them through it, but it was a scene we couldn't duck if we wanted to take the story seriously. All I can say in mitigation is that it wasn't as bad as it looks.

Was Cathy Come Home *going through your mind while you were making* Ladybird, Ladybird?

We were very aware of it. There are obvious surface similarities, but the stories are very different. *Ladybird, Ladybird* is a study of a person and the relationship she's in. *Cathy Come Home* was a much more diagrammatic description of how a family becomes homeless. The scene in which Cathy's children are taken away happens right at the end of the film, whereas it's the thing Maggie's fighting right from the start. We did think long and hard about whether or not we dare show this happening to a woman again, even though there was a twenty-eight-year gap between the two films. In the end, it would have been silly to walk away from this very real story because we'd filmed something akin to it that long ago.

After Ladybird, Ladybird, *you collaborated with Jim Allen again on* Land and Freedom. *However, the idea of your making a film about the Spanish Civil War was not a new one, was it?*

It was something we'd had at the backs of our minds for ages. It was first formulated in 1988, after a production company had turned us down on *Hidden Agenda* but offered us a commission on something else. We suggested three subjects to them, and one was the Spanish Civil War. They commissioned us to write a script, we did a draft of it, and then went back to *Hidden Agenda*. When it came up again, it just seemed the right moment to do it.

The Spanish Civil War is holy writ to people on the left because it was the first big war against fascism. There was great international solidarity between working people who went to Spain to help the Spanish people against Franco. And there was also, in the first few months of the war, when the peasants took over the lands and the factory workers took over the factories, a critical moment when there was a real possibility of change. It looked as though there would be a social revolution in Spain, as there had been in Russia, with the people taking control of their own lives with optimism and strength. So for a few months everybody was clear where they stood and there was no hiding place for anybody. That's why it's such an exciting story and why we wanted to tell it. But, inevitably, the film would have to be about why the political tendencies resisting fascism fell out, and the consequences of their falling out.

The Spanish war is also one of those events that unlocks the twentieth century. When the mists had cleared, it was apparent that the British, French and American governments had supported the fascists in Spain because the revolution there was going to benefit the working class. It was, therefore, hypocritical of them when they posed as the great anti-fascist nations during the Second World War. The Communist Party, meanwhile, had been desperate at all costs to do a deal with Britain and France at the expense of the workers' revolution in Spain.

What were the main problems Jim Allen faced in writing the script?

The war was fought by people who were very political, particularly the international volunteers. You couldn't make a film about that without engaging with why it happened and the reasons why it went wrong. It was very important to us that these conflicts were reflected through the relationships, that they didn't exist in the abstract, that it wasn't a film about 'ologies' or 'isms', that it was really a film about David and the betrayal of his group, and his relationship with Blanca and why she felt betrayed. All that has more resonance with people than a lecture would.

There was very little in the script at the beginning that was there at the end. Several things had to be resolved. The main one was that essentially it was a political story about the struggle between the Communist Party and the anarchists for the leadership of the Republican side. It raised a lot of questions: Is having a revolution an essential part of winning the war? Do the revolutionaries try to win the war against fascism first and then try to win the revolution? How do we show all that? The only way to begin to answer those questions – and I'm not sure we did – was to incorporate all that into a personal story of a group of people and the various tensions that emerge among them, without making good guys and bad guys, without falsifying history, and without doing anything that one couldn't justify absolutely as something that could have happened to this person or that person. It took a long time, going backwards and forwards, to work all that out.

Is David naive in his idealism?

David's fired with enthusiasm, but that doesn't make him naïve. He's from Liverpool, which is a very politicized city, and he's in the Communist Party – so he's political. Remember, the Spanish Civil War happened less than twenty years after the Russian Revolution, and the Communist Party was still seen as a revolutionary party. If you wanted change and you wanted a better world, you joined the Communist Party. What's important about the journey that David makes in his mind is that he is in the Communist Party at the beginning and that he goes to fight the fascists as an individual. When he's on his way to Barcelona he meets somebody by chance on a train and ends up joining a group called the POUM,* which was a small Marxist party in Barcelona. When the fascists raised their standard, it was ordinary people organized by trade unions or different political parties like POUM who went to the front line to fight them. The point is that David is proud of being one of those ordinary people and he's proud that he was a member of the Communist Party before it got organized into the International Brigade.

Originally, we had David going out to Spain not as a communist, but as a member of the Independent Labour Party, which supported the POUM all the way through. But that would have meant he wouldn't have had to tear up his party card, which was essential. Blanca was originally going to be a German girl, because Jim thought it'd be good that she be somebody who had a knowledge of what fascism meant. In the end we felt one of the main characters had to be Spanish and must in some way embody the revolution. That's why we made Blanca Spanish, and when she is killed you know that the revolution has died with her.

Doesn't her death also symbolize the tragedy of the Communist Party selling out the Trotskyists?

Really it was about the selling-out of all those people who had taken the opportunity to say, 'The land is ours, factories are ours,' to stand up repeatedly and say, 'We're taking control of our own lives. Why should we fight to put the landlord back in power?' The

---

* Partido Obrero de Unificación Marxista. Formed in 1935, a party of Trotskyists and communist dissidents committed to the notion of 'permanent revolution'.

Land and Freedom: 'One of those events that unlocks the twentieth century.'

communists weren't just betraying a small sect. They were actually betraying the opportunity for the people as a whole to liberate themselves from the class struggle. It was the end of that dream. Incidentally, the POUM claimed not to be Trotskyists, although one could debate that.

David is made aware of what's happening in Spain when he sees a newsreel. Your films could scarcely be described as self-reflexive, but I wondered if, in a way, you were acknowledging the power of film to stir people up?

Yes, in a way. It was the best and simplest way of communicating to David and the audience what fascism meant. An old film is very evocative, isn't it? You really have to peer at it because there are jump cuts in it and no sequences, just odd moments. It has a stronger impact because of that very fragmentation, rather than if it were a more technically adroit piece.

Partly for budgetary reasons, I believe, you had to introduce framing sequences. They deal with David's passing away in modern-day Liverpool and his granddaughter finding his letters and mementoes of the war. Through them, she becomes his witness and the carrier of his memory. How did these framing sequences enhance the narrative?

We didn't want to tell the story with a straight A–B narrative, but in a fragmented way that would allow us to comment on it from a contemporary perspective. Having the girl read the letters enabled us to show that the Spanish Civil War is part of our history now. But it was also a way of condensing some of the events through the letters – instead of showing them through dialogue scenes – and letting the protagonist, David, reflect on them as he experienced them. The letters were very important because they didn't just come to his girlfriend in Liverpool, but to two generations later.

There's also a little mystery that goes along with the letters. Among David's things, the granddaughter finds the picture of the long-dead girl – who was she? There's often something special about old people, but we don't always take the trouble to find out. Because our grandparents are elderly, we think they're boring and out of touch, but they've probably all got extraordinary stories, if we did but know it.

There's a hint, but no more than that, of what the failure of the Spanish revolution had left David with and has left us with now. It makes you think about the present in a way that isn't, I hope, too heavy-handed. The situation today is that there is mass unemployment, as there was at the time of the Spanish Civil War, and the far right is on the march again, as it was then. We wanted to show that connection. It makes me think of the oft-quoted Orwell remark, 'Who controls the past, controls the future,' the gist of which is that history is written by those who are in power now, and so, in that sense, history is contemporary.

At the centre of the film there's a long debate about land reform. Was that a structural risk?

To us, it seemed great drama, great conflict, a very human struggle put forward in concrete terms. One guy says, 'Look, I work harder than you lot. Why should you share what I have?' Then there's the old fellow who's seen it all, and who says, 'The revolution's like a pregnant cow, and if you don't help it at the moment of delivery, the thing will die,' which is very true. Another says, 'Look, if we band together, we can get a tractor. But we can't do that if we stay separate.' So it's not a battle of ideologies. That would be a major turn-off, and nobody would want to go and see it. The scene shows people struggling in a very practical, human way, just to see how they can move. When they do make a decision, to me that's a very moving thing, because these are people who have been on their knees all their lives. They're saying, 'This is us – we can take these decisions.'

How much of that scene was scripted?

Jim had written some good speeches and interaction between the participants, but as it developed people obviously took off from the script and got into the cut and thrust of it.

The POUM was betrayed by the communists – once again it's that theme of the left betraying the left that recurs in your films.

Yes. One of the abiding themes of politics on the left in this century is that ordinary people, working-class people, however you

Land and Freedom: the left betraying the left.

describe them, have shown immense potential to make changes, but not only have they constantly had to struggle for wages, against factory closures, welfare provision and health services, but they have always had problems of leadership. The twin evils they're beset with, it seems to me, have been social democracy and Stalinism. If the social democrats haven't betrayed the workers, then the Stalinists have. The left has consistently been led down paths that disorganize and disorientate them, and which lead them up blind alleys. One set of workers will start to lead a struggle, and everyone else will be held back until they're defeated. Then there's always that political tendency that says, 'Go back home, boys. Not today. Do it tomorrow.' And, of course, tomorrow never comes.

Why do you think the right wing is better organized?

The right's interest is in maintaining the status quo, so it doesn't really deal in ideas. It might deal in populist slogans, but it doesn't have to make an analysis of the situation in order to see how to change it, which is what the left has to do. If you look at what ideas there are on the right, they're fairly derisory, and you can't formulate an analysis from them. The left has always been about ideas – conflicting ideas.

Ultimately, what is the contemporary resonance of the Spanish Civil War that you tried to get across in the film?

I think if one has to pick one thing, it is, in the end, the idea of working-class loyalty – to use an old-fashioned term – and solidarity. The enemy is internationalist and has no problem in slipping its capital from one economy to another, which keeps the working classes divided into nations and countries and makes them compete with each other or they're out of work. That international solidarity was something that was expressed so graphically in Spain, and it's something we need to remember now.

This was an epic film, compared with the things you'd done in the past.

It was very exciting to do it because of that. We tried to suggest the breadth of the struggle, while keeping a sense of intimacy among the people. There's no mystique in shooting battle scenes. You do them just like any other sequence, and if what you put in front of the camera is exciting, it's exciting – provided you shoot it right and cut it to a proper rhythm. The only criterion is accuracy.

Was it a coincidence that Ladybird, Ladybird, Land and Freedom *and* Carla's Song *had Spanish or Hispanic protagonists?*

It was entirely coincidental. The real woman we based *Ladybird, Ladybird* on was pulled through, insofar as anyone could pull her through, by a man from South America, and therefore Jorge had to be South American, too. Long before that, Jim and I had started talking about the Spanish Civil War. Then *Carla's Song* came out of the blue. Paul Laverty, who had been working as a civil rights lawyer in Nicaragua, got in touch with us about doing a script after he had been there. They all came quite separately and independently. Obviously, having worked on the Spanish film, we had to think of a way of telling a story about Nicaragua in a very different way.

You weren't consciously seeking, with Land and Freedom *and* Carla's Song, *to internationalize the issues you keep coming back to in your work?*

Definitely there was the sense that I'd just done a few films that were set in working-class situations in Britain, so it was good to get a different perspective on things. But it was no more than that.

When you were on location in Nicaragua, did the Nicaraguans embrace the film?

There was a great tide of emotion and interest and concern about this subject that they were very anxious to pour out, so, yes, they took us to their hearts. That fact alone was very moving and it kept me going. It was Crissy times a hundred, if you get my meaning, and that was much more than what I expected. I anticipated an uphill struggle, but it was the Nicaraguans who carried the film along.

How did the Nicaraguan actors respond to your working methods?

From the Spanish films I'd seen, I guess I feared that Hispanic acting would be histrionic and that they'd be declaiming all the time, but Nicaraguan people aren't like that. When we were doing auditions, I would try to set up scenes of conflict for them to improvise, just as a way of trying to find the right actors. But I realized that I was asking them to do things that were foreign to the way they express themselves. I've noticed that the British, Spanish and other European actors that I have auditioned slip very easily into scenes of rows and arguments because they're easy to act – you strike off the other performer and the thing takes on a momentum. Nicaraguans tended not to do that. They were very polite and they listened to each other before they spoke. It made for an interesting challenge.

When George is talking to some of the campesinos on the bus, one of them tells him that the land once owned by one man is now owned by forty families. Was the collectivist theme – which is expressed more ardently in Land and Freedom *– something you brought into the script?*

No. It's very central to what Paul was writing about and very central to the reason for making the film. Even in the situation many Nicaraguans are in now – with ex-Contras lurking in areas close to the people they were fighting and killing – there is this great attempt at reconciliation. There's still a lot of violence in Nicaragua, but on the whole it's not expressed through debate or through rows. The scene on the bus touched Oyanka particularly, because of the transparent honesty of the *campesinos* and the fact that many had lost family members in the war.

Did the fact that the Sandinista government was no longer in power make it difficult to get across the progressive achievements of the revolution in the film?

Yes. We met a lot of people who are still committed to the ideas of the revolution, particularly people in the countryside: it was a revolution of *campesinos*. But undoubtedly the mood of the country had changed. I'm sure if we had made the film ten years earlier, it would have been more vehement.

Some observers felt that the film lost narrative momentum once it left Glasgow for Managua. Can you describe how the romantic story was supposed to facilitate the political one?

Carla's Song: Oyanka Cabezas.

I can only talk about intention, and the intention here was to show George caught in a dilemma. Here's this bus driver from Glasgow, a cheerful guy who's completely apolitical, and he's become involved with a woman who fought for the Sandinista Revolution and was traumatized by the war. As George gets deeper, he wants to pursue a full relationship with Carla. He's obviously very attracted to her and has a sense of who she is, but there's a whole area that he can't touch. In order to really know who she is and have a viable relationship with her, he has to help her explore what happened to her so that she can come to terms with it. He takes her back to Nicaragua to help her search for her lover, Antonio, knowing there's always the danger that she will stay with him. Despite that, he has to help her lay that ghost.

As it unfolds, the more George gets to know Carla, the more she slips away from him; the more she returns to who she is and to her struggle, the more unfathomable she becomes to him. Which is why in the end he tells her that this isn't his world and he's going back. We hope that, as the audience witnesses this, it sees all kinds of parallels: like how a struggle in a foreign land of which we know little becomes a struggle that we kind of understand. The fact that George is a bus driver was obviously not an accident, because the kinds of people he gets on his bus and enjoys meeting and jokes with are exactly the same kinds of people he meets in Nicaragua. Except for the fact that they've all got guns, the girl soldiers he's chatted up and is kidded by are just like his sister and her schoolfriends. We tried to thread all those little resonances into it. Oddly enough, the rhythm of the film is different from some of the others we've done in that it's quite discursive; it's like a journey. That was a big gamble, and I don't know whether it comes off or not.

Do you think George is politicized at all?

Politicized is probably too strong, but he learns a lot.

Scott Glenn plays Bradley, the renegade CIA man in the film. Like Harris in Hidden Agenda, *he's crossed over because he wants no more blood on his hands, but I'm not certain how well integrated into the film he is. Not to criticize Glenn's performance – he looks*

Carla's Song: Glasgow (Robert Carlyle).

Carla's Song: Nicaragua (Robert Carlyle and Oyanka Cabezas).

the part – but Bradley's denunciation of the CIA's sponsorship of the Contras' atrocities is shrill.

It may be that we slightly misjudged the narrative around that point in the film. If we were doing it again, I think we'd structure it differently, particularly towards the end. We trimmed a little from that scene in the version we showed in Britain.

Did the experience of working in Glasgow on the first half of Carla's Song *prompt your return there for your next film,* My Name Is Joe?

It was prompted more by the chance to work with Paul Laverty again. He's a terrific writer, and we see the world in the same way. It seems a very good partnership at the moment. We wanted to carry on working together, and to do something on a domestic scale. *My Name Is Joe* is another film about what's going on in Britain, or Scotland in this case. It's a film that explores people's three-dimensional humanity rather than just their harder edges.

Joe is an alcoholic who's off the booze and he's running a football team for the unemployed in the housing scheme where he lives; that's his project, as it were. He meets this woman who's a health visitor working out of a doctor's surgery; she's a well-organized

Carla's Song: Scott Glenn as the renegade CIA man.

professional who keeps a tight grip on her life. The film is really about their love story, and it's quite light in some ways.

These are characters in their late thirties. Do you feel this is an age group that doesn't usually get heard in the cinema?

Absolutely. I think older people tend to be more interesting, by and large. They are more complicated by life. But then all generalizations like that are daft in the end, aren't they? You know, Hamlet's a youth, King Lear's an old man.

What dictated the look of the film?

It's a continuation of trying to distil everything down to its essence and to work in the most economical, simple, direct way. The area in Glasgow where we filmed it is very hard and has the highest incidence of intravenous drug use in Europe. A lot of the people there are in very bad shape. But, as you'd expect, there are also people there performing acts of heroism on a daily basis, just to try to make something viable happen.

What specifically has driven the work you've done in the 1990s?

My Name Is Joe: Peter Mullan.

My Name Is Joe: Louise Goodall and Peter Mullan.

As Britain emerged from the spell that Thatcher had put on it, I and perhaps some other film-makers felt very dissatisfied with ourselves. We felt we hadn't really put on the screen the appalling cost in human misery that aggressive Thatcherite politics had brought on everybody. We should have made films in the early 1980s that really showed what was happening, but I know that I didn't. I think the last few years have been an attempt to remedy that.

CHAPTER 6

Some Reflections

GRAHAM FULLER: *Do you feel that the political analysis you made in the 1960s still applies?*

KEN LOACH: I think it applies even more strongly. It just grows ever more apparent that there are two classes in society, that their interests are irreconcilable, and that one survives at the expense of the other. In the 1960s, we didn't have the mass unemployment we have now. We didn't have such alienation. We didn't insist that the workforce should be ever more flexible, ever more exploited. All that was endorsed by Thatcher. Her politics were inverse Marxism in a way: the working class must pay; the organized working class must be disorganized. And that's exactly what she did.

Now, with the global economy, the struggle is relentless. All the propaganda is aimed at keeping working people divided by their country. You know, 'You've got to work hard or all the jobs will go to Germany. Your conditions have to undercut the conditions in Germany.' People are kept divided, but nevertheless their interests are global, so it's very difficult to think of subjects that are restricted by country.

In Britain, the recurring themes don't go away. The human cost of the experiment in free-market economics that Thatcher inflicted on us is still working itself out because the policy hasn't changed, and it won't change drastically under Tony Blair. The human cost is something that never goes away. It's always in front of your eyes and it's always something that draws you to try to deal with it. You walk through the cities, especially the outskirts of cities, and you see that people are not having a good time. The underlying observation of what people are experiencing is that things don't have to be this way. There are better ways to live.

Have you ever felt that you could have perhaps reached a wider audience for the kinds of ideas that you and your writers have tried to get across if you'd made more obviously commercial films or television programmes? Would it have been unacceptable to you to make, say, a film like Reds *or, at the opposite extreme, a soap like* Brookside, *each of which has its own kind of marketable socialist agenda?*

For me, it's unacceptable because politics is reflected through the aesthetics of film-making. If, say, you get a well-known film star to play a working-class guy, it's like saying, 'There's no working-class man who's capable of doing this.' You can also deconstruct it and say, 'What's a film star doing in the middle of a working-class area of Manchester?' In other words, it invalidates the proposition. The reason we only went to one classroom in one school in Barnsley to pick a boy for *Kes* was part of the thinking behind the project, the idea being that there's a kid in every class like Billy. The way you make a film is an important way of validating the ideas in it.

Are the means of production, and especially the communal spirit in which you make the films, an intrinsic part of the democracy of the process?

I can't use the word 'democracy' really because what I do is quite manipulative in the end – it has to be. Only one or two people are looking through the lens, and so only one or two people can make the judgements about what needs to happen. But it has to be an inclusive process. It's a cliché, but it's true, that everybody can fuck it up and everybody has a contribution to make.

Is that because it benefits the work, or is it also a principle?

I think it's the only way to behave; anything else is just intolerable. It's important that everybody's comfortable in what they do, and so everybody must be respected. The actors, in particular, must feel able to take any risk and they need the confidence of knowing they're among friends. I think that's the only way you get good work, otherwise people become defensive and inhibited and shy.

In terms of getting across the ideas that you and your writers wanted to get across, do you feel you've been more successful with fiction films or with documentaries?

More with the fictional pieces, especially as most of the documentaries haven't been shown anyway. Fiction is about more than a political analysis, which can often be very dry. Fiction is about the expression or the lines on somebody's face when something happens. It's about the way light falls in a room. It's about the way people walk down the street after a lifetime's work. It's about how they live in their rooms, how they've got the food they put on the table. It's about the fabric of life, the product of all those details of the way we are. Politics is implicit in all that, but it can't be dragged out of it.

If approached to work in America, would you?

I think it would be interesting. I think it's always very difficult to work in a country other than your own, as I found in Spain making *Land and Freedom* and in Nicaragua making *Carla's Song*, because you don't have the same intuition about the culture and about the way people are. There has to be a very powerful reason to work outside your own country, I think.

Robert Duvall says that the films he's directed were influenced by yours. I believe he invited you to direct a project at one point.

Yes. We first met just after he'd directed that film about the gypsy lad [*Angelo, My Love*, 1983], and when I was doing *Carla's Song* he suggested a script to me. I appreciated the offer very much, but I just felt that it needed an American sensibility. The problem now is that the idea of working in the States is sitting there like a challenge, and I'm starting to feel that if I duck it, it'll seem like I bottled it. Sooner or later I feel I've got to have a go and just do one there. I feel I can't walk away from it before I fade to black.

Which of your films have given you the most personal satisfaction in terms of getting their ideas across?

You remember films by the people you made them with and not the finished product. It's like having sets of families, and they're all good in different ways. I was very lucky to work on *Cathy Come Home*. *Kes* was obviously very important to us; *Land and Freedom* was perhaps the most memorable. It marked all who worked on it. *Ladybird, Ladybird* has a special kind of resonance, as does *Riff-Raff* because of Bill Jesse. That's not to say the others weren't also full of good memories.

Where do you see your targets arising from in the next few years?

It's dangerous to think in those generalized terms because you start making films about issues rather than a particular person or situation or a precise image. For a film to work, you've got to be excited by it cinematically, as well as by what it's saying. The essence is always to find the humanity in whatever situation you're exploring, and to find moments of resistance and moments of dilemma and choice in which there's inherent drama, inherent struggle. I think a lot of cinema now touches situations that are quite profound or important, but it reduces them to a facile cinematic style. I believe the challenge now is to push all that aside and just say, 'Look, where is the common humanity between the audience and the people in the film?'

Are you optimistic or pessimistic about the state of society?

In the short term, you can't be optimistic because people are faced with this spiralling decline. In the long term, I guess I'm optimistic because people always fight back. The reason to make films is just to let people express that, to share that kind of resilience because that's what makes you smile. It's what makes you get up in the morning.

Do you think you'll go on until you drop?

Well, it certainly feels like it.

CHAPTER 7

Lessons

More on *Perdition*; a new era

As a quarter of a century had passed since the interviews comprising Chapters 1–6, a reorientation was in order. This chapter revisits the censoring of Jim Allen's play *Perdition* (1987) and Loach's disappointment with his direction of *Fatherland* (1986) – setbacks that he considers instructive – and the processes of making *Hidden Agenda* (1990) and *Riff-Raff* (1991). The latter pair revitalized his career as a director in the cinema and presaged the formidable run of films he made with the producer Rebecca O'Brien and the screenwriter Paul Laverty, along with other regular collaborators, from *My Name Is Joe* (1998) to *The Old Oak* (2023).

GRAHAM FULLER: *I'd like to renew our conversation by looking back a little. Forming Sixteen Films with Rebecca and working consistently with Paul have enabled you to be enormously productive since the mid-1990s. What were the long-term lessons of the difficult time you went through in the 1980s?*

KEN LOACH: I tend not to look back very often because you've got to keep your eyes to the front. The 1980s was a very harsh decade and, for me, in terms of work, an extraordinary lesson, in that almost everything I touched got banned. As you know, even when I did Jim Allen's *Perdition* in the theatre, it was banned. We've talked about it briefly, and it's certainly important because it was the springboard for the next phase – I've been lucky to keep going for more than thirty years since. I learned that everything we'd said politically in the 1960s, based on the books we'd read and political theory in the abstract, was actually true: namely, that, in Marx's words, 'The executive of the modern state is nothing but a committee for managing the common affairs of the whole bourgeoisie.'*

The issue is the dominance of big business over workers' rights. When Thatcher came into power, she was determined to put the economy back in a shape suitable for capital to make profit at the expense of the working class. So set-piece strikes were set up that Thatcher was prepared to win, and unions were picked to do battle with, starting with the weakest, which was the steelworkers' union, and ending with the strongest, which was the miners' union. It was planned like a military campaign, and it allowed unemployment to rise from less than a million to over three million very quickly. This meant people were desperate for work, which further weakened the unions, because if someone's outside your door willing to do your job for half the money, inevitably you lose because you can't negotiate. Then legislation followed that formalized rules to keep unions weak. It was a conscious, very carefully worked-out plan that you could see unfold throughout the decade, and alongside that you could see how the news was absolutely and precisely manipulated.

It was the same in all the press, but particularly visible in the BBC, which is set up as the state broadcasting company, literally. It parades its independence, but the editing of the BBC news crew's footage of the Battle of Orgreave† gave the lie to that. It was the

---

* Karl Marx and Friedrich Engels, 'Bourgeois and Proletarians', Chapter 1, *The Communist Manifesto* (1848).
† British Steel's Orgreave coking plant, near Rotherham, South Yorkshire, processed coal into coke. On 18 June 1984, 5,000 pickets from the National Union of Miners, striking to protest threatened pit closures, attempted to stop coke from being transported from Orgreave to the Scunthorpe steelworks in Lincolnshire. They were confronted by 6,000 officers from the South Yorkshire Police and seventeen other police forces. Three hundred and forty-five officers were armed with riot gear (batons and short shields); police dogs and their handlers were deployed to hem the pickets into an open space between Orgreave village and the coking plant. During the ensuing violence, which included three charges on the pickets by forty-two mounted officers, fifty-one pickets and seventy-two policemen were injured. One miner who speaks in the film likens the police brutality to that inflicted by the Black and Tans

biggest confrontation between miners and police. What happened in real life was that the police charged the miners on horseback, and then the miners, who were wearing T-shirts and plimsolls mostly, retaliated by lobbing whatever was to hand at the police in self-defence. The BBC showed the miners throwing stones, and then the police charging. It's accepted now that the BBC reversed the footage.

The constant refrain in the BBC, and in the press at large, was picket-line violence, the pickets beating up the police. That was the only story. I remember Kate Adie, the celebrated BBC journalist, reporting it. Well, I stood on the picket line. I saw the police going in, in their vans, holding £5 notes at the windows to show the overtime they were getting. And then, if the miners did anything, they were charged by mounted police, struck with batons, arrested, beaten up in the back of police vans. As you know, we made a little film called *Which Side Are You On?* for [London Weekend Television's] *The South Bank Show*. It was the only film at the time that showed how the miners' strike was part of the campaign to weaken the trade unions. We got some footage of the police beating up the miners and put it in the film, which is why ITV refused to show it. It was only shown on Channel 4 towards the end of the strike. Seeing the role of the media so sharply was a real education. It endorsed the ideas that we'd had in the 1960s, which said that the media is in the hands of the ruling class, to use the old language.

So all that was a huge lesson. And then, when I did *Fatherland*, from an interesting script Trevor Griffiths wrote, I completely

---

on Irish civilians between 1920 and 1922 (see pp. 217, 220 and 229). Daniel Gordon's 2024 documentary *Strike: An Uncivil War*, which contains archival footage and first-hand accounts of the battle by former miners, police officers and lawyers, follows Loach's *Which Side Are You On?* in detailing how the Battle of Orgreave was pre-planned by the Conservative government to break the NUM and redress its successful strike for improved pay in February–March 1972 and subsequent strike for an increase in February 1974. The credibility of his Conservative government having been damaged by the miners' victory in 1972, Edward Heath called a snap general election for 28 February 1974, under the slogan 'Who governs Britain?' The election led to a hung parliament, Heath's fall from power and the return of a Labour Party government under Harold Wilson.

messed it up. I didn't do it well. It's my fault. I don't blame anyone else for that. It had good people in it, Chris Menges shot it, everything was right, but my work was rubbish. Then I worked with Jim Allen on *Hidden Agenda*, which came out of a long period of failing to get the right ideas. Between us we didn't come up with a really strong idea. I was still involved in trying to get documentaries made that told what was happening, but at every corner I was turned back.

What are your reflections now on Perdition?

That was another extraordinary lesson. Jim's play was based on the true story of Rudolf Kasztner, one of the leaders of the European Zionist movement in Hungary towards the end of the Second World War. In 1944, Adolf Eichmann did a deal with Kasztner's group [the Relief and Rescue Committee of Budapest] to select over 1,600 Jews to leave by train for Switzerland, with the aim of going to Palestine, provided the information about where the other Jewish people would be sent was kept secret.*

Jim used this story to examine the validity of the Zionist project. I was new to this subject and read some of the research Jim had done, though not all of it. There were Jewish academics who supported us, books written that detailed the facts of the case, and a Jewish man, Uri Davis, made certain the play was

---

* Between 15 May and 9 July 1944, 434,000–437,500 Hungarian Jews were deported, mainly to Auschwitz, where 80 per cent of them were gassed on arrival. The 'Kasztner Train' left Budapest on 30 June and was diverted to the Bergen-Belsen concentration camp, arriving with 1,684 passengers on 9 July. Between August and December, 1,670 survivors arrived in Switzerland. In 1953, when Kasztner was living in Israel, he was accused by the journalist Malchiel Gruenwald of collaborating with the Nazis. On Kasztner's behalf, Israel's government sued Gruenwald, who was acquitted by Judge Benjamin Halevi in 1955. In a statement, Halevi said that Kasztner had 'sold his soul to the devil' by collaborating with Adolf Eichmann and his SS deputy Hermann Krumey by betraying thousands of Hungarian Jews in order to save those who escaped to Switzerland. Kasztner was assassinated near his home in Tel Aviv on the night of 4 March 1957 by three veterans of the right-wing militia group Lehi. Nine months later, Israel's Supreme Court overturned all but one of Halevi's rulings against Kasztner.

published afterwards.* So we were surrounded by Jewish people who said it wasn't a racist or anti-Semitic work but a play about a political idea. But just before it was due to open at the Royal Court, the theatre's director, Max Stafford-Clark, gave the text to the historian Martin Gilbert, a hardline Zionist, and within a few days there were leading articles in all the main newspapers – led by the *Guardian*, of course – suggesting it was anti-Semitic. Then, as the campaign grew, the charge of anti-Semitism was made quite openly in everything from the *New Statesman* to the *Evening Standard*. Some said it denied the Holocaust, which, of course, couldn't be more wrong because it was based on the fact of the Holocaust, but that didn't seem to matter. It was just abuse, and the attacks got more generalized and more inaccurate. The play was taken off, and ever since then I've been a marked man for those attacks. This resurfaced when Jeremy Corbyn became leader of the Labour Party, because I was supporting him, along with hundreds of thousands of others. Anti-Semitism was the weapon that was eventually used to remove Corbyn from the party's leadership.†

To get back to your original question, the general point I've been making is that the 1980s was a tough time financially for making films, but it was a hell of a lesson and it just clarified politics. I think it was Lenin who said capitalism can survive any crisis, provided the working class pays the price. And that was the period when the working class did pay the price, and we've seen it in more recent times as well. The role of the media could never be clearer, and it's remarkable that so few people seem to have learned that lesson. You know, the great and the good, the people who parade themselves as being on the left, the people you looked to for support for Jeremy Corbyn, for example, suddenly disappeared. All these people who made their reputations as leftists, suddenly where were

---

* *Perdition* was published on 8 July 1987 by Ithaca Press, Reading, England, in collaboration with the Jerusalem & Peace Service, a consulting office on the question of Palestine headed by Davis. Born to Jewish immigrant parents in Jerusalem in 1943, Davis is a civil rights activist and academic who describes himself as an 'anti-Zionist Palestinian Hebrew'.
† Corbyn was leader of the Labour Party and Leader of the Opposition from 12 September 2015 until 4 April 2020.

they? They'd lived through the 1980s like I had, and how could you not have that imprinted on your mind?

Though we talked before about Hidden Agenda, *I think it's worth readdressing it as the film that rekindled your career as a director in the cinema. Significantly, it was the first film on which you worked with Rebecca O'Brien.**

Jim had the idea of doing a film on 'shoot to kill', where the 'British' (in inverted commas) security forces – the military and the pro-British Ulster Unionists who wanted to keep Ireland divided – collaborated, obviously in a secretive way because it couldn't be public, in a policy not of arresting Republicans whom they suspected of taking part in the armed struggle, but of shooting them.

It was a good story. But from the point of view of film-making, I still had an idea of feature films being something rather elaborate and felt I had to shoot them in a different way. I'd forgotten the lessons of *Kes*, really, and certainly forgotten the lessons of the TV work we did with mobility and speed and spontaneity. Everyone else's work on *Hidden Agenda* was fine. Frances McDormand, Brian Cox and the Irish people we worked with were all terrific, and I've stayed friends with them. Fran and I still exchange Christmas cards. The cameraman, Clive Tickner, is a lovely man, and his work was good. But my work was a bit laboured, I think. The way we shot it felt too heavy, and I emerged from that film thinking I didn't get it right.

As we were finishing it, I met Bill Jesse, a Scotsman who had been a merchant seaman. He was working on building sites and writing down incidents that occurred. There wasn't a story, but we worked on one about a gang of builders, and I gave it a framework. Then we introduced the character, Stevie, really based on Bill, whom Bobby Carlyle played. A Scottish guy comes down to London, meets a girl and works with a bunch of Scouse builders and others, led by Ricky Tomlinson. It was a very simple story that just had an energy. And that was *Riff-Raff*. I realized I had to get back to making films with speed and mobility, that allowed things to happen, rather than try to nail them down so anxiously, as I'd

---

* O'Brien was co-producer on *Hidden Agenda*.

done on *Hidden Agenda*. Just work with much more freedom. It pushed me on in terms of film-making. It was a whole other step, and it was immensely helpful.

Riff-Raff has the flavour and energy of some of your late-1960s television films, like The Golden Vision.

They're both Liverpool films as well, and the Liverpool lads bring their own comedy and fun and laughter. We shot *Riff-Raff* in five weeks on 16mm. It was the first feature film I did with Barry Ackroyd, whose skill as a cameraman is very precise. It emerges from Chris Menges's way of shooting, but is a development of it. I wanted to work with Barry again, so *Riff-Raff* led to *Raining Stones*, which was written by Jim and produced by Sally Hibbin.

I had had many sound recordists up to that point, but Rebecca had worked with Ray Beckett and recommended him, so Ray came on board. *Raining Stones* was also the first time I worked with Susanna Lenton, who was . . . well, I always say 'continuity', but the job is called script supervisor now. Susanna stands by me throughout the shoot. Martin Johnson had already been with us as production designer for many years, and Fergus Clegg came as his art director on *Raining Stones*. Film-making is a series of partnerships where you share the same basic aesthetic, and there was something about the team that just clicked. Everybody, in their own taste and judgement, gravitated to a way of shooting that is quick and fluid when you're on set. I will have a basic little plan for how the shooting will work each day, which I sketch on the script but don't show to anyone. I will have talked it through with Barry on the phone, so when we do the recces, he will know where the camera's going to be. The light will be minimal, and the camera positions allow the light to fall pleasantly on the people in the shot, without him having to overcompensate by shooting into the light too much or with the light behind us.

In terms of Ray's approach to sound, the guiding principle is that, as an audience member, you are a witness, in a corner of the room or out of sight on the street. The camera is a human presence, placed where an observer could be standing, so the sound reflects what that observer would hear, without a change of perspective. The camera might end up taking two positions, but that's the maximum. It's always an unobtrusive presence so that the audience is unaware of it, and it's positioned so that the people are the most important element in the shot, unless there's a specific plot point that needs to be made. By and large, it's about the people. If there's a bright red or something that would catch your eye and draw attention to something that isn't important, you remove it. The colours are modulated so that it's the people you watch and are drawn to. And the camera is never positioned on the ceiling or on the floor or in the sky or anything!

Barry has great skills. If we were filming a discussion around a pub table – or any classic situation like that – he'd be able to pan from one speaker to another, maybe from a two-thirds rear profile of one person to the other person, who's looking at them and seen more in full face. The camera would go where your eyes would go naturally. Just by following what's going on, Barry would get a good composition at the end of it. We would work out the positions around the table so that he could get all those moves, very unobtrusively, and each time he would land a good frame. We wouldn't end up with someone's nose in the corner of the frame, which would have meant we had to do it again. So it became a very precise partnership.

Likewise, when we were much more dependent on the boom than we are now, Ray would work very carefully, paying great attention so that the boom could be in the right place without disturbing the line of the camera. We've had one or two really brilliant boom operators. Pete Murphy, a terrific Scottish guy, worked with us for ages. He'd hold the boom for long periods, knowing where to go with it, and he'd never make eye contact with the actors, only seeing them out of the corner of his eye so as not to put pressure on them. Little things like that are important. Ray isn't dependent on the boom because the personal mics are so efficient, but I like the boom, and we still use it.

Have you always shot on 35mm film in recent years?

Not always. We went back to 16mm on one or two films. *The Navigators* [2001] and *Sorry We Missed You* [2019] were on 16mm. It has advantages if you're in a confined space, because the gear is smaller and you can move it around more quickly.

Have you ever been tempted to shoot a film digitally?

No. I like the discipline of the ten- or eleven-minute reel. It means you shoot less, and it's much more precise because you've got to contain a scene within that time, which makes you consider what its structure will be when you put it together: can you get the shots that will give you the balance and shape of the scene, visually, that you want? You don't just shoot endlessly as you do with a digital camera, simply because it's cheap to use.

Some of the old Hollywood directors – John Ford, 'One-Take Woody' Van Dyke – used to cut in the camera.

I would never do that because what you're filming is part of a long day in someone's life, and the idea that they suddenly speak without anything leading up to it is false. Often you cut into a scene, however. If it had been in real life, it would have begun some time before, so if you're one of the people playing it, you've got to know, 'What's in my head? What's in my guts when I come to the piece that they want to use for the film?' But you don't know – you haven't done it. So I always try to do a lead-in. Though the actors don't know which bit we're going to use, they will then feel it's as close as it can be to a real scene that's happening. Otherwise, you've got to work with them and say, 'Right, imagine you've been doing this. Start now in the middle of it.' But that goes against the idea of making what you see on film as close to a real experience as we can get it.

You mean you can't isolate an emotion from what produced it?

And you can't rationalise it. I don't want people to say, 'I'm feeling this, that or the other.' Just respond. Follow your instincts so they carry you beyond the end of the scene. You always let a scene run on afterwards, otherwise people play the end of it. If you ever listen to *The Archers* [the BBC radio serial], you can tell which is the last line of a scene because it's spoken like a punchline. Well, that's obviously false.

Another key member of the team for many years was David Gilchrist, who was a terrific first assistant director. David understood that, for a scene to work, the director's got to keep in contact with everyone in it. I tend not to relay requests or suggestions through the first AD because your tone of voice is important and the words have got to be very precisely chosen. Don't say too much, don't say too little. Just find words that indicate something or leave a question. It's got to be very subtle, so you can't relay that through someone because it would change and become Chinese whispers. David always showed great sensitivity in that area. It's very important.

What about hair and make-up?

We haven't always had the same person, or people, doing the make-up and hair. We don't use much make-up, apart from a bit of blood now and then, and the actors' hair should be as natural as possible. The people doing those jobs are the first to meet the cast in the morning. They've got to be good at their work in terms of skill and technique, of course, but also because the mood that they set first thing is key. They're not too boisterous and not too hale and hearty. They're certainly not miserable. They're comforting, and [cast members] can talk to them if they've got problems. The care work is a key part of what they do. Everyone we've worked with in those jobs has been a friendly face, cheerful but not imposing.

This sensitivity also applies to the gaffer and the sparks.* You only need one person yawning or looking uninterested and the energy falls. For a long time we had a penalty box on the set – 10p for a yawn. I haven't maintained it on the last film or two – and it was a joke anyway. But the point is, you don't want anything to affect that collective concentration, which isn't oppressive but is something we share and is really central.

I've certainly never made a speech about any of this. Everybody in the team is drawn to this sensibility. The communication between all the departments is very easy and friendly, and everybody consults. Nobody has been presented with anything on the day that has made them say, 'Oh, God, I can't work with this.' Everybody interacts well, and we become a really happy team at every level.

---

* On a film production, the gaffer is the head of the electrical department and the technician responsible for the execution (and often the design) of the lighting plan. The sparks are electricians who look after and ensure the distribution of power to the lighting equipment.

You are under stress sometimes, but if you're shooting fast and have that ease, it's like driving a car, where everything is well oiled and all the parts interconnect, which is such a joy. And when things go wrong, you take it seriously, of course, but in the end it's only a film, so you share a laugh and get on and make it better.

Is this level of sensitivity still important when you're working primarily with, say, a cast of self-assured blokes who constantly joke and kid each other, as on The Navigators?

Oh, yes. Everybody responds to kindness. There's got to be a sense of welcoming and valuing everyone. Some were railway workers, some were actors and some were comics in the Sheffield area. You just find the common denominator really, and on *The Navigators* everybody shared the laughter, particularly at the beginning of the film. And, of course, the comics were great because they were throwing in lines, and everyone fell about. It was infectious, and the point was to capture that laughter. When you've got a situation like that, no one's competitive in a bad way and no one's looking over their shoulder.

I would say I make more mistakes than anyone, but if you make a mistake, it doesn't matter. It's just a bit of film in a camera, so do it again. It's a question of finding the right pressure, but it's never destructive pressure or the fear of failure. It's creative pressure, and we're going to get there however you wind up the energy because everyone's on their game.

CHAPTER 8

Looking to Scotland

My Name Is Joe, Sweet Sixteen, Ae Fond Kiss, Tickets, The Angels' Share

Throughout his career, Loach has elected mostly to follow the story ideas and characters created by the writers of his films. 'If you go where the writer writes well, where he understands the idiom and where the language rings true, you tend to get the better work,' he told David Archibald in 2002.* He has, of course, worked only with writers with whom he shares strong social and political values, at the core of which is a burning sense of injustice over capitalism's exploitation and impoverishment of ordinary people.

This chapter looks at the five Loach films, from *My Name Is Joe* (1998) onwards, that were written by Paul Laverty and either set in his native Scotland or, in the case of their strand of the anthology film *Tickets* (2005), foreground Scottish characters. Though the duo's first collaboration, *Carla's Song* (1996), opens in Glasgow and shares the subjectivity of a Glaswegian bus driver, its focus on the tragic experiences of a young Nicaraguan woman following the Sandinista Revolution means Loach's commentary on it dovetails with his thoughts on *Bread and Roses* (2000) in Chapter 9 and his and Laverty's segment of *11'09"01 – September 11* (2002), which are rooted in Laverty's familiarity with the Los Angeles Justice for Janitors movement and knowledge of the 1973 military coup in Chile. (To preserve the organic flow of the interviews, the discussion of *Carla's Song* remains in Chapter 5.)

Of the Scottish films, the tragic dramas *My Name Is Joe* and *Sweet Sixteen* (2002) and the uplifting heist comedy *The Angels' Share* (2012) confronted the ongoing drugs crisis that spiralled

---

* David Archibald, 'Match Made in Heaven', *Sunday Herald*, 29 September 2002.

in Scotland in the 1980s. The Thatcher government's monetarist and fiscal policies included lowering taxes to boost free-market capitalism and increasing unemployment to lower wage inflation, which in Scotland was facilitated by the accelerated, policy-driven contraction of jobs in shipbuilding, coal mining, steel and jute production, engineering, manufacturing (including textiles), docking and the railway industry, though engineering and shipbuilding had been declining since after the First World War. A savage blow was dealt to the Scottish working class by the 1981 closure of the Linwood car plant in Renfrewshire, which resulted in 6,000 immediate job losses and 7,000 more in the vicinity. Mass unemployment caused widespread poverty, mental ill health, the collapse of communities, dereliction and depopulation, with cities like Glasgow, Dundee and Edinburgh among the worst hit. The availability of cheap heroin from Iran and Afghanistan caused crime and addiction to surge.

Introduced in Chapter 5, *My Name Is Joe* tells the story of Joe Kavanagh (Peter Mullan), a jobless but optimistic recovering alcoholic with a history of domestic abuse who coaches the unemployed lads (some played by addicts) in his housing scheme's football team, including Liam (David McKay), a former drug dealer and junkie who cleaned up in prison. Joe has befriended Liam and through him meets Sarah (Louise Goodall), a health visitor with a steady income and a nice flat, who is helping Liam's partner, Sabine (Annemarie Kennedy), with their toddler Scott, who has learning disabilities.

Joe persuades Sarah to let him and his pal Shanks (Gary Lewis) wallpaper a room in her flat, despite their limited decorating skills. Joe interrupts the job to pour paint on the car of an unemployment benefits office investigator, who has taken photos of him working that will stop him receiving his dole money. He loses it for a week, despite Sarah writing in to explain that Joe did the job for her as an unpaid favour. After he thanks her, they go on a date and start a romance.

Sabine and Liam's life becomes increasingly unstable. Sabine steals a prescription pad from the clinic where Sarah works and is told to leave, despite Sarah's protests. Joe sees Liam being menaced by thugs working for McGowan (David Hayman), a drug baron who grew up in the same scheme as Joe and once employed him.

Finding condoms in Sabine's purse, Liam accuses her of having an affair, but she is secretly working as a prostitute to pay for heroin. Joe realizes she has become an addict when he visits the couple at home and finds her shooting up. While Liam was inside, she took over his dealing but still owes McGowan £1,500. McGowan threatens to have Liam crippled unless he is paid.

Laverty's 'reveals' in his screenplays frequently expose how politically compromised working-class people betray one another in order to survive. Like Joe and Liam, Sabine is a victim of the government's callous (and low-interventionist) anti-industrial imperatives, which despoiled Scotland in the 1980s no less than it did at the time of the Highland Clearances (as the Scottish rock duo the Proclaimers ruefully observe in their 1987 song 'Letter from America'). But she is also culpable, thanks to her addiction, for Liam's plight. To wipe out Liam and Sabine's debt and make £500 on the side, Joe agrees to pick up a drugs consignment for McGowan from a northern Scottish harbour town (though it was filmed west of Glasgow in Tarbert, Kintyre). After Liam lets slip to Sarah – who is pregnant – how Joe got McGowan off his back, she breaks up with Joe, appalled that he would bring drugs to Glasgow, knowing that she works with addicts. In a speech that encapsulates the film's critique of the unbridgeable gulf in class between Joe and Sarah, he bitterly explains to her how people of his social stratum are economically hamstrung and, unlike Sarah, have no financial resources. Having given Liam £300 to leave town, Joe visits McGowan to tell him that he refuses to do another drug run. When McGowan's son threatens to rape Sarah, Joe bottles him and floors McGowan. Back home, Joe gets drunk. When Liam comes seeking help, Joe reviles him and his family. Sabine phones to warn Joe that McGowan's men have smashed up her home and are coming to kill him and Liam. Joe is too incapacitated from the booze to stop Liam hanging himself. Sarah and Joe stand apart at Liam's funeral, but as she's leaving she waits for him.

Sweet Sixteen tells another initially upbeat story of a well-intentioned male 'schemie' inevitably derailed by his social circumstances. Another Liam (Martin Compston), this one aged fifteen, has been raised in Greenock, on the upper Firth of Clyde, twenty-six miles west of Glasgow. The town has been depleted by the closure of most of Clydeside's shipyards and heavy engineering works.

Like Billy Casper in *Kes* and Mick in *Looks and Smiles*, Liam has become, as far as society is concerned, an expendable youth who has no likelihood of finding a decent job. Thrown out of school, he and his best friend, Pinball (William Ruane), whose father is a junkie, survive by selling contraband cigarettes in pubs.

Liam's mother Jean (Michelle Coulter) is a heroin addict controlled by her violent partner, Stan (Gary McCormack). She took the rap for Stan's drug dealing and has served most of the resulting prison sentence. Later in the film, it's revealed that she is a victim of domestic violence at the hands of her father Rab (Tommy McKee) and her ex-husband. Stan and the alcoholic Rab, who are Stan's partners in crime, make Liam conceal heroin in his mouth for smuggling to Jean in prison, but because she's in rehab he refuses to give it to her. Stan beats up Liam outside the facility; Rab throws Liam's belongings out of his house. Liam's sister Chantelle (Annmarie Fulton), a self-reliant single mother who's studying at college, agrees to put him up.

Liam sees a caravan overlooking the estuary and sets his hopes on buying it for Jean. He and Pinball steal Stan's drug stash and sell it on the streets. Liam puts down a deposit on the caravan. After a gang of rival dealers beat Liam up and steal his gear, he gets it back by threatening them with a baseball bat. Tending his wounds, Chantelle recalls when they lived in a kids' home, and how scared she was by the sight of Liam recklessly fighting three bigger boys who broke his arm.

The local drug kingpin, Tony Douglas (Jon Morrison), whose front is a health club, offers Liam a regular supply of drugs to sell, and Liam uses a friend's pizzeria as a front for his dealing. Thanks to him and his mates using mopeds, business is brisk. Douglas warns Liam to drop the unstable Pinball and tests his nerve by seeing if he would kill an associate of Stan in a nightclub, Douglas's henchmen stopping him at the last moment.

Finding the caravan burned down, Liam goes after Stan, but merely liberates Rab's false teeth from their irate owner. Pinball picks up Liam in Douglas's stolen car and rams it into the plate-glass door of the health club, on the wall of which he sprays the word 'cocksuckers'. His rage at Douglas's approval of Liam hints at homoerotic jealousy. When Douglas meets with Liam, he tells him he's bought the pizzeria and put it in Liam's name, and that he will buy Liam a flat for Jean to live in, as long as he 'takes care' of 'that wee prick Pinball'. It is unclear what Liam will do when he visits Pinball, but Pinball pre-empts him, admitting in his anguish that he burned down the caravan and gashing his own face with a knife. Liam calls an ambulance for him.

Liam's drug business continues to thrive. Three months later, he holds a party at the flat, which overlooks the estuary at Gourock, to celebrate Jean's release, but the next morning he discovers she has gone to stay with Stan, who is again supplying her with heroin. Liam learns from her and Stan that she mocked the caravan and doesn't want the flat. In his distress, he stabs Stan. He winds up on a beach, alone, like another compromised youth, Antoine Doinel (Jean-Pierre Léaud), in François Truffaut's *Les Quatre cents coups/The 400 Blows* (1959). Chantelle phones Liam to tell him the police are seeking him and that she loves him. Having turned sixteen that day, the age of full legal capacity in Scotland, Liam is certain to go to prison. He walks towards the water; only Chantelle (who has just passed an exam and taken a job) seemingly has the capacity to escape the pervasive social decay.

Like *My Name Is Joe*'s Liam and Sabine, Jean and Pinball are birds of a feather tarred by Scotland's urban malaise and their social disenfranchisement by the government; despite their best efforts, so, too, are Joe and *Sweet Sixteen*'s Liam. Laverty, as the writer, and Loach, as the director of the actors, ensure that their behaviour is conveyed with psychological accuracy, desperate feelings predominating over rational thoughts.

The Loach team's next Scottish-based film was *Ae Fond Kiss* (2004), a romantic drama about generational conflicts and the ongoing problems of assimilation faced by a Glaswegian Pakistani family. However, the brutal environments and bleak endings of *My Name Is Joe* and *Sweet Sixteen* prompt a look first at *The Angels' Share* (2012), in which a schemie with a criminal history, but also a connoisseur's nose for whisky (a talent equivalent to Billy Casper's in *Kes* and Liam's in *Sweet Sixteen*) and a supportive partner (a positive young mother like Chantelle), escapes the pall of drugs and violence bequeathed by deprivation.

Robbie (Paul Brannigan), who's in his early twenties, has served time in prison for committing grievous bodily harm, when stoned, on a student, Anthony (Roderick Cowie), during a night out. Now trying to go straight, he has been sentenced to community payback with fellow young offenders Mo (Jasmin Riggins), Rhino (William Ruane) and Albert (Gary Maitland), under the kindly supervision of the avuncular Harry (John Henshaw). Robbie is beaten up on the instructions of Matt (Gilbert Martin), the father of his pregnant girlfriend, Leonie (Siobhan Reilly), and misses the birth of their son, Luke, but Harry cleans him up and helps him celebrate becoming a father with his first glass of whisky. (Harry is a whisky aficionado, but not a heavy drinker.)

Liam and Leonie attend a restorative justice meeting with Anthony, whose academic and professional prospects were ruined when Liam half blinded him in the attack, and Anthony's parents and girlfriend. Despite Liam's awareness of his guilt, he cannot bring himself to apologise, but Leonie warns him she won't allow Luke to grow up amid violence. Harry takes his charges to a whisky distillery as a treat for good behaviour. Robbie discovers during the visit that he can differentiate between different whisky flavours. Though Matt rescues Liam from a beating by his old adversary, Clancy (Scott Kyle), and his crew, he tries to bribe him to leave Leonie and Scotland for £5,000. When Harry takes Liam, Mo, Rhino and Albert to Edinburgh – the capital an alien place to them – for a whisky-tasting, they learn of the imminent auction of a rare bottle of the prized Malt Mill brand at a northern Scottish distillery. Impressed by Liam's nose for whisky, the collector, Thaddeus (Roger Allam), who covets the Malt Mill, gives him his business card.

As astonished by the sight of the Highlands as Albert was by Edinburgh Castle, Robbie heads to the auction with Mo, Rhino and Albert. He has concocted a plan to conceal himself in the distillery's warehouse and siphon into four empty Irn-Bru* bottles 'the Angels' share' of the Malt Mill that would be expected to evaporate in an oak barrel, replacing it with inferior whisky from another barrel. The four friends' teamwork and a hosepipe enable them to pull off their audacious heist. Thaddeus fails to beat an American bidder at the auction.

Back in Glasgow, the gang is stopped by police, and two of the Irn-Bru bottles are accidentally smashed, thanks to Albert's

---

* Scotland's 'other' national beverage, Irn-Bru (originally Barr's Iron Brew) is a rust-coloured soft drink that contains iron hydroxide. It was launched in 1901.

gormlessness, their Malt Mill contents lost. Liam privately trades one of the remaining bottles to Thaddeus for £100,000 and a job offer in a Stirling distillery. He divides the cash with his friends, who plan to get drunk, and drives away with Leonie and Luke in his newly acquired Volkswagen camper van. Harry comes home to find the fourth Irn-Bru bottle and a newspaper article with a photo of Liam, Mo, Rhino and Albert at the auction. He sniffs the Malt Mill in the bottle with amazement.

The student Anthony's tragedy is collateral damage in *The Angels' Share*'s depiction of Scotland's post-industrial social breakdown. Though Loach and Laverty do not mitigate Liam's culpability, the film prioritises his rehabilitation by giving him a fresh start. To some extent, the making of the film embodied the storyline's premise, even as it strove for authenticity in the casting of the first-time actor Paul Brannigan to play Robbie. Eschewing artifice, his portrayal of the pensive Liam justified their choice.

Born in 1986, Brannigan grew up in working-class Barrowfield, in east Glasgow, which – long dominated by gang warfare – in the 1980s became the neighbourhood with the city's highest rate of drug abuse, overdoses and suicide. Brannigan's parents were heroin addicts, and his mother's family were dealers. He was twelve in 1999, when a nineteen-year-old male cousin was violently murdered. When he was sixteen, he was sentenced to four years and three months in prison after a violent incident (in which no one was hurt). After incarceration at the Young Offenders Institution Polmont, Brannigan was discovered coaching football at Strathclyde Police's Violence Reduction Unit by Laverty, who was doing research for *The Angels' Share*. Like his character Liam, he was in a relationship and had become a father. 'He was a fantastic kid and you think "let's give him a chance" and we were at a casting session with him yesterday. He was absolutely marvellous,' Laverty told David Archibald during pre-production.[*]

The Angels' Share brought Brannigan more acting opportunities, notably opposite Scarlett Johansson in *Under the Skin* (2013), in *Sunshine on Leith* (2013, with Peter Mullan) and in *The Nest* (2020, with Martin Compston and David Hayman). Beyond the

---

[*] David Archibald, *Tracking Loach: Politics, Practices, Production* (Edinburgh University Press, 2023), p. 111.

compassionate and agitational nature of Loach's cinema, it would be misleading to suggest the dramas and comedies are intended as interventions, but Harry's giving Liam an opportunity to develop his gift – mirrored in the film-makers' belief in Brannigan – demonstrates how the potential of some young people born into politically decimated communities can be unlocked.

By depicting Liam's crew as Scottish 'fishes out of water', *The Angels' Share* uses humour to illuminate the gap between the grim reality of their lives and the mythical Scotland sold to tourists, augmenting Joe's wry comments on the Scottish piper in *My Name Is Joe*. (The same subject is broached in Danny Boyle and screenwriter John Hodge's 1996 film of Irvine Welsh's *Trainspotting*.) To allay suspicions while on their larcenous expedition into the Highlands, the quartet disguise themselves in kilts (the boys in sporrans) as 'whisky train-spotters'. It takes a French tourist to tell Rhino that he's wearing his kilt backwards. Albert's sporran inflames his genitals. The crew's disconnection from the tourist industry's commercial assets – whisky, tartan, tins of Walker's Shortbread decorated with romanticized paintings of Bonnie Prince Charlie – satirizes capital's exploitation of what Laverty terms 'the quaint view of Scotland' and Loach calls the 'Walter Scott image of kilts and sporrans [which] bears no reality to the lives of ordinary Scottish people'.* Comedy is to the fore as the four friends' street smarts enable them to outwit the system, and Liam, crucially, to overcome his victimhood by securing a job. Yet by invoking Scotland's clans, which were politically disempowered and ethnically cleansed by the British government after the defeat of Bonnie Prince Charlie's Jacobite army at Culloden, *The Angels' Share* pointedly draws a line from 1746 to the human cost of deindustrialization in the 1980s, as surely as *The Wind That Shakes the Barley* draws a line from the Irish War of Independence to the war in Northern Ireland.

Like *Carla's Song*, *Ae Fond Kiss* is a Glasgow-based film with an internationalist, post-colonial perspective rather than one that confronts directly the class war's creation of unemployment, addiction and poverty. The film's star-crossed lovers, the Irish teacher Roisin (Eva Birthistle) and first-generation Scottish Pakistani

---

* Graham Fuller, 'Beneath the Kilt, a Modern Scotland', *New York Times*, 5 April 2013.

entrepreneur Casim Khan (Atta Yaqub), are children of former British Empire countries that suffered partition, war and mass emigration. However, in contrast to the protagonists of *My Name Is Joe*, *Sweet Sixteen* and *The Angels' Share*, who are tempted into crime because they live without jobs or resources in forsaken Glaswegian communities, Roisin and Casim are insulated from Scotland's working-class wasteland, having acquired degrees and jobs they like. Roisin clearly has a middle-class Irish background. The Khan family's newsagent business has afforded them a degree of prosperity and a nice house. Casim, who has an accountancy degree, is a DJ and is planning to launch his own nightclub with his friend, Hammid (Shy Ramzan). Casim's older sister, Rukhsana (Ghizala Avan), has a master's degree in psychology. Their younger sister, Tahara (Shabana Akhtar Bakhsh), intends to do a journalism degree after leaving school. Kristine Chick notes that 'more than a third of Scottish Muslims are self-employed, and a proportionately higher percentage of young South Asian Muslims than white Scots have higher education degrees'.*

Written by Laverty partially in response to the increase in Islamophobia that followed the 9/11 attacks, *Ae Fond Kiss* depicts Casim and Roisin's struggle to maintain their romantic relationship when pressured by external forces that make them question religious belief as a defining aspect of their individual cultural identities and allegiances – Casim as a Muslim, Roisin as a Catholic.

Casim is the middle child of Tariq (Ahmad Riaz) and Sadia Khan (Shamshad Akhtar), who emigrated from Pakistan over forty years earlier. They have arranged for him to marry his Muslim cousin, Jasmine (Sunna Mirza), and for the couple to live in the extension that Tariq is adding to the Khans' house. Rukhsana is anticipating her arranged marriage with the PhD graduate Amar (Pasha Bocarie). Though Tariq is concerned for his family's honour and standing in the Muslim community, there is a psychological component in his need to keep his children close: when very young, he was traumatized by the killing of his twin brother during the slaughter that followed the Partition of India in 1948.

---

* Kristine Chick, 'Crossing Enemy Lines in Ken Loach's *Ae Fond Kiss/ Just a Kiss*: Representing Muslims and New Ethnicities in the Shadow of 9/11', *OpenEdition Journals/Angles*, October 2020.

Eva Birthistle and Atta Yaqub during the filming of *Ae Fond Kiss*.

At the start of *Ae Fond Kiss*, the informed, articulate and conscientious sixth-former Tahara briskly condemns America's and Britain's post-9/11 fostering of Islamophobia to justify the Iraq War. Participating in a school debate about terrorism, she rejects the West's definition of terrorism for excluding 'the hundreds and thousands of victims of state terror', the West's claim of the moral high ground, because 'two of its main Jesus-lovers [George W. Bush and Tony Blair] tore up the UN charter' [by backing the Iraq War] and 'the West's simplification of a Muslim'.

She proceeds to describe proudly her own multifaceted, multicultural identity as a first-generation Glaswegian woman of Punjabi descent, a position that brings her into conflict with the rigidly traditionalist Sadia. Whereas Tahara is determined to embrace this self-defined identity, her oldest sibling, Rukhsana, compliantly accepts the identity she has been given by her parents.

When Casim comes to pick up Tahara from school, he follows her as she chases classmates who are antagonizing her with racist slurs into the room where Roisin, who has a part-time job, teaches music. A guitar is broken in the scuffle. Casim returns the next day with a replacement guitar and gives Roisin a lift home; she has to duck down en route to avoid Casim being seen with a white woman. After Casim and his friends help move a piano for Roisin (who is separated from her husband), they start dating and become lovers. Casim doesn't tell his parents, knowing they would be horrified to discover that he is involved with a non-Muslim woman.

The film's central conflict springs from Casim's vacillations between being Tariq and Sadia's dutiful son and Roisin's romantic partner. Owing to the unbending laws of the Catholic Church, Roisin is, meanwhile, confronted with choosing between Casim, the Muslim man she loves, and the teaching job she also adores. Laverty's screenplays specialise in showing how corrupt or coercive social situations squeeze each of the films' protagonists between a rock and a hard place, so that a crucial decision they are forced to make will cost them.

During a short Spanish holiday that Casim and Roisin take to celebrate her being offered a full-time job at the school, Casim confesses to her that his parents expect him to marry Jasmine. Roisin is hurt and offended, assuming that he considers her a last fling. Despite assuring Roisin that he loves her, on returning to Glasgow he breaks up with her after learning of Rukhsana's engagement, fearing his relationship with Roisin will alienate Amar's family and destroy the Khans' reputation. But when Casim learns that Tariq has forbidden Tahara from studying journalism at Edinburgh University, he angrily refuses to marry Jasmine and leaves home. Roisin and Casim reunite and move in together.

Roisin goes to her parish priest to get the certificate of approval that she needs to teach full-time at the school. He grills her about her personal life. Because her marriage hasn't been annulled and she is therefore a Catholic wife having an adulterous sexual relationship, she is contravening Church law. The priest rebukes her and denies her the certificate. He makes it clear that Casim's religion is behind his reasoning when he says to Roisin, 'I mean, what are you thinking? You think you can get into bed with any Tom, Dick or Mohammed and then teach wee Catholic kids?' Roisin is subsequently transferred to a non-denominational school.

When the Muslim community learns that Roisin and Casim are living together, the Khans are disgraced. Amir calls off his engagement to Rukhsana, who at a fraught meeting with Roisin in a café appeals to her in vain to leave Casim. Owing to a misunderstanding,

Roisin locks Casim out of their flat. To convince Roisin that Casim will marry Jasmine after all, Rukhsana drives her to the Khans' house to show her Casim, lured there by his mother, being introduced to Jasmine. After Roisin leaves in despair, Casim, who was unaware of her visit, berates his parents for keeping Jasmine's family in the dark about his decision not to marry her. He asks Tariq to give Roisin a chance. In his frustration, Tariq starts to smash up the house's extension.

Typically, Loach and Laverty justify every character's feelings in *Ae Fond Kiss*. The priest who withholds the certificate of approval from Roisin is following the letter of Church law. Rukhsana urges Roisin to leave Casim because their relationship will end her marital hopes and tear her family apart. While forced marriages are not ordained in the Quran and have no legal validity in Islam, as a patriarch of Punjabi origin Tariq adheres to the tradition of arranged marriages that goes back at least 2,500 years; his entire social fabric is founded on it and he cannot accept Casim choosing a partner of whom he has not approved. The conflict is constructed to make viewers empathise with Casim – who needs to be with Roisin as much as she with him – and with Tahara, who is determined to study in Edinburgh, as both she and her brother free themselves from Tariq's control. Yielding to his demands would have cost them their integrity and forced them to live dishonestly. Yet the scene in which Tariq, knowing he is defeated, vents his rage on the extension he has built for Casim and Jasmine should elicit sorrow in even the most hard-hearted viewer.

Tariq is unable to stop Casim and Tahara evolving as self-willed, assimilated Scots. Tahara asserts that she will do her degree in Edinburgh. Casim seeks out Roisin at their flat. She fears he has come to pack his belongings, but he convinces her that he will still want to be with her when they are old. The film's title, taken from Robert Burns's 1791 poem lamenting the end of his unconsummated love affair with the poet Agnes Maclehose, raises a doubt: will Casim and Roisin's romance survive, given the difficulties they will continue to face as a cross-cultural couple? Loach considers the film's optimistic ending appropriate, he said at the Berlinale. 'The process of assimilation will happen eventually. There might be some pain on the way, but nevertheless . . . we just recognise our common humanity.' It was a belief Loach and Laverty would emphatically put to the test again in *The Old Oak*.

GRAHAM FULLER: My Name Is Joe *addresses alcoholism and the drug culture in a Scottish urban setting, as would* Sweet Sixteen *and* The Angels' Share, *which is a more optimistic film than the first two.* My Name Is Joe *and* Sweet Sixteen *show that once people are trapped by addiction, there's often no way for them to escape. Do you think questions of individual responsibility are moot, given that the root causes of these problems are social and political?*

KEN LOACH: When you say 'moot', how do you mean it?

I'm just wondering if it is impossible for people to take responsibility for their lives if they are being destroyed by alcohol or heroin, and when mass unemployment, which invariably results from political decisions, is creating widespread despair. It's in that circumstance that people often find short-term solace in drink or drugs and become addicted.

People struggle, and some have got the capacity to get through the darkest times and some don't. It's not a question of blame. It's just about individuals' capacity to respond and how deep they are into the problem. Whether it's humanly possible to escape after a certain time, I honestly don't know. It's like people struggling in a swamp. Some have the will to get to dry ground and some will sink. It depends on such a myriad of different circumstances that it's impossible to generalize.

But I think, as you say, the overall situation is that if you have an economic system that creates poverty, that creates a lack of security, families break up because lack of money puts pressure on relationships and fractures them. Kids especially are caught up in those splits. Rows, arguments and fear can lead to bullying and violence because people are desperate and can't articulate their frustration. And all those different fractures and pains that people go through in trying to deal with things that are very hard to deal with can lead to them finding a method of relief, whether it is through alcohol or drugs.

I've been lucky. I've led a charmed life and have never been in that situation. Who knows who will survive and who won't? Objectively, in the social situations where addictions and violence emerge, yes, you can identify that the economic system that creates that has to change. And you can analyse that. Thatcher and her gang produced that society of inequality, poverty, hunger, hardship, fractured families, destroyed communities. We saw that it was a conscious decision, and we've absolutely had to oppose it. But how people struggle and survive within it, who's to say?

It's interesting talking about blame, because we see children as victims, and when they're in their late teens, we put the blame on them or blame their parents for the child's fears, phobias and anxieties. Well, in one sense, yes, the parents are in a protective role, but they themselves are victims from their early years. So the problem goes back in time. I think responsibility is a very elusive thing to pin down because it's a balance, isn't it? There is individual responsibility, but there's also a predisposition to not being able to sort things out because your childhood hasn't equipped you in that way.

If people are deprived, they're more likely to self-medicate through drugs or alcohol, but the issue of deprivation is a social issue. Doesn't it come down to whether you've got a caring or an uncaring society?

Absolutely. We built a welfare state on the principle that everybody would be taken care of and there would be security for everyone – a

My Name Is Joe: Joe (Peter Mullan) warns off a DSS investigator (Sandy West).

home and job, care when you're old, care when you're sick. This security was consciously destroyed in the 1980s by Thatcher. I remember at the time, the right-wing press wrote that the welfare state had made us soft, and asked, have we taken away responsibility from the parents? The 'nanny state' encapsulated, in a phrase, the right-wing attitude towards a caring society. Mind you, the wealthy buggers in the Tory party are the only people who have nannies, so if anyone's been softened, it's them. They reveal themselves just by their term of abuse. But, as you say, the social situations produce deprivations, addictions and all the domestic issues that insecure communities face.

It's striking that in My Name Is Joe *and* Sweet Sixteen, *you show that supplying drugs provides an alternative form of employment. In those parts of Scotland where once there was shipbuilding, steelworking, mining and other industries offering employment, trafficking drugs mimics capitalism.*

The drug industry is raw capitalism. The people at the top ruthlessly exploit those whom they have trapped, and the people who are doing the dirty work for them have their own addictions to satisfy. The irony of *Sweet Sixteen* is that the lad [Liam] has to deal drugs in order to help his mother, who has got an addiction, because that's the only way he can get the money. And in *My Name Is Joe*, the only way Joe can raise money to help the young father [also named Liam] who desperately needs his help is by transporting drugs. He hates doing it, but he's faced with an impossible choice. One of the themes of Paul's writing is that, by examining the choices that people in desperate circumstances have, he shows that often there's no good choice available to them. Whatever choice they make is a bad one.

In My Name Is Joe, *Sarah, the community health worker who has become involved with Joe, understandably expresses her fury at him for collecting a drugs consignment for McGowan because it's going to undo her work with addicts, who include Sabine. Joe replies, 'I'm sorry, but we don't live in this nice, tidy world of yours. Some can't go to the police. Some can't go to the bank for a loan. Some can't move house and fuck off. Some of us don't have a choice.' This suggests that Sarah and Joe are irrevocably divided by their class differences, doesn't it?*

I wouldn't put it quite like that. George Bernard Shaw talked about middle-class morality [in *Pygmalion*] and people pontificating from on high about how the working class should behave. Sarah isn't like that. As a social worker, she's fighting on the front line. Social workers are not middle class as a rule. Sarah and Joe are both working-class. But, as you say, she sees the terrible cost of what Joe is doing. She says she works with drug addicts every day and spells out graphically the consequences of addiction. Joe's just the other side of that fence, and Sarah says he should have found another way of helping the young couple. She doesn't know what that way is, but in doing what he's done he's inflicted more pain on others. But he's trapped. Given his situation, he doesn't know what else he could have done, and that's why he lets fly at Sarah. 'What am I to do? I cannot just leave this lad to get broken up and destroyed, which is what McGowan's men will do to him. The couple have a little child. I did the only thing I could do.' It's a genuine dilemma, and the fact that they're both right in a way shows Paul's brilliance as a writer. Your heart bleeds for both of them, and that's what makes it a very strong piece of writing.

Like Cathy Come Home, Ladybird, Ladybird *and* I, Daniel Blake, My Name Is Joe *casts the social services in a negative light – specifically, through the figure of the Job Centre snooper who gets his just deserts when Joe splatters his car with paint. It made me wonder if you have seen a marked difference in social care since it began to be privatized.*

Obviously, the general attitude to social workers in *Cathy*, *Ladybird* and *Joe* is from the point of view of people who are on the receiving end, so it's a very subjective view of them. The social workers are in impossible situations, particularly in *Ladybird*, where, I think, we got a bit more nuanced. You can see they're under instruction to take the child away from Maggie because they fear for its safety, which has got to be the priority, though they don't know what the outcome will be. The audience knows that Maggie is in a positive relationship [with Jorge], as opposed to the kind of violent relationship that has been her history. But the social workers don't know this and they're absolutely not enjoying what they're doing. They're not like the insensitive middle-class social workers who punish Cathy for her poverty. The ones in *Ladybird* have a more genuine difficulty because they can't communicate with Maggie, who's raging at them because her anger and distress are so great. They are trying to do their best, but they have preconceptions, as there were in the real case the film is based on. The research we did suggested that there was a blindness to the qualities – affection and care – that a working-class woman like Maggie could give to her children, albeit not in a way that a well-off middle-class family would be able to. And sometimes middle-class values are, or were, incorporated into the actions of social workers.

As more and more social work was privatized, its priorities changed. The prime concern of the companies that accept the contracts for it has to be to make a profit. If they don't, they go out of business. Talking to social workers, we learned that they'd been encouraged to take short cuts, to tick the boxes, rather than investigate cases as fully as they maybe should. Also, because the companies cut their work forces to enable them to profit, the workloads for individual social workers increased, which led to crude decision-making.

My Name Is Joe: Joe (Peter Mullan) and Sarah (Louise Goodall) get to know each other.

The idea that social work and care work should be subject to market forces is incompatible with a decent society, as you also show in Sorry We Missed You. *It makes a mockery of welfare in Britain, as does the explanation in* I, Daniel Blake *that capability assessments to determine whether people are fit to work have been outsourced to American-owned companies.*

Yes, the capability assessments to determine if someone is fit for work. A GP and a consultant might say this person is not fit to work and their health will be impaired if they're made to look for a job. In which case they get what we used to call a doctor's note and can't work for the moment. Then the government imposes an assessment by a so-called healthcare worker. These assessments are subcontracted to private companies, and, of course, they're not based on the claimants' interests. They're based on ticking boxes for the sake of the government, so it can reduce benefits. The claimants can only get their full benefits if they appeal. Some people who get the wrong assessments haven't got the strength or are too mentally frail to appeal, so in those cases the government wins.

When Joe is on the return leg of his drug run, he stops for a cup of tea at a catering van in the south-west Highlands (filmed in a car park on the Rest and Be Thankful Pass). A piper is there playing 'Scotland the Brave' for Japanese tourists. Joe and the tea vendor joke about the piper only knowing flag-waving tunes – 'The Skye Boat Song', 'Flower of Scotland', 'Bonnie Scotland' – and Joe asks the vendor if the piper sells shortbread, too. The point, of course, is that the tourist fantasy of Scotland veils the poverty and hardships endured by at least a fifth of the population.

It's like the English selling the Changing of the Guard. It's the cosy view of a nation offered by tourist companies and the hotel industry, from which the people who live there don't make a lot of money. There's comedy to be had in the shortbread and the kilts, of course.

You get laughs out of sporrans and kilts in The Angels' Share.

Yes, but all that is more egregious when the people have been exploited.

In My Name Is Joe, *it seems at first that the young father, Liam, Joe's friend, who's been in prison, has endangered his family. But it emerges that it's his heroin-addicted wife, Sabine, who has racked up the debt to the drug dealer and gang boss McGowan. Why was that more effective dramatically than making Liam responsible?*

You expect it to be Liam, so it turns expectations on their head. It's something different, a more complex situation than the stereotype would be. You feel great sympathy for the girl as well. She's a lovely kid, but very lost, and there's an extra sadness to that. It's wasted potential, isn't it?

Because Joe fails to save Liam in the end, he falls off the wagon and gets drunk. There's a shocking transformation in him. His voice deepens. The Mr Hyde in him appears. I wondered if you and Peter Mullan discussed how Joe would change, or did you leave it entirely to him?

I wouldn't discuss it. Peter's a very fine actor. This is a community he knows well, and he would have seen people like this. He was very absorbed in his performance, so I didn't need to say anything. He's a man with a lot of depth, so to spell it out would have been crude and would have encouraged a kind of drunken acting, which is the last thing you want. You spell something out to an actor as a last resort if your plan isn't working, or you might nudge them towards it. But it's always got to come from their instinctive response. I knew Peter's would be spot on, and it was. It's a wonderful performance, and very deeply felt.

Is there any hope for Joe and Sarah at the end of the film, or is it best left unsaid?

I think it's best left unsaid. I mean, who knows? I think you've seen enough in both their characters to know that they're not trivial people. Both have a capacity for understanding and for weathering storms. At the beginning, Joe shows a lot of interest and commitment in supporting the young men in his football team. There's a lot of strength there. Maybe the drink will get him in the end, or maybe he'll come through. We didn't decide, so it's completely open-ended. You cross your fingers for the two of them, sure. But it's not hopeless.

Sweet Sixteen is set in Greenock and Port Glasgow, in Inverclyde, one of the most deprived areas in Scotland. Just as Joe does the drug run in My Name Is Joe *to help Liam, Sweet Sixteen's Liam becomes a dealer with similarly good intentions – to buy his mother Jean a decent place to live after she leaves prison. Though the caravan he buys her on the Firth of Clyde is burned down, the gangster he works for provides him with a new house, also on the Clyde, for him and Jean to live in. But Jean, whose addiction has destroyed her moral will, rejects Liam's plan and the house, instead moving back in with her boyfriend, who will keep her on heroin. Her rejection of everything Liam has worked for is one of the cruellest of the many acts of betrayal in your films.*

Yes, it's devastating for the lad. His sister says their mother just can't do it – she hasn't got the strength, she hasn't got the understanding. She hasn't even got the compassion for her son to make the right choice because of everything else that's dominating her life. She's in thrall to her boyfriend. Their whole relationship is drug-dependent, and the guy uses that dependence for his own ends. The tragedy of that whole way of life is built into it. Where can Liam go, what can he do? He stabs the boyfriend, and then the police are after him. Now that he's turned sixteen, he's become more legally culpable for his misdeeds than before, so he's going to go to prison for a long time.

Though Liam deals drugs, we feel for him because he's been trapped, like Joe, into making a bad choice, the only one really available to him. In previous decades, he and his mates might have expected to get jobs on Clydeside, but Britain's shipbuilding industry declined because it couldn't compete with Korea's, Japan's and China's. Liam is bright and ambitious. He shows initiative in setting up his friend's pizzeria as a front for dealing drugs – just as his boss uses his health club – and getting his mates to deliver them on mopeds. Someone with his wit and leadership skills would surely have prospered if they hadn't been born and raised in this blighted, post-industrial world.

This is down to Paul's depth as a writer. He shows that some people who do bad things have great qualities. Liam is driven to help his mother, but he puts his wit, his intelligence and his ability into a

Sweet Sixteen: Martin Compston as Liam.

low-life criminal activity that will produce more people like his mother. One of Paul's strengths is to unravel these kinds of contradictions everywhere you look. Liam has a good intention, an intention we cherish: a son caring for his mother, trying to get her out of a damaging relationship. But the only way he can do it is by damaging more relationships, because that's the society he was born into. Wherever you look in that film, like in *My Name Is Joe*, it's contradiction after contradiction after contradiction.

Liam's sister, a young single mother who's getting an education, urges him to forget their mother and find a meaningful direction for his life, but there isn't a character in Liam's world, or Joe's either, who offers a political or social remedy in the way that, say, the Ricky Tomlinson character in Riff-Raff *urges his fellow builders to unionize. Is that because there's no one like that around?*

Most kids don't have that experience, really. We know there are some brilliant people around, but the tragedies recur despite that, and [in *Sweet Sixteen*] it just seemed a more naked way of presenting the story. In *Riff-Raff*, yes, Ricky does advise the others to unionize, but they take the piss out of him all the time. He's a comic character who makes you laugh and whom the film makes fun of, not a serious character who shows them the way to the light. We tend to shy away from characters who are political and argue things out, or who come along and preach a sermon on the way forward but aren't integrated into the story or aren't themselves compromised. The interesting characters are the ones who are compromised in some way by their own contradictions, otherwise it can be really glib.

Joe and Liam are in criminal situations, not industrial ones. And, as you say, it's a post-industrial world. A few decades earlier, they would have had jobs. And having a job gives you respect. It gives you income. It makes you stronger, and the stronger you are, the more independent you are and less likely to get drawn into dependence.

In contrast to Billy in Kes *or Robbie in* The Angels' Share, *Liam in* Sweet Sixteen *lacks a father figure or concerned adult, and there's no social mechanism in place that can guide or rescue him, anymore than there's a political party invested in representing Liam's class and generation.*

The consequence of Margaret Thatcher and Tony Blair together was to depoliticize people. A lot of people opposed Thatcher and went for the alternative, but Blair was in the same tradition and nearly as bad.

The drug kingpin in Sweet Sixteen, *like McGowan in* My Name Is Joe, *embodies the Scottish hard man. Do you and Paul give much consideration to the tropes of an archetype like that, or does your assessment of the socio-political world of a film always take precedence?*

There's the same tradition in London with gang leaders like the Krays and the Richardsons and the rest of them. There's a bit of flash in their clothes and they pretend to live the life of the class above them, but it's always comic in the end because their working-class origins and cultural characteristics undermine their attempts to be the lord of the manor. The guy who runs the health club and recruits Liam in *Sweet Sixteen* is a typical Glaswegian hard man and, typically, he's got henchmen who will go and do his dirty work, but I'm not sure we gave him or McGowan consideration beyond that. They were just the guys who ran the gangs.

Masculine pride implodes in these films. McGowan in My Name Is Joe *says the reason he won't let Joe off the hook is because he doesn't want to lose face, but that leads eventually to his undoing. Losing face is exactly what Robbie fears in* The Angels' Share, *when he's being chased by the thugs.*

Losing face is just not acceptable, hence they will do the most terrible things. You see it recurring among kids in today's society. The equivalent of losing face now is what they call 'being disrespected' and, I suppose, being humiliated in their eyes. They say, 'No one makes fun of me,' and then someone gets stabbed.

Just as it's a shock to learn that Sabine racked up the debt to McGowan, it comes as a surprise when Liam's friend Pinball reveals that he, not Stan, burned down the caravan that Liam bought for his mother. When it's disclosed that Pinball's father was a junkie, we realize that Pinball is foredoomed. He eventually cuts his own face; there's little hope for him. Then Jean crushes Liam's hope that she will stay clean by returning to Stan. Again, do you attribute these betrayals to individual failings or to all-pervasive social breakdown?

When does one cease to be a victim and become a villain? It's just that cycle of deprivation, lack of security, lack of affection, lack of care, and the way in which kids in the midst of that deprivation – and the people before them who had similar childhoods – lean on addictions of various sorts. Inevitably, the cycle will keep going, and that's why we need a massive change in the whole way we live together, economically and socially.

It needs a massive intervention to break that cycle. But the people in charge have no intention of doing that because their profits and their way of life depend on it. At the bottom, they have poverty, whether it's the workhouse back in the nineteenth century or the dole office or the Job Centre or whatever it is. And out of the poverty and hardship come these terrible stories.

There has been a long tradition of resistance in Britain – the Peasants' Revolt, the cotton riots of 1878, the Corn Laws protests after the Napoleonic Wars, the Jarrow March, the miners' strikes, and so on. That tradition now seems weaker than it's ever been. Close to three million people used a Trussell Trust food bank in 2022–3. How can a fairer society with a greater distribution of wealth be achieved?

The moment of resistance came with Jeremy Corbyn. It's easy to forget now because the media, politicians and all aspects of the state wiped him from the story. The BBC was central to destroying him. It's always going on about preserving its independence, but it contradicted that by slaughtering the only left-wing Labour leader there's ever been. Clement Attlee [Labour prime minister, 1945–51] wasn't on the left. He was a right-winger, and the post-war settlement was achieved almost in a consensus with the Tories. Certainly, the Tories didn't reverse it or dismantle the welfare state when they returned to power [in 1951].

Corbyn and John McDonnell [the Labour Party's shadow chancellor of the exchequer] had a substantial left-wing social democratic programme. It proposed a big increase in public ownership; trade union rights from day one; moving towards the ending of outsourcing and subcontracting in the NHS; ending the marketization of education; kicking private investment out of the railways, the post office and public utilities; and a foreign policy based on human rights and international law, which we've never had, as witness the Iraq War. They would have established a publicly owned bank to regenerate neglected areas like the north-east, the northwest and the West Midlands. They would have introduced a huge council housing programme led by the councils, not speculative builders, to create planned communities, with infrastructure, work and schools all in place.

There was to be a Green New Deal. It would have been more than just tinkering at the edges but would have taken energy into public ownership through collectives and community organizations in order to plan the generation of energy, as well as its use, which you can't do if you're dealing with big corporations because they do what they want. Jeremy would also have cut back profits in big business and shifted power back to the trade unions. It would have meant parliamentary reform in the interest of the working class. Just read the Labour Party 2017 election manifesto. The

2019 manifesto was more chaotic, but it was all there in 2017. The elements of it were very clear, and it went as far as it could. But the ruling class killed it, stone dead. People in Europe who follow politics underestimate the significance of that. It shows that the British ruling class is the cleverest and most sophisticated in the world. They destroyed Corbyn through an invented anti-Semitism smear, though Brexit played a part.

Hostility against the Labour Party had been building because of Tony Blair and rowing Labour councils. But in 2017, Corbyn almost won the election. A few thousand votes in different constituencies and we would have won. That's when the ruling class clearly took the decision that 'This man's got to go.' It coincided with Corbyn's support for the Palestinians, which antagonized Zionists within some organizations. The Jewish Labour Movement [formerly Poale Zion] attacked him, and right-wing MPs attacked him on television day after day after day.

Tactically, Jeremy and John made mistakes, for sure, but there was such determination to uproot him. The BBC and the *Guardian*, the so-called liberal paper, led the way, and so the right just piled in. It's worth digging out some of the press. They said Jeremy was too old, that his brain was going, that he was dodgy. But there's something immaculate about him. He's a straight-down-the-middle English guy who's got an allotment and supports the National Trust. We needed a street fighter and got a saint, really, so no mud stuck until they fired the anti-Semitism thing.

Do you firmly believe the allegations of anti-Semitism against Corbyn were contrived?

Yes. The smear campaign was built on very thin evidence. Sometimes you misjudge your words and use them too loosely when you're speaking and having meeting after meeting and conversation after conversation, and if someone is trying to pick a hole in something you've said publicly, they'll find a phrase you should have phrased differently. You make a mistake like that every now and then, and I'm sure I've done the same. Jeremy Corbyn is the least racist person in Parliament, I would say. I think everyone knows that, but his opponents used the allegations to wage the campaign against him. Jewish people in the Labour Party, in human rights organizations, in pre-existing organizations of support for the Palestinians or simply in progressive Jewish organizations supported Corbyn, but you rarely heard them in the press.

The selfie incident was unfortunate.*

I don't claim any prominence at all, but I know if I go to a meeting, everyone wants a selfie, and there might be a hundred in an evening and there's no way you can check everyone who comes up to you and asks for one. And, of course, you want to be friendly, so you say yes, stand beside someone, and they click their phone. Maybe one in a thousand has said bad things in the past or been associated with certain groups. Someone scrutinizing all those may well say, 'Why are you associating with this person?' and make a story out of it.

[In 2012] Corbyn endorsed a cartoon† that could be interpreted as anti-Semitic because of the way it was drawn, but it wasn't

---

* A keynote speaker at an Oslo event held in support of Julian Assange on 4 June 2023, Corbyn posed for a selfie with Hans Jørgen Johansen, a Holocaust denier and founder and leader of the neo-Nazi Alliance–Alternative for Norway political party. Corbyn subsequently tweeted: 'I am approached for selfies on a daily basis from strangers. I had no idea know [*sic*] who this individual was. Naturally, I condemn his abhorrent politics in the strongest possible terms.' Before Corbyn became leader of the Labour Party, he had been criticized for attending a 2014 wreath-laying ceremony at the Hammam Chott cemetery, near Tunis, Tunisia, for victims of the Israeli airstrike that destroyed the Palestine Liberation Organization's headquarters in the resort town on 1 October 1985. A photograph showed Corbyn standing near victims' graves and those of two Palestinian activists, Salah Khalaf and Atef Bseiso, who had allegedly been members of the Black September Organization, which was responsible for the killing of eleven Israeli athletes at the 1972 Summer Olympics in Munich. A Labour Party spokesperson stated, 'Jeremy did not lay any wreath at the graves of those alleged to have been linked to the Black September Organization or the 1972 Munich killings. He of course condemns that terrible attack, as he does the 1985 bombing.' Khalaf and Bseiso had denied they were members of Black September.
† 'Freedom for Humanity', a temporary mural painted on a wall in Hanbury Street, London, by the American street artist Mear One (Kalen Ockerman, b. 1971), showed, he said, six 'Jewish and white Anglo' bankers playing a Monopoly-like board game supported on the backs of mostly dark-skinned naked figures.

intended like that. It wasn't until years later [in 2018] that they dug that up. Because he hates conflict, Jeremy apologized for it and other things he didn't really need to apologize for. But once you've done that, you've admitted culpability. Apologizing might just be good manners – you want to be approachable rather than digging your heels in – but the moment you do it, from the other side's point of view it's 'Right. We've got him now – he's admitted his guilt.' And in Jeremy's case, it happened time after time and the pressure built, until everybody was convinced he was a racist. But nothing could be further from the truth.

Your documentary In Conversation with Jeremy Corbyn *(2016), based on Q&A sessions during the Labour Party leadership election that Corbyn won, captures the same sense of optimism for socialist change that infuses* The Spirit of '45 *(2013). Retrospectively, that what-might-have-been quality resonates in the England of* Days of Hope, *the Spain of* Land and Freedom *and the Ireland of* The Wind That Shakes the Barley, *in all of which leftist resistance is subverted or crushed. There are no historical accidents, of course.*

No. The British, the French and the Americans gave tacit support to the fascists in the years immediately prior to the Second World War, when Hitler and Mussolini were arming them. The British stood back from arming the anti-fascists because British companies had investments in Spain that the Republicans could well have taken. Principles are one thing, but money's money and business is business. Then, of course, the language of anti-fascism entered the Second World War, which was a just war against the most monstrous expressions of fascism in Germany and Italy. But in Spain in 1939, Britain offered no principled objection to the fascists at all, until they threatened British interests.

Why has there been a catalogue of missed opportunities on the left?

It's the balance of class forces. The lesson to learn from history is why we lose. It's about what struggles you engage with and how well you can prepare to win. What you also have to put in the balance is that the other side has to keep on provoking. As I said, they have to keep increasing the weight of exploitation. Their system never reaches equilibrium, so they're constantly on the attack.

When all those trade union rights were won, you thought they were won for ever. But now here we are with the gig economy. The eight-hour day has gone, sick pay has gone, holiday pay has gone. The other side has to keep it up, and now they've got to find other ways of exploiting people.

Jumping ahead a little, the hours worked by Ricky and Abby in your gig-economy film Sorry We Missed You *made me think of the twelve-hour-plus shifts worked by millhands during the Industrial Revolution.*

Now, as you walk around London you'll see kids on bikes delivering a pizza or something, and they'll be going the wrong way down one-way streets, through red traffic lights, up on the pavements. They're paid so little by the agencies and work in such a competitive environment that they have to break every rule. And people are getting killed. It's real madness.

Why do you think the middle class broadly tolerates such exploitation? Is it because they've been softened by materialism, or do they just not care?

It's the manipulation of consciousness, isn't it? Freedom is equated with doing what you want, regardless of the cost to others. Capitalism equals freedom to make money, to set up a company. Every week we've got TV programmes like *Dragons' Den* and *The Apprentice* that worship entrepreneurs. Their basic premise is that the people who make money out of others are the creators of wealth and the heroes of our society. That's how they generate that consciousness. There is no political voice against it because they've removed it. It's never represented.

Do you think unions have lost sight of their age-old principles?

By and large, even when people are on strike. Mick Lynch [general secretary of the RMT, the National Union of Rail, Maritime and Transport Workers] is probably the best of the current leaders. The RMT has got a policy of public ownership of the railways. Lynch leads a great strike, but he never says that we can only solve this by taking the railways back into public ownership. He restricts himself to saying, 'We need a decent wage, the railways need to be more efficient, we've got to end the chaos of private ownership,' and he barely says that now; he just talks about the loss of income and loss of services – you know, the companies want to close all the ticket offices. Lynch fights on a trade union basis, but the next step is to fight on a political basis and a social basis, which he isn't doing. So if he isn't doing it and people never hear the alternative position, then, of course, consciousness is being manipulated. And that's at the heart of the [right wing's] success.

Keir Starmer is right-wing Labour, and if he is elected, he will make no structural changes.* He's already paving the way for changes in the health service to include the private sector. For example, he's proposing community medical hubs that will be privately run. The moment you talk about a role for private health companies, that's the green light for the big American health insurance companies to come in and clean up. And the code people like him and Wes Streeting† put forward is, 'We've got to get more money into the health service,' by which they don't mean through progressive taxation but through those who can afford it to take out health insurance – which means people spending much more on health than they do now, for a much worse service. You don't have to pay for public healthcare currently, but if they starve the National Health Service, people will say, 'I can't tolerate this. I need my operation. I need my teeth done, I need this, that and the other. I'll take out insurance.' People don't realize that if they're paying for those things through their taxes, they'd pay half of what they'd pay for private insurance and get a much better service – and everybody would get it.

Your next Scottish film, Ae Fond Kiss, *depicts the struggle faced by a young Irish Catholic woman, Roisin, and her Pakistani boyfriend, Casim, to sustain their romance in the face of his parents' insistence that he marry the Muslim woman they have chosen for him. Was it prompted solely by the Islamophobia that erupted after 9/11?*

---

* Starmer was elected prime minister on 6 July 2024.
† At the time of the interview, Streeting was the Labour Party's shadow secretary of state for health and social care.

I don't think we identified it specifically as a film made in the wake of that event, but you are right – 9/11 did become an excuse for racism against people with a Muslim background. It's a film that looks at the whole question of identity. Paul encapsulated it in Tahara, Casim's younger sister, when she makes humorous points about the complexity of identity in her school speech by describing herself as a Glaswegian Pakistani teenage woman of Muslim descent who supports Glasgow Rangers [traditionally a Protestant football club] at a Catholic school. People have many elements to their identity, and they're all valid.

Tahara is the most integrated character in the film, the one who holds up a standard of acceptance for everybody else. In his book The New Scottish Cinema, *Jonathan Murray notes that* Ae Fond Kiss *privileges Casim's subjectivity over Roisin's because of her inability to understand the forces that have shaped Casim's life. Since Casim is caught between his love for Roisin and the needs of his family, he is the one with the dilemma, so it makes sense that you would follow his perspective a bit more than hers. Were you conscious of that?*

Yes, I think we were. That was the story we wanted to tell. The irony is that she's more of an immigrant than Casim because he was born in Scotland and she came across from Ireland. Of course, there are so many Irish people, or people with an Irish background, in the west of Scotland that she doesn't stand out as an immigrant at all. He was born in Glasgow, yet he's the one who's seen and treated as an immigrant. It needs time for that absorption to take place.

Just as Casim has to deal with his Muslim family trying to force him into an arranged marriage to a Pakistani woman, Roisin has to deal with the moral control of the Catholic Church. The parish priest who refuses her a certificate that would allow her to take a full-time position teaching at a Catholic school is as puritanically restrictive as Father Sheridan in Jimmy's Hall *(2014). Both these young people are subject to doctrinaire teachings that are out of step with the lives they want to live. Do you consider that kind of religious pressure an arm of state control?*

There's a coincidence of interests between some aspects of religion and tradition, though Paul, who was a seminarian, would say that there's an alternative to that even within the Catholic Church, which is liberation theology. The priests who supported the Sandinistas actively worked for revolutionary change. So there are different elements within the Church. The dominant one, I guess, has conformed to the interests of the state. For example, the Catholic Church supported Franco during the Spanish Civil War, and we know Christian elements supported the Nazis during the Second World War.

By and large, the majority of clerical teaching has supported the status quo through selective reading of the scriptures. The traditional views of the Church have supported the class structure, which it's the role of the state to uphold. But this is a roundabout way of speaking. It's too simple to say the Catholic Church supports the state.

Ae Fond Kiss is sympathetic to Casim, but sympathetic also to his traditionalist father, Tariq, whose twin brother was one of thousands of Muslims killed following the Partition of India. That kind of trauma is bound to make someone adopt an entrenched position on traditional family life. Having lost his brother, Tariq despairs at the thought of losing his son.

Exactly. Again, this is where Paul's writing is so good. Everyone has their reasons. You can understand why Tariq is desperate for his family to stay together: so the good things he sees in the tradition are maintained; to make a dignified life for them; to be a success; to be accepted for who they are and not to lose their separate culture, which he values; and to be seen as equals. You can see, too, that he's quite a vulnerable man, but the consequences of what he does are oppressive. In the end, Casim says, 'Look, I have to be who I am. I can't be who you want me to be necessarily.' I think that first-generation immigrants face genuinely difficult choices, as expressed in the film.

I was going to suggest that the film is less sympathetic to Casim's older sister, Rukhsana, whose advantageous upcoming marriage to a successful Pakistani man is threatened by Casim and Roisin's relationship. But, of course, it depends who's watching the film. If you're in a similar position to Rukhsana, you would naturally sympathize with her.

I think she wants to do her best for her family. She's respectful of the tradition. Probably some of the marriages that she's seen in this country haven't worked out because of the clash of cultures. If you're culturally very different, it's difficult to sustain a long-term relationship because you're being pulled in opposite directions. I think she knows the limitations of her situation, but she's a traditionalist, and there are many like her. Casim isn't, and I think Rukhsana tries to explain to Roisin in what she thinks is the gentlest way that this relationship that Roisin wants isn't going to work, and that in the struggle the family will win. So it's an attempt to let Roisin down gently, but, of course, it backfires.

The issue for people raised traditionally is that if the culture they've been born into has been transplanted to a pluralistic culture – in this case, one that permits marriages between people of different ethnicities and religions – they can't fight against its freedoms. The tide of change will come, inevitably it will. In the end, societies do tend to become more homogeneous once second or third generations of immigrants have relationships with people in the country where they've arrived. Often it's the indigenous people, not immigrants, who oppose that integration.

That it's Tahara, the progressively minded younger sister, who's instrumental in bringing Roisin and Casim together at the end makes for a satisfying conclusion. But was there a danger that someone who expresses her heterogeneity vocally – who's proud of being a mixture of so many things – could be perceived as an idealized citizen?

There was a danger of that, but really it's just the cheek of a kid, I think. She's very bright and delights in provoking the people who want to put her in a box, and there's a sense of fun about it. I hope that stops her being idealized. She sees things sharply and is not afraid to express herself.

Ae Fond Kiss *has the most erotic love-making scene in all your films. Does so honestly depicting the passion that exists between*

A break during filming on *Ae Fond Kiss*: Ahmad Riaz, Gary Lewis and Raymond Mearns.

Roisin and Casim – the desire to love and be loved – suggest that it's a life force that can't ultimately be suppressed by dynastic or religious traditions?

It's Romeo and Juliet, isn't it? Their passion for each other transcends the hostility of their parents. I'm not good at those scenes. I don't find them easy to do, and I know the actors find them tough. But I think we felt at the time that the strength of Roisin and Casim's desire for each other is really powerful and an essential part of their relationship, and that was something we couldn't short-change because it would be cheating to leave it out. Paul and I both said afterwards, 'Were we right to show it, or could we have cut the scene earlier?' I don't know if the more you show, the more the audience comes outside the film because they're embarrassed or see the scene differently. Whether that decision was right or not, I don't know, to be honest. I haven't seen the film for a long time, but I know we were torn then and are still torn now. All credit to Eva Birthistle, who is a brilliant actress, and Atta Yaqub, who was a terrific young man to work with. Real respect, because it was a difficult thing to do, and they did it without compromise, and certainly it's only the camera that sees what's happening.

The film's commentary on identities extends to its use of spaces, whether they're seen or not. The nightclub Casim plans to build with his best friend and business partner will be a multicultural space. It's echoed in Tahara's mixed self-identity, which augurs the mixed-race children Roisin and Casim would have. In contrast, the annexe Tariq builds onto the family house as a home for Casim and his arranged Pakistani bride symbolizes isolationism.

And the idea of the family staying together. The father is pursuing something that can never be, which is that the family stays and integrates but remains separate. It's an impossible contradiction, but you can see where it comes from – cherishing the life he had and wanting to reproduce it in a country where that can never happen. It's like building a sandcastle and then being surprised when the waves smooth it out.

It's deeply upsetting when he starts to smash up the annexe.

You feel sympathy for the man, but sad he's caught in a situation where he can never win.

The characters in Ae Fond Kiss *are more middle-class than those in the films in which you've focused on the struggles of the industrial or post-industrial working class.*

Teaching used to be thought of as a middle-class profession but, given their status and wages now, teachers are very much identified with the working-class struggle. The family are tradesmen on a fairly low level in terms of their income. It's just that they've grafted, worked really hard, and they've got a decent house, but they're barely petty bourgeoisie, and in the grand scheme of things they're fairly ordinary.

Up to 3.4 million migrants were killed following the Partition of India. Hindus, Muslims and Sikhs all suffered ethnic violence. Towards the end of Ae Fond Kiss, *Roisin shows her school class images of lynchings of African Americans during the Jim Crow era. Does this suggest she's developed a greater understanding of what Tariq has endured as a persecuted Muslim?*

Yes, absolutely. We play the Billie Holiday song ['Strange Fruit'] over those images. Because of what she's going through, Roisin is very aware of the racist implications in people's presuppositions about her relationship with Casim. She's saying to the class, 'Look, this is racism, and this is what can happen if we demonise people of different colours, different cultures, different backgrounds.'

Despite being named after a Robert Burns poem, Ae Fond Kiss *doesn't feel particularized as a Scottish film. Could it apply to any city where there are immigrant communities?*

I hope it would apply to every immigrant community and every host indigenous community where people come and there are tensions. In the end, the alternative to integration is apartheid and separate development. So it applies generally, but it's important that the details are specific because you can't make generalized films. Language is pivotal. The members of the Pakistani family are all at different stages of integration, which is reflected in how they speak. Casim and his sisters are obviously very Scottish, but the mother hardly at all. The way Tariq speaks with a Scottish accent while still struggling with the language is touching because it epitomizes his separateness. When we were casting him, we looked really hard to find someone who could speak that way. Ahmad Riaz is one of the very few who could, because Glasgow's Pakistani community is significant but not overwhelmingly large. There are a number of well-known actors you would expect to have played Tariq, but they didn't have that precise way he uses words. And finding people from that background capable of considering doing a fictional film is very small. So we were lucky to find Ahmad, and he made a good contribution.

After Ae Fond Kiss, *you and your fellow directors Abbas Kiarostami and Ermanno Olmi collaborated on* Tickets, *which is set on a Rome-bound train. In the section Paul wrote and you directed, three young Celtic fans (played by William Ruane, Martin Compston and Gary Maitland) heading to the game of their lives have to decide whether to give up one of their train tickets to a young Albanian refugee who is travelling with his mother and siblings to reunite with his father, or let him face deportation. Was it British hostility to Albanian refugees from the war in Kosovo that prompted you and Paul to have the Glasgow lads do the right thing by the Albanian boy?*

It was a very simple story, really, about helping somebody who was going to be in trouble. We remembered the comedy of the little team [led by Compston's and Ruane's characters] in *Sweet Sixteen*. It was very funny how *Tickets* came about. Abbas was the motivator. He had the idea of us doing a joint film with Ermanno Olmi because he thought we all shared an idea of film-making. I mentioned it to Paul straight away, of course, and we were very happy to join in. Abbas was living in Paris at the time, so we planned to meet there and near Ermanno's house in Italy, or in London. We'd take it in turns and travel to each place. Ermanno said, 'Why don't we start in Italy, because there's a really nice little restaurant that we can all sit down in and get to know each other?' So we all went to his place in Italy and had a very nice dinner and talked rather generally. We needed to meet again because we hadn't found a way of unifying the film. So we said, 'Shall we go to Paris, where Abbas is living?' And Ermanno said, 'This meeting worked very well. There's another little restaurant I know that's really nice, and it's just as easy coming to me.' We said, 'OK,' but with more reservation. And each time we met it would be in a little restaurant that Ermanno had a very good relationship with. We'd eat very well but didn't progress very much.

It emerged that a railway journey could encompass three stories, and Paul came up with the idea of the Celtic fans helping the Albanian family, which was good. But the train idea indicated how different our criteria were from Kiarostami's and Olmi's. I said, 'Right. Where's the train starting from? Where's it going to? Where do the people get on it? What's the timetable? Let's look it up and make it work.' And the other two didn't see it like that. They said, 'It's a train. It's an image of travel, of voyaging, and it doesn't matter where it's going to.' And me being an old northern European social-realist, I said, 'You've got a scene in the night-time. What long journey does it happen on? Because our story takes place in the daytime. It can't be happening at night.'

'Listen, it doesn't matter,' they said. 'Just tell the story of a train.' [*laughs*] I guess our interest in the details, in being accurate, was not matched by the other two at all. They saw the train journey more as a kind of metaphor for movement or travel. It was an interesting clash of ideas. There was an apparent similarity in how we did films, but underneath there was a rather major difference.

Do you think the film succeeds as a whole?

I'm not sure it works. It was really nice to meet Abbas Kiarostami – he was a terrific man – and Ermanno Olmi, too. His film *The Tree of Wooden Clogs* [1978] is magnificent. It's illuminating to find out how other directors work, though I didn't see Ermanno filming, and only a bit of Abbas. Ermanno put another voice on the woman character in his film, and it didn't seem to bother him that the voice didn't match the lip movements at all. That says a lot about Italian neo-realism [*laughs*]. I found that quite shocking.

Did you shoot on a moving train?

We did. I don't know about Abbas and Ermanno [*laughs*]. I do know that both of them directed from monitors. The idea of sitting further down the train and looking at a monitor, rather than crouching in a seat near the actors and trying to overhear them, was something I could never have done.

Was the restriction of working in such a confined space challenging?

It wasn't a big issue. It was like doing the 9/11 film* in terms of discipline. But we had a *Mr. Hulot's Holiday* [1953] moment doing one of the exterior shots. [Jacques] Tati has that scene where the passengers can't understand what the announcer is saying and keep missing the trains because they go to the wrong platforms, and they have to keep carrying their luggage up and down the steps of the underpass. We were trying to film a shot of a train travelling under one of two bridges. It was near to where we were doing other filming, so it was an easy place to get to, but the line diverged and the information kept changing about which bridge the train would go under. We set up to film the train arriving and going under one bridge, but we saw to our horror that it was approaching on the other line a hundred yards away, and it went under the

---

* See pp. 200–3.

other bridge. We were told that the next train would go under that bridge, too, so, of course, we moved the camera and, lo and behold, the train went through on the first line [*laughs*]. The shooting was full of those irritating, in retrospect comedy moments. But at the time, when you're trying to finish a film on a tight schedule, they can drive you to distraction.

Did you and Paul choose to make your story about Celtic supporters because they would have been exposed to sectarian rivalry, or does that read too much into it?

It's too much. Yes, they would have been [exposed to sectarianism in Glasgow], but it was just about three lads on their way to support their football team. Paul is forever telling me about Celtic's glory days, when they won the European Cup [in 1967], so it was a light-hearted folk memory of that and about how they react to the Albanians, which introduces the serious element of the story.

This might sound fanciful, but it faintly recalls E. M. Forster's Where Angels Fear to Tread, *in which you've also got a trio of Brits in Italy, placed in the position of either helping or hindering*

Tickets: Loach directs William Ruane, Martin Compston and Gary Maitland as Celtic fans.

someone. Your story boils down to the moral decision the three lads have to make about giving the train ticket to the Albanian boy. It asks viewers what they'd do in that situation.

Yeah, in a very simple way. They're there for the football, not to get involved in other people's difficulties. It's about them teasing out what to do to resolve that dilemma, but not in a portentous way. Just in a human way.

The Angels' Share also follows a group of lively Glasgow teenagers. Though it's more comic and hopeful than My Name Is Joe *or* Sweet Sixteen, *its main character, Robbie, comes from a similar background to Joe and the two Liams; the difference is that he's able to break free from a cycle of drug addiction and violence. Robbie leads his friends Rhino, Mo and Albert in pulling off a low-tech whisky heist. The title refers to the portion of a spirit – about 2 per cent – that is lost to evaporation when it ages in oak barrels, the same share the gang steals from a cask of priceless whisky being auctioned in a Highland distillery. In a sense, is Robbie himself 'the angels' share' – the one in a thousand kids who have had a wretched start to life and gone wrong but are able to make a fresh start?*

We didn't think of it like that; we just thought about the amount of whisky that evaporates. The four of them steal a little bit of whisky, and no one knows, so they are collectively the angels. Underneath their mischief and sometimes seriously dangerous behaviour, there's something redeemable about them. We'd done so many heavy films; we just wanted to do one with a smile on its face. William Ruane and Gary Maitland, who were in *Sweet Sixteen* and *Tickets*, were with us again in *The Angels' Share*. Gary's very funny. You can just see his brain working. He's slower than everybody else, but he's totally unselfconscious about it. I don't know what he's doing now, but after we made the film and went to Cannes with it, he went back to working on the bins [as a refuse collector]. He just liked the job and having a laugh with the other binmen. He was in the street emptying the bins with the gang when a bus came by with an advert for the film on it that featured his face. It was a beautiful counterpoint – as a binman you don't expect to be starring in a film.

We talked earlier about symbols of Scottish culture that have been commodified by the tourist industry. Did you and Paul want to enjoy the irony of Robbie and his mates pinching from the Scottish whisky industry?

It didn't feature largely in our conversation [*laughs*]. It just seemed a suitable target for the four of them to make some money from to help them solve their problems. And I think Paul likes a dram or two. Whisky's not to my taste – I prefer the grape to spirits.

Was Alexander Mackendrick's Ealing comedy Whisky Galore! *(1949) an influence on* The Angels' Share?

No. Haven't seen it actually, to my shame.

What about Bill Forsyth's comedy That Sinking Feeling *(1979), which is about four unemployed young Glasgow lads who steal stainless-steel sinks from a warehouse, with the idea of selling them?*

No, I haven't seen that either.

Early on, you made Tap on the Shoulder *(1965), a gold-bullion heist film that addresses the thin line between organized crime and legitimate business.*

Yes, it was my first *Wednesday Play*. Jimmy O'Connor was the writer. It was about a London villain who aspired to respectability and being one of the gentry. The 'tap on the shoulder' refers to his [impending] knighthood. But there was no link between *Tap on the Shoulder* and *The Angels' Share* in our minds at all. The crime the kids commit in *The Angels' Share* is not a crime in which anyone suffers. Nobody notices it because the whisky they take is [assumed to be] the angels' share. So it's a cheeky thing to do. To have an adventure, you have to travel. Their alibi is that they're Scots on a hiking trip, so they all dress up for it. It all fitted into that narrative.

The symbols of Scottishness have always been joked about. When Rhino is trying to impress a couple of girl tourists, he claims he's the grandson of a Highland chief and wears his kilt with pride, but one of them notes that he's wearing it back to front.

Yes. And Albert gets sore from the chafing of the kilt where the sun doesn't shine. When the police inspect the group on their return to Glasgow, they advise him to apply a little cream [*laughs*]. Again, it was making fun of the tourist image of Scotland.

When Albert sees Edinburgh Castle, he doesn't know what it is. Then, when the four are travelling to the distillery in Balblair, there's a close-up of Robbie, amazed by the sight of the Highlands. As someone who's been confined to Glasgow, that landscape is outside his realm of experience. He can't relate to it. One suspects that's true for many urban Scots.

We found this a lot. Paul noticed first that many Scottish people had barely moved more than a few miles away from where they were born. They're locked within their communities. It was the same when we did *Sweet Sixteen*. Kids had never been away from the estates where they lived overlooking the Clyde. A murder happened very close to where we were filming – one lad against another – and they found the guy who'd committed it. He was still in one of the houses in the area. He hadn't left. Those communities seem almost closed; there's been poverty for generations. Even when there was

The Angels' Share: Jasmin Riggins, Gary Maitland, Paul Brannigan and William Ruane.

work there, they were still very poor. And as we've said, without jobs there's no respect, just drugs, violence, all the rest.

In David Archibald's book Tracking Loach, *he records a conversation you had with* The Angels' Share's *cameraman, Robbie Ryan. Robbie said he had time to get a shot of a 'nice vista' at Loch Lomond, where the kids were hitch-hiking. You told him not to bother because such a shot wouldn't help the story. You tend to be sparing with visual poetry.*

It depends what you mean by 'poetry', really. I think it's got to be embedded in the film through the framing and the lighting. It's also got to carry the central point of what the scene's about rather than be decorative. That quality should be in the shots themselves and essential to telling the story. I don't think there's space to say, 'Oh, by the way, look at this.' I mean, tell the story – and tell it as precisely and as economically as you can, but allow it its full complexity. Don't simplify, but clarify it. I think the important distinction is that the images should be eloquent. They should be shot in such a way that they reveal the people. You can understand the people when you can see their eyes and read what's in their minds.

Did you hope to strengthen the viewer's identification with Robbie through the way you positioned the camera, so that we share in his vicious attack on the student in the flashback, but also enjoy being with him when he pulls off the heist?

The intention always is that the camera is a sympathetic observer, but from the point of view of understanding someone rather than condemning them or putting them on a pedestal, like in Hollywood cinema, and maybe in other film industries, where the stars are the heroes.

You seldom use high- or low-angle shots, which – similar to the way music is used in many films to intensify specific emotions – can manipulate the thoughts and feelings we have about specific characters.

The criterion is, could someone be standing here or sitting there? If you're in a car, where on earth is the camera when the car is being driven at great speed? Is it on the bonnet or is the cameraman flying along, looking through the passenger window or something? That's nonsense. Immediately, it invalidates the reality of what you're looking at. So you put the camera where the cameraman can actually be. I've probably said this before, but the lenses are the lenses of the human eye. Normally, the camera should be in a standing position, at eye height, which is how you meet people, though they might be a bit taller or a bit shorter. The camera is a human presence, with a position of equality. It doesn't take sides but just observes what's there. Let the audience judge.

A character filmed from a low angle invariably wields power over whoever is looking at them.

Or by being made to look up at them you think they're heroic. In most of the films we've done, there are no villains. We want to engage equally with people. Everyone is caught up in dilemmas, in making choices. Everyone has a context that indicates why they are who they are, so we try to understand that context. Conventional cinema sees people as heroes and villains, or as the good guys and the bad guys, as the Americans say. Nothing sets my teeth on edge more than that, because it indicates the crudity of what they're doing. It penetrates their politics. Donald Trump and Joe Biden* love this idea of the world turned into good guys and bad guys, and each claims he's the good guy, of course. Look at history, and you realize that anyone who uses that crude definition is on the other side.

How do you go about juxtaposing comedy scenes and darker scenes, and would it be different for a mostly upbeat film like The Angels' Share, *compared with, say,* Sweet Sixteen, *which becomes increasingly bleak?*

The driving force is always the story, the people in it and the inherent comic nature of what they're trying to do. With regard to the Scottish films, Paul is very good at understanding and enjoying the

---

* This interview took place before President Biden was replaced by Vice President Kamala Harris as the Democratic candidate in the 2024 US presidential election. On 5 November, Trump won comfortably.

Glaswegian sense of humour. It's very much in the vein of the young Scottish comedian Kevin Bridges or Billy Connolly, whom everyone knows. I'd diminish it if I tried to explain it, but you know it when you see it and hear it and smile at it. Paul's enjoyment of it is in his writing, and my enjoyment of it is through him and through meeting the people who bring it to life.

That humour's a big part of *The Angels' Share*, so we just told the story and didn't minimise the dark side of what the main character's been through. He's clearly a very intelligent, imaginative lad, yet with an appalling history. It's the struggle between all those contradictions in his character that you see, but without us making it melodramatic. It's just there, implicit in who he is. Just assembling the cast for the gang of four, we knew they were going to be funny between themselves. The characters' disagreements and how they express them is partly funny, but should also be revealing.

When Harry, the community payback supervisor, takes the crew on a tour of a whisky distillery, Robbie absorbs what the guide tells them, then hangs back. While we're listening to the others chatting and joking, we can see that he's silently thinking about what he's learned. It's an evocative moment because a light has been lit.

Yes, he's very bright. Again, it's a theme that runs through a lot of our films, not only the ones we've done with Paul, but going back to Billy Casper in *Kes*. In Billy, you see a lad with great sensitivity, thoughtfulness, talent, ingenuity, though the world sees him as useless, or that he has limited use as unskilled labour. It's the same with the lads and the girl in *The Angels' Share*. They're perceived as being of little value, with nothing to offer, whereas we can see they've got huge value as very rounded, thoughtful, bright people.

When I interviewed Jim Allen for the first edition of this book, I asked him if he was conscious of using the three-act structure of classic cinema. He said, and I quote, 'That's all bollocks.' Obviously, as a seasoned writer, the means of telling a story had become ingrained in him.

The irritating thing about the people who promote this way of storytelling – the three acts – is that it's unique to cinema, but it's nicked from the theatre, from Aristotle and the earliest classics.

And the old tradition of fairy tales shows you how to tell a story with surprises and expectations that are denied, moments of unconscious humour, set pieces, the remorseless series of events interrupted by a diversion that enables you to recover your appetite for the next serious bit. It doesn't belong to cinema but is an inherited understanding of how you tell a story.

When you and Paul are devising the stories for the films, do you map them out episodically?

No. What happens is, we talk about the basic situation, and as we knock it backwards and forwards, Paul proposes the characters. Then we say, 'Yes, I think this will make a good film,' or that it'll make a film – I don't know about a good one [*laughs*] – and Paul will go away and do a first draft. I think that's right because, in the end, you can't write by committee. So many ideas go round in your head that to laboriously explain them to someone and then argue them through would kill them. I know from the little bits I write – newspaper articles or whatever – that there's a point where you just have to sit down and do a first draft, and then you knock it about. Paul writes very quickly. He'll take four, five, six weeks max. to write the first draft, and then we'll look at it, I'll make suggestions – or not – and we'll go to and fro.

The great thing about Paul as a writer is that he's very collaborative, but that's based on my respecting his writing and the necessity of him writing the first draft without my chipping in. He's such an imaginative, creative writer. There are always lots of strands. Each screenplay is like a huge pudding – it's brilliant stuff – and I suppose my role has tended to be to thin it out a little bit, but the essence of the film is always what Paul's written. That's why it upsets both of us, I think, that directors get all the credit for films. The credit 'A film by', followed by the director's name, is absolutely fraudulent, because if a film belongs to anyone, it's the person who sits down for a number of weeks and writes the story. The director's job is to interpret and clarify and try to put on screen what the writer's written in the clearest, most available and most easily communicated way. But the essence of the creativity is in that first draft.

You have always disparaged the cult of the auteur.

Absolutely. You can't look at the people you work with in the eye if you believe in all that. Also, I don't like the use of the word 'film-maker' for a director, because everyone who works on a film is a film-maker. The person who is working in design is making the film. Sound recordists, editors, the cameraman – which is a shorter, less pretentious word than 'cinematographer' – we used to call the 'camera operator'. The person who runs up with a message is helping to make the film, and so to call some people film-makers and not others devalues and denies the work of everyone else. Yes, I direct the film, but all that means is that I'm involved in a series of partnerships. It's not telling people what to do. It's working with them to create a harmonious, integrated piece of work. Calling yourself 'the film-maker' smacks of egocentricity and a failure to acknowledge that you are in a team. Sadly, it's common practice to pay lip service to the team and pay too much attention to [the hierarchy implied by] the credits, and I hate that.

But because you've worked with different teams on a series of films over—

Sixty years – God help us!

—and because you're the common denominator in those films, with their recurrent themes and consistent political analysis of the social problems faced by working people, inevitably the media has landed on the idea of what some journalists have described as a Ken Loach 'brand', awful shorthand though that word is.

It is an awful word because it's a kind of post-Thatcher word, where everything is for sale. A brand is something you sell, and that's not how we think of the films. We think of them as communications.

Undeniably, your films are associated with a realist style – a more helpful term than 'brand'.

Yes, I can see that. On the cinematic side, I've obviously worked with a series of brilliant cameramen – and they have all been men, I'm afraid – and sound recordists and designers and a certain kind of actor, but the collaboration with the writers is at the heart of everything. And, of course, the producer plays another absolutely essential role, but it's a different kind of role.

You mentioned the dark side of what Robbie's been through in The Angels' Share. *A flashback shows him coked up and attacking a student. He half blinds the boy, Anthony, costing him his university place. Robbie goes to prison and gets clean. In the present, he and Leonie, his girlfriend, have a newborn. They attend a meeting with Anthony and his parents. The mother is enraged by what Robbie did, and he himself is mortified, but unyielding. It's a pivotal moment of self-reckoning. Did you hold back information about the encounter from the actors to maximize emotional intensity?*

I think we followed the script pretty well, but I usually try to keep the end of a scene hidden, and I imagine we did it that way. When the people in a film play a scene, there needs to be something at stake so there's an unexpected quality about what they're doing. The actors don't know exactly how the scene is going to end, but they've got an interest in it ending in a certain way.

So there is that dependence on each other in the scene, each person looking to the others to see how it's going to end. The camera must be as unobtrusive as possible, and my presence totally unobtrusive, too. I'll just be crouched in the corner somewhere, with my head turned away from them so they become absorbed in each other and try to read what the outcome is going to be.

There was a huge amount at stake for the characters in that meeting. The family needs to know that Robbie knows about the catastrophic damage he's done. That would enable them to move on, as they say. Are they going to get what they want? Robbie's overwhelmed by it, but something in him says, 'I can't grovel,' so there needs to be tension in this confrontation.

On a different note, at the end of the film Albert accidentally smashes two of the priceless bottles of stolen whisky when the police are questioning the gang. I believe you told Gary Maitland, who plays Albert, that he'd do this, but not the other actors, so that they'd be shocked.

Yes – appalled by it! Acting's about suspending disbelief. You are acting, but you are living in the world that is being created and responding instinctively to what's happening. Your instinct can be in tune with words you've learned, and it can also follow the same path as your feelings about a situation, as articulated by the writer. All this can flow together, and sometimes when something happens that you're just not expecting, you believe it, even though you're acting in a film. That's what acting is, isn't it? It's believing in something as you're experiencing it. It's caring, it's feeling, it's believing in that world you're in, so you respond as the characters would. [As the director], you never quite know how the actors will respond, so you just have to mould it a little bit. Usually it's spot on, because if you cast the right people, when they reveal themselves they reveal the characters.

Do you always hope to get a shot on the first take?

Usually we shoot very quickly, but we might get two or three takes out of a set-up. You've got to be prepared to get it on the first take. Often, you need more than one shot, so occasionally you'll use two cameras. But usually you can get it in one because you get the key reaction on the first take, looking one way, or possibly the second. Then you'll pick up the camera and whizz round to the other side and turn over the complementary shot on the other people in the scene responding to the person who's instigated the surprise. You have to make certain you've got the right lens; you might need to change it, but you've mentioned that to the cameraman and the focus puller beforehand, so you've got both shots lined up. Then you'll go back and do it again the other way. You just judge it moment by moment. What do you need? Who's going to come to the boil in the next take? And what will last for a couple of takes and what won't? You always have both set-ups ready. You can't have a long gap between takes, because the sensation of the surprise will last with the people in the film for just a few minutes, and you have to be sure they're still in the moment.

It's amazing that the purity of the actors' emotions isn't diluted by repetition, or that a few minutes' delay doesn't diminish the spontaneity of their reactions.

It is a diminishing asset, but the comedy or sadness of a scene – whatever it is – isn't totally transitory. If you've had some shocking news, or something comic or funny has occurred, it stays with you for a bit. Obviously, it gradually diminishes, but it's there long enough for the actors to know how they first reacted, and strong enough in their minds for them to recreate it.

Though it isn't your custom to give the lead actors in a film the full script in advance, you did give a copy of The Angels' Share *screenplay to Charles MacLean, the whisky connoisseur and writer who plays a version of himself. Were you confident he'd be OK with the film poking fun at the Scottish whisky industry?*

Definitely. He's a great man with a great sense of humour and a huge enjoyment of whisky. In the nicest sense of the word, he's a Falstaffian figure of mischief and fun, and very good company. The warmth of his presence spread across the film.

Would working with someone like that be different to how you worked with, say, Grace Cave, a strict traditionalist in real life, who, as the domineering mother in Family Life *(1971), crushes her fragile daughter (Sandy Ratcliff)?*

Yes, but that doesn't mean we'd treat someone like Grace with hostility. We treated her well, and got on well when we were filming. You can't work with somebody if you are antagonistic to them because of who they're playing. I knew that a lot of what Grace said was what she thought, but I didn't challenge that. I didn't want to challenge it because I wanted it represented in the film and wanted her to express it without fear of being undermined; I wanted to believe in it as we were making it. The film itself challenged the role of parents in disciplining and shaping how children should be, but on a personal level you get on well with the people you work with and have a smile with them.

Did you partially see The Angels' Share *as a story of redemption or forgiveness? Though Anthony's parents can't forgive Robbie for brutalizing their son, the film celebrates the fact that he gets a second chance.*

It says more than that. It says this is a lad who has never had a chance. Do you say to him, 'You are a victim and need all our

The Angels' Share: a production shot of Robbie (Paul Brannigan) among the whisky casks.

support,' or 'You are a villain and need to go back to prison'? It's the same person, after all. It's our understanding that who people become depends on their earliest years. What is it the Jesuits say? 'Give me a child until he is seven, and I will give you the man or the woman.' You don't suddenly become a different person at eighteen, as criminal law would suggest when it says, 'Right. You are old enough now for us to lock you away for the rest of your life.' As always, the cliché is that a mix of nature and nurture determines how we turn out, but for someone like Robbie, the poverty of every aspect of his life has been imprinted on him since he was a kid. And that's an understanding we want society to acknowledge and to act accordingly to redress.

Talking about second chances is almost inheriting that idea of 'Right. You're to blame now. We've given you one chance,' or 'You're lucky. We're giving you a second chance.' The issue is more about understanding and creating a whole social structure in which people can live well. It's good housing, good employment, education and healthcare, producing something, contributing in a useful way, being properly rewarded, having sport, the arts, leisure available. When everyone has those opportunities, the people who make the judgements – usually the middle class, who don't have those privations – can go ahead and make them. But don't make them before people have those opportunities to lead a decent life. In fact, we know they have never had them. Looking back in history, we got close sometimes to the prospect of a universal better life, but whenever that happens the right wing steps in and says, 'No. Get back to where you belong.' It's 'the rich man in his castle, the poor man at his gate'.

Thatcherism was a case in point in the 1980s. It was the decade in which the gross national product – the value of what we make in our industries – was more widely shared than in any other decade. And the attitude from those in power was: create mass unemployment, drive down wages, weaken trade unions, destroy the welfare state. The consequence of that is generations of people like Robbie, because that's the atmosphere they've grown up in. 'Look after yourself,' because that's what the rich do. Selfishness, ruthlessness, greed – those are the characteristics our society develops. In fact, according to Thatcher, 'There's no such thing as society,'* so we shouldn't be surprised when the people who suffer from that say, 'Right. That's how we'll operate.'

---

* The full quote from Douglas Keay's interview with Margaret Thatcher, published in *Woman's Own* magazine on 23 September 1987, is as follows: 'We've been through a period where too many people have been given to understand that if they have a problem, it's the government's job to cope with it. "I have a problem, I'll get a grant." "I'm homeless, the government must house me." They're casting their problem on society. And there is no such thing as society. There are individual men and women, and there are families. And no government can do anything except through people, and people must look to themselves first. It's our duty to look after ourselves and then, also to look after our neighbour. People have got the entitlements too much in mind, without the obligations.'

CHAPTER 9

In the Americas

Bread and Roses, 11'09"01 – September 11

Loach was sixty-three when he made his only American-based film, *Bread and Roses*, written by Paul Laverty and produced by Rebecca O'Brien. Shot in Los Angeles in the autumn of 1999, it depicts a Service Employees International Union's Justice for Janitors campaign, inspired by the three-week strike in April 1990 that resulted in a 22 per cent pay rise over the following three years for office cleaners, many of them illegal Latino immigrants. By using innovative, militant tactics mobilizing women workers, the strike revitalized labour action in the US.

It is a measure of Loach's political commitment and personal sympathies that he is probably the only well-known international director who has travelled to the profit-obsessed industry town – where about $4.5 billion is spent annually on producing trivial mass entertainments – to make a film about cruelly exploited workers from a marginalized community organizing to fight for employment rights. Loach consciously abstracted *Bread and Roses*, which is confined mostly to the claustrophobic interiors of steel-and-glass office towers in downtown LA and the streets outside, from the architecture and iconography of Hollywood and Los Angeles's other wealthy neighbourhoods. The faceless, well-heeled white-collar workers seen going to and from their workplaces are oblivious to the cleaners' existence.

Laverty initiated the film. Between 1994 and 1996, he was in Los Angeles, after winning a Fulbright scholarship to study at the University of Southern California. 'I used my money to live in a crazy area in downtown Los Angeles where all the gangs were and, as usual, I got to know political people,' he said.* Riding the

---

* Interview with author.

early-morning buses, Laverty chatted to Hispanic office cleaners, who told him about the Justice for Janitors campaign. 'They were all young trade unionists. What they said in essence – and this is what I loved – was: "It isn't the employers against the employees, it's the corporations against the community." They were brilliant people, and what was so great was that they connected with students, other trade unions, churches, women's groups – the whole spectrum.

'All of them were working for big corporations and, as they were all illegal, they were working like dogs, cleaning the offices of banks, lawyers, and luxury buildings. Many of the people I met were working three jobs. They hardly saw their children, and as a result their children would often end up in gangs. Obviously, they wanted to get trade union recognition so they could get health insurance for their families – that was key – and other minimal rights. The stakes were very high because the corporations said, "We'll set the Migra* on you. You'll be picked up and sent back to where you came from," and that's what the bastards did. If that happened, it had a devastating effect on the families.

'But the janitors had these guerrilla tactics,' Laverty continued. 'They said, "Where does power operate?" They would find out where the heads and owners of these big buildings were and track them down, and, of course, they said, "Oh, it's nothing to do with us. You've got to deal with the cleaning companies." And we'd say – because I'd volunteered [to help the janitors] – "No, it's you. You fucking choose them. You subcontract the work out – you are responsible." We'd go target them. I remember going into restaurants where the building owners were eating, and saying, "Oh, look at that lovely shrimp there. How much did that cost you?" Or we'd go outside their homes and play music, winding them up, you know? It was great fun. There was a sense of *joie de vivre* in it.

'The other thing is that some of the old trade unionists were white racists who tried to ban Spanish, but the young Hispanic activists said, "No, this is our union, and you're not going to touch it." I loved everything about them, and I thought, "Fuck, this is

---

* 'Migra' or 'La migra' is Mexican and American Spanish slang for US Immigration and Customs Enforcement and the US Border Patrol.

what we need." So I wrote to Ken, suggesting it'd make for a feisty film, and he said, "Let's have a crack at it." So that's how *Bread and Roses* came about.'

The film's protagonist, Maya (Pilar Padilla), is an illegal Mexican immigrant newly arrived in LA who, as an office cleaner, is politicized by her involvement in the Justice for Janitors campaign. Maya's youthful idealism is contrasted with the pragmatism of her careworn older married sister and fellow janitor, Rosa (Elpidia Carrillo), who cannot afford to jeopardize her job by joining a union.

In the opening sequence, Barry Ackroyd's jerky hand-held camerawork captures Maya and other 'illegals' scrambling over the rough vegetative terrain of the border, where a people trafficker is waiting to ferry them to LA in a van. On arrival, she is prevented from meeting Rosa and kidnapped by the trafficker, but she pretends to go along with his attempt to seduce her and escapes, stealing his fancy cowboy boots into the bargain. She takes a taxi to the house where Rosa lives with her unwell husband, Bert (Jack McGee), and their daughter and son. Maya is subjected to more unwanted male attention while working as a bartender, but gets Rosa to bring her to Perez (George Lopez), her boss at the Angel Cleaning Company, for an interview. A working-class exploiter as self-serving as Maloney in *Sorry We Missed You* (2019), Perez is also a bully and lecher who asks Maya to tighten her overall so he can assess her figure. He hires her, but tells her he's going to take her first month's salary in two instalments.

Sam Shapiro (Adrien Brody), the white, educated Justice for Janitors rep, makes a Chaplinesque entrance in the film, causing Perez and the security guards to take pratfalls on a floor onto which he's tossed cleaning wax as they chase him. Maya hides him in her cleaning cart. That evening, he turns up at Rosa's house to enlist Maya, telling her that in 1982 cleaners were paid $8.50 an hour and, as union members, had healthcare coverage, paid sick leave and holiday pay. He reminds her that, in the absence of a union deal, they are now paid $5.75 and have no benefits. Rosa scorns him – 'When was the last time you got a cleaning job?' – and throws him out.

After Perez fires the elderly Teresa (Estela Maeda) for lateness, Maya asks Sam to address the Angel cleaners, who are mostly a mix of Latinas and African American women, but including a few men and a Russian, Maria (Elena Antonenko). He tells them Angel has outbid unionized cleaning companies by cutting wages. He wants the Justice for Janitors protesters to block intersections across LA so as to cause disruption to businesses, which will force the building owners to meet the cleaners' demands. In the heated exchange that follows, Maria denounces his plans. Some of Maya's colleagues are resistant to joining the union, and Perez threatens to fire anyone who does. He tells the cleaner Berta (Maria Orellana), who has been sending money to her family in El Salvador for seventeen years, that he will raise her wages and give her a supervisor's job, and health insurance if she agrees to inform on union joiners; when she refuses the bribe, he fires her (off-screen). Sam leads a night-time meeting of cleaners and welcomes Maya and other non-union members to the campaign's ranks. Rosa, who isn't among them, looks on in dismay.

Sam, Maya and a few others march in the street with placards, then Sam leads them into a restaurant, where he taunts a building owner by taking a chop from his plate and drinking his wine. The protesters watch footage from 1990 showing police beating up striking janitors (fifty were jailed and sixty injured, among them a pregnant woman who consequently miscarried her baby). At a cleaners' social evening – where Maya and Sam kiss for the first time – Bert collapses and is taken to hospital. He has a renal condition and probable retinopathy requiring an operation.

Sam's boss reprimands him for his subversive tactics, which have earned the union three injunctions in two days. Sam still intends to lead the cleaners in crashing a party being held in one of the office towers to celebrate the merger of two law firms. Maya's friend and admirer Ruben (Alonso Chavez), who is about to enter law school, needs to use his cleaner's earnings to supplement his private foundation grant. He quits the janitors' campaign because he cannot risk missing his tuition deadline. He also antagonises Maya by jealously accusing her of supporting Justice for Janitors because she likes Sam (and because Sam is white). Critics who argue that *Bread and Roses* musters only one emotional scene – the climactic conversation between Rosa and Maya – neglect how angrily Maya upbraids Ruben for insulting her. She explains how incensed she is by rich Americans exploiting the Latinos whom they hire as servants and nannies for a pittance: 'Remember what you said when they fired Teresa? "She reminds me of my mother." That's why I'm doing it. I'm doing it because my sister has had to work sixteen hours each day. I'm doing it because I had to pay Perez two months of my wage and beg him for a job. I'm doing it because we have to feed those bastards. We wipe their asses, we get everything ready for them. We raise their children, and they look right through us.'

Several film stars, playing themselves, and glamorous white models arrive at the law firm's party. Sam presents one of the partners with a golden turkey because the cleaners earn only $12,000 a year, and they swamp the room to sabotage the occasion. Maya and Sam hold hands as they watch the news report of the event on TV. The next day, Perez, backed by security guards, fires half of the cleaners, including Maya and Ruben. Some of them blame Maya, who learns that it was Rosa who phoned Perez and named the protesters, for which she has been awarded the supervisor's job in a new building. At home, Maya asks Rosa why she sold them out. Stung by being called a traitor, Rosa reminds Maya that, after their father walked out on them, she moved to Tijuana when she was seventeen. She bitterly explains that, in order to send money back to Maya and their mother so they could eat, she spent five years 'whoring', night after night. She adds that she doesn't know who fathered her daughter, who was born in a brothel, that she had sex with Perez to get Maya her job, and that she pays Bert's medical bills by continuing to work as a prostitute. Having known nothing of Rosa's sacrifices on her behalf, Maya is distraught. Wrenchingly delivered by Carrillo, Rosa's tirade – crafted by Laverty so that her memories pour out in a disordered rush, such is her feeling of degradation and her sense of self-betrayal – gives the lie to the allegation sometimes made against Loach that his films lack a feminist consciousness.*

Maya steals money from a garage and uses it to pay for Ruben's law school registration papers. Union members from around the city stage a large demonstration to protest the cleaners' dismissal; Barry Ackroyd's roving camera, Jonathan Morris's montaged

---

* Leading feminist activist-authors such as Kathleen Barry and Andrea Dworkin have argued that prostitution is oppressive and forced on women by necessity, as in Rosa's case. Other prominent feminists, including Carol Leigh and Margo St. James, have argued that sex work is a viable choice. See also pp. 332–3.

cutting and the sounds of a Mexican band and singing combine to convey the joy in community action. A banner bears the slogan: 'We want bread but roses too'.* As Sam gives a rousing speech on the ground floor of one of the office towers, LA riot police march up. The scene briefly recalls the Battle of Orgreave during the miners' strike, as well as Sergei Eisenstein's *Strike* (1925), but though Maya is pulled to the ground, the cleaners and their supporters are quelled with less violence than were the miners of 1984 or the striking Russian factory workers of 1902–3.

The police arrest Maya, Sam and other protesters. In his cell, Sam learns from a phone call that Angel has agreed to reinstate the fired cleaners and grant them health insurance and holiday pay – a victory for collective action. Identified as the garage robber, Maya is deported, under the threat of receiving a three-year prison sentence. Carrying a letter from Sam, she leaves on a bus that will take her back to Mexico, in much the same way that another deportee, Jimmy Gralton, starts his return journey to America in a horse-drawn cart at the end of *Jimmy's Hall*. Keeping apart from the other cleaners who have come to see Maya off, Rosa runs after the bus, waves at Maya and tells her she loves her.

Following al-Qaeda's terrorist attacks on the United States on 11 September 2001, the French producer Alain Brigand invited eleven directors from different countries, including Loach and Claude Lelouch, to contribute a short film to the omnibus project *11'09"01 – September 11*. It was inspired by *Far from Vietnam* (1967), an anti-war assemblage organized by Chris Marker, with contributions directed by Lelouch, Jean-Luc Godard, Agnès Varda, Alain Resnais and Joris Ivens. Each segment commissioned by Brigand was to last eleven minutes, nine seconds and one frame, a fastidious constraint for a subject of such magnitude, though

---

* The slogan 'bread for all, and roses, too' was first used by the American suffragist and labour activist Helen MacGregor Todd (1870–1953), in a speech supporting women's right to vote in Illinois in June 1910. Todd explained in a 1911 *American Magazine* article: 'Not at once; but woman is the mothering element in the world and her vote will go towards helping forward the time when life's Bread, which is home, shelter and security, and the Roses of life, music, education, nature and books, shall be the heritage of every child that is born in the country, in the government of which she has a voice.'

it allowed for a range of perspectives. Beyond recommending a reflective approach and inclusivity, there were no other restrictions, Brigand favouring 'freedom of expression'.

The overall result was not a success. Though Samira Makhmalbaf's and Idrissa Ouédraogo's segments pointedly implant consciousness of the World Trade Center attack into the minds of children in Burkina Faso and Afghanistan respectively, most of the other short films were variously deemed self-indulgent, whimsical, nationally inward-looking, polemical, guilty of bleeding-heart liberalism or tastelessly arty.[*] Loach's film, which he devised with Laverty, was acclaimed across the board. It shows the activist, musician and performer Vladimir Vega,[†] who had played Jorge in *Ladybird, Ladybird*, sitting alone in a room and reading in voice-over the letter he is writing to the parents and loved ones of those who died on 11 September in New York. He says that, as a Chilean living in exile in London, he 'maybe' has something in common with them. He invites them to think about the consequences of the Nixon administration's and the CIA's[‡] roles in the military coup, led by Augusto Pinochet, that overthrew the Chilean president Salvador Allende's democratically elected, progressive socialist government on 11 September 1973. Allende nationalized the copper mining industry (which the government expropriated without compensating the American multinationals who owned the mines), coal mining and healthcare, and introduced welfare, education and agrarian reforms (including the unionisation of rural workers), some of his policies echoing those of the British Labour government that Loach celebrated in *The Spirit of '45*.

Archival footage depicts the jubilation that greeted Allende's 1970 election as the leader of Popular Unity, the left-wing coalition he led as a moderately inclined, pro-democracy Marxist, and the

---

[*] See the Filmography for the other directors on this project.
[†] The Chilean Vladimir Vega (1953–2013) was imprisoned and tortured as a student activist following Augusto Pinochet's coup. He was released into exile in the late 1970s and settled in London.
[‡] Alarmed by Allende winning 28.58 per cent of the vote in the 1958 Chilean election, the CIA, which feared another Cuba, covertly spent $5.6 million (including $3 million on anti-Allende propaganda) on helping his opponent, Eduardo Frei Montalva, leader of the Christian Democratic Party, win the 1964 election.

chaos and carnage caused by the coup. There is disturbing footage of people who have been herded into Santiago's National Stadium waiting to see what will happen to them; many would be tortured and executed there. Shots of corpses strewn across wasteland appear towards the end of the film. The National Commission on Political Imprisonment and Torture and the Commission of Truth and Reconciliation have reported that 40,018 people were tortured and 3,065 were executed during Pinochet's dictatorship from 1973 to 1990. Prisoners of both sexes – but primarily women – were subjected to sexual torture, which Vega's letter unflinchingly describes.

Though Vega sings and plays some of his plaintive folk songs and is seen walking peacefully with his family in a London park, the short film is Loach and Laverty's most mordant work. On 11 September 2001, they suggest, the US reaped a whirlwind for its decades-long pursuit of a geopolitically driven foreign policy aimed at protecting global capitalism. The *Observer*'s film critic, Philip French, observed on 29 December 2002: 'Loach's message is that the Americans had it coming or, as he has put it in a production note: "This was a symbolic attack on a power represented by the World Trade Centre and the Pentagon." Whether or not you agree with that, Loach's film is like being kicked in the guts by an Andean mule.' Peter Matthews concurred in his review in the January 2003 issue of *Sight and Sound*: 'Despite Vega's earnest attempts to look respectful, the WTC [World Trade Center] attack is clearly regarded as a historical quid pro quo – the devil of American foreign policy has at last come home.'

As Loach explains below, he was appalled by the horrific scale of the attacks on the World Trade Center, the Pentagon and United Airlines Flight 93. He demonstrated outrage at the US government's hypocrisy, however, by juxtaposing in the short film a clip of President George W. Bush telling the American people in his post-9/11 address that 'enemies of freedom committed an act of war against our country . . . and night fell on a different world, a world where freedom itself is under attack'* with shots of Hawker Hunter

---

* Address to a joint session of Congress and the American people, 20 September 2002. The clip of Bush, which includes an invisible cut, comprises two segments that are approximately thirty-five seconds apart in the same section of the speech.

planes bombing La Moneda palace, Allende's Santiago residence, on the morning of the coup. Anticipating the invasion of Iraq two years later, Bush's speech was, of course, a trigger for the events the Loach team unfold in *Route Irish* (2010).

GRAHAM FULLER: *When I interviewed you for the US release of* Bread and Roses *in 2001, you said that you felt you would have bottled it if you hadn't taken the opportunity to make a film in the US. Did you find it a very different experience to making films in Britain?*

KEN LOACH: In the details, it's very different. I think we all felt Los Angeles was the most difficult place we'd ever filmed in, and that included shooting [part of] *Carla's Song* in Nicaragua, with its mosquitoes. In Los Angeles, they think they know everything about making films, but the way we work is very different. The determination to impose the American way of doing things on us was very oppressive.

Just to take a simple thing, the way we work is to involve everyone in the crew as much as possible. So, in Los Angeles, I'd talk to everyone, and not in a pattern, I hope, but just as you would normally. I'd talk to the sparks, to the drivers, and they'd know the actors and everyone on the team. I'd maybe tell the guys driving us to the location what we were going to do that day. It's just a friendly way of working. Well, then the drivers would disappear. You'd ask, 'Where's so-and-so?' 'Oh, he's on another job.' And he wouldn't have said, 'Cheerio, I'm off,' he wouldn't have signed off – he just didn't turn up. Some of them seemed to actively resist a connection to the content of the film. They were just there to drive, and they'd say, 'You are Mr Loach, and that's what I'll call you. You call me by my first name.' Well, OK. That was so much the norm and how they were expected to be, and it was difficult to escape it. People would just come and go, even when you thought you had made a connection or had a relationship with them. But sometimes we'd have more drivers than we had vehicles.

Because we were filming in the States, we had to have a producer from an American company involved, and that person was actively subverting what we were doing because she was answerable to the company, not to us. When we asked for something to be put through, like a driving licence for one of the crew, it just wouldn't happen because she didn't want them to drive. We'd never had to deal with that kind of conflict of interest before from somebody who, though apparently working on the film for us, wasn't answerable to us but was working for someone else and feeding it back to her bosses, who'd obviously say, 'Don't let them do this, don't let them do that.' So that went on. Against that, we did work with a lot of brilliant people.

Were the unions co-operative?

Rebecca and I went to them and said, 'Look, this is how we've worked before, and this is how we'd like to work. We pay union rates and, of course, we want to include you [in the production]. We won't do anything behind your backs. It's a very modest film, and this is the money we've got. Can we work together?' And they were very helpful, by and large. We had a lot of office cleaners in acting parts in the film – they're called 'janitors' in America – and the unions were very understanding about that. So it was much better than I thought it might be.

Some elements made it hard. The location manager, who was a nice guy, got permission for us to film a little demonstration by the janitors in the street outside some big office blocks. We started filming the demo, but then somebody came out of one of the blocks and said we'd got to stop. We said, 'Why? We've got permission.' He said, 'You're interfering with our business. You're putting people off.' We weren't at all. It was one of these areas where there's just traffic, no one on the pavement at all, but he insisted we stop. The location manager said, 'I've got to ask you if you will stop. We are in the right, but if he reports me to the municipal office that gave me the permission, I won't get the permission again, and it'll blight my career.' So in deference to him we backed down and went somewhere else. But business rules. Another thing is that Americans like to say, 'We kick ass. We don't stand for any nonsense.' Well, they do. In contradiction to their public image, we found it more bureaucratic than working in the UK.

Had you previously received offers to work in Hollywood?

I did in the 1970s, after *Poor Cow* and *Kes* and one or two others. It wasn't for a particular project; it was to join a group of young directors there. But we had a young family, and I didn't want to go. I'd rather work here [in the UK]. I don't understand American culture very well and thought I wouldn't be doing good work, so I didn't go. I think the stuff we've done is different to what the American film culture produces in so many ways.

Was it the specifics of the 1990 Justice for Janitors strike that impelled you and Paul to make the film, and did you see it as part of the continuum of union struggles going back to the United Mine Workers of America in the 1890s and the Wobblies (Industrial Workers of the World) in the 1900s?

Absolutely. Again, it was Paul's idea. He'd been in Los Angeles for a year, ostensibly doing a course on screenwriting but mainly spending his time with people like those in the film. As you know, he's a lawyer by training and had been in Nicaragua as an observer of the human rights abuses by the American-backed Contras. He'd learned Spanish there, and when he was on the buses early in the morning in Los Angeles with the Mexicans and Salvadorans and the rest of the Central Americans going to clean the offices, he got to know them well, and out of them came the story for *Bread and Roses*. He was particularly attracted to the janitors' strike because of the unorthodox way in which the young organizers [of the Los Angeles Justice for Janitors movement] went about it. They tore up the rule book and said, 'Right, we are going to nail the people in the businesses in the offices so that they put pressure on the agencies [building service contractors] that hired workers to do the cleaning and all the dirty work. It'll be intolerable for them, until they give way.' They didn't go down the usual path but had an inventive, energetic way of working and thinking laterally to get their demands met.

So that was very attractive. And, of course, the stories of the Wobblies and their legendary battles were inspiring. The film's title comes from the Lawrence textile workers' strike [Massachusetts, 1912]: 'We want bread, but roses, too.' A side of America we never hear of over here is the struggles of the labour unions. Sometimes they had victories, but the powers that be don't want us to hear about victories. So that was very much in our minds.

The film shows the conflict between the two Mexican immigrant sisters: Maya, a newly arrived illegal immigrant, and the older Rosa, who gets Maya a job working alongside her cleaning offices. Whereas Maya eagerly joins the janitors who unionize in hopes of getting a better wage and working conditions, Rosa refuses because she has family responsibilities and fears losing her job. Eventually, Rosa betrays the union members to their supervisor.

It was a terrific script again from Paul. He's very good at encapsulating the core struggle of a film in terms of personal relationships; in the story of the struggle between the two sisters, both their viewpoints are understandable. Rosa takes care of her family, but her actions have terrible consequences for some of the other workers. Maya, the younger one, is naïve in not realizing what Rosa has had to go through. The climactic scene was slightly different to what we'd planned. The strike has been betrayed by Rosa, who has passed on the names of some of the strikers to the management. When Maya realizes this and comes back to the house and rounds on her, accusing her of betrayal – 'Do you know what the consequences will be for all the people that are going to lose their jobs? Their families will suffer. How could you do it?' – we'd imagined that she would have then said, 'It's too awful – I can't live with you,' and leave.

Actually, when we played it, Pilar Padilla, the actress playing Maya, didn't know what she was going to be told. I'd just given her the first part of the script. The key thing was Maya hearing the revelation that Rosa had had to work as a prostitute in the border towns to get money for her family back in Mexico to live on. And when Rosa got herself into the States, she had to go to bed with the manager of the cleaning agency in order to get hired, as she did later to get Maya her job. That corruption is endemic in the whole thing. Rosa's got a husband who's got diabetes and can't afford medical insurance. If she'd joined the strike, she would have lost her job. She just couldn't risk it. And when put under pressure, she gave the names of some of those involved just for self-protection.

Pilar didn't know any of this, so when Rosa tells her [Maya] what she's had to do to survive, she just wept – and, of course, it brings the sisters together and cements the bond between them. Paul quickly rejigged the script at the end of the film to accommodate it. It's much stronger than what we'd imagined because [Maya's response] actually came from Pilar's instinct, and that instinct was dead right. She just wanted to put her arms around Rosa. It was an extraordinary scene to shoot. It was all in the preparation. Elpidia Carrillo, who plays Rosa, got the script, so she knew everything, knew what she was going to say. Though Pilar had no idea what was going to happen, she really listened. It's quite a long scene: we shot it in a couple of hours, just very simply, with the two actresses in a small room, Barry Ackroyd behind the camera and two or three of us crouched behind doors so we weren't in their eyeline. Elpidia and Pilar were terrific, both really brilliant.

Like Rosa, Katie in I, Daniel Blake *also turns to prostitution to support her family, and it's implied that Joy in* Poor Cow *does, too. This is a difficult subject to discuss, but do you think third-wave feminists' reclaiming of prostitution as an empowering form of labour is a rationalization of a transaction that, in the wrong circumstances, can be degrading and dangerous?*

I can't say it's OK. I can see that people are driven to it through desperation. I assume there are often other psychological issues involved; I'm not competent to speak about it. But from the outside you can't help but see it as humiliating and degrading for the people involved, women or men. I'm not sure that saying it's acceptable is relevant really – acceptable to whom? If people are driven to it, then that's a terrible indictment of the situation they're in and the society that creates it. If there's anything else involved, I don't know. It's way beyond my pay grade to talk about it.

The alternative for Katie, as it was for Rosa, is to let her family go hungry.

And sometimes, obviously, addiction is involved, and then that imposes another imperative on someone's life.

As is the case with Sabine in My Name Is Joe.

Yeah. But who am I to talk or pontificate about this?

The broad context of Bread and Roses *is corporate America's exploitation of, and dependence on, minimum-wage workers, illegal immigrants usually. In the janitors' group in the film, there's a Russian woman, Maria. Was there any significance in making her one of the workers who resists joining the union?*

No, we weren't making a point about her. We just picked the people whom we thought would play the individual roles the best.

How did you go about staging the Hollywood legal firm's party, in which Tim Roth, Benicio del Toro and other well-known actors appear – and look totally bemused when the union organizer Sam and the janitors disrupt it?

Nobody knew what was going to happen. I didn't get the right location for the scene. It should have been much bigger, but we hadn't got the finances to get somewhere that would have been right and fill it. So I ended up in too small a place. Some good friends, and friends of friends of people I know, or was able to make contact with, were prevailed upon to come along and were very generous with their time. Then we just staged the demo in the office. I should have done it better. It's one of the scenes I kicked myself about. We didn't get the scale right, and that was a pity. We shot the film in six five-day weeks, and it needed a bit more time and money than we had.

The film's environment embodies the class war. The offices the janitors have to clean are contained in a cold, forbidding tower of glass and gleaming metal. Their overalls are contrasted with the smart business clothes of the few office workers we see. But when the janitors hold a demonstration in the street, there's an explosion of colour and vitality. Is it true the scene was inspired by similar scenes in Soviet films? Eisenstein's Strike *and Dovzhenko's* Earth *(1930) come to mind.*

No. Obviously, I saw those films years ago – and they're stunning. But we just did what was right for the story. Again, it's about scale. It's difficult, on our budgets, when you need a lot of people, so you do the best you can by indicating it. In a way, I don't mind the limits. I'd sooner have that discipline than spend a lot of money and then have that affect the casting. Casting is more important than the mass crowds. If we are economical, then we have freedom in

Bread and Roses: Maya (Pilar Padilla) and Sam (Adrien Brody) on a Justice for Janitors protest.

casting, but the cost is that sometimes you need a bigger scene than you're able to put on film.

When Sam visits the union's office, his boss complains about the injunctions and legal costs accruing from the protests Sam has organized with Maya and the other janitors. It's not the first time you've shown a union officer who's reluctant to rock the boat or whose motives are suspect. I know we discussed this in the last series of interviews, but is it inevitable that unions and labour movements harbour individuals driven by self-interest?

It's a familiar tendency, and it's been a pattern in British trade unions. The unions start as rank-and-file organizations, and as they get bigger they need bureaucrats to run them. The bureaucrats gain power and start to negotiate with the employers. They get to know the employers better than they know the workers they're representing. In the end, they tend to say to the members – when the members want a dispute – 'Very good. You demonstrated your strength. Now go back to work and leave it to us.' Then they'll do a deal, and often the members are not satisfied with it, but the union leaders have sold them out, to use a traditional term. They maybe negotiated compensation for a factory closure and people losing their jobs, but they won't have kept the factory open, which was the demand that drove the members to strike or occupy the factory, or whatever action they took. Of course, there are union leaders who don't do this. Arthur Scargill* is a case in point.

Union leaders often adopt a lifestyle that is closer to the employers' negotiators than to their own members. As you know, we did a series of films, *Questions of Leadership* [1983], which never saw the light of day, about this very subject. And we showed union leaders who became lords of the realm. We had shots of them looking militant, and then showed them in their robes. They were meant to be working-class representatives but had become members of the aristocracy in the House of Lords. Right-wing union leaders, by and large, have kept the Labour Party on the right. It used to be that the NEC [National Executive Committee of the Labour Party] was dominated by the right-wing unions. And the right-wing unions kept Tony Blair and Gordon Brown [Blair's successor as Labour prime minister] in power.

Because you're identified with Marxist values, sometimes even critics who admire your films conclude that your characters aren't rounded people but mouthpieces for militant positions, as one review of Bread and Roses *argued. What are your thoughts on this?*

You wonder if the people who have said those things have ever met people who have been in a union or political meeting and heard how people speak and talked to them afterwards and have them as friends. Because people who argue for positions will have read the books of socialist history. They'll know the analysis, they'll speak the language of that position and they'll use the terms of

---

* Scargill (born in 1938 in Worsbrough Dale, Yorkshire) worked as a coal miner from 1953 to 1973. He served as president of the Yorkshire area of the National Union of Mineworkers from 1974 to 1981 and president of the NUM from 1982 to 2002. A key organizer of the miners' strike in 1974 that precipitated the February general election and defeat of Conservative prime minister Edward Heath, Scargill subsequently led the 1984–5 strike.

the political left and Marx in their speech. They're far more dogmatic than, I think, our characters are. People on the left do have strong positions. They articulate them and they're often brilliant. Sometimes they're tedious, sometimes they're boring, sometimes they're speaking clichés, but, far more often than people think, you'll get people with a working-class background who haven't been formally educated but have read more books than probably half a dozen critics put together. And they speak with plain eloquence based on a theory of class struggle that's absolutely defensible. It makes complete sense.

There's a guy I know – I haven't seen him for a bit because he's getting on, like me – called Alan Thornett. He was a shop steward at the Cowley car works in Oxford. Brilliant speaker, self-taught, been through the Trotskyist movement. He's written books on the struggles of the left, new trade union history and how ecosocialism can help save the planet.* There are many, many workers like that. Ricky Tomlinson got into politics through reading Robert Tressell's *The Ragged Trousered Philanthropists*;† Jim Allen read it, too. For many, their political education came from the Communist Party and the Trotskyist groups, not the Labour Party. When I was involved in some of them in the 1960s, we would have a book set each week, read it and discuss it at the end of the week. It was much better than anything I got at Oxford University because people were passionate about it and fought over the ideas. The people who write, 'Oh, these are stereotypes,' should get out in the world, you know? If you're involved in radical politics, you'll know these characters in the films are genuine people. And if the story is about the working-class struggle to fight the interests of big business, why wouldn't you have characters who know what they're talking about, who have read the books?

---

* Thornett's books include *From Militancy to Marxism: A Personal and Political Account of Organising Car Workers* (1987), *Militant Years: Car Workers' Struggles in Britain in the 60s and 70s* (2010) and *Facing the Apocalypse: Arguments for Ecosocialism* (2019).
† Robert Tressell was the pseudonym of Dublin-born painter–decorator and labour activist Robert Noonan (1870–1911). His semi-autobiographical novel was first published in an abridged version in 1914; the unabridged version was published in 1955. See also reference to Sam Watts on p. 299.

Critics like working-class people who are victims: 'Oh, I feel sorry for them. They're put upon.' But you hardly ever see them with power in films. That is one thing we've tried to show – that the working class do have power and ideas, and that there's a whole way of understanding how society works that shows our collective strength. It goes back to the Middle Ages, when John Ball said during the Peasants' Revolt, 'Good people, things cannot go right in England and never will, until goods are held in common.'* You heard the same during the English Civil War, in the 1960s and in recent politics. That tradition obviously carried on into the nineteenth century with Marx and the people who followed him, and with Chartism, which was a coherent intellectual movement that hasn't been given any credence at all.

British pop culture has often patronized or made fun of ordinary people with socialist or radical leanings – the shop steward Fred Kite (Peter Sellers) in I'm All Right Jack *(1959),* Wolfie (Robert Lindsay) in Citizen Smith *(BBC, 1977–80) . . .*

And if they are presented, they're presented as caricatures. The communist is always the scruffy guy looking sinister on a railway platform, like in that dreadful Richard Attenborough film *The Angry Silence* [1960]. These types are always plotting against good people who just want to go to work – strike-breakers, in other words. The people who make or praise these things like to see workers downtrodden. They choose not to understand the workers' strength, the substance of the intellectual basis for what they're doing, their understanding of the society that produces the conflict, the demand for common ownership, democratic control, workers' control, and so on. They choose not to understand it because it doesn't fit their interests.

Watching Bread and Roses, *one knows that the union organizer Sam, who is an educated white man, will have a much easier path*

---

* The sermon reportedly addressed to the rebels by the itinerant radical priest Ball (born *c.*1338) at Blackheath, London, on 12 June 1381 is recorded in the section on the Peasants' Revolt in Book II of Jean Froissart's fourteenth-century *Chroniques* (*Chronicles*, translation by Geoffrey Brereton, Penguin Books, 1968). Following the collapse of the Revolt, Ball was executed before King Richard II in St Albans.

than the janitors. Adrien Brody is good in the role – earnest but with something of a clown about him.

Yes, he was fine. George Lopez was, too [as the tyrannical agency boss, Perez]. We cast him because he was really good when he came in. I hadn't realized he had a whole history before that and was well known [as a stand-up comic, actor and pro-Democrat champion of Los Angeles's Hispanic community]. We were very happy with the cast. The actors were terrific.

Did you feel you accomplished what you set out to do in the film?

Oh, well, you never feel that, really. There are things I kick myself about on every film, and I got some things wrong on that one. Barry [Ackroyd] did a brilliant job, and so did all the team. Filming is always the art of the possible, isn't it? On our schedule, we didn't have an hour to spare. Every day you've got to get the scene done, and sometimes you miss things that would have made it a bit better here, a bit better there. But always you've got to get the guts of it right, and get it in a way that you can cut a sequence out of it so that you get the essence of it and you've respected what's written. Kicking off at eight o'clock in the morning and finishing by six o'clock at night, you've got to get all that on that day, in that weather, in that place, with this group of people, with this gear. Obviously, things go wrong sometimes, so what you film is always an approximation.

In 2002, you and Paul contributed to the anthology film 11'09"01 – September 11. In effect, were you saying with your piece that, no matter how horrific the terrorist attacks on America on 11 September 2001, the United States must be held accountable for the Pentagon's covert support of Augusto Pinochet?

Put boldly, yes. I think it's the case that the United States doesn't acknowledge its role in Latin America. There's a famous little piece written by [Major General] Smedley Butler [of the US Marine Corps].* He talks about his role as an agent for American capi-

---

* In 'America's Armed Forces: 2. "In Time of Peace": The Army', published in *Common Sense*, vol. 4, no. 11, November 1935, Butler

talism throughout all the countries where he served and the violent suppression of any movement that threatened the dominance of the United States in the economies of South America, where the big American corporations extracted vast amounts of profits from unregulated 'factories over the border'. That was the case in Chile, Cuba, Nicaragua, obviously, and other countries in Central America. The United States is hypocritical to claim to defend peace and democracy when it's the epitome of oppression across the world.

How did you first meet Vladimir Vega?

I auditioned a lot of people, everyone we could find, for *Ladybird, Ladybird*. We met some lovely people, musicians mainly, and Vlad was the one we chose. He was a kind, generous man. I didn't know all his history when we were doing *Ladybird, Ladybird*, but we stayed in touch, obviously, and saw each other from time to time. After 9/11, I was speaking to him on the phone, and he mentioned that it was the same day – 11 September – that the attack on Allende happened. Paul was also aware of this. So the information came from these circumstances, and it coincided with being asked to do this short piece in the 9/11 film.

Each segment was eleven minutes, nine seconds and one frame. It's like chamber music, with very precise limits. Paul and I thought we would tell Vlad's story – and use his beautiful songs – in the form of a letter to the American people, saying, 'Look, this is what

---

wrote: 'I spent 33 years and 4 months in active service as a member of our country's most agile military force – the Marine Corps. I served in all commissioned ranks from a second lieutenant to Major General. And during that period I spent most of my time being a high-class muscle man for Big Business, for Wall Street and for the bankers. In short, I was a racketeer for capitalism. Thus I helped make Mexico and especially Tampico safe for American oil interests in 1914. I helped make Haiti and Cuba a decent place for the National City Bank boys to collect revenues in. I helped in the raping of half a dozen Central American republics for the benefit of Wall Street . . . I helped purify Nicaragua for the international banking house of Brown Brothers 1909–12. I brought light to the Dominican Republic for American sugar interests in 1916. I helped make Honduras "right" for American fruit companies in 1903. In China in 1927 I helped see to it that Standard Oil went its way unmolested.'

you did. Please remember this. As we mourn for your dead' – and there's no question that it was an atrocity, those planes being made to fly into those buildings and all those innocent people dying – 'please remember that thousands died from what you did.' Alexander Walker in the *Evening Standard* said we were a disgrace to our country for pointing this out. It's interesting that the sharpest political pieces we've done have got real abuse, as was the case with both *Hidden Agenda* and *The Wind That Shakes the Barley*.

Did Paul and Vladimir Vega develop the letter for the script together?

Paul talked to Vlad extensively, and then Paul wrote it. They're basically Paul's words as written, but they became Vlad's words, and he embodied them. I don't know if he changed anything, but Paul used words Vlad would have used. Paul's experience in Nicaragua, of course, was central to this. The atrocities of the American-backed Contras he'd recorded as a human rights lawyer [mirrored] exactly the attacks in Chile and Henry Kissinger's support for the murders and tortures by Pinochet, whom Thatcher later supported. She called him a friend. Disgusting – really disgusting.

Vlad became very sad. The story in the little film is about how he desperately wanted to return to his own country, but his wife and their children were at home here. He felt increasingly alienated. He worked in the health services towards the end. He took his own life by jumping off a tall building in a hospital.

Pinochet was responsible for his death, forty years after the coup.

Absolutely. He'd been horrendously tortured. He didn't tell me much about it when we were doing *Ladybird, Ladybird*. But as the years went by, he must have become haunted by that. It was desperately sad. He was a lovely man.

CHAPTER 10

Ireland's Manacles

The Wind That Shakes the Barley, Jimmy's Hall

Having addressed British imperialism in Ireland in the first episode of *Days of Hope* (1975) and *Hidden Agenda* (1990), both written by Jim Allen, Loach returned to the subject in *The Wind That Shakes the Barley* (2006). Written by Paul Laverty, the film dramatizes from a Republican perspective the Irish War of Independence (1919–21) and the start of the Irish Civil War (1921–3), showing how Crown forces prevailed, despite the democratic vote in the 1918 general election that established the Sinn Féin-led Irish Republic proclaimed during the 1916 Easter Rising. The Free State Army's eventual defeat of the anti-Treaty IRA in the Civil War enforced the terms of the Treaty, confirming Ireland's status as a dominion of the British Empire and enabling the six counties of Northern Ireland to maintain their union with the United Kingdom.

Filmed mostly in and around Bandon, Timoleague and Coolea, and among the verdant mountainlands near Ballyvourney, in County Cork, *The Wind That Shakes the Barley* is a grimly realistic war film that depicts lightning guerrilla strikes by an IRA flying column and reprisals by Crown forces, as well as a lament for the opportunity the Irish people had to resist economic exploitation by political means. In two heated Republican discussions that recall the collectivization debate in *Land and Freedom*, the IRA volunteer Damien O'Donovan (Cillian Murphy) and his friend Dan (Liam Cunningham) stress the need to respect the authority and democratic programme of the revolutionary Dáil parliament and protect the workers and the poor through public welfare and common ownership, in an Ireland that has been dominated by landlords.

At the outset, County Cork villager Damien plans to complete his medical studies in London, despite the terrorizing of the old farm woman Peggy (Mary O'Riordan), her daughter Bernadette (Mary Murphy) and her granddaughter Sinéad (Orla Fitzgerald), and the beating to death of his friend, Sinéad's brother Micheál (Laurence Barry), during an unprovoked raid by the Black and Tans, the brutal paramilitary force raised to augment the Royal Irish Constabulary in suppressing the rebels. But after seeing British troops assault railwaymen for refusing to transport them, Damien joins the non-uniformed IRA flying column led by his brother, Teddy (Pádraic Delaney). The brigade executes four officers of the Auxiliaries, the RIC's elite counter-insurgency division, but all its members are captured after the Anglo-Irish landowner Sir John Hamilton (Roger Allam) forces Chris Reilly (John Crean), an IRA volunteer employed on his estate, to betray them to British intelligence. Behind bars, Damien befriends the beaten train driver Dan, a union organizer who stood with the Marxist revolutionary leader James Connolly during the 1913 Dublin lock-out. Together, Damien and Dan admiringly quote from Connolly's essay 'Socialism and Nationalism' (1897): 'If you remove the English Army tomorrow

The Wind That Shakes the Barley: Cillian Murphy and Pádraic Delaney as Damien and Teddy – brothers in arms.

and hoist the green flag over Dublin Castle, unless you set about the organization of the Socialist Republic your efforts will be in vain. England will still rule you. She would rule you through her capitalists, through her landlords, through her financiers, through the whole array of commercial and individualist institutions she has planted in this country and watered with the tears of our mothers and the blood of our martyrs.' Teddy's screams can be heard from an adjacent cell, as his fingernails are torn off by an interrogator. Helped to escape by an Anglo-Irish guard (William Ruane), Damien leads the brigade in seizing Hamilton and Chris as hostages, while Teddy recuperates. When news comes that the three remaining IRA prisoners have been tortured and shot, Damien has no alternative but to execute Hamilton and Chris, whom he has known since the boy's birth.

At a Republican court hearing held under the judiciary of the Dáil, the judge, Lily (Fiona Lawton), rules in favour of a penniless woman (Clare Dineen) who is being sued by a merchant (Kieran Aherne) for the non-payment of extortionate interest on a loan. Teddy sympathizes with the widow but protests the court's decision in case it deters the merchant from donating to the IRA's fund for the purchase of arms. Approving of the court's decision, Damien and Dan oppose Teddy and the IRA stalwart Finbar (Damien Kearney) for favouring financiers over the poor. The clash of political principles opens a split in the Republicans' unity, echoing the rift in POUM in *Land and Freedom*.

As the war escalates, the flying squad massacres Auxiliaries on a hilltop (in a version of the Kilmichael ambush of 28 November 1920). In revenge, the Auxiliaries burn Peggy's farmhouse. Sinéad, who's a member of the women's paramilitary group Cumann na mBan and Damien's girlfriend, has her hair hacked off by three of the attackers, one of whom labels her a 'Fenian whore' as he departs.

After the ceasefire, a cinema newsreel proclaims the partition of Ireland and the creation of the Irish Free State, as ratified by the signing of the Anglo-Irish Treaty (6 December 1921). The Republicans' debate where their loyalties lie. Remembering their martyred comrades, Finbar refuses allegiance to the Crown. Sinéad fears Loyalists will terrorise Republicans in Belfast. Teddy and others support the Treaty. Damien argues that fealty to Britain will sustain the class war, enslave factory workers and accelerate unemployment. Dan champions the people's ownership of Ireland's industries and land and says the Treaty will deny that. Soon afterwards, Teddy is seen marching with other Treatyites who have joined the Free State Army.

With seven in ten Republican volunteers opposing the Treaty, Damien trains recruits for the anti-Treaty IRA and tends the sick and starving. The Irish Civil War begins (28 June 1922). Sinéad reports that the Four Courts in Dublin, occupied by the anti-Treaty IRA leaders and their men, including Finbar, are being shelled by the Free State Army using 'borrowed' British eighteen-pounders. Damien's comrade Rory (Myles Horgan) and his men ambush a Free State Army truck and shoot former colleagues. In church, where Damien and Teddy sit on different sides of the aisle, a pro-Treaty priest decries Republican socialism and cites Cardinal Logue's pastoral letter accusing the anti-Treatyite 'Irregulars' of wrecking Ireland and excommunicating them, claiming the recent general election (18 June 1922) had endorsed the Treaty. Damien declares that the election was unfair because the voters feared a war with 'the most powerful country in the world'.

Free State troopers menace Bernadette on the farm while searching for the rebels' hidden weapons. Dan is shot dead and Damien seized when they try to burgle guns from an army barracks at night. In the cell where Damien was previously held, Teddy begs him to reveal where the arms are and offers him an amnesty if he'll disclose Rory's whereabouts. Ruefully recalling that he executed Chris for the Republican cause, Damien refuses to sell out. The following morning, Teddy orders Damien's execution by firing squad, in a scene filmed in Kilmainham Gaol, Dublin (where the leaders of the Easter Rising and other rebels were executed). Teddy brings Damien's last letter to Sinéad. She hits him and tells him she never wants to see him again, echoing what Chris's mother told Damien when he showed her Chris's grave.

The Wind That Shakes the Barley hews closer to the facts than Neil Jordan's romanticized biopic *Michael Collins* (1996), which was shot by Loach's frequent collaborator Chris Menges. The historical record was not, however, germane to the reporting of the right-wing British press, which reacted hysterically to *The Wind That Shakes the Barley*'s depictions of the violence and aural evidence of torture meted out to Irish civilians and IRA prisoners by the Black and Tans, the Auxiliaries and the Free State Army. Tim Luckhurst, a columnist for *The Times*, compared Loach to Leni Riefenstahl, the Nazi propagandist film-maker.* Chris Tookey, the *Daily Mail*'s film reviewer, quipped that Luckhurst's judgement was harsh because 'Riefenstahl was far more visually talented'.†

Documented murders, house burnings, gang rapes and instances of 'bobbing' (the agonizing and permanently traumatizing removal of women's hair as a form of sexual policing), often with the use of toxic substances that caused sickness, were perpetrated by both sides in the War of Independence and the Civil War.‡ Though the film does not minimize or whitewash lethal Republican violence in the film, Loach felt justified in emphasizing – whether through showing or indicating through sound – the sadistic actions of the Crown forces over those perpetrated by the IRA. As he told David Archibald, 'The idea of "balance" is wholly skewed because the British stood for opposition to democracy, for oppression of the people, for the brutal destruction of their homes in many cases and their lives.'§ Loach and Laverty chose not to replicate on screen the bloodiest non-lethal atrocities (including teeth-pulling) committed by the Tans, Auxiliaries and Free State troops, but the film-makers' restraint was lost on conservative British journalists and film critics unable to look past the bombings and killings carried out by the IRA during the 1968–98 war in Northern Ireland, which was still fresh in the memory.

Also contentious was Loach and Laverty's focusing of *The Wind That Shakes the Barley* through a socialist prism. The film shows

---

* *The Times*, 31 May 2006. Luckhurst wrote: 'During the de-Nazification of postwar Germany Leni Riefenstahl, Hitler's favourite film director, was classified guilty of the lowest degree of complicity with the regime. Riefenstahl did not fully understand the evil cause to which her work contributed. Ken Loach does not deserve such indulgence. He knows precisely what he is doing.'
† *Daily Mail*, 23 June 2006.
‡ See Linda Connolly, 'Sexual Violence and the Irish Revolution: An Inconvenient Truth?' *Women's History Review*, vol. 30, pp. 126–43, 2021. https://www.tandfonline.com/doi/full/10.1080/09612025.2020.1735613.
§ David Archibald, 'Correcting Historical Lies: An Interview with Ken Loach and Paul Laverty', *Cineaste*, vol. 32, no. 2, spring 2007, p. 30.

Damien's growing sense that his socialist views must be adopted by the Republicans and translated into action – as *Days of Hope* shows Ben's evolution from a passive army volunteer to a communist who protests against the Labour Party and trade unions for betraying the workers during the General Strike; as *Land and Freedom* shows David's transition from card-carrying communist to member of the Marxist militia POUM; and as *Bread and Roses* shows Maya's emergence as an active janitors' union member. In contrast to Damien, David, Ben and Maya, neither the casual building worker Stevie, who is exposed to labour exploitation in *Riff-Raff*, nor George, who is awakened to the CIA-backed Contras' tortures and killings in Nicaragua in *Carla's Song*, fully articulate their changed consciousnesses.

At the time of *The Wind That Shakes the Barley*'s US release, Laverty said in an interview with the *New York Times** that it was the cogency of the Republicans' arguments in the film that irked the right-wing press. 'They were furious that ordinary people could be so articulate about what they were fighting for,' he said. 'To be truthful to the times during those debates, we researched all the arguments that were made and tried to imagine what they would have actually felt, not what they should have felt or debated.' Loach has said that the film tells one story from those turbulent times, which explains why he and Laverty were careful not to depict real-life participants or name events like the hilltop ambush.

Influenced by Dan, a trade unionist and veteran of the Irish Citizen Army who represents its founder James Connolly's Marxist position, Damien adopts a sympathetic, proto-Marxist, humanist stance that prioritizes ending the people's suffering; he backs up his words by tending the half-starved child of a woman who has summoned him in his capacity as a student doctor. Damien's brief speeches, devoid of ideological rhetoric, contrast with the militarist statements of Finbar and Teddy, who seek to oust the British from Ireland at all costs. Until, that is, Teddy changes his allegiance. Believing that opposing the Treaty will cause greater bloodshed, as he argues during the second debate, he joins the Free State Army (a political surrender that echoes the socialist Philip Hargreaves's

---

* Graham Fuller, 'In This Corner, a Leftist, Riling the Right Again', *New York Times*, 4 March 2007.

switch to the Labour right in *Days of Hope*). Dan points out that all the Treaty will change 'is the accents of the powerful and the colour of the flag' – a prediction that is seen to have come to pass in *Jimmy's Hall* (2014).

In an article published in the *Dublin Review*,* the Irish historian Roy Foster wrote: 'The idea that [anti-Treaty leaders] de Valera, [Erskine] Childers, Cathal Brugha et al. were motivated by socialism is baroquely wishful thinking. The film's historical advisor, Donal Ó Drisceoil, gives a more accurate and judicious version in [the published screenplay of *The Wind That Shakes the Barley*†], referring to revolutionary socialism as "a tendency within the national movement".' In the *New York Times* article, Foster added that the film's 'history was badly skewed – particularly the idea that opposition to the Treaty was based on the wish to complete a socialist revolution, a feeling shared by very few of the revolutionaries'. Interviewed for the same piece, Loach said he and Laverty had seen papers in the course of their research that countered this view and cited the socialist leaders Connolly, Liam Mellows, Peadar O'Donnell and their followers, who carried 'their experiences in the labour movement into the struggle'.

In any case, Loach added, socialism was not the dominant idea in the Republican movement 'and it isn't in the film, I would argue. The slogan of the time was "Labour Must Wait", and the Labour leaders consciously decided to put their demands on the back burner. But there were people who objected to that. We wanted to make certain that that point, which was largely ignored by the establishment historians, had an outlet through characters like Dan and Damien.'

In *Ken Loach: The Politics of Film and Television*, John Hill meticulously analyses the socio-political values for which the pro-Treaty and anti-Treaty forces fought and how Loach and Laverty relay that information.‡ Hill sees a correlation between Fergus Campbell's suggestion that the 'Irish revolution' may properly be regarded as 'a period of flux, during which a number of different

---

* Roy Foster, 'The Red and the Green', *Dublin Review*, autumn 2006.
† Paul Laverty, *The Wind That Shakes the Barley: A Screenplay* (Galley Head Press, 2006).
‡ John Hill, *Ken Loach: The Politics of Film and Television*, pp. 216–21.

outcomes were possible', thus 'Loach's polemic . . . is not as far-fetched as some historians have suggested',* and Ó Drisceoil's contention that it presents 'the "what-might-have-beens" of the Irish revolution, not in a romantic, counterfactual manner, but by highlighting or foregrounding spurned radical political and historical possibilities'.†

'What kind of Ireland are we fighting for?' Damien says, distraught after shooting Chris. How the Irish are governed and whether their rights are protected, particularly in relation to land, are central issues in *Jimmy's Hall*, which depicts a moral and political struggle in 1932–3 between the real-life communist organizer, IRA recruiter and community-hall owner Jimmy Gralton‡ (Barry

---

* Fergus Campbell, 'Reviews in History', March 2009, https://reviews.history.ac.uk/author-response/response-to-review-no-734. Commenting on Patrick Cosgrove's review of his book *Land and Revolution: Nationalist Politics in the West of Ireland 1891–1921* (2005), Campbell prefaced his comment on *The Wind That Shakes the Barley* as follows: 'I argue that the land agitation of 1920 – which was carried out in a collective fashion and which benefitted whole communities – aimed to create a new kind of society that was fairer and more equitable for the poor tenant farmers, labourers and their families in the west of Ireland. I further argue . . . that some sections of the leadership and the rank and file of the republican movement (Sinn Féin and the IRA) supported the popular agitation to seize and redistribute land that swept across the west of the island during the heady months of early 1920. I also propose that the outcome of the Irish revolution might have been different if the radical sections of the republican movement had been able to influence the policies eventually adopted by the republican leadership. If the anti-Treaty IRA had supported a popular campaign for land redistribution in 1922 then we do not know which side would have won the Irish Civil War (1922–3) . . .'
† Donal Ó Drisceoil, 'Framing the Irish Revolution: Ken Loach's *The Wind That Shakes the Barley*', *Radical History Review*, no. 104, 2009, p. 10.
‡ James Gralton, born in Effrinagh, County Leitrim, on 17 April 1886, was one of seven children of Micheál Gralton, an old Fenian who farmed twenty-five acres, and his wife Alice (née Campbell), an agent for a small circulating library. Gralton enlisted as a teenager with the British Army but deserted after being disciplined for refusing to serve in India. He worked as a docker, miner and stoker in the British Merchant Navy. Emigrating to America in 1907, he acquired American citizenship through serving in the US Navy. Back in Ireland in 1921, he trained volunteers for the IRA during the War of Independence and

Ward) and a fictitious priest, Father Sheridan (Jim Norton), who represents the state power invested in the Catholic Church and the Church's opposition to communism. Jimmy's continued efforts to restore smallholdings to poor tenants who have been evicted by wealthy landowners assume much greater significance in the film than the danger he poses to the youth of his County Leitrim village by corrupting them with the jazz records he's brought back from New York City and plays at dances in his revived Pearse–Connolly memorial hall.

After a ten-year exile in America, Jimmy has returned to Effrinagh to support his mother (Aileen Henry) and farm her land. The fame and popularity of his hall goes before him. When he encounters local teenagers dancing on a road, he's approached by one of them, Marie O'Keefe (Aisling Franciosi), the daughter of Dennis O'Keefe (Brian F. O'Byrne), a Free State Army veteran and adversary of Jimmy who 'married into land' and now commands the local branch of the fascist Army Comrades Association.*

---

opened the Pearse–Connolly Hall on his parents' land as a social club, education centre and Dáil court for settling land disputes. His Direct Action Committee having supervised seizures of land from large owners to restore it to evicted tenants, Gralton was sought by the Free State Army and, in 1922, left for America again. Following the death of his brother Charles, Gralton returned to Ireland in 1932 to run the family farm, reopened the hall and ran Leitrim's Revolutionary Workers' group. Gralton was denounced by priests for his communist activism, amid allegations that the hall was a den of vice. After it was destroyed by arson on 24 December 1932, he went into hiding, but was arrested and deported 'as an undesirable alien' to America on 13 August 1933. In New York City, Gralton raised money for the international brigades in Spain, stood unsuccessfully as a Communist Party electoral candidate and lectured on James Connolly's teachings at the Irish Workers' Club. Late in life, Gralton married Bridget 'Bessie' Cronogue (1890–1975), from Drumsna, County Leitrim, four miles south of Effrinagh; it is unknown if they knew each other in Ireland. Gralton died of stomach cancer in Bellevue Hospital, Manhattan, on 29 December 1945. The Irish president Michael D. Higgins pardoned Gralton in 2016.

* O'Keefe is *Jimmy's Hall*'s equivalent of Eoin O'Duffy (1890–1944). After leading the Monaghan Brigade of the IRA during the War of Independence, the pro-Treatyite O'Duffy served as chief of staff of the Free State Army during the Civil War. He became leader of the fascist

Marie urges Jimmy to reopen the hall because she and her friends have got nowhere to dance or enjoy any other social activities. Despite Jimmy's reluctance to revive the now dilapidated hall, he is prompted to change his mind when he visits it alone and finds there his dusty copy of *Labour in Ireland*, James Connolly's posthumously published explication of the Irish class war as a battle for land rights.* He glimpses another opportunity to revive the spirit of working-class solidarity by giving the people a place to meet, talk, learn and enjoy themselves. In a flashback to spring 1922, Jimmy tells a reporter that he and a few volunteers have built the community-run hall on his land, the Black and Tans having burned down the church hall in nearby Gowel (a reprisal for the Sheemore ambush of 4 March 1921, during the War of Independence).

Back in the present, villagers of all ages – including Jimmy's old flame Oonagh Dempsey (Simone Kirby in a fictional role) – help him refurbish the hall. Soon it is hosting not only dances, but art and literature classes (Yeats's poetry is taught) and boxing lessons. Jimmy and Oonagh, who married another man during Jimmy's absence, are still drawn to each other romantically, but they rekindle their relationship chastely.

Sheridan, O'Keefe and the Gardai fear that Jimmy will again use the hall as a pulpit for disseminating his communist beliefs and for

---

Blueshirts of the Army Comrades Association in July 1933 and renamed it the National Guard. He headed the new conservative political party Fine Gael in 1933–4, after it absorbed the National Guard. During the Spanish Civil War, he raised an Irish brigade to fight for Franco.

* Connolly wrote: 'As we have again and again pointed out, the Irish question is a social question, the whole age-long fight of the Irish people against their oppressors resolves itself in the last analysis into a fight for the mastery of the means of life, the sources of production, in Ireland. Who would own and control the land? The people or the invaders; and if the invaders, which set of them – the most recent swarm of land-thieves, or the sons of the thieves of a former generation? These were the bottom questions of Irish politics, and all other questions were valued or deprecated in the proportion to which they contributed to serve the interests of some of the factions who had already taken their stand in this fight around property interests.' Originally published in Chapter 16 of *Labour in Irish History* (1914), which was combined with Connolly's *The Reconquest of Ireland* (1915) and republished in the single-volume *Labour in Ireland* (Maunsel and Roberts, 1922).

fomenting agitation to fight landlordism. They are proved right. In a recreation of an incident involving Gralton at Drumsna in 1922, Jimmy and his supporters, including the old rebels Mossie (Francis Magee) and Tommy (Mikel Murfi), reverse a land grab that is judged illegal by a Republican court. By the closed gates of the disputed farm, they face down Sheridan and O'Keefe, with guns drawn on both sides. After Sheridan tells O'Keefe's men to hold fire, Jimmy's people drive the tenant's cattle back to his plot to reclaim it for him.

Loach and Laverty opted not to portray Gralton as the bluntly spoken ideologue he was said to be. Barry Ward plays him as a common-sense-talking socialist, akin to Damien in *The Wind That Shakes the Barley*, and a genial man of the people – worldly but clean-living – whose wish to nourish an inward-looking community starved of culture threatens Sheridan's iron control of it. Sheridan's curate, Father Seamus (Andrew Scott), offers him liberal counsel: 'Repression breeds belligerence . . . Jimmy Gralton's not Karl Marx. He's just a worker now.' Though Sheridan allows that Jimmy isn't greedy or selfish, he sermonises against the hall as a dangerous bastion of pleasure, materialism and paganism that conflicts 'with our own true Irish values', exaggeratedly invoking Oliver Cromwell's attempt 'to burn all the harps in the land' and 'murder our priests'. In his authoritarian puritanism, the guileful Sheridan is the Cromwell of *Jimmy's Hall*.

After Sheridan names those who have attended the dances, O'Keefe takes Marie home and thrashes her, drawing blood. Though Sheridan and Jimmy are well matched as opponents, their conversations, which reveal each man's intellect and keen grasp of their differences, comprise one of the strongest political dialectics in Loach and Laverty's films. When Jimmy visits Sheridan's home to try to work out a compromise, he sees that the priest owns a copy of John Lavery's 1922 propaganda painting *The Blessing of the Colours*, which shows a Free State Army soldier genuflecting before an archbishop beside the furled tricolour. It emphasizes Sheridan's attitude to the Church's dominance of the then newly formed state and his role within it.

The forcible eviction of a tenant couple and their five children by an aristocratic landowner who has the protection of the army, Gardai and politicians brings a deputation from a sympathetic wing of the divided Roscommon IRA to seek help from Jimmy as a figurehead of solidarity and resistance. The ensuing debate among Jimmy and his supporters to decide a course of action typifies Loach and Laverty's commitment to the processes of democracy. Seán (Karl Geary), an educated man of Jimmy's age, advocates that they seize the opportunity to teach the establishment a lesson, and because its enforcers will 'be coming for us anyway'; Mossie, just out of prison, urges caution, fearing as he does for the hall's future; Molly (played by Leitrim poet Sorcha Fox) worries that an action will incur the wrath of the bishops, flush with power following the Eucharistic Congress (22–26 June 1932), which brought over a third of Ireland's three million Catholics to Dublin. Oonagh remains silent, fearing Jimmy's endangerment. A march goes ahead, resulting in the tenant family's reinstatement after the IRA men and some of the marchers drive off the landowner's thuggish agent and his men. Asked to say a few words, Jimmy, not the greatest orator, decries how American capitalist greed has spread around the world. 'We need to take control of our lives again. Work for need, not for greed.'

In one of Laverty's subtlest scenes, Sheridan, in his dressing gown, listens admiringly to one of the records – Bessie Smith's 'Weeping Willow Blues' – that Jimmy has strategically left on the priest's porch, and invites Father Seamus, woken by the music, to take 'a wee drop' with him. He tells the curate that Jimmy entered the confession box that day and told him, 'You have more hate in your heart than love.'

'What do you think of that?' Sheridan adds, with the suspicion of someone who senses he might be in the wrong. Even as he says the words, Jimmy's hall is engulfed in flames, as a quick cut reveals. Though the arson was blamed at the time on the right wing of the IRA, the film implies the fascists were responsible, possibly with priestly connivance. When, the next day, Sheridan (tellingly silent), O'Keefe and the local Gardai chief hold a summit, the enraged Father Seamus, who is also present, condemns the hall's destruction as 'the tactics of the Ku Klux Klan' and refuses to drink in O'Keefe's company. Obsessed with the persistence of communists like Jimmy, O'Keefe, referring to a newspaper report from Belfast, rails against the uniting of the Catholics of the Falls and the Protestants of the Shankill, who have joined the 100,000 unemployed people on the city's streets to support the 20,000 pickets upholding the Outdoor Relief Strike.* O'Keefe sneers at 'the Reds' for stirring up attacks on the union leaders who have intervened to limit the workers' benefits demands, but Father Seamus retorts that poverty is the cause of the turmoil. Oonagh's fears for Jimmy are realized when he is arrested. As he is driven away for deportation, Sheridan commends his courage and decency.

When Damien storms out of the church service at the onset of the Civil War in *The Wind That Shakes the Barley*, he berates the Catholic Church for siding with Ireland's rich, their unholy alliance the fulcrum of Jimmy Gralton's expulsion from Ireland eleven years later. It is also the rudder that steers *Jimmy's Hall*, above and beyond the opening of a place where village folk could dance and learn. The two films fit together like a jigsaw, the smaller piece no less trenchant than the larger one.

GRAHAM FULLER: *Was* The Wind That Shakes the Barley *long in the planning?*

KEN LOACH: Since I've known Paul Laverty, we've talked about Ireland, Britain's first colony, and now – a remnant of the North still being separated from the South as part of Britain – its last. I'd been introduced to the story of Irish politics by Jim Allen, who, as you know, wrote *Days of Hope*. There's an episode in it where, during the First World War and after the Easter Rising, the British troops in Ireland are trying to keep their hold on the Irish. I knew about the War of Independence and the consequent Civil War and the role of James Connolly [1868–1916], the great Irish socialist, from that

---

* Leading to riots and the deaths of two men, the Belfast strike (3–14 October 1932), which was joined by the unemployed of the twenty-six southern counties, protested the draconian means test for the Labour Exchange's distribution of unemployment benefits under Stormont's continuation of the Poor Law, which was not repealed in Northern Ireland until 1948. According to *Workers Solidarity* (no. 21, October 1986), Gralton spoke on behalf of the Irish Unemployed Workers' Movement at a demonstration in Longford, County Longford. Though in the film Gralton's hall is destroyed a day or two after the start of the strike, in reality it survived for seventy-one days after the strike ended.

time onwards and read the relevant books. Paul's mother's family comes from Ireland, and his father's family came from there earlier, and he was also fascinated by the War of Independence and the Civil War. I think we always knew we would try to tell that story.

The simple essence of it is that, as I said, Ireland was a colony within the British Empire, which is an interpretation the British establishment doesn't like. It claims the British are there to stop the Irish fighting themselves. Our story, of course, is quite different. It shows the brutality of the British in oppressing the Irish, and how the Irish victory in the War of Independence was manipulated by the British, led by Winston Churchill, to divide Ireland. And that division has been maintained at the point of a gun ever since, at great cost to the Irish people and through the treachery of the British so-called security forces, whose interventions have always been malign. So *The Wind That Shakes the Barley* incurred great hostility from the right.

The film begins with the Black and Tans terrorizing women in a Cork farmhouse and their beating to death of a friend of Damien for refusing to say his name in English. In prison, Damien hears his brother, Teddy, screaming in an adjacent cell as his fingernails are torn off. Personally devastating killings follow. Damien executes Chris, a young lad who's known him all his life, for betraying the IRA to the British Intelligence Corps. At the end, Teddy – by then a Free State (or National) Army officer defending British and pro-Anglo-Irish Treaty interests in the Civil War – orders a firing squad to shoot Damien. Is the point that internecine and civil wars are especially brutalizing?

I think it's a generalization that wars brutalize people. Civil wars brutalize people in an extreme way because you are forced to ignore the ties you have with the people you have to fight. It's different to when you go to a foreign land and kill people, or when people you don't know invade your land and you kill them. In its cruelty, civil war is particularly vicious and horrendous. But I don't think we went beyond that generalization.

I know the fearless Republican flying-column leader Finbar, played by the actor Damien Kearney, was partially based on Tom

Barry (1897–1980), who commanded the IRA volunteers in the Kilmichael ambush and was responsible for the execution of sixteen civilian informers in 1921. Kearney looks a little like Ernie O'Malley (1897–1957), the assistant chief of staff of the anti-Treaty forces during the Civil War, but I wondered if O'Malley, who was a medical student at the time of the Easter Rising, was more an inspiration for Damien O'Dovovan.

Damien wasn't based on O'Malley, but his training as a doctor accounted for why he was leaving Ireland for London and then decided to stay and fight. That's the only connection between them, apart from the fact they're both Republicans who chose to fight against the Treaty. Other than that, Damien is a character in his own right.

He decides to stay after seeing British troops, who are trying to force their way onto a train because of the unions' boycott of military transport, intimidate its driver, Dan, and his stoker. Was Dan, who later reminisces to Daniel about the Dublin lockout,* inspired by Patrick Bradley,† a close friend of Connolly?

---

* The industrial dispute resulted from the capitalist William Martin Murphy's opposition to the Irish Transport and General Workers' Union (ITGWU), founded in 1909 by James Larkin and organized by James Connolly from 1911. Led by Murphy, a newspaper baron and owner of the Dublin United Tramway Company, 300 employers banded together in July 1913 to fight unionization in Dublin. After Murphy had dismissed 340 suspected ITGWU members, the employers barred 20,000 workers from entering their workplaces between 26 August 1913 and 18 January 1914. Two workers were killed and 300 injured during a police attack on a workers' rally on the first 'Bloody Sunday', 31 August 1913. The lockout ended when, desperate to feed their starving families, most workers pledged not to unionize and returned to work.
† Bradley (1893–1972) worked as a boilermaker at the Great Southern Railway depot in Inchicore, west Dublin. A member of the ITGWU and Irish Republican Brotherhood, Bradley participated in the general strike that precipitated the Dublin lockout. One of the first men recruited by Connolly for his Irish Citizen Army, Bradley was briefly imprisoned in England and Wales after the Easter Rising. He went on the run in 1918, after serving with the Irish Volunteers. He was subsequently an active member of Éamon de Valera's Fianna Fáil party.

Again, we weren't referring to Bradley specifically. Dan is just a follower of Connolly. The [IRA] flying columns [small military land units comprised of volunteers] were mostly in County Cork, which is rural, and we wanted to have someone from Dublin – from the cities – with an industrial background and a socialist perspective who supported Connolly. He's an individual who happens to have that background.

It's Dan, powerfully portrayed by Liam Cunningham, who puts forward Connolly's Marxist beliefs at the court hearing of the old woman. Would a socialist government have been feasible if a united Ireland had won full independence?

Who knows? After being wounded in the Easter Rising, Connolly was, of course, executed by the British, but the socialist tradition was very strong in Ireland. Whether the balance of forces would have allowed that element to dominate a settlement after the War of Independence, I don't know. The whole thing was distorted by the British politicians who bullied some members of the Irish delegation to London into accepting the Anglo-Irish Treaty,* which the British offered only because they knew they couldn't sustain a war. Churchill and [Lord] Birkenhead thought they could see a way in which the interest of the British Empire would be maintained, even if the Irish had a measure of independence. To cheat the Irish people of the united independent Ireland the Dáil had declared in 1919,† they threatened to use the full weight of the British state to

---

* The Anglo-Irish Treaty, signed on 6 December 1921, ended the Irish War of Independence and created the Irish Free State as a dominion of the British Empire. The following day, the Northern Ireland parliament approved an address to King George V to confirm the exclusion of its six north-eastern counties from the Irish Free State. Northern Ireland had been created by the Government of Ireland Act (23 December 1920), informally known as the Partition Act. The act was repealed by the UK's 1998 Northern Ireland Act and the Republic of Ireland's 2007 Statute Law Revision Act.
† Following Sinn Féin's landslide victory in the 1918 Irish general election, Éamon de Valera (1882–1975), who had been a commandant of the Irish Volunteers during the Easter Rising, became president of Dáil Eireann on 1 April 1919. He founded the Fianna Fáil party in 1926 and served as Taoiseach (prime minister) from 1932 to 1948, 1951 to 1954 and 1957 to 1959, and as president of Ireland from 1959 to 1973.

crush them yet again and convinced Michael Collins and others to support the Treaty.

It's remarked in the film that Collins's Republicanism softened after he was wined and dined by the British in London. Some Irish leaders were reportedly in an agony of indecision about whether to accept the Treaty. Given the British threats, could it be that Collins and other Irish co-signatories feared there'd be greater loss of life if they didn't agree to the terms?

I'm sure some of them did; it was an honest decision. The British saw the people they could do a deal with – that is, the pro-Treatyites who were on the right of the independence struggle and were not going to change the basic economic model. They were not a threat to British business interests in the way some of the anti-Treatyites were. The anti-Treatyites were nationalists, like Patrick Pearse* had been, and socialists in the Connolly tradition. They were uncompromising in wanting a united independent Ireland, which was the wish of the Irish people. The pro-Treatyites would have been more pragmatic. They would have opposed the anti-Treatyites because the [forming of] an anti-Treaty government with socialist policies and a radical new state might threaten their own status in society. There seemed to be a connection between the class interests of those who accepted the Treaty and the British, who wanted to do a deal with people they could trust to protect their own investments, so that comes into it. We didn't make a major issue of Collins being wined and dined at all, because that would have undervalued the interest shared by the pro-Treatyites and the British, socially and economically, and the principled opposition to the Treaty from people in the Connolly tradition and in the nationalist tradition.

---

* A barrister, writer and educational reformer, Pearse (1879–1916) was commandant-general of the Army of the Irish Republic, president of the provisional government and main author of the Proclamation of Independence, which he read in front of the General Post Office in Dublin, the Republican headquarters, at 12.45 p.m. on 24 April 1916, at the commencement of the Easter Rising. Following heavy British bombardment, the rebels surrendered on 29 April. Pearse was among the first of the fifteen leaders of the Rising, including his brother William and Connolly, executed by firing squad between 3 and 12 May.

Those who opposed the Treaty could see it was a sell-out to go against the democratic decision the Irish people had made [by electing Sinn Féin in 1918 and 1921] in favour of a united independent Ireland. And quite rightly. The map of Ireland clearly shows it's an island, and historically it was one country. Why would you want to divide it up? Many people said that partition wasn't acceptable or sustainable.

At the point in the film when the Civil War is imminent, it gives voice to both Damien, who joins the anti-Treaty IRA, and Teddy, who has become an officer in the Free State Army. The film's sympathies are with Damien.

I think Teddy is a very honest man and absolutely torn and destroyed by the ultimate choice he has to make, which is to supervise the execution of his own brother. But, yes, we are clearly with the anti-Treaty side because, I suppose, Paul and I could see that that was a more consistent argument. We've also got the benefit of hindsight following a hundred years of violence in the north, which was a direct consequence of partition. History has shown that it was a bad treaty to accept, and the killer fact was that the British acted out of self-interest in ignoring the democratic decision of the Irish people. Their response, as Damien says in the film, was to close down the parliament [the revolutionary Dáil Éireann, 1919–22], close down the newspapers and send in the troops. There were many cases of families splitting, and I think Paul found one instance, in particular, of two brothers who fought on opposite sides. But, again, that is the only connection between actual brothers and Damien and Teddy.

Were you drawing a parallel between the British forces in Ireland from 1920 to 1923 and the British Army and the security forces in Northern Ireland from 1969 to 2007?

Yes, of course. I'd done *Hidden Agenda*, about the British and the 'shoot to kill' policy in Northern Ireland. But what was there in our minds with *The Wind That Shakes the Barley* was the way that the British Army has been an instrument to enforce British rule in foreign lands, and an extraordinarily brutal one. We knew about the nineteenth-century horrors and the concentration camps in South

Africa during the Boer War, but it has come to light only in recent years what brutal, brutal stuff they did in Kenya* after the Second World War.

When Damien is in prison and demands to be treated as a political prisoner, were you reminding us that Thatcher had denied political status to the IRA prisoners in the Maze?

Yes. That was a more recent example of it. Political prisoners are regularly denied that status because the people who put them in prison don't want to recognize their politics. A similar case is Julian Assange. The Americans and the Brits didn't want their crimes in the Iraq War exposed, so their response is not to deny the message but to punish the messenger. It's a tactic used by people who, at that moment, are winning. But will they win in the long term? We'll see.

In the scene in the Republican court, which represents the authority of Dáil Éireann, a gombeen *man, or usurer, demands that a poor woman pay him extortionate interest on money she borrowed from him to buy groceries. Dan defends her right not to be exploited, and the judge agrees with him. But Teddy remonstrates that the plaintiff will feel he doesn't have the town's backing and will stop paying for the weapons the rebels need to fight the British, and that other local bigwigs will follow suit.*

Once the Civil War began, the British armed the pro-Treatyites to fight the anti-Treaty forces, which demonstrated it was a class war, but that's not in the film because you break the unity of the story and the characters if you keep throwing in facts.

The British wanted the pro-Treatyites to win because that way they'd get their divided Ireland and there'd be no social upheaval in the new republic, which would remain a kind of capitalist economy.

---

* Loach is referring to the covered-up torture and other forms of ill-treatment inflicted on Kikuyu detainees and sanctioned by the British colonial administration during the suppression of the Mau Mau rebellion (1952–60). See Caroline Elkins's *Britain's Gulag: The Brutal End of Empire in Kenya* (Jonathan Cape, 2005); Marc Parry, 'Uncovering the Brutal Truth About the British Empire', *Guardian*, 18 August 2016 (originally published in the *Chronicle of Higher Education*, June 2016).

The courtroom dispute turns into a row about land agitation and class inequality, with Dan claiming that the IRA's support of landlords and businessmen makes them as bad as the English. How would you translate the 'landlordism' that Dan is railing against in contemporary terms?

It's the essence of the social democrat argument – big business must succeed because only then can we raise the taxes for our public services – and the essence of its flaw. Because if your priority is for business to make a profit, then you can't stand up for improved wages and working conditions. That's why the social democrat position is not a position for a party of the working class, because their priorities are not in the interest of the working class, but in the interest of those who exploit them. It's a heresy, and it's why, along with the Stalinists, the social democrats are the enemy of working-class progress.

In its vigour and polarizing effect, the courtroom scene recalls the land reform debate in Land and Freedom. *Was it directing Jim Allen's scripts for* The Big Flame *and* The Rank and File *that alerted you to the dramatic power of such debates and their potential for representing watershed moments in people's lives?*

For me, it was sitting in the Shakespeare Memorial Theatre [now the Royal Shakespeare Theatre] in Stratford [-upon-Avon] and being entranced watching Shakespeare's history plays – the political arguments fought out about power, war, tactics, who should fight whom and who's betraying whom, the guilt and the innocence. And because Jim had lived his life as an activist, he knew intimately what political arguments were, as well as the language they were couched in, so that was really invigorating. Paul, too, loves the cut and thrust of political discourse. He was actually in the land reform scene and makes a contribution as one of the militia in *Land and Freedom*.

When it's a situation where there are huge issues and people's lives at stake, and the success or failure of the project they're engaged in is at a critical moment, these debates come from a desperate need to determine what to do and how to progress. They are not academic debates but discussions that contain all the political principles that are at odds with each other, what you can get away with and what you can't, and they contest those factors that will eventually destroy you if you accept them rather than fight them.

It's a matter of life and death, literally, in the Irish conflict and the Spanish conflict, so it is absolutely the stuff of drama. Conflict is visible and tangible and articulated. People always talk about film as a visual medium – you know, you've got to rely on images. Well, you don't have to rely on images totally. These are characters, they speak, and the eloquence and language they use and the precise nature of how they put forward their ideas and fight for them are absolutely right at the heart of drama. And film can do that, as well as just being images.

I think we undervalue in cinema generally the power of language and articulated thought. One aspect of bourgeois criticism and the bourgeois understanding of cinema is that that class likes to see the working class as victims. The attitude is, 'Pass that hat around for the poor man begging in the street. Oh, he's unemployed – give him a helping hand. Put an extra can of soup in your trolley for the food banks, the poor buggers can't eat.' But they don't like to see the working class organized, articulate and formidable, and that it can win. And that's one of the key things that Jim and Paul and I and the people we've worked with have wanted to show in a number of

The Wind That Shakes the Barley: Auxiliaries seize Sinéad (Orla Fitzgerald).

films – certainly in *Land and Freedom* and *The Wind That Shakes the Barley*.

We talked earlier about your sparing use of poetic images. To take another element of poetry, the Black and Tans' attack on the farmstead is rhymed by the later attack on it by the Auxiliaries, while Chris's execution is rhymed by Damien's. Do you think of narrative or visual rhymes as poetic?

No. Poetry isn't necessarily lyricism. You wouldn't have Wilfred Owen if it was lyricism. 'Poetic' is a very difficult word because it's a word of praise, isn't it? To say a film is pure poetry is a way of praising it rather than a way of precisely defining it. You can talk about a move on a football field as pure poetry, but it's a very imprecise use of language. You know what people mean – it's very beautiful or beautifully executed. There's a symmetry or a kind of simple accuracy about it. To talk about the poetry of film is, in a way, a metaphor for something done with precise economy that says a lot and is pleasing.

It can be pleasing in the framing, in the movement and the juxtaposition of images, and in the moments of personal exchange that you see between the people in the film – the truth of a performance and the way it's set within the framework of a scene or film. To me, it's about economy, precision, authenticity; aesthetically pleasing images juxtaposed in a way that is coherent and has a rhythm to it and an inevitability about it. I think that's a key point. It's like good music. If you listen to Beethoven, you're surprised every few bars, but you realize the sequence of chords and the progress of a movement or symphony is inevitable. It's the same with film. Every shot after the first one might be surprising, but in retrospect couldn't have been anything else. It should be satisfying, maybe, rather than pleasing, if it works at all. These are all aims, but not necessarily what we manage.

Cillian Murphy gave a haunting performance as Damien. Can you tell me about working with him?

He's a brilliant man. As always, we began casting with a blank sheet of paper and no commitment to having an actor with a well-known name, only to find the best person. This was the part of a young man who has trained to be a doctor and gets drawn into the conflict. The film is set in County Cork, and we tried to restrict the casting to actors from Cork. Cillian was one on a whole list of people from there who were suggested to us. I hadn't seen his work, but obviously other people had, and they said he'd be good. I asked him to come along to the hall in the city of Cork where we were seeing people. He turned up and sat on a bench with the other lads, some of whom were farmhands or apprentices or whatever. He just waited his turn and came in. He was very friendly, and we sat and chatted. The modesty of the man and his lack of pretension and his enthusiasm for what we were doing was not calculated at all. That is who he is. I liked him immediately and was impressed by the fact he didn't make a fuss about anything. And to his credit, the agent didn't make a fuss or demand anything. We then tried out various little improvised bits, as we always do, and Cillian was terrific from day one, like Frances McDormand was when we worked with her on *Hidden Agenda*. Cillian wasn't such a big star then as he's become – it was a long time ago – but he enjoyed just being part of the gang, as did the other young lads on the film. He was just Cillian to them and he didn't get special treatment. He slotted in immediately, which was very impressive, but he's also a very fine,

The Wind That Shakes the Barley: Cillian Murphy and Pádraic Delaney as Damien and Teddy – brothers divided.

nuanced actor. He seemed to be very happy with the way that we shot the film in sequence, and the fact that the plot developed for him, as for the others, day by day, week by week, as it unfolded; he entered into that way of working very happily. He was very supportive always, so it was a great experience.

Since you mentioned Hidden Agenda, *I'd be remiss not to ask you about your memory of working with Brian Cox, for decades a formidable stage, TV and film actor who only became a household name in his seventies.*

I knew Brian from the Royal Shakespeare Company. He's also a fine actor, of course, but a very different one. He was about to play Lear when we did *Hidden Agenda*. In some ways, *The Wind That Shakes the Barley* was tough just because of what we had to get on film, but I'd learned a few more tricks by the time I did it. *Hidden Agenda* came after a decade of my not doing good work at all, so I was much less secure, still trying to keep to the basic principles that I'd learned before, which was difficult. It was difficult not being able to shoot in Belfast, too. But Brian was good fun to work with. I see him from time to time at events, and we have a laugh.

In The Wind That Shakes the Barley, *Dan raises the issue of poor farming people being hurt by IRA volunteers carrying out land seizures and cattle drives to support the landlords. In* Jimmy's Hall, *set in 1932, eleven years after the Anglo-Irish Treaty, the communist activist Jimmy Gralton gets involved in land agitation to help poor tenant farmers. What was the origin of the film?*

Paul's got a very good friend whom he knows from his Nicaraguan days: Donal O'Kelly, a politically committed actor and director in Irish theatre who wrote a play about Jimmy Gralton.* He told Paul the story of Jimmy, who had opened a Republican hall in 1922 but had been forced to flee to the United States. James Connolly went to the States, too – it was a familiar passage. When Gralton came back, he reopened the hall, knowing, I think, that it was

---

* O'Kelly's play is *Jimmy Gralton's Dancehall* (2011). O'Kelly first interested Laverty in Gralton when he sent him a poem that he had written about him.

quite a dangerous thing to do. Then he was expelled for being an alien, when, in fact, he was an Irishman born in Ireland. The perversity of that struck Paul. He told me the story, and we agreed it was extraordinary. What's liberating about it is that the politics are already there. There's no need for speeches, no need to spell it out, because all the class forces are arraigned in front of you. And it's about dancing and music and the joy of that. So Paul did the research, and we made the film.

The central conflict is between Jimmy and Father Sheridan, the Catholic priest who wants to shut down or take over the dancehall, ostensibly because he fears his flock will be corrupted by dancing to the jazz records Jimmy has brought back from America. Sheridan is modelled on the anti-communist priest Father O'Dowd of Gowel, who conspired with Father O'Donoghue of Carrick-on-Shannon to have Gralton deported, and he's also close in spirit to the Dublin author–priest Richard Devane (1876–1951), self-appointed moral guardian of Irish youth, who campaigned against nightclubs and commercial cinema. They call to mind the '. . . Priests in black gowns, [who] were walking their rounds, / And binding with briars, my joys & desires' (from William Blake's 'The Garden of Love' in Songs of Experience, *1794), which is quoted in Damien and Dan's prison conversation in* The Wind That Shakes the Barley.

Yes, it's brilliant, simple, clear verse.

Jimmy's Hall *shows that the authoritarian Irish priesthood saw no separation between Church and state and would suppress anything it considered subversive. This agenda is more political and secular than religious.*

Absolutely. From Henry VIII onwards, religion was used to sustain the power of the monarch or state. The Church controls people in the interest of the established economic order. It's about power and maintaining the status quo. Bound into it is the strand of liberation theology that identifies non-conformity and urges, 'Just read what's there in your own language in the Bible and be empowered by it.' But that can tip over into puritanism. Obviously, the opposition of the Catholic Church to what it regards as licentious is at the other end of the ecclesiastical scale from hard-line puritanism. You know, the Wee Frees* now close all the shops on a Sunday and observe the Sabbath. For many years, I carried around a leaflet from the [Irish] Anti-Jazz Campaign,† a movement that opposed jazz as an ungodly form of music. It wasn't just prejudice; it was quite a formal organization within the Catholic Church. The message was, 'You must not have anything to do with jazz. Chase it out!'

That campaign was implicitly racist given jazz's African American origins.

It's obviously not expressed as that, but rural Ireland was an all-white culture, so I'm sure there are hints of it. Racism always occurs when something comes from another part of the world.

As a land agitator, Jimmy leads marches to remove cattle imposed upon one man's land and reinstate the tenant farmer who's been evicted from his cottage. It's the fight for land rights that ultimately lead to the hall being burned down and Jimmy's deportation.

People take power over their land. This is what was so interesting about the story. It's about a simple hall where people meet to enjoy themselves, and it's linked to land, which has always been a thread in revolutionary demands. 'Peace, land and bread'‡ were the Bolsheviks' three central demands. Fair distribution of land, the right of people to own their own land and not be serfs or chased

---

* Members of the conservative evangelical Free Church of Scotland, which is second only to the Church of Scotland as the country's largest Presbyterian denomination. It practises Calvinist theology.
† Led by the cultural nationalist Father Peter Conefrey of Cloone, County Leitrim, the movement dates to 1 January 1934, when over 3,000 protesters marched through Mohill, carrying banners decrying jazz music and dancing. The Public Dance Hall Act, passed without debate in 1935 in the Dáil and still in effect with amendments, directed district courts to regulate the licensing of premises where public dances were held and imposed a tax on admissions.
‡ The slogan, adopted by the Russian masses during the July Days of 1917, was distilled from Lenin's article 'The Tasks of the Proletariat in the Present Revolution' (a.k.a. 'The April Theses'), published in *Pravda*, no. 26, on 7 April of that year.

off it, or [used as] just agricultural labour, have been fundamental needs since time immemorial. The threat of eviction is everywhere. It was in the mining villages, where the mine owners built the miners' houses, then evicted them when they couldn't work.

The Woody Guthrie song 'This Land Is Your Land' expresses a universal theme, and universality is what you hope films can carry. If you can get to the heart of the subject while being precise in the details of the time and the place and the people, you can communicate core ideas that are universal. It's a constant aim.

The film doesn't present Jimmy as a psychologically complex character. Barry Ward plays him as a steely, intelligent man who's kind-hearted and affable when he's with his friends.

I think that was the case. The complexity is in his politics. It's difficult to know from the history books what Jimmy Gralton was like. There's not much information about him, but he clearly liked to see people enjoy themselves, and Barry's instinct was to show his warmth. The real Jimmy loved his home. After he went back to the States finally, he married a woman who came from a neighbouring village in Ireland.

So we wanted somebody with a generosity of spirit. Paul had written this scene where Jimmy teaches jazz dance moves. Barry is not a great dancer, and to his credit, he'd be the first to say it, and the dance lessons were quite comic, but that was OK. He's a working man – he isn't Fred Astaire. He doesn't compromise on his politics, but he wears them lightly. I think that was important for the film. We didn't want a lead character who was dogmatic and making political speeches all the time. If he were that kind of man, I can't see that he'd enjoy the dancing so much. The place would be a platform for him, and we didn't want that. We wanted to share the fun and the enjoyment of it.

For all his convictions, Jimmy isn't a practised orator in the film.

There's a tradition of brilliant working-class men and women who can stand up and speak with clarity and power. But that wasn't Barry. A mistake I used to make back in the early days was, if I had an idea in my head, I'd push it at all costs, but that's wrong. It's much better to go with the grain of the person you've cast in the film and

Jimmy's Hall: the outdoors dance that prompts returned Irish exile Jimmy Gralton to reopen his community hall.

make it work through them. Otherwise, if they're pushed too hard in a direction that isn't easy or natural for them, it becomes false. The important thing with Jimmy is the sincerity and commitment and connection he has to the people. He's a good actor, Barry, and was a real treat to work with, as was Simone Kirby as Oonagh – both terrific and capable of a lot. I was impressed with all of them, including the kids [playing the young Irish adults]. As always, you meet wonderful people. But there was something about Simone I thought was really special.

You'd previously directed Jim Norton, who plays Father Sheridan, as another authoritarian figure: the RUC police chief in Hidden Agenda.

Yes, he was fantastic in that, very dry and hard. I remembered he was an excellent actor to work with.

After Jimmy is arrested, Father Sheridan admits his admiration for his integrity. Why is it important that they respect each other, despite their antipathy towards each other's values?

They're equal combatants, and neither underestimates the power or commitment the other has. Sheridan isn't a wheeler-dealer. He's got his principles. He knows which side he's on and he's going to fight to the death for it, but he recognizes that Jimmy is somebody who will stand on his principles, too. He's fundamentally opposed to them, but he knows he's a worthy opponent. You respect and understand your opponent, don't you? For example, it's a lot easier to respect a hard-line Tory than it is a Labour leader like Tony Blair or Keir Starmer, who believe in nothing. They're just shallow opportunists. They have what old Jim Allen used to call 'jungle agility'. They see the opportunity and swing from branch to branch to get through the undergrowth. They seek leverage wherever they can to find a way to power, manipulating whatever circumstances they're in. I have absolute contempt for people like them. It's much easier to respect Margaret Thatcher. Like many others, I hate everything she stood for, but, nevertheless, you knew where she stood. She was on solid ground in her own mind. Her class loyalty was undisputed; it was clear. People on the left have all always said, 'My God, we need a leader who will fight for our class the way she fought for hers.' People like Starmer and Blair are trivial by comparison – and treacherous, I think.

In fact, Sheridan has more respect for Jimmy than he does for Dennis O'Keefe, who's ostensibly his ally. O'Keefe is a big shot in the Army Comrades Association, the fascist Blueshirts. Notwithstanding the brutality of the Tans in The Wind That Shakes the Barley, *your films are wary of moral absolutes, but O'Keefe is little more than a thug.*

All the evidence is that that's how those people were. His principles are to defend the status quo, defend what he sees as his inalienable rights over his land and property. The difficulty comes when he beats his teenage daughter [Marie, whom Sheridan has upbraided from his pulpit for dancing in the hall]. Again, the evidence for the beating of children and teenagers in Ireland was so overwhelming that it wasn't something Paul wrote lightly. That's how discipline was beaten into you. We know the horrific stories of what happened in the homes for orphans and the Magdalene Laundries in Ireland. It was a culture of brutality, and physical beatings were just part of it. O'Keefe has a moment of remorse after the beating, when he thinks, 'Christ, what have I done?' He wouldn't admit it to himself and almost certainly wouldn't admit it to his daughter, but there's a sense of shame in him. It's important that people, whoever they are, are seen as human.

The newsreel of the 1932 Eucharistic Congress in Dublin, which Jimmy and Oonagh and their friends see in a local cinema, demonstrates the enormous power and sway of the Catholic Church. It's mentioned afterwards that the bishops have the Irish government in their power. O'Keefe and his cronies, who are also in the cinema audience, mock Éamon de Valera for genuflecting to Cardinal Lauri, the papal legate at the congress. O'Keefe derides de Valera as a communist. What are your thoughts about de Valera?

He was a very canny, clever politician on the anti-Treaty side, but he avoided a lot of the key arguments during the War of Independence because he was away in America.*

He also avoided the Treaty talks in London in 1921, probably for strategic reasons.

Yes. In the end, he kept Ireland together for much of the century, apart from partition, obviously. He negotiated the various problems, but he didn't really change the [political] character of Ireland in the way people needed him to.

The Roscommon IRA – whose spokesman is played by Donal O'Kelly – turn up to help Jimmy and his supporters restore an evicted tenant to his cottage, but their role in the background of the film is otherwise ambiguous. At a hearing over Jimmy's removal of a land-grabbing farmer's cattle from the rightful tenant, O'Keefe reads a letter from the IRA supporting his view that the removal of the cattle was unauthorized. What are your perceptions of the IRA's role in the post-Treaty years?

The role of the IRA is very difficult to assess because the propaganda that we get is so intense against the Republican struggle. For

---

* From June 1919 until November 1920.

me, you just go back to first principles. In any other colony, the struggle for freedom and independence is now applauded – people approve of it. But the British ruling class cannot allow that the Irish were involved in an anti-colonial struggle, which happened over centuries, or that the Republican Army was a legitimate resistance movement fighting against their imperialism, because Ireland is so close – it's next door. The corollary of that view is that Britain continues to maintain a military presence in a foreign country.

Since the ruling class can't allow that it was an anti-colonial struggle, they can't say, 'The Republican Army was a movement for freedom and independence, legitimately involved in an anti-colonial struggle, but at a certain point it ceased to be that.' That's an untenable position. But the Republican Army does inherit that anti-imperialist role, and if that's the perspective you see it from, at what point do you say they're not in that role? Obviously, individual acts of terror should be opposed. They not only kill innocent people, but also they're ineffective. They're horrific acts that alienate more people than they bring to your cause, so they're not only wrong, but politically a mistake. But differentiating that struggle from the legitimate struggle for Irish unity and true independence from Britain, and tracking how that struggle developed year by year, are very difficult.

At the time of the war in Northern Ireland, any sense that the IRA was fighting a war of resistance was lost on the average British person in the street because of the civilian casualties, and because the media labelled the Republican forces – whether the Official IRA or the Provisionals – as terrorists.

It's still the case today. When they talk about Irish terrorism, it's always the IRA they mention, rarely the Loyalist terrorists. They never mention the Loyalists' collusion with the British military and the RUC. The propaganda continues. When we made *The Wind That Shakes the Barley*, one headline in the *Daily Mail* was: 'Why Does Ken Loach Loathe His Country So Much?'[*] The article made

---

[*] *Daily Mail*, 30 May 2006. The first paragraph of the article by Ruth Dudley Edwards read: 'Accepting the Palme d'Or award in Cannes for *The Wind That Shakes The Barley* – a pro-IRA film made in Ireland and partially funded by the National Lottery – the director Ken Loach

the point that our productions have received money from the National Lottery, i.e. state money. The thought behind that – and it was personalized against me – was: 'Why are we giving them money to make films that attack us, the hand that feeds them?' In the *Daily Telegraph*, Simon Heffer, a noted right-wing commentator, said he hadn't seen *The Wind That Shakes the Barley*, but that he didn't need to, any more than he needed 'to read *Mein Kampf* to know what a louse Hitler was'.* And there was a piece in *The Times* that said I was a worse propagandist than Leni Riefenstahl. The attacks were intense, and this was for our trying to tell accurately, not from a pro-British point of view, what had happened in the War of Independence.

Those journalists were writing from fixed political positions, not objectively.

They're never held to account. The discussion in the Irish press was obviously very rounded. There were some [journalists] opposed to the film and many who supported it. But finding the equivalent in the British press was almost impossible. People would like it as a film, but they wouldn't argue the case. Michael Gove, who would become the education secretary, went on a full-frontal attack.† He wrote that the Republicans had always ignored the democratic route. He failed to mention that the only time the Irish were able to vote as a united people, they voted overwhelmingly for a united

---

explained that it was "a little step in the British confronting their imperialist history".' In reference to *Hidden Agenda*, the article recalled that 'In a memorable phrase, the then Tory MP Ivor Stanbrook described the movie as "the IRA entry at Cannes".'

* *Daily Telegraph*, 3 June 2006. Heffer prefaced this statement by saying that Loach 'hates this country, yet leeches off it, using public funds to make his repulsive films'.

† Gove wrote in *The Times* on 31 May 2006: 'The truth is that films like Loach's [*The Wind That Shakes the Barley*] that glamorise the IRA give a retrospective justification to a movement which used murderous violence to achieve its ends, even though the democratic path was always open to it. They help legitimise the actions of gangsters who have been torturing innocents for decades, and lend enchantment to an organization which aspires to govern part of the UK although it remains enmeshed in criminality.'

independent Ireland.* He ignored the only democratic test of what Irish people think. The guy who claimed to be holding the film to account for its lack of history had missed the main fact.

That the press would use inflammatory rhetoric invoking Hitler and Leni Riefenstahl to criticize the film is iniquitous, because those references, in turn, invoke the Holocaust.

You see this when the chips are down. If the basic beliefs they want to perpetuate and to permeate consciousness are challenged, they are ruthless. If you attempt to compare anything to the rise of Nazism, they say, 'Oh, no, nothing can compare to that. You can't use it.' But when they want to use the parallel – a false parallel, obviously – it's no problem. You know, 'Call him a worse propagandist than the Nazi propagandist.' The level of abuse is just extraordinary. It's a kind of visceral hatred.

The verbal duels between Jimmy and Father Sheridan are heated. And then you have Father Seamus, played by Andrew Scott, who tries to palliate Sheridan's views, and who comes across as a voice of reason.

It's tempered by the fact that he's a junior. He can only say or hint so much. He knows the response he's going to get, so it's more that he's storing up experience for when he has control over his own parish one day.

Did you feel that the political struggle embodied by Jimmy Gralton and Sheridan succeeded on screen?

I can't judge, really. You're looking from the ground up, doing it as you think fit. Paul was keen on the Andrew Scott character because, as he rightly said, the Catholic Church isn't monolithic. It's like the BBC or anything else. The big institutions are seldom monolithic. There are always people who are critical of the accepted leadership or what they're saying. They fight them as best they can. The

---

* In the 1918 Irish general election, Éamon de Valera's Sinn Féin won seventy-three of the 101 seats. The results of the popular vote were Sinn Féin 497,107; Irish Unionists 257,314; Irish Parliamentary Party 220,837.

Jimmy's Hall: in 1932, Mossie (Francis Magee, left) drives Jimmy Gralton (Barry Ward) back to their Irish village after his exile in the US.

Jimmy and Oonagh (Simone Kirby), his former sweetheart, chastely rekindle their love in Jimmy's reopened Pearse-Connolly Hall.

Apprehended by the Gardai, Jimmy accepts he will be deported from Ireland.

Labour Party was a case in point. It was never monolithic, though since Starmer ruthlessly eliminated all the people with opinions he doesn't like, it has never been as intensely undemocratic as it is now. I think that the need to have a voice saying, 'Look, some of us don't agree with you,' is important. As to whether the argument works in *Jimmy's Hall*, I'd have to see it again. I rarely see these films again after they're done. You just move forward. When I go to a screening and see the last twenty minutes or so, before I go and talk about it, some of it is quite surprising. And the further away you get from a film, of course, the more you see the mistakes.

CHAPTER 11

Perfidious Albion

The Navigators, It's a Free World . . ., Route Irish

Loach's analysis of how the nature of work and worklessness for ordinary people has been manipulated, to their detriment, by successive uncaring governments and unscrupulous employers continued in three films based in and around English cities: Sheffield, in *The Navigators* (2001), written by railwayman Rob Dawber; London, in *It's a Free World . . .* (2007), and Liverpool, in *Route Irish* (2010), both written by Paul Laverty. These films preceded Loach and Laverty's damning statement on the same issue in their north-eastern trilogy: *I, Daniel Blake* (2016), *Sorry We Missed You* (2019) and *The Old Oak* (2023). Blighted English lives are contextualized by Middle Eastern catastrophes in *Route Irish* and *The Old Oak*: the first traces the disastrous involvement of two Liverpudlian mercenaries in the Iraq War; the second examines the impact that the arrival of refugees from the Syrian Civil War has on residents of a poverty-stricken former mining village in County Durham.

One of Loach's least-seen and most under-appreciated films, *The Navigators* echoes *Riff-Raff* – Bill Jesse's story of a London construction crew working without safety measures or union protection – and, thematically, *The Flickering Flame* (1997), which documents the Liverpool dockers' strike resulting from the introduction of casualized labour. It also anticipated *Sorry We Missed You*, which shows the destabilizing effect that a Gateshead couple's exacting work in the gig economy (by definition, casual and unprotected by union membership) has on their school-age son and daughter.

A men-at-work comedy that builds to a tragedy, *The Navigators* focuses on the travails of five mates working as rail maintenance crew for a Sheffield depot: the old-left union rep Gerry (Venn Tracey); the pragmatist John (Dean Andrews); the young father Paul (Joe Duttine), who's separated from his wife and is worried about providing for his two daughters; Mick (Thomas Craig), a stickler for safe work procedures; and the sensitive Jim (Steve Huison). Will Hemmings (Nigel Harrison), the aggressive managing director and glib public face of the private company that has just absorbed the depot and the local lines, threatens to fire the crew's protective manager, Bill Walters (John Aston), when he mentions, in their first meeting, the union agreements that had been established with BR. He orders Walters to 'let the troublemakers go' and punishes him by withdrawing the 'clocking-off' concession he had negotiated with the workers. Walters's foreman, Harpic (Sean Glenn), is obliged to issue absurd directives, such as telling the men to smash usable equipment on the trackside. Reduced in personnel by company pay-offs, the depot loses business, causing the remaining workers to clock in to do non-existent work.

Because Paul has no other choice – the habitual predicament of embattled workers in Loach's films – he takes a pay-off so he can continue to pay child support. Eventually, all but Gerry opt for better-paid but unsafe, unprotected, disorganized agency work, for which they're augmented by jobbing unskilled builders who have driven up from Essex. When John, Paul, Mick and Jim team up again on a night-time concreting job, they proceed without posting a lookout on the line, an illegal action forced on them by the company's cost-cutting. This results in Jim being struck by a passing train, which presents the others with an appalling dilemma. Rather than face prison sentences and a loss of income for their families, Paul and Mick hurriedly move the dying Jim (while John is calling an ambulance) onto a road to indicate he was killed in a hit-and-run incident and cover up their crime. Their remorse will not be so easily assuaged.

Dawber had approached Loach with the idea of writing a script about the break-up of British Rail into private companies and subcontractors. Loach suggested he type up some speculative scenes and discovered that he was a talented, naturalistic writer with a strong sense of character and an eye and ear for robust comedy and pleasing domestic scenes. *The Navigators* would touch on Mick's contented marriage and on Paul's relationships with his angry estranged wife and his daughters, and his dalliance with the depot's secretary, Fiona (Juliet Bates).

Like *Riff-Raff* and such Laverty-scripted films as *Sweet Sixteen*, *Looking for Eric* (2009) and *The Angels' Share*, *The Navigators* revels in workers' camaraderie and mickey-taking. The cast, played by a mixture of actors and northern club comedians and singers, extemporized 'all the quips and innuendos', Dean Andrews claimed. 'We were all like tennis players batting each other lines, with people thinking of new jokes all the time. One of the takes must have gone on for 10 minutes, even though Ken only used about 10 seconds.'* The main targets of the crew's ridicule are the officious but clueless Harpic and the foul-mouthed works janitor, Jack (Charlie Brown), who – as gullible as Malvolio – is kidded into believing he can claim a free tin of sardines when he buys fish and chips.

Britain's 'Big Four' railway companies† were merged as British Rail (BR) on 1 January 1948, under the Labour government's nationalization policy. The rail workers' unions afforded safety and job security for drivers, guards and maintenance workers. BR was rarely profitable, however, and though it survived the Thatcher government's wave of privatizations, it was dismantled during its 1994–7 privatization by John Major's government. The consequences were disastrous. Though fewer accidents occurred than under BR, the number of fatalities increased, from eighteen in 1990–6 (inclusive) to thirty-eight in the first three years (1997–9) after Railtrack, a privatized group of companies, became responsible for infrastructure. There were tragic accidents at Southall in 1997, at Ladbroke Grove in 1999 and at Hatfield on 17 October 2000, when a known problem concerning metal fatigue in the rails caused a derailment and four people were killed and seventy injured. Railtrack had subcontracted track maintenance to companies employing workers who lacked skills, experience and knowledge of safety. As a result, huge delays were caused by Railtrack's decision to impose hundreds of speed restrictions throughout the national

---

* Sheila Johnston, 'How to Make a Drama Out of a Crisis', *Guardian*, 17 November 2001.
† Great Western Railway (GWR); London, Midland and Scottish Railway (LMS); London North Eastern Railway (LNER); and Southern Railway (SR).

network so that rails could be checked for possible cracks. In May 2001, Railtrack announced a £534 million loss, and the government put the company into administration in October of that year. The British rail system is now run for the Department of Transport by the publicly owned Network Rail, which owns the infrastructure, is responsible for maintenance and ploughs its profits back into the system, not into shareholders' pockets. The trains are still operated by private companies, but a full return to nationalization is planned, under the rubric 'Great British Railways'.

The Navigators was timely: a scene showing the aftermath of a train derailment was filmed two days after the Hatfield crash. The finished film was screened briefly in Sheffield, but it did not get a proper theatrical release in the UK. However, it performed well in France and Italy, where audiences have a much greater appreciation of social-realist films. Its bleak conclusion cannot efface its raucous humour, its discreet dabs of Eros or its visual grace notes. Paul and his daughters try their luck among the happy punters at an indoor skating rink. A strolling cat is caught in the yellow light of single mum Fiona's backyard, just before she relieves her daughter Rose's babysitter. Fresh from an outing to a disco, Fiona and Paul are feeling amorous, but their love-making is interrupted by the sudden appearance at the sitting-room door of Rose (Charlotte Hukin), in her angelic innocence reminiscent of the footballer Alex Young's five-year-old, Jane, whom Loach gently interviewed at the start of *The Golden Vision*. Rose has been woken by a nightmare. While Fiona is heating some milk for her in the kitchen, Paul patiently advises her to read about fairies rather than monsters before going to sleep. The film doesn't belabour the point, but the economic security of kids like Rose and Paul's two daughters is what's at stake in *The Navigators*.

Dawber died on 20 February 2001, aged forty-five. The cause was mesothelioma caused by working with asbestos as a railwayman, as Loach explained in the obituary he wrote for the *Guardian*, published two days later. 'Last year, he won a significant victory in establishing his employers' culpability for his illness,' Loach added.

Dawber studied politics and English at Leicester University and began his eighteen-year career as a rail worker and trade union activist, Loach's obituary continued, 'partly because of his political commitment; Rob was of that generation of socialists who were inspired by the trade union struggles of the 1970s. Also, as he said, he wanted to work alongside people he liked . . . He became a branch secretary for the National Union of Railwaymen, and wrote for *Socialist Organiser* and *Off the Rails*, a bulletin for rail workers. His Fat Controller column mercilessly lampooned the rail managers who squandered the opportunities of the nationalised industries.'

Loach said Dawber showed no self-pity about his illness and 'took great delight in seeing his film completed, and became the centre of much laughter on the set . . . His strength, good humour and integrity were an inspiration to all who knew him.'

As would *Route Irish*, *It's a Free World* . . . follows a dynamic, effective but uningratiating protagonist who is driven by past experiences to transgress moral and social laws in tyrannical pursuit of a goal. *It's a Free World* . . .'s east London entrepreneur, Angie (Kierston Wareing), overcomes her kinder impulses to maintain her business at all costs. *Route Irish*'s elite soldier of fortune Fergus Malloy (Mark Womack) resorts to brutal vigilante justice to avenge the killing of his lifelong best friend, Frankie (John Bishop). Loach and Laverty trusted that audiences would recognize that the faults lie less in these characters as individuals than in the politically diseased environments that they are forced to operate in.

The enlargement of the European Union in 2004 to include Cyprus, the Czech Republic, Estonia, Hungary, Latvia, Lithuania, Malta, Poland, Slovakia and Slovenia opened the floodgates to migrants coming to Britain, desperate to find work and ripe for exploitation. At the start of *It's a Free World* . . ., employment agent Angie is herself exploited. While working for a British firm on a hiring trip in Katowice, Poland, she is threatened with dismissal after she complains about being sexually harassed by a male colleague. Back home in east London, she enlists her roommate, Rose (Juliet Ellis), in starting up their own agency. A single mother, Angie demonstrates the determination, guile and organizational skills that distinguish her from Carol White's characters in *Cathy Come Home* and *Poor Cow*, films that reflected their era's paucity of opportunities for working-class women. In the context of Loach and Laverty's work, Angie's zipping between appointments with employers on a motorcycle and her comfort with summoning male sexual partners, via texts, for herself and Rose are details that suggest that women's acquisition of professional and personal power coincided with the metaphorical emasculation of the male workforce resulting from the decline of British heavy industry instigated by Thatcher.

In the rear of a Leytonstone pub, Angie and Rose begin recruiting mostly East European migrants and deliver them to construction and factory jobs. Angie uses her charm and looks to persuade employers to hire her and Rose's clients, all of whom are exploited as casuals without workers' rights. To Rose's consternation, Angie increasingly hires illegal workers. Despite her tendency to treat them like cattle when they throng the pub car park each morning, and also to gouge rent for the room she lets to them, she is capable of compassion, finding caravan accommodation for the homeless Iranian dissident Mahmoud (Davoud Rastgou), who's hiding from the police with his wife and two daughters. After a crisis results from an employer bouncing cheques worth £40,000, which is needed to pay the wages of Angie and Rose's desperate workers, Rose's suggestion they should have paid them with their rental earnings is scorned by Angie. A child of Thatcher's free-market ethics and selfish individualism, she replies: 'It's a free world – I don't give a shit.' When Angie reports the caravan site's illegal dwellers to the police so that she can house her workers there, Rose ends their partnership.

Angie's unscrupulousness also alienates her younger Polish lover, Karol (Lesław Żurek). Retribution comes when her son, Jamie (Joe Siffleet), is kidnapped and briefly held for ransom by a few of the furious unpaid workers, who, disguised by balaclavas, bind and menace Angie in her flat, causing her to lose control of her bladder. As John Hill suggests,* the degrading nature of the assault, echoed in the brutishly macho horror film *Dog Soldiers* (2002), which Angie and Jamie had been watching on TV, embodies misogynistic revenge for Angie's usurpation of the traditional male role of breadwinner. Despite these terrifying experiences, the unrepentant Angie is last seen recruiting illegal workers in Ukraine. Like Margaret Thatcher before her, 'The lady's not for turning.'

The Navigators ends with a cover-up of a death for which otherwise honest men were responsible because their working conditions

---

* John Hill, *Ken Loach: The Politics of Film and Television*, p. 195.

were compromised by their profit-focused employer. *Route Irish* begins with the funeral of the former British paratrooper Frankie, whose elimination was engineered and covered up by the private military contractor Tyree, which deployed him in Iraq and feared he would blow the whistle on his unit's slaughter of an Iraqi family and two young boys. The harrowing conspiracy thriller condemns, in microcosm, the US's and UK's prosecution of the Iraq War in order to benefit Western oil companies and the corporations that would profit from multi-billion-dollar reconstruction projects. Recalling the ops he took part in as an SAS man with US Special Forces, Fergus tells Frankie's grieving girlfriend Rachel (Andrea Lowe) that the hunt for terrorists, which supposedly justified the US-led coalition's occupation, was a fallacy, because the locals were 'chicken farmers mostly', and 'if they didn't support al-Qaeda before [we invaded], they did after, I can guarantee that'.

Loach and Laverty's disgust at the capitalization of a conflict that caused approximately 460,000 excess deaths in Iraq (60 per cent of them attributable to violence) from 2003 to June 2011[*] is filtered in *Route Irish* through flashbacks to ferocious engagements, rendered through night footage, phone video and news clips. This disassociating mediation of war is complemented by the gradual dehumanizing of Fergus, who, haunted by images of dead babies and soldiers clubbing children, seeks to discover the circumstances around, and perpetrator of, Frankie's killing.

Guilt-ridden because he had persuaded Frankie to sign on with Tyree, Fergus is angered by the self-serving eulogy to Frankie that his boss, Andrew Haynes (Jack Fortune), delivers at the funeral and his attempts to use the occasion to recruit operatives. Marisol (Najwa Nimri), a fellow mourner, passes to Fergus a package containing a mobile phone – sought by Haynes's fixer, Alex Walker (Geoff Bell) – that Frankie had used. At a multicultural community centre, the Iraqi techie and musician Harim (Talib Rasool) helps Fergus to access video footage on the phone, which reveals that Frankie anguishedly witnessed the unhinged Nelson (Trevor Williams), who was on a mission with Frankie and three Colombian mercenaries, murdering the Iraqi family and the two boys.

---

[*] According to the journal *PLOS Medicine*. Its study, based on household survey data, indicates that an estimated 55,000 Iraqi migrants also died.

Rachel, with whom Fergus starts a long-delayed affair tinged with sadomasochism, tells him bitterly that Frankie went to Iraq to be with him – 'I think he loved you' – not for the tax-free £10,000 he'd earn monthly, though the lack of work in Liverpool was clearly a factor. Both men have Rachel's name tattooed on their arms, the love triangle an unusually dark psychosexual element for a Loach–Laverty film. Chris Menges's cool observational cinematography, which contrasts the sombreness of Liverpool (filmed in 35mm) with the glaring light of Iraq (filmed in Super 16mm, at locations in Jordan), underscores the film's disorienting effect and the anomaly of a happy-go-lucky Scouser like Frankie, whom Nelson sneeringly called 'Florence' and 'Goody Two Shoes', being sent to Iraq to help protect the interests of American multinationals.

On the rampage back in Liverpool, Nelson hospitalises Harim in his search for the mobile phone but is taken at gunpoint by Fergus in a golf-club car park. Suffering PTSD, his moral compass destroyed, Fergus waterboards Nelson and kills him off-screen. Contacted by former associates Tommy and Craig, Fergus learns that Nelson was in Afghanistan at the time of Frankie's death, and that it was Haynes who issued orders for Frankie to patrol – fourteen times, and in a defective car – the 12-kilometre-long road from Baghdad airport to the Green Zone; 'Route Irish', as it was nicknamed – after the Troubles – was lethally plagued by roadside bombings and drive-by shootings following the invasion. After exacting vigilante justice on Haynes, Fergus throws himself from the Mersey ferry, on which, as hopeful youths, he and Fergus had shared their desire to travel.

GRAHAM FULLER: *We've come to* The Navigators.

KEN LOACH: Rob Dawber, blessed memory.

The film reflects the disastrous effect the privatization of British Rail had on workers' rights and safety in the late 1990s. Did you seek out a story or did Rob come to you with his script?

He wrote in. He was a very nice, interesting man. He'd been to university, but he'd chosen to work on the railways as a political act, rather as Jim Allen used to work on building sites to recruit people to the [construction workers'] union. Rob was two generations younger than Jim, but he was of the same mindset of working in an industry where he could organize and take part as an activist. He wanted to write something about how the railways were privatized.

What he began with was that, at every turn, the propaganda [that management presented to the workers concerning their futures] said, 'You can choose.' One choice would be made to look very attractive, and the other would be made to look very unattractive. And what was advertised as the attractive option was joining an agency and doubling your wages, [among other] con tricks companies use to get people to sign up to their own annihilation as a workforce.

Rob had lots of stories, so we talked about what the storyline of the film might be. He'd written some stuff before he came in, and the dialogue was good. The first thing you always look for is if somebody can really write, or is he somebody who would like to write but isn't a writer? Rob wrote really well, and he'd got some great characters. Harpic, the manager of the depot and the workforce, was one of them. The joke was, 'Why is he called Harpic?' 'Because he's clean round the bend' [*laughs*]. Obviously, we talked a lot, but Rob wrote the script. He was very imaginative and had a great sense of humour, but very sharp politics. He'd written for some of the left-wing papers. So he was a good guy. When he first worked on the railways, which he eventually worked on for eighteen years, he'd had to break up asbestos items in a shed with an asbestos roof, and, tragically, he contracted mesothelioma, which killed him. It was devastating – he was just a young man.

In the film, the railway maintenance workers at the Sheffield depot are told they're now working for a private company that will ban union agreements. So they have no job protection and no guarantee of safety. Presumably, it was always intended that the film would focus on the group rather than a single protagonist, which is the norm in most films.

It was always intended. The film is about the team and its interaction and the friendships and jokes that bind people who work together – the piss-takes, the nicknames, the running gags. Somebody's always

The Navigators: Dean Andrews, Venn Tracey, Thomas Craig, Steve Huison and Joe Duttine.

late, somebody's always got a special kind of food, somebody's in trouble with their missus. Everyone has some defining characteristic that means everyone else can take the mickey. Rob was very funny about that, and that was a key thing. I've always enjoyed and found interesting the dynamics of the group.

Were they based on real people?

They were characters that Rob came up with, having known people like that, but nobody was a copy of anyone.

The crew of five that you focus on in the film fragments, but eventually four of them reunite as an agency skeleton crew, working without safety measures. Jim is struck and killed by a train because they were unable to post a lookout on the line when doing a night job. Even their integrity is compromised, because Paul and Mick move Jim's body up onto the road to make it seem like a hit-and-run. This makes it a double tragedy, in a way, because these are good men who'd been doing honest work, until the new conditions prompted them to cut corners.

Rob's writing – as does Paul's – shows how the whole morality of a situation gets muddied when people are compromised. There's no clear shining hero who speaks the truth from the first shot to the last, which would be boring. Everyone gets compromised in *The Navigators* because they're all in danger, if it's only the financial danger of being blacklisted. In the end, no one is going to put their head above the parapet. They could if the case [of Jim's fatal accident] came to trial, but in the heat of the moment, despite reservations, people try to cover up things that shouldn't be covered up because they don't know the exact consequences. There's a confusion about it. You don't know what's at stake. You know you shouldn't do the wrong thing, but that's how people are, by and large, when the waters are muddied.

It's dramatically right because it shows the corrupting nature of the whole system, which forces people to be individuals instead of a team. If the railways were under common ownership and there was proper respect for life and safety, nobody would be inhibited about saying, 'Look, this is what happened.' In a situation like the one we show, the whole crew would be held to account because there would be something in the small print [of the work order or company regulations] that would exonerate the manager who was really responsible and making a profit out of the particular job. It would mean he'd escape, so everyone is contaminated by this corrupt way of working.

The hiring in The Navigators *of unskilled labourers as casual workers, which appals the survivors in the regular crew, recalls the building industry 'lump', which was the subject of Jim Allen's first TV drama.**

Exactly. It's back to the nineteenth century, when workers were easy to exploit. Everything now springs from Thatcher's attempted destruction of the trade unions and the easier-to-exploit diminution of workers' rights. We've done several films where each is a step down from [union-protected employment]. *The Navigators* is a step down, then *It's a Free World . . .*, and then it's another step down to the gig economy in *Sorry We Missed You*. It's all to do

---

* *The Lump* (1967; see note on p. 31).

with the transformation of work, the removal of workers' rights and the capacity for employers to make profits. But the contradiction within their system is that their profits decrease because each company is trying to undercut the other. On the one hand, they need to exploit workers more to maintain their profits. On the other, they need to be as cheap as possible to get the contracts with the customers. They keep having to lower their prices, so they're trapped in this eternal conflict.

Maloney, the manager of the delivery depot in Sorry We Missed You, *boasts about how aggressive he's being in trying to win contracts from Amazon and other corporate giants. And, of course, he's pushing the drivers to their limits.*

And safety goes out the window. The more safety is the last consideration, the more the drivers talk about it.

In the making of The Navigators, *were there any dangers for the cast and crew on the railway line, or was it completely safe?*

It was always safe. We got possession of lines [located] in Doncaster sidings, so we weren't on lines that were live. The biggest danger was the rain. It rained almost continuously for six weeks.

It feels like a docudrama, for want of a better term. It's hard to believe that it's fiction.

The actors were a great bunch, very funny. It was one of those films where you began chuckling the moment you arrived in the morning, and they kept you going the whole day, until towards the end of filming, when the story got darker.

Sean Glenn, as Harpic, the ineffectual foreman, reminds me of Will Hay's stationmaster in Oh, Mr Porter! *(1937). He's the same kind of officious, incompetent boss who's laughed at for being in over his head. Glenn is a pantomime legend. Over the years, you've worked with a number of comedians – people like Bill Dean, Lynne Perrie, Crissy Rock and Dave Johns – who weren't trained at RADA but who act truthfully, without tics or affectations, often in very serious roles. How is it that you're able to get people from the world of entertainment to give performances that trained actors couldn't deliver?*

They're working a different way. For a part like Harpic, you look for people who are funny when they get cross. They don't have a deep anger that frightens you. They make you smile. Ricky Tomlinson is one – the crosser he gets, the more you laugh. Willie Ross, the very funny actor who played the site manager in *Riff-Raff*, was the same. So is John Henshaw, a brilliant performer who came to acting late. Sean is certainly that in *The Navigators*; so was Arthur Lowe, a traditional actor, in *Dad's Army* [1968–77]. It's a real quality, and it's to do with timing. Comics can do it because to succeed as a club comic you've got to be rooted in the working-class experience of the people in the audience. People working in that idiom have that shared understanding of laughing at what's familiar and shared recognition of the stupidity of the things everyone does, including the bloke on stage. They share their humanity, as well as the laughter.

When we try little auditions or improvisations, you can spot very quickly the people who have it, so it's just about finding them and making it easy for them to perform. They thrive on surprises and things being thrown at them, because when they're in the vein, things just flow. It's like having a heckler in the audience. Good comics love that because they've got a few lines in their head and can always put a heckler down, which adds to the comedy of the moment. It's about working in an atmosphere that clearly welcomes that kind of interchange and has the people around the camera chuckling away.

There's not only the badinage at the depot and the fooling of the janitor into believing he's going to get free sardines with his fish and chips, there's marital-sex comedy with Mick and his wife, and the tryst between Paul and the depot's office assistant Fiona, a single mother, which is interrupted by her little girl coming downstairs because she's had a nightmare, meaning Paul has to cover his chest quickly. He then chats sweetly with the girl, but after Fiona has taken her back to her room, he thoughtfully uncovers his chest again, hoping he and Fiona can carry on from where they left off. Do such comic moments come from simply observing and enjoying how people are, or are they created to balance the social and political concerns you're addressing?

It's never that calculated. I don't think of them as balances. It's just that ordinary life is full of comic things that happen. Paul tries to make up with his wife, but she won't see him, and when he pushes the flowers he's brought her through the letterbox, their heads fall off. It's funny but sad. His efforts to get off with Fiona are also funny. I think it would have been wrong to have had a tragedy in the crew's private lives, because that would compete with the tragedy on the railway, which is the story. Showing their private lives is necessary because everyone's got a private life, and you want to know who the main characters are and what their situations are, but you can't be too heavy, otherwise you take away the ultimate tragedy of the main story.

Some scripts lend themselves to the comedy of everyday life more easily than others, and some performers make you smile more than others. I think those moments of warmth are still there in the last three films [*I, Daniel Blake, Sorry We Missed You, The Old Oak*], but they're harder to find because the people are so stressed and under such pressure. At the time of the rail privatization, people's characters were still in the traditional mould. Confronting privatization and its practical details, the railway workers knew it was plain stupidity, and they were sufficiently well grounded and confident to take the mickey out of it. Whereas now people have had several decades of insecurity, anxiety, poverty and food banks, that space for finding the simple comedy of everyday life is being squeezed out. There aren't so many laughs in the food bank [in *I, Daniel Blake*] as there are in a railway depot, when the men are being told things that are obviously stupid. There has been a shift. It's my hunch that a lot of the laughter has gone out of daily life. Certainly, for us, it seems to have done.

It's a Free World . . ., *which also examines labour exploitation in Britain, depicts the plight of migrant workers following the expansion of the European Union in 2004. Why did you and Paul choose to tell the story from the perspective of an ambitious recruiter, Angie, who becomes more and more corrupt as the story goes on?*

Again, it's not about bad people doing bad things. It's about the system, which demands that in order to succeed, you have to do things that exploit others. Exploiters are traditionally seen as hard-faced men, but in this case it's a bright, clever girl from a working-class background whose father is a socialist, an old dock worker who experienced the struggle on the docks, whose principles are solidarity and fighting for workers' rights. Despite that background, because Angie has been exploited as a worker – and, as a young woman, refuses to continue being humiliated by men at work – she starts her own agency. The only way a small agency can succeed is to provide workers who will work for less than the other agencies it competes with. Why should people recruit from her agency when there are better-established ones? Because her workers are cheaper, and she can drive them to be on time at their jobs and do as they're told. So she has to collude in their exploitation for her agency to succeed. As the competition gets harsher, she then, of course, has to get into other things she originally couldn't have imagined doing, such as forging her workers' passports. She knows she's doing all this, but that's the way the world is. If you want to succeed, you have to do it.

Angie's father, who has lived through the workers' struggles of the 1970s, says he didn't think he'd ever see such exploitation of labour again. But Angie is unscrupulous about how she gets ahead. She grew up during the post-Thatcher era of free enterprise. Her ruthlessness can be identified with neo-liberalism.

She is a child of Thatcher, absolutely. Not consciously, but in the sense that she's a child of the consciousness of the society that's been developed. What creates consciousness in a society – understanding the way people see the world – is an idea we've referred to time and time again in the films. Thatcher's achievement was not only to reduce the power of organized labour, it was to change consciousness. Her message was: 'Trade unions are old-fashioned. You don't need to be a member of a union. Every man for himself. You're on your own, so look after yourself and your family. The entrepreneur is king and queen, and that's all that matters. We're in a global economy. Just fight hard for what you want and do what you need. The collective is meaningless.' Blair inherited that shift of consciousness and carried it on. Starmer is promoting it

It's a Free World . . .: employment agent Angie (Kierston Wareing), a child of Thatcher.

effectively. Though he and his people use different rhetoric, their actions – and increasingly what they say – is about the individual. That's the essence of the society they build, isn't it?

Angie's trajectory is largely defined by her gender. Early in the film, she's sexually harassed at work by one of her male colleagues. When she starts up her agency with her roommate Rose, she uses her feminine charms to get ahead. She flirtatiously tells the male shirt manufacturer whose business she wants that the good thing about her company is, 'We're all girls under thirty.' She also takes the sexual initiative in her private relationships with men. Since she becomes more and more unprincipled, do you think the film risks inviting criticism that it's sexist, especially as not all viewers will glean how the political climate has shaped her?

Men use masculine tricks, and women use women's tricks. It's as old as Beatrice and Benedict. Angie is a very attractive young woman. She knows she can use that. Men use what they see as male strengths. They bully and do all kinds of things. People use their assets to get what they think they need.

Why did you choose to make the character a woman rather than a man?

Because it's not what you expect. The figurehead for economic exploitation, in this instance, is another woman, Thatcher, but it's the issue of exploitation that matters, not the gender of the person doing the exploiting. Making the character a woman stands expectations on their head, because you can't just say men are responsible for it. People are responsible for it, and they're driven by the economic system they're in.

At one point, Angie shows compassion for an Iranian worker and his family. She brings them to her flat, feeds them and finds them a home on a caravan site, which puts her in legal danger. Yet the goodwill we feel towards her evaporates when she has them evicted so she can house other illegal workers.

She's full of contradictions. It shows how self-interest can ruin good intentions. In order to run a successful agency, she depends on getting people she can control in order to provide reliable cheap labour. It's the same in *Bread and Roses*. If the workers can't declare themselves publicly, those in charge have got a much greater hold over them. Illegality works in the agencies' favour because the workers are in no position to make complaints about their working conditions.

At the end of It's a Free World . . ., *Angie goes to Ukraine to sign up more workers. She's continuing to capitalize on people's needs and misfortunes. The overarching message is that greed begets more greed.*

I think so. Alan Sugar is quoted as saying, 'There's nothing wrong with being greedy. If you're a businessman, that's what it's about.'* There's the 'greed is good' speech in that Hollywood film.† Greed is the driving force for a successful business now. The idea of a stable family business that lasted a long time, that treated everyone well,

---

* Alan Sugar, 'Our Children Need Enterprise', interview with Rachel Sylvester and Alice Thomson, *Daily Telegraph*, 9 February 2008.
† *Wall Street* (1987), directed by Oliver Stone, from a screenplay by Stone and Stanley Weiser.

that was socially responsible and behaved with a degree of honour – that idea hasn't survived because those businesses are taken over by entrepreneurs who strip their assets or absorb them into a bigger corporation. That's the pattern, isn't it? That's the game of Monopoly.

You see this on British high streets, where the chains have taken over. Those old family businesses would have once had a presence at country fairs or driven a float in a town parade. They were advertising themselves, of course, but they were integral to their communities.

There would still be a hierarchy. The boss would pay himself a lot more than the people he employed, but it was comparatively benign, whereas the business model now is an inevitable development of the system in which profit is the yardstick of success. Smaller companies are taken over by big ones, and the intense competition demands greater sacrifices from those who sell their labour.

Angie and her son Jamie, whom she's neglected because of work and who is suspended from school for hurting another kid, are watching an action–horror film on TV at home when migrant workers wearing black balaclavas burst in, seize the boy and tell Angie she won't see him again, unless she pays them what she owes them. Was anything metaphorical intended in your use of such sensationalistic genre imagery, or was the scene factually based?

I don't think we ever consciously refer to other forms of cinema. Pretty much everything is based on what Paul finds in his research. People do crazy things when they're driven to desperation, and the point here was to show the outcome of the rivalry that existed between agencies fighting for the same business.

That desperation comes across, too, in the way you orchestrate the crowd of migrants pleading for work. They don't know where they're getting their next meals from.

Many of them are strangers in a strange land and out of their depth. They don't have that intuition about how the world works around them, and that always makes people anxious. They know they're being cheated, but they don't know how the system works. The system forces you to be ruthless, and if you're not, you're not in the game. It's a bit like *Sorry We Missed You*. You begin with the value of being an entrepreneur and a great landscape opening up in front of you, but bit by bit you're dragged into doing things that you know are wrong.

Angie starts treating her personnel like cattle. I see in her intimations of the contempt for foreign workers that played a part in the Brexit vote ten years later. Eastern European plumbers and lorry drivers were the archetypes that got the brunt of it. It doesn't matter where you're from, many British people will resent your presence.

That, again, is a contradiction. The right wing want foreign workers to provide cheap labour, but they don't want their foreign ways and they don't want them in our land. The *Daily Mail*, on the one hand, represents the class that exploits foreign workers for profit and, on the other, fans the prejudice against them. So they're caught in that contradiction: Do we want them or not? It's a pattern with immigration, isn't it? We needed the *Windrush* generation* for their work, but some people didn't want them, or didn't want the character of their neighbourhood to change.

A strain of British exceptionalism also factored into the Brexit vote.

It's always an undercurrent in our politics because we're an island nation, not part of the European mainland. I think our idea of ourselves as a country – 'this blessed plot'† – is that we are something else. We are very different. We had the empire. We've got all these

---

* African Caribbean people from the West Indies who, starting in the late 1940s, were encouraged to immigrate to the UK, where there was a labour shortage following the Second World War. HMT *Empire Windrush*, the third immigration ship to sail from Jamaica, arrived at the port of Tilbury, Essex, on 22 June 1948, with 1,027 passengers (and two stowaways) on board. They included 802 passengers who had resided in Caribbean countries and sixty-six Polish refugees – Soviet deportees from Siberia – who had lived at a camp in Santa Rosa, Guanajuato, Mexico.
† From John of Gaunt's deathbed speech in Act 2, Scene 1 of Shakespeare's *Richard II*, which emphasizes England's proud isolation and warlike nature.

specific jokes, clichéd jokes about everyone else – the French, the Germans, the Italians. Those jokes are very close to expressing a prejudice that turns serious very quickly.

What are your recollections about the filming of It's a Free World . . .?

Faye Wareing – she became Kierston Wareing – was the main part of it. She was very good, very reliable. She embodied Angie and was funny and bright and easy to work with. The guys around her in the film were good, too. Going to Ukraine was interesting, in the light of what's happened since. There was no shortage of people in the film who were experiencing what we were filming; most of the workers in it were doing that kind of work through agencies. And it was interesting working in east London, because I haven't worked in London much at all.

When Route Irish *was shown at Cannes in 2010, at the press conference and in interviews you and Paul expressed your anger about Britain's involvement in the Iraq War. You both remarked on the irony of Tony Blair being made a peace envoy to the Middle East in 2007, given that hundreds of thousands of people perished in Iraq. Did the lies told about the cover-up of Frankie's death in the film resonate with the lies told to justify the Iraq War – namely, that Iraq had an arsenal of weapons of mass destruction, and that Saddam Hussein was in league with al-Qaeda? Was that your thinking behind the film?*

Yes, it was, but we wanted to go a stage further. Paul felt, and I agreed with him, that the truth about the weapons of mass destruction had been exposed so comprehensively by the time we were doing the film that simply to say that again wouldn't be new. What concerned us was the privatization of war and how the contractors that went into Iraq operated with a level of impunity and violence that endorsed all the worst aspects of the illegal invasion.

The attitude of the security firms was: 'Iraqi lives don't count. This is a commercial venture, and we are gonna make the most of it. There'll be money available for rebuilding. It's gonna come our way, and the world will turn a blind eye to whatever we do.' In the chaos of war and the aftermath, they could get away with anything and have a public face that enabled them to get government grants from the West – money that should have gone to the Iraqi people. So it was a strong idea.

I just watched the film again, which confirmed my memory that I'd made a number of mistakes on it, but the core of it isn't too bad. One thing we were afraid of was that, because it's about British people, it would be seen as a film about a British problem, but Paul's script does centre on the Iraqis' suffering. So often you see films about Americans who have been to war, and they're all about the problems they have when they come home, but the poor people who have been shot up in their own countries don't get a mention. So Paul got that right. Then, as you say, it's about the tangled web of the cover-up, and how these private companies control communications and everything else in the interest of profit. I think the journey of the main character, Fergus, is OK.

Like Land and Freedom, *it begins with the funeral of a working-class Liverpudlian who has fought in a foreign war. Though Frankie's operating as a mercenary in Iraq is ignoble compared to David's fighting for the Republican cause in Spain,* Route Irish *empathizes with Fergus's and Frankie's girlfriend Rachel as she and Fergus grieve for Frankie. He followed Fergus to Baghdad because he needed the money, but he died out there trying to protect an Iraqi family.*

Yes. Those firms are made up of real people, so, of course, everybody will react differently. It's not like these firms are armies of robots. Some are more committed to making money and doing what they have to in order to make it, and others are appalled by what they're doing. It must be that way.

Was the film set primarily in Liverpool because the high unemployment there is what caused Frankie to join Fergus in Iraq?

No. We weren't certain where to set it at first, but we narrowed it down to Liverpool. It's one of four or five places we've always returned to because they have very rich pools of talent, and I knew we'd find good people there to act in the film. Liverpool's also an area where the army frequently recruits from, and the port, the Mersey and the ferries became part of the plot.

After 9/11 and the start of the so-called 'War on Terror', the privatization of military operations led to some eighty British firms sending private contractors, or mercenaries, to Iraq and also to Afghanistan, Somalia, Libya, Egypt and Syria. The British state has paid these companies about £50 million annually since 2004.

Parliament just declared [on 15 September 2023] the Wagner Group* a terrorist organization for doing what British and American contractors were doing. After the Nisour Square incident,† what more evidence did you need? It's extraordinary how no one holds them to account.

Did you and Paul meet with private contractors who had been in Iraq?

Paul met more than me, but they're quite reluctant to talk, obviously. We also met some soldiers who had fought in the war and then become very politically active in opposing it. One or two spoke really well about the whole British presence and the brutality and disregard for life. Craig,‡ the lad who is playing blind football in the film, was an ex-soldier who lost his sight when an explosive device struck him.

---

* The Russian state-funded private military company, which first appeared during the 2014 annexation of Crimea, is currently deployed in the war against Ukraine.

† On 16 September 2007, employees of the American private military firm Blackwater Security Consulting killed seventeen and wounded twenty Iraqi civilians in Nisour Square, Baghdad, while escorting a US embassy convoy. The four Blackwater guards convicted in 2019 for participating in the massacre were granted unconditional presidential pardons by Donald Trump in 2020.

‡ On 22 March 2007, Corporal Craig Lundberg, twenty-one, a section commander in the 2nd Battalion, Duke of Lancaster's Regiment, was serving his second tour of duty in Iraq. During an operation to arrest known insurgents in Basra, Lundberg was struck in the chest by two rocket-propelled grenades. He lost his left eye and most of his teeth, and his left arm was almost severed. He continued to give orders and return fire until he collapsed. Doctors could not save the sight in his right eye. A Liverpudlian, Lundberg has since played for England in the European Blind Football Championships, climbed Mount Kilimanjaro and run the London Marathon. In 2019, he cycled from Land's End to John O'Groats in the Blind Tandem Challenge.

Were some of the contractors remorseful about what they'd done?

I don't think they were proud of it necessarily, otherwise they wouldn't have spoken to Paul. There can be a certain fatalism about doing that kind of work.

Fergus is a complicated protagonist. Because Frankie's death touches him personally, it's the catalyst for him not only to unravel the security firm's cover-up of it, but also to confront his own guilt and shame. The tragedy brings out both his humanity and his ruthlessness. His quest to expose the conspiracy accelerates the changes he goes through.

Towards the end, he can communicate only by shouting at people. At one point, he engages in the torture that the British have used: waterboarding, as deemed acceptable by the American president – Bush[*] said he had no problem with it. Fergus does what he does to get to the truth of what happened. And, of course, it doesn't work.

---

[*] 'Getting Away with Torture: The Bush Administration and Mistreatment of Detainees', published by Human Rights Watch (hrw.org) on 12 July 2011, reports: '[President George W.] Bush acknowledged on several occasions that he approved waterboarding of detainees, including Khalid Sheikh Mohammed and Abu Zubaydah.' The first acknowledgement came on 11 April 2008, in an interview with Martha Raddatz of ABC News:

> Raddatz: ABC News reported this week that your senior national security officials all got together and approved – including Vice President Cheney – all got together and approved enhanced interrogation methods, including waterboarding, for detainees.
> Bush: Yes.
> Raddatz: You have no problem with that?
> Bush: No. I mean, as a matter of fact, I told the country we did that. And I also told them [national security officials] it was legal. We had legal opinions that enabled us to do it. And, no, I didn't have any problem at all trying to find out what Khalid Sheikh Mohammed knew.

Bush wrote in his 2010 memoir *Decision Points*: 'Had I not authorized waterboarding on senior al Qaeda leaders, I would have had to accept a greater risk that the country would be attacked. In the wake of 9/11, that was a risk I was unwilling to take.'

Route Irish: Fergus (Mark Womack, right) and Tommy (Russell Anderson), British mercenaries in Iraq.

The victim, Nelson [Frankie's unit leader in Iraq], tells him what he wants to hear, which is that he set up a hitman [Mad Max] to shoot Frankie because he'd got information Nelson didn't want revealed. Of course, it wasn't true. Actually, they just sent Frankie in a dodgy car onto the dangerous road, Route Irish, between Baghdad airport and the Green Zone time after time after time so in the end he'd get shot.

When Fergus is hearing what he's hearing when he's doing the waterboarding, he's losing control of himself. It's a sort of breakdown, and as it develops, he gets the feeling, 'I'm so compromised as an individual, I can't live with myself any more.' He can't be aware of his own redemption, and so, in the end, the only way he can live with himself is to kill himself. It's that paradox, isn't it? 'I can only live with myself if I'm dead.' He has self-loathing, I suppose, for what he has become, and he says all the time, 'I wish I could be like I was.'

There's that glimpse at the beginning of Fergus and Frankie in a ferry crossing the Mersey, when they were two young lads with the world in front of them. They're thinking, 'Where shall we go? Which countries? Oh, yeah, we'll join the army, see the world.' The army goes to Iraq, you get involved in killings. That's your skill. You can make a decent few bob by going there again to work for a private company, which is endorsed by the government with grants. Why not? And then that's where you end up. It just destroys them.

The Chinese army used waterboarding on British POWs during the Korean War, as the film Captured *(1959) shows. Soldiers of the British Parachute Regiment and detectives of the RUC Special Branch used it during interrogations of IRA suspects in Northern Ireland in the early 1970s. The waterboarding you filmed for* Route Irish *wasn't faked for the camera. Mark Womack (as Fergus) waterboarded Trevor Williams (as Nelson) for real. Was that a gruelling experience to film?*

It was tough. It had to be realistic, but obviously it had to be safe. We put protection over Trevor's mouth, and when Mark was pouring the water down, he wasn't always pouring it on the poor man's face. But even though we did it safely, Trevor still had nightmares and panic attacks afterwards. Yes, it was very difficult.

Did you feel the film succeeded in condemning the security firms, and the governments behind them, for their billion-dollar commercial exploitation of war, as opposed to condemning mercenaries on the ground like Fergus and Frankie?

I think Paul got the important balance right in not allowing the villain, Haynes, to get away with it, which is why he's blown up in the car at the end, but also in nailing the British security firms profiting from the war. Sometimes in American films and others made in the West, the bad guys suffer, but the system survives because it's the system itself that destroys them. We were very aware that we had to differentiate ourselves from that and not say that the system put things right, because the system is fully implicated.

How was your experience of filming in Jordan?

Films had obviously been made there before, and we filmed in an area that had previously been used for making war sequences, working with someone who'd arranged them before. So there was a well-trodden path for the process. I thought it would be daunting, but the people were terrific, as always. I mean, it's always a struggle, for me anyway. It wasn't like filming three people in a council flat. For one thing, we were out in the heat, so it was a very different experience. But it was OK. We went to a Palestinian refugee camp there as well, which was extraordinary. As far as the eye could see, as far as you could walk, there were little huts full of refugees who'd lived there all their lives. It was a very vivid image of what the Palestinians there have been through.

You've been especially critical of your direction of both Fatherland *and* Hidden Agenda. *Did you feel on* Route Irish *that you did a better job of handling the mechanics and tensions of a conspiracy thriller?*

My response is that a film is always the director's responsibility, and I didn't do *Fatherland* well at all. On *Hidden Agenda*, we made a mistake by putting two stories together as one. It would have been better as just one. *On Route Irish*, I think I did the later part better than the earlier part and certainly edited it better with Jonathan [Morris]. One problem is that the conventional thriller demands a certain kind of acting, which is not the temper of an observational film. On a conventional thriller, it's: 'Here's a clue, something unexpected, cut, what's the next scene?' Then you're somewhere else and something happens there, and you cut again. And that's not the temper we usually work to. Our style of film-making is usually more reflective. In a conventional thriller, there's a heavier narrative, and you have to emphasize the storyline and drive it. I think I got caught in the early part of *Route Irish* by not being tight enough. I don't know if that occurred to you?

I was carried along by Fergus's investigation, the contrast between hi-tech and old-fashioned detective work, his burrowing into those dark corners of Liverpool, and the disorienting flashbacks to Iraq, with all that light. Mark Womack is very strong; so is Andrea Lowe as Rachel.

It was a difficult part for Andrea because she doesn't have much agency in the story. I think we'd imagined a more complex connection between Rachel and Fergus. Again, it was something I didn't get quite right. In the beginning, they should have had a stronger relationship before either Frankie had interrupted it or she'd simply become close to him and become his partner. If I'd sufficiently established that Fergus and Rachel had been more involved to start with, there would have been something to reawaken at the end.

There's a sadomasochistic quality to their relationship, which struck me as psychologically accurate, given that they're grieving for the same man. It's tangled up with Fergus's guilt over Frankie and what Frankie felt for him.

Yes, it's a complex relationship, and I didn't quite pull that off. It was nothing to do with the actors. They did everything that they could. It was a directorial thing.

Did you get complaints from government figures about Route Irish?

It didn't get much screen time. They usually keep their heads down on things like this. They've learned the lesson that they get more attention for complaining than for what it is they're complaining about. I don't think it's a film they would have loved. They won't be showing it when they're at the Cenotaph on Remembrance Day.

CHAPTER 12

The People's Game

Looking for Eric, Another City: A Week in the Life of Bath's Football Club

'Eric Cantona or Angelina Jolie? They've both used it,' Loach said with a smile, when the editor of this book asked to use the WC in Sixteen Films' modest offices near Wardour Street, in Soho, London, before the second set of interviews began. The question – unlikely to produce a materialization, however answered – was prompted by the French ex-footballer-turned-actor and the American actor–film-maker having visited Loach on separate occasions: Cantona for meetings to discuss their collaboration on 2009's *Looking for Eric*; Jolie (a Loach admirer) to seek professional advice as she went about making films with a social conscience. Recorded below, Loach's comment on how he responds differently to great footballers and people in his own industry is instructive.

Whether subject matter or story or character detail, football is a social force to be reckoned with in Loach's films. It is a working-class passion not to be denied in *The Golden Vision*, the 1968 Neville Smith-scripted docudrama about a group of fervent Everton supporters and the players of Harry Catterick's successful team, some of whom Loach interviewed on camera.

If football brings out the worst in bullying games master Mr Sugden (Brian Glover) in *Kes*, the sequence on the school pitch (with its Brechtian scoreline caption) is deservedly famous. It's not just a comic interlude, but a metaphor for the education authorities' callous neglect of working-class kids. Mr Sugden's antipathy towards hapless goalie Billy Casper (David Bradley) contrasts with the respect his colleague Mr Farthing (Colin Welland) shows Billy for tending and training a kestrel.

In terms of football, Sugden's opposite is the recovering alcoholic Joe (Peter Mullan) in *My Name Is Joe*, who coaches the younger lads in his Glasgow housing scheme's team. The players' theft from a sports shop of enough Brazil national kits for the entire team – Joe unwittingly acting as getaway driver – provides a moment of hilarity in a film that addresses heroin addiction and its exploitation by organized crime in one of Britain's most socially deprived cities.

It's unsurprising to learn that the County Durham publican TJ in *The Old Oak* has also been a local football coach – a sign of his communal values. TJ's friendship with the newly arrived Syrian refugee Yara (Ebla Mari) is triggered by a drunk (Neil Leiper) in a black-and-white-striped Newcastle United shirt breaking her camera. Loach previously cast Dave Turner, who plays TJ, as a belligerent Newcastle diehard – or 'Magpie' – in *Sorry We Missed You*. He trades barbs with Mancunian delivery man Ricky (Kris Hitchen), who has had the temerity to show up with a package while wearing the shirt of his beloved Manchester United.

At the start of *Ae Fond Kiss*, a billboard for the *Daily Record* tabloid carrying the headline 'Church Tells Celtic Fans No Nookie in Seville' issues a warning to the 80,000 Catholics travelling to the Spanish city – to see their team's May 2003 UEFA Cup Final match against Porto – not to visit brothels. In keeping with the film's attitude to the parish priest who later denies the Irish Catholic music teacher Roisin (Eva Birthistle) a necessary certificate because she's living with her Muslim boyfriend, Casim (Atta Yaqub), a boxer dog urinates on the billboard. Moments later, Casim's younger sister, Tahara (Shabana Akhtar Bakhsh), the most fully assimilated member of their Glaswegian Pakistani family, gives a witty speech at her Catholic high school, during which she reveals that she's been wearing under her blouse the royal blue shirt of Rangers – traditionally, the Protestant club in sectarian rivalry with Celtic.

In Loach's segment of *Tickets*, written by Celtic supporter Laverty, a trio of young Glaswegians played by Martin Compston (who played professionally for Greenock Morton), Gary Maitland and William Ruane head by train to Rome for a European Champions League match. Naturally wearing their team's green and white hoops, they encounter a younger Albanian boy clad in David Beckham's Manchester United shirt. It is not only an excuse for Laverty to have one of the lads make a 'Golden

Balls'* quip, but leads to the three risking arrest by saving the boy from deportation by giving him one of their train tickets. One of the beleaguered railwaymen in *The Navigators* wears a Sheffield Wednesday shirt; the two unemployed lads in *Looks and Smiles* attend a Sheffield United game – a break from the dole queue. Football puts 'hope in your hearts', to quote Liverpool FC's anthem, so it resonates in the predominantly masculine environments of Loach's films about the decline of industrial work, though the director is wary about categorizing it as a proletarian sport.

Anyone faced with a choice between going to see a brainless Hollywood movie or attending a football match on a Saturday afternoon would do well to seek out *Happy Ending*. This is the cheeky three-minute satire Loach and Laverty contributed to the anthology film *To Each His Own Cinema* (2007), which Gilles Jacob commissioned for the sixtieth anniversary of the Cannes Film Festival. The short's spine-tingling final sound effect sucks its father-and-son duo towards a place of worship.

Loach has for fifty years been a fan and occasional programme-seller for the semi-professional Somerset club Bath City, whose games he watches from the terraces. Also the honorary president of the club's foundation, he was a prominent voice in its move towards community ownership. In the autumn of 2016, the Supporters' Society raised enough money to become the club's controlling shareholder, holding 55 per cent of its voting rights and a majority of seats on the board. Early in the fans' struggle to become owners of the club, based since 1932 at Twerton Park, in a working-class suburb of Bath, Loach directed and Rebecca O'Brien produced the affectionate twenty-six-minute documentary *Another City: A Week in the Life of Bath's Football Club* (1998). It includes bracing excerpts from matches, archival footage, team meetings, interviews with players and fans involved in the ownership initiative, and anecdotes told by club legends Malcolm Allison and Tony Book during a celebratory promotional week.

---

* Victoria Beckham disclosed her nickname for her husband, which she gave him for improving his media image, on the *Parkinson* talk show that aired on 22 September 2001. Seized on by the British tabloids, the nickname enhanced the celebrity couple's marketability.

Among *The Golden Vision*'s actors, Neville Smith and Bill Dean were Evertonians. Ken Jones started out as an Everton fan but, risking both blue and red ire, later also followed the club's Merseyside rivals across Stanley Park. When a fan of Leeds United's Eric Cantona moved across the Pennines after Cantona signed for Manchester United in 1992, he not only became a friend of the virtuosic French forward, but gave him an idea for a film about fan obsession that Cantona, who became a film actor after quitting football in 1997, later brought to Loach. As excited to work with Cantona – known for his arcane philosophical pronouncements – as Loach, Paul Laverty reworked his idea (about a French fan who gives up everything to follow Cantona in England) for the script of *Looking for Eric*, which proved Sixteen Films' most popular comedy.

Its theme is the need for teamwork, an ideal the depressed Manchester postman Eric Bishop (Steve Evets) learns to trust while overcoming his demons. Eric crashes his car after driving the wrong way round a roundabout. His daughter, Sam (Lucy-Jo Hudson), a hard-working single mother and student, like Liam's steadfast sister (Annmarie Fulton) in *Sweet Sixteen*, had asked Eric to pick up her infant, his granddaughter Daisy, from his estranged wife Lily (Stephanie Bishop), who babysits her. The thought of seeing Lily for the first time in nearly thirty years caused Eric to panic.

A later flashback shows that Eric (played in his late teens by Matthew McNulty) and Lily (Laura Ainsworth) met and fell in love at a rock 'n' roll dance contest in 1979, when he was sporting American-made blue suede shoes and feeling relatively confident. They married and became parents, but Eric abandoned Lily and Sam after having a panic attack at the baby's christening. Consumed by guilt and regret, he lives in a cramped terraced house with his unruly teenage stepsons, Ryan (Gerard Kearns) and Jess (Stefan Gumbs), from another relationship. Eric's only solace in his passion for Manchester United. He worships retired United idol Cantona and sometimes converses with the poster of him that dominates his bedroom.

Eric's workmates gather to help him with an informal group therapy session, their ringleader, Meatballs (John Henshaw), drawing on a self-help book, with its 'possibility generator'. After Eric smokes cannabis he has pinched from one of his stepsons, he hallucinates Cantona (playing himself) into existence. (In an earlier touch of magical realism, rare in Loach's films, Ken Jones's Joe Horrigan, in *The Golden Vision*, fantasizes scoring a goal for Everton and being mobbed by the team's real players.) Cantona becomes Eric's guardian angel, dispensing wisdom and telling him to clean himself up and visit Lily to apologize to her. When Eric and Lily meet, he realizes he still loves her.

The sleek Mercedes that picks up Ryan to take him to a Manchester United Champions League tie against Barcelona raises Eric's suspicions about the boy's acquaintances. He and Meatballs watch the match in a pub, where their friend Spleen (Justin Moorhouse), who has switched his allegiance to FC United of Manchester, berates Manchester United loyalists. FC United is the fan-owned club founded in 2005 by Manchester United supporters angered by the club's takeover by the American billionaire Malcolm Glazer (1928–2014), in a deal that loaded it with debt and enabled his six children to extract massive dividends. Aligning *Looking for Eric* with *Another City*, the pub argument posits common ownership as the alternative to ruthless capitalist exploitation of a beloved working-class institution.

Eric returns from the pub to see Ryan being beaten up by the gangster Zac (Steve Marsh), a rich, intimidating drug lord who employs teenagers as lackeys, as do *My Name Is Joe*'s McGowan and *Sweet Sixteen*'s Tony Douglas. Cantona instructs Eric to start disciplining his stepsons and be braver in his decision-making, sharing with him that his best moment as a footballer was not scoring a goal, but making an audaciously risky pass that enabled United left-back Denis Irwin to score against Tottenham Hotspur in 1993. 'What if he'd have missed?' Eric asks him. 'You have to trust your teammates – always,' Cantona says. 'If not, we are lost.' Another risk Cantona took was digging deep within himself, as he tells Eric, and learning to play the trumpet, after he was banned from playing football for nine months after notoriously karate-kicking an abusive Crystal Palace supporter. To prove it, he scratchily plays 'La Marseillaise' to Eric.

Teamwork and solidarity come into full force after Eric finds the incriminating handgun that Zac has forced Ryan to hide in his room. He realizes that he has to break Zac's hold on Ryan. Advised by Cantona to play on the gangster's fears, Eric, his mates and a large party of Manchester United fans don Eric Cantona masks and march on Zac's house, smash his Mercedes, television and furniture, spray red paint on him and his lieutenant, and threaten to post footage of this humiliation on YouTube. With Zac defeated, one of the marchers pulls off his Cantona mask to reveal that he is Cantona himself.

Ryan and Jess visit the hospital where Lily works as a nurse and tell her about Eric's courage in rescuing Ryan. Cantona's mentoring of Eric – as imagined by him – has, meanwhile, enabled Lily to look kindly on him again. When she and Eric, his mates and Ryan and Jess come to celebrate Sam's graduation – they line up for a 'team' photograph – it seems likely that Eric, who's wearing his talismanic blue suede shoes, and Lily will become close again. United they stand.

GRAHAM FULLER: *In* Looking for Eric, *the postman Eric Bishop, a Manchester United fanatic, conjures up the United legend Eric Cantona as a figment of his imagination, and Cantona becomes his philosophical adviser, as Humphrey Bogart does for the Woody Allen character in* Play It Again, Sam *(1972). Cantona and a French producer originally approached you about doing a different film, didn't they?*

KEN LOACH: Yes. It was very funny. I had a call a year before I met Eric, and the message on my phone said 'Eric Cantona' is trying to get in touch, but it wasn't in Eric's voice. I thought, 'This is a piss-take.' I tried to phone back, and nothing came of it. And then the French producer Pascal Caucheteux, whom we've worked with ever since, came in with Vincent Maraval from Wild Bunch, who's an old friend. Pascal said he'd been contacted by Eric about making a film. So Eric came to our office, and we met him. I think we were quite shy of each other. I'm not impressed by film people at all, but football is something else, and Eric Cantona was the supreme footballer of his time. So I think there was a certain apprehension on both our parts. Anyway, we sat around the table downstairs and soon got chatting. Eric was interested in doing a film about his relationship to the fans and had a story. Obviously, I spoke to Paul, who's a great football fan, like me. Normally, you start a film because you feel you have to tell a story, but this was different because it came from Eric and was a unique opportunity. I went to a game with Eric . . .

I watched it on TV – Manchester United against Roma in the Champions League (9 April 2008).* The camera spotted Cantona, and the commentator remarked on him, but not you. I said, 'Just a minute – that's Ken Loach with Cantona!'

How funny! Arriving at the ground with Eric, I saw grown men weeping, literally weeping, when they saw him. The crowd was singing the Cantona songs before they realized he was there, and this was many years after he'd left. Then, of course, when they realized he was there, the wave of emotion across Old Trafford was extraordinary.

Paul had a thought about the film we could make and spent a long time talking to Eric, just trying to have an easy relationship with him to understand his ideas and how he thought and getting the rhythm of his speech. Then Paul had this idea of the other Eric, who was a failure in every aspect of his life, even a failed postman [*laughs*]. The idea was the contrast between him and Eric, this supremely confident, beautiful man, the greatest footballer of his generation, or the greatest footballer of the time in the fans' imagination. The interaction between them became the basis of the film, and the story grew out of that.

Little Eric's marriage has failed, his stepsons are out of control, his place is a wreck. Nothing had worked for him. After smoking a cigarette, into which he's mixed an illegal substance found in his stepsons' room, he imagines Eric Cantona is with him. As you say, their relationship is a figment of his imagination, but Eric Cantona assumes an independence in the film and gives him advice and shows him the way. That's the comedy of the film, but one of Little Eric's stepsons has real problems, and Big Eric gives Little Eric the strength to fight back.

There's a flashback to postman Eric and his future wife Lily meeting at a rock 'n' roll dance contest when they were young, a scene

---

* See Simon Hattenstone, 'The Awkward Squad', *Guardian*, 8 May 2009.

that shows he once had some fire in his belly. But in the film's present tense they've been separated for years because he abandoned Lily and their daughter Sam just after she was born. They begin to draw together again through sharing the care of their granddaughter while Sam is trying to finish her degree. Do you see it as a film about healing?

It's about how Little Eric puts his life back together again. Big Eric gives him some advice on that, as a man who could obviously be successful with women, if he so chose, and helps him rediscover his confidence and capacity to cope, so that he can deal with people and say no when he needs to say no and not allow people to exploit him.

Is Steve Evets a Manchester United fan?

I don't know. He was happy to become one. 'Evets', of course, is 'Steve' backwards. His real name, Steve Murphy, was already used by an actor on Equity's books. Steve was a musician, basically,* a talented, very funny man with a surreal sense of humour. He was imaginative in the part and very easy to work with. There's a warmth and frailty in him that lets you see that, underneath everything and all the mistakes he's made, Little Eric is a good guy. Big Eric enables him to get on his feet again and find the affection that he lost through his own stupidity, I suppose, and through the chaos. It's a very simple story.

John Henshaw, who plays postman Eric's friend, colleague and fellow Manchester United fan Meatballs – the one who comes up with the self-help-derived 'possibility generator' – is a lifelong Manchester City supporter . . .

Yes, John really struggled with that [*laughs*].

I believe Paul incorporated some of Cantona's aphorisms into the script?

Yes – the wisdom of Eric Cantona. He made some up as well. He took delight in writing little epigrams that he knew Eric would not

---

* Evets played bass with The Fall, Mark E. Smith's Manchester-based post-punk band, from 2000 to 2002.

Ken Loach and Eric Cantona during the filming of *Looking for Eric*. 'He's a team player,' Loach says of the ex-footballer's contribution to the film.

be able to say. The classic one – we fell about as Eric tried to say it – was, 'He who sows thistles shall reap prickles,' which, of course, is very hard for a Frenchman to say. That was a great amusement, shared by Eric, who tried to get his tongue around this thing that was impossible for him to say.

Was Cantona easy to work with?

Yes, he's a team player. Under Alex Ferguson at Manchester United, he was a natural team player anyway, so he was just one of the gang and joined in the fun. He's a great giggler and enjoyed making fun of his public persona, which I think he'd done all along when he was playing football. He took the mickey out of the press. But he had a real connection to the genuine fans. He's a lovely man. We've stayed in touch. When I've been attacked, he's done everything he could and got some seriously influential people from football to support me. So he is a good friend. I wouldn't say he's political in the way Paul and I are, but he's very principled and speaks very simply. If he has a principle, you will never shake him, which is terrific.

Cantona's a good sport in the film. The script refers to his darkest hour, when he famously karate-kicked a Crystal Palace fan who abused him. He'd acted in a few films before, of course. He was a dignified presence in Elizabeth *(1998) and memorable in* The Children of the Marshland *(1999).*

Because I hadn't worked with him before, I thought, 'I'm going to have to do a bit of improvisation with him first so that we know we can work together.' John Henshaw and Justin Moorhouse came along to a little practice with Eric in a room in Manchester, and I set up a little improvisation. The idea was that they were three workmates. I said, 'Let's imagine that one of you' – I think it was Justin – 'is in domestic trouble. Your wife's fed up and she's left you – you're a pain in the neck and you've been caught with a woman at work. You want your wife to come back to you, so you put the problem to Eric and John, and they talk it through with you and give you advice.' And they all chipped in and it was quite funny, and it was obvious Eric could do it. At one point, Justin collapsed laughing and said, 'I can't believe I'm discussing marital arrangements with Eric Cantona.' The whole thing was monumentally absurd.

Looking for Eric *is more than a domestic comedy. Postman Eric's second wife left him with the two teenage stepsons. He's had to become both their mother and father, and, despite his limitations, he does his best for them. He doesn't know what to do when one of the boys gets involved with a gangster, but Meatballs rallies their mates and other Manchester United fans to help. The film celebrates teamwork, a vital theme in your films.*

Yes. When Big Eric is talking about his favourite moment as a player, it isn't an individual goal he scored, it's a pass. He says, 'You must trust your teammates, always.' It's about the collective, the group, not the individual. The point is, trust your friends, and together you can make a wrong right. It's the opposite of one man with a gun can solve it for you.

With Little Eric being a postman, were you consciously drawing on British postal workers' long history of industrial action?

No. That would have been too manipulative. Referring to the postal disputes would be us making a point to the audience rather than part of the story.

Another – probably far-fetched – idea that occurred to me was triggered by the memory that the United crowd's 'ooh-aah Cantona' chant was sung to the tune of 'La Marseillaise'. When the fans in the film raid the gangster's house in their Cantona masks, are they storming another Bastille?

You're reading too much into it [*laughs*]. They're just raiding his house.

At the end of The Golden Vision, *the Everton fan played by Ken Jones fantasizes (or dreams) of scoring a goal for them. Did that occur to you or Paul when you were conceiving the fantasy aspects of* Looking for Eric?

That was another very enjoyable film to make and it was very well written by Neville Smith, but I doubt Paul's ever seen it, and I never speak to him about other films. The golden rule is that you always go back to basic research and what you know to be true, and then everything springs from that.

As a predominantly realist director, you've rarely incorporated fantasy elements in your films.

The coexistence of fantasy with straightforward realism in a realistic film is awkward, for obvious reasons. It's not an easy match of styles, but you just hope the audience will make that leap with you.

How did you make the magical realism work in practice?

I wanted to keep it a secret from Steve Evets that Eric Cantona was going to be in the film until he appeared in Little Eric's room. We were filming in a bedroom in this comparatively small terrace house. Eric, who's a big lad, was secreted in another room. We'd just done a scene, and Eric was going to appear in the next one. I said to Steve, who was a smoker, 'Steve, you can have a cigarette. We've just got to rejig the lights.' So Steve went outside, Eric came

Eric Cantona as himself (left) and Steve Evets, as postman Eric Bishop, in a poster for *Looking for Eric*.

in, and we put a black cloth over the camera in the corner of the room, and Eric crept under it. Then Steve came back in.

At the crucial moment, Eric stepped out and was behind Steve's head. Steve spoke his line and was facing away from Eric when Eric spoke. The first take didn't quite work because Steve thought Eric was one of the French–Belgian crew that we had. I said to Steve, 'You have to turn round and see him.' And when he did, he was completely stunned, just transfixed, when he saw Eric there for the first time. It was a sweet moment, because I don't think he'd met him before that.

Making the film was a happy experience?

A very happy experience, with a lovely cast. All films are exhausting to do, but we had good fun doing it with Steve, John Henshaw, Justin Moorhouse and all the comics in the post office team. Comics are always great to work with because they begin laughing at eight o'clock in the morning and they're still laughing at six at night, with a bit of luck.

Until the mid-1960s, Manchester United was, in spirit, if not in reality, a football club with a communal, local identity. Any lingering sense of that ended when the American billionaire Malcolm Glazer and his family bought it in 2005. In Looking for Eric, *it's FC United* that carries the banner for football as the people's game.*

The sad thing is that the people who started FC United were passionate Manchester United supporters. They just couldn't stand having the club taken away from them. Also important is the whole image of a celebrity footballer. On the one hand, there's hero worship, and, on the other, there's that affection for a footballer who is just a working-class bloke like themselves. That relationship is very human.

Club ownership by foreign billionaires threatens to turn football into an elite sport. The European Super League, with no

---

* Football Club United of Manchester, based in Moston, was founded in 2006 by Manchester United supporters alienated by the Glazers' ownership. Completely fan-owned, FC United competes in the Premier Division of the Northern Premier League (as of the 2024–5 season).

promotion and relegation, that was proposed in 2021 would have violated the pyramidal structure of the national leagues. You'd never get a Luton Town or a Brentford in the Super League. If – or when – it comes about, people who have supported their teams all their lives will be priced out of attending live games. If that wasn't bad enough, there's the sportswashing of human-rights abuses by the Saudi sovereign fund's ownership of Newcastle United and the Abu Dhabi United Group's ownership of Manchester City. This leads us back to Another City *(subtitled* A Week in the Life of Bath's Football Club*), your 1998 film about your local team, Bath City.*

It's just a little half-hour film I made for the local TV station that tells a few good stories about the club. It was good fun to make. I got into the dressing room with the players and listened to the manager talk, which is a fan's dream. A French company bought the film, and the club captain, Nick Brooks, and I went to France for a day to do some press. It was remarkable – a bizarre experience – to see the captain of a non-league football club talking about it to French journalists near Gare du Nord.

Why did you make the film?

I did it when a group of us – supporters from the terraces – became directors on the board. There was a previous owner who was pretty useless, but he was dissatisfied with the board, which was also pretty useless, and he wanted to get rid of it. It was arranged that a group of supporters would take over the board, which we did. Some of the people involved had no concept of how to run the club, and the board fell apart because we had no power over big decisions, which were always made by the owner. Anyway, we administered the board on behalf of this owner, who was a local businessman. I'm not sure why he owned it, because he wasn't a passionate football supporter. Most of the things that needed to be done we couldn't do because of his control, but we did do a relaunch and had a relaunch week, with all kinds of initiatives. One was an event where some of the old players and managers who had become famous returned to the club for a day, so I filmed that.

The film's star turns include Malcolm Allison, still exuding the old charisma, who managed Bath (1963–4), and Tony Book, a Bath bricklayer and the team captain (1962–4). Allison brought Book to Plymouth Argyle when he was manager, then to Manchester City when he was Joe Mercer's assistant. Book captained City to four major trophies under Mercer and Allison. You filmed him telling a great story about 'Big Mal''s gambling habit.

Allison was the big catch, but I didn't make enough of him or his stories in the film. He said that on the first day he arrived at the club, he didn't know what to do. So he hung about for a bit and looked through some of the paperwork, and then he went to the pictures. I forget which film he said he saw, but he said it was excellent [*laughs*]. That was his first day in his first job as a manager. As a non-league club, they trained only two nights a week, so the daily routine of a professional club wasn't there yet, but Allison doubled the training, and the team started to do well.

He was on great form and totally beguiling at the event. He talked all day and all evening, and then tried to lure some of the weaker spirits to go and have a few beers with him. I think he was still standing when they were under the table. It was an amazing evening. Brian Godfrey, the player–manager who nearly took us into the Football League in 1978, was there. So was the local lad, Alan Skirton, who went on to play for Arsenal. And, as you say, Tony Book, who comes from a very old Twerton family.

The great thing about Bath City – and it's still the case now – is its ground, which is in the old working-class area of Twerton. That's why we called the film *Another City*. It's the city that the tourists don't see. It's always been the poor area, though now, of course, most of the kids who were born there can't live there because house prices are so high. It has all the problems that other poor areas in other cities have. There are a number of charities and good people working there.

Does Bath City have majority fan ownership now?

We're only partly community-owned at the moment, but, of course, the club should be completely. We got part of the way there at the time, but we had financial problems and were partly bailed out by a benefactor, who bought a fair number of shares to get us over the limit and gave their voting power to the Bath City Supporters Society, which owned [sufficient shares] for the supporters to have the voting majority now.

The club still has debts, though they're not as high as Everton, say. Can fan ownership keep Bath City afloat?

This is a problem because the thing about private owners is that they're usually wealthy and can bail a club out, if they choose. The group of businessmen who own shares in the club aren't that wealthy. They have put their hands in their pockets to keep it afloat, but now it is in quite considerable debt. There are no more private loans coming in. A lot of supporters volunteer – you know, 'I'll operate a turnstile,' 'I'll sell programmes,' 'I'll help steward the crowds,' 'I'll serve behind the tea bar,' all kinds of things at that level of organization. They're certainly clever and sharp, but they don't have managerial experience in business or know how to deal with debt, and even if they did, the resources aren't there. Nobody's got deep pockets. You can raise a certain amount of money through community activities, but that goes to help keep the club afloat anyway. Almost all football clubs are losing money on the playing side, so you have to have a source of income alongside that to balance your expenditure. But if you're carrying a burden of debt in addition to that, it's very hard to chip away at it. So that's an ongoing issue.

Your conversations with the team recall those with Everton players in The Golden Vision, *though the Bath players are more relaxed.*

It was a similar experience. The Bath players were a great bunch, constantly taking the mickey out of each other. I hadn't seen [the film] since I made it, so I watched it again when I knew we were going to talk about it. I was struck by the fact that we had a player called Rob Skidmore – an unfortunate name for a footballer [*laughs*]. Then, in the part where the players describe the jobs they do outside football, Rob says he works for the Ministry of Defence, 'but I'm not supposed to say that'. And everyone collapsed in laughter. If any of the players in the team were to be responsible for national security, Rob was the least likely. They were just nice lads really, good mates, and that's one of the joys of smaller football clubs. We've been very lucky with the spirit of the club. If we're on a particularly bad run, and then you have a real stinker of a game, there might be the occasional boo or jeer or whatever, but there's nothing like the abuse you get with the big clubs in the Premier League. The crowd always gives a big round of applause for effort and commitment. As long as the supporters see that, they'll cheer you to the echo. It's a very friendly atmosphere.

I've experienced the same at Stevenage FC, where the Supporters' Association has a golden-share veto over home colours and the location of the stadium. Taken together, Looking for Eric *and* Another City *make a persuasive case for community ownership of football clubs, which works successfully in the German Bundesliga, with its '50 + 1' (50 per cent plus one share) ownership by member associations.*

Yes, the German model of club ownership builds a strong connection to local people and their families. The idea that the major clubs should be owned by foreign billionaires and nation states is clearly wrong. It can't go on and on. Teams were once supported by local people in their towns and cities. Now they're global brands, and the owners regard the supporters as decoration in the grounds. Their real income comes from television and merchandise. The product the clubs sell is full stadiums with passionate supporters, but the fans are part of what is sold rather than being the owners and main protectors of a club.

The great quality of all these clubs is their connection to their locality. They represent that town, that city or that part of the city, each of which has a very distinct character that comes from the supporters. Newcastle is a case in point because it has such a strong local identity, and the character of Newcastle United is drawn directly from the Geordies. The anomaly of the club being owned by a foreign state is anathema, which is very sad. The problem comes because the money from football is so huge that investors naturally see it as a source of revenue or, in the case of certain countries, a source of kudos to cover up unacceptable practices. They bargain that their identification with a great football club that people love and take pride in mitigates the effect of their violation of human rights, their reckless pursuit of profit or anything else they do that people wouldn't view so kindly.

You directed the courtroom re-enactments for Franny Armstrong's documentary McLibel: Two Worlds Collide *(1997). I was reminded of sportswashing by the film's commentary on how McDonald's manipulated its image and child-friendly advertising of unhealthy fast food that – as claimed by the environmental activists Helen Steel and David Morris, the defendants in the case – was unethically produced, harming animals and violating workers' rights.*

I had little to do with the film, though I was happy to be identified with it because it made very good points. I just found two or three actor friends who read some lines. The film belongs to the two film-makers,[*] and I wouldn't want to detract from their work. I was just on the outskirts, giving a small helping hand.

Do you think the legal help Keir Starmer gave Steel and Morris was one of the better things he's done?

Those two were always very popular figures for their heroic stand against McDonald's – certainly among people of the left and campaigners for the environment and against junk food – so Starmer didn't risk anything by supporting them.

Starmer seems to have been on a journey. He may have been an opportunist all along. Certainly, now I think he's revealed as a shallow opportunist whose principles disappeared the closer he got to power. Has he ever had any principles? I don't know. He was Director of Public Prosecutions [2008–13] when Julian Assange was first detained [in 2010]. He could have done far more, but I think he's always bent with the wind.

Now we see Starmer's indifference to the terrible suffering of the Palestinians. He has nothing to say . . . nothing to say. In fact, he petitioned the Speaker of the House of Commons [Lindsay Hoyle], enabling the Labour Party to put forward a watered-down version of the SNP's motion – a motion Labour would have found very difficult not to vote for and could well have passed, had it been debated – condemning the collective punishment meted out to the Palestinians in Gaza. Collective punishment, of course, is a crime against international law, and consequences would have followed. Starmer didn't want Labour to have to vote on that, so he had the

---

[*] Producer–director Armstrong and assistant producer Sharon Davey.

alternative motion introduced, which meant the motion proposed by the SNP fell.* It saved Starmer's Labour Party from having to show whether they accepted his evasive action on collective punishment.† It was really shocking trading of Commons business.

You said in a recent Variety *interview‡ that in the past you'd been interested in making a film about Palestine. Now that the death toll in Gaza is catastrophic, what do you think can be done to stop the killing? Protests are crucial, but they won't stop the killing.*

The United Nations should send in a task force to intervene, separate the combatants and instruct Israel to withdraw from Palestinian land. That's what should happen, but as long as America and Britain refuse to support the United Nations wholeheartedly, then the United Nations is too politically weak to do that. So it needs a global authority to step in, knowing it has support across the world, and say that this is what must happen. It's the only way to solve issues, I think, and the United Nations has done it before.

In this case, it means Israel ultimately withdrawing from all the occupied territories, going back to the 1948 borders and allowing Palestine to be recognized as a state and to contribute as one. Then there will be a proper negotiation between two states – both with security issues, both with long-term interests – to find a way for both sides to live in peace.

---

* Whereas the SNP motion would have called for 'an immediate ceasefire in Gaza and Israel . . . and an end to the collective punishment of the Palestinian people', the Labour motion called for 'an immediate humanitarian ceasefire'.
† The debate on 21 February 2024 ended with many Conservatives and SNP members walking out of the House of Commons. The Labour version of the ceasefire motion passed on a voice vote.
‡ In an article by Alex Ritman published in *Variety* on 2 April 2024, Loach said: '[Palestine] was a subject that I would have liked to have worked on, but I didn't quite know how to tackle it. It would have had to be a documentary, but it was a big project and certainly beyond me for the last decade.'

CHAPTER 13

Labour Gains and Pains

The Spirit of '45, Clement Attlee, Aneurin Bevan, Tony Benn, Jeremy Corbyn, Keir Starmer

Loach's documentary *The Spirit of '45* (2013) looked back to the temporary realization of common ownership, via nationalization, of Britain's major industries by Clement Attlee's post-war Labour government and forward to how it might be restored. The film was prescient. Jeremy Corbyn's election in 2015 as Labour Party leader reawakened the spirit of '45 among the rapidly increasing party membership. The possibility of a UK governed along socialist lines seemed plausible after Labour narrowed the Conservative Party's majority in the 2017 general election, but was ended by Labour's rout in the 2019 election. The Labour Together group attributed the defeat to Corbyn's declining popularity following his mishandling of allegations of anti-Semitism within the party, an erroneous belief that he supported terrorism, Labour's evasive attitude to Brexit and its unrealistic or unaffordable policies.* Indisputably, Corbyn had been traduced by the right-wing press and his opponents on the left. Still, there had been a moment of hope for his support base.

In 1945, hope resided not in the kind of militancy that emerged in Britain following the Russian Revolution, but in the idea that the people who had won the Second World War together could build the peace together. Constructed from archival footage and on-camera oral reminiscences of socialist front-liners who were mostly in their eighties and nineties when they were filmed, *The Spirit of '45* presents the halcyon moment when equitability seemed as valid a prospect as those of jobs, free medical care and good housing

---

* Peter Walker, 'Key Points from Review of 2019 Labour Election Defeat', *Guardian*, 18 June 2020.

becoming available to all. After describing the despair of the 1930s, when the free-market economy benefited only the elite, and touching on the Blitz and VE Day, the film celebrates Labour's landslide victory two months later, on 5 July, Attlee taking power with the party's first electoral majority. Miners weeping with joy is one of the more vivid images recalled by a witness.

In depicting the run-up to the election, Loach pointedly cuts in footage of Winston Churchill, the wartime coalition leader and Conservative candidate, looking confused as he's heckled by a crowd. Troubled by his reading of Friedrich Hayek's *The Road to Serfdom* (1944), Churchill did not endear himself to voters by making the alarmist assertion in his first election broadcast that 'No Socialist Government conducting the entire life and industry of the country could afford to allow free, sharp, or violently worded expressions of public discontent. They would have to fall back on some form of Gestapo . . .'

The blueprint for the welfare state was drawn up by the liberal social economist Sir William Beveridge (1879–1963), who had been instrumental in implementing labour exchanges (1909) and state insurance for the unemployed (1911). Commissioned by the wartime coalition government, Beveridge's 1942 report 'Social Insurance and Allied Services' recommended expanding national insurance contributions, which would enable the payment of benefits to people who were unemployed, sick, retired and widowed, the aim being to eliminate 'idleness, ignorance, disease, squalor and want'. The report further recommended the introduction of 'comprehensive health and rehabilitation services for prevention and cure of diseases', which was realized in 1948 by Labour minister of health Aneurin Bevan's creation of the National Health Service. Attlee's government also nationalized utilities, transportation and the mining and docking industries. These measures and the expansion of council housing were received as practical manna by the ageing survivors of the inter-war slump, returning combatants and home-front workers.

Loach's film logs the successive acts of nationalization without triumphalism, but offers few statistics (fewer, for example, than his groundbreaking 1966 housing docudrama *Cathy Come Home*). We learn that after the NHS Act passed, some people got spectacles and dentures for the first time. This section of the film ends with footage of the summer 1951 Festival of Britain. That October, Churchill returned to power: the Conservatives were elected with a seventeen-seat majority, despite losing the popular vote. After acknowledging Labour's achievement of full employment and a functioning National Health Service under Attlee, Loach logs the Thatcher government's aggressive privatizing of the key industries, which ended the era of public ownership. The concertina structure of the movie is dramatically powerful.

The Spirit of '45 is invaluable for the revealing and deeply moving testimony of the interviewees. Ninety-year-old Eileen Thompson, a nurse whose hospital was bombed during the Blitz, recalls accompanying her union organizer father, with his orange box, from their home in the slums of Liverpool's 'poverty park' to the docks. The shop steward and communist activist Sam Watts, an eighty-eight-year-old Liverpudlian, remembers sleeping with his siblings in a vermin-infested bed in 'a house of death' in the 1920s and '30s; he was politicized in his mid-twenties, he says, by the first book he ever read – Robert Tressell's *The Ragged Trousered Philanthropists*. Ray Davies, eighty-three, a Welsh left-wing activist and miner's son, himself a much-injured former miner and steelworker, was thirteen and one of eight children when he was politicized by the death of his mother for want of an abortion. There are many more.

Loach's off-camera interviewing is discreet; one of his interviewees calls him 'Ken', but we neither see nor hear him. His evocative calibration of the footage – which concludes with a spectacular colour rendering of the VE Day image that started the film – makes one wish there was more to come; Loach, in fact, has hinted that he might recut the film to integrate and contextualize Corbyn's role in reviving the aspiration for a fairer, more egalitarian Britain.

GRAHAM FULLER: The Spirit of '45 *captures the voices and faces of people who endured extreme poverty in Britain in the 1920s and '30s, were on the front line of the political struggle and lived to vote in a government that put people's welfare first. It's an important act of memorialization because most of them are gone now.*

KEN LOACH: They were remarkable, and it was a real privilege to meet them. Sam Watts, the Liverpudlian in the flat cap in the pub, told brilliant stories. Maybe [other interviews with them] exist in an archive somewhere, but there has been little interest otherwise in reviving them. It's the old story, you know – working-class history is not told properly.

The film was timely because the election of David Cameron as prime minister in 2010 had reasserted the grip the Old Etonian upper-class network has on British politics. By looking back at what Clement Attlee's government accomplished, were you also looking forward to what might be possible again, with the right attitudes and leadership?

That's the implication of the film. The ending isn't satisfactory, because shortly afterwards Jeremy Corbyn became leader of the Labour Party, with, as I've said, the project of re-establishing the welfare state, based on the development of the principle of the 1945 settlement, but, of course, he was never given the opportunity to fulfil it. So, yes, the film was to remind people that, before Thatcher, we owned all the public services and utilities and a large part of the infrastructure of the country, and it had worked well. The creation of the National Health Service was the epitome of what a socialist public service could be, until it started being privatized. It fell short originally because senior doctors had been reluctant to take part, but in the intervening years the medical profession had become more inclined to embrace it. Thatcher started to destroy the NHS in the 1980s. Blair and Cameron continued the destruction, and so will Starmer.

In 1945, there was a sense that the war was being won by everyone pulling together. The pre-war years, the 'Hungry Thirties', had been years of poverty, hardship and mass unemployment, and the people who fought the war vowed that we'd never go through that again. The spirit of '45 was: 'We've won the war, now we can win the peace, and we'll do it together.' The sense of the collective had never been stronger, and the will of ordinary people to win had never been stronger.

The Labour Party had been in the wartime coalition, so there had been Labour government ministers, including Attlee and Ernest

Bevin, during the war. A lot of them served in Attlee's first ministry* and gave concrete existence to the spirit of '45, so it was an easy transition. It wasn't like people had to elect politicians who came in with wild ideas. They weren't ideological socialists by and large, but right-wingers perpetuating what had been necessary solutions in the war. The pressures of the wartime economy and the need for munitions meant a lot of what had been privately owned, such as the mines, had become publicly owned. Attlee's government simply continued the move to collective ownership. It was much tougher for Jeremy Corbyn, who, in 2015, came in after nearly forty years of a right-wing consciousness prevailing to say, 'Here's an entirely different programme.'

Do you think The Spirit of '45 *enshrined a true socialist moment in British history?*

Attlee talked about it being a government with a socialist programme, but it was really a social democrat programme with an infrastructure for private business to succeed in so Britain could be rebuilt. Private business needed a well-housed, healthy workforce, which led to the council house programme. This was all achieved in the way we had won the war: through joint collective ownership and effort. That's the spirit that was destroyed progressively by Thatcher and the prime ministers who followed her. The Thatcherite ideological transformation had promised: 'The market will solve your problems. Let the market operate, and if there's a need, it will satisfy it.' But we know that didn't happen, because where there was a need but no profit, the need remained unsatisfied. The north-east of England is a glaring example of that: massive poverty, communities destroyed, people out of work. Everything there collapsed, and the market just ignored it, so people were wrecked.

---

* The ministers who served under Winston Churchill in the wartime coalition and also in Attlee's first ministry were A. V. Alexander, Bevin, Stafford Cripps, Hugh Dalton, Arthur Greenwood, William Jowitt, Herbert Morrison and Frederick Pethick-Lawrence. The coalition's junior ministers who joined Attlee's first cabinet were James Charter Ede, George Hall, Joseph Westwood, Ellen Wilkinson and Tom Williams.

The film recalls that it was Nye (Aneurin) Bevan rather than Attlee who was the champion of state ownership.

Not to be confused with Ernest Bevin, who'd led the Transport and General Workers' Union and was a hard-nosed ass-kicker from the right wing of the party and became foreign secretary. Nye Bevan was the Welsh leader of the left wing of the party who became minister of health and founded the National Health Service and instigated the housing programme, because that was part of his remit. So there was a clear party split, and Bevan resigned from the government partly because it introduced NHS charges for glasses and dentures.

One of the major catalysts for change in 1945 was soldiers coming back from the war determined to have a share in what they had fought for, along with the workers who'd fought on the home front and didn't trust the old political order. Although Britain is approaching Victorian levels of poverty again, the decimation of industry by Thatcherism and New Labour means the working class no longer wields or assumes the power it once had to fight for working people's rights. Nor has any upheaval as cataclysmic as the war apparently occurred – neither Brexit nor the pandemic – to effect political change.

Yet the catalyst for change was exactly that poverty. The rise of the food banks, the rise of the gig economy, the fragmentation of the National Health Service, the failure of the economy and the sense of society fragmenting over the last decade . . . People realize there's an urgency. Climate change is a massive emergency. There's the homelessness question. People trying to rent places will never own a house. People in the middle class are struggling, never mind the working class. There's a real sense of alienation and despair. Communities are collapsing. I think that urgency in some way matches the need to rebuild after the Second World War. It's certainly not the same as before. You're right: if you demand change, you're presented as a militant or a hothead by the press, but many people are desperate.

All these effects on people's lives have intensified. That's what led to Corbyn's election as leader of the Labour Party. It's true a large part of the population will never be ideologically committed, but many people did say, 'This is not right. We have to have change.' Corbyn came to power on that wave, and the programme he and John McDonnell put forward was based on the utilities – gas, electric, water – transport, the infrastructure industries, the energy companies and the Post Office all being returned to public ownership. It would have begun a process of clearing out all the private contractors and subcontractors from healthcare and the public services. So there was a surge of support for the spirit of '45 and a mass movement behind Labour. It became the biggest party in Europe: 590,000 members under Corbyn, from just over 200,000 under Blair. With a few thousand votes in different places in the country, we could have won the general election in 2017. We *were* very close to winning. Labour was going to tackle whole areas where the big corporations were making money: energy, the railways, health companies and education with the academy schools. That was when the ruling class said, 'No way. We will not tolerate this,' and the campaign against Corbyn came into play.

The issue of Brexit also turned people against Labour. Corbyn and McDonnell, sadly, made a big mistake on Labour's policy on Brexit. There was some doubt as to whether or not a Labour government would rerun the Brexit vote, and the architect of that confusion was Starmer.*

When I was growing up in the 1970s, Tony Benn – one of your interviewees in The Spirit of '45 *– was vilified in the media as a left-wing crank. Under the right circumstances, could Benn have been a more dynamic Labour leader than Harold Wilson, James Callaghan, Michael Foot or Neil Kinnock?*

Undoubtedly. He was in the centre of the party to begin with, then he became a socialist in his later years. He was a very clever man, obviously, and a very warm-hearted, generous man as well. A good writer. Whether he had 'the jungle agility' that Jim Allen always

---

* Labour entered the 2019 general election promising a second Brexit referendum, a stance identified with Starmer, who was shadow Brexit secretary. The Conservative Party, which stood on a 'Get Brexit Done' ticket under Boris Johnson, won a landslide victory on 12 December. Corbyn promptly resigned. Starmer won the vote to become Labour leader on 4 April 2020.

said you needed to be a political leader, I don't know. He had huge qualities, but he wasn't a street fighter. He needed to be part of a team that would manage the street fighting and political chicanery for him and give him good advice, like Jeremy Corbyn had. Benn didn't have that, but I think he could have been part of a leadership team with others who were committed to the same project. In the end, he was undone by the fact that he was a social democrat and stuck with the Labour Party. There's a brilliant quote, which I've got written down somewhere, by Ralph Miliband, the socialist academic who was a very authoritative figure when I was young in the 1960s. He said, '. . . the Labour Party will not be transformed into a party seriously concerned with socialist change'.* It's the illusion that bedevils people on the left – that the Labour Party would ever be able to make fundamental changes.

The other great quote was Lenin's, when he said he wanted to support the British Labour Party 'in the same way as the rope supports a hanged man'.† You know – as an agent of change the party

---

* Ralph Miliband, *Parliamentary Socialism: A Study in the Politics of Labour* (1972, second edn), p. 376.
† Lenin wrote: 'At present, British Communists very often find it hard even to approach the masses, and even to get a hearing from them. If I come out as a Communist and call upon them to vote for Henderson and against [Lloyd George, prime minister of the Liberal government] they will certainly give me a hearing. And I shall be able to explain in a popular manner, not only why the Soviets are better than a parliament and why the dictatorship of the proletariat is better than the dictatorship of Churchill (disguised with the signboard of bourgeois 'democracy'), but also that, with my vote, I want to support Henderson in the same way as the rope supports a hanged man – that the impending establishment of a government of the Hendersons will prove that I am right, will bring the masses over to my side, and will hasten the political death of the Hendersons and the Snowdens just as was the case with their kindred spirits in Russia and Germany.' From the chapter '"Left-Wing" Communism in Great Britain' in the pamphlet *Left-Wing Communism: An Infantile Disorder* (June 1920), Vladimir Lenin, *Collected Works*, vol. 31, pp. 17–118 (Progress Publishers, USSR, 1964). Lenin was referring to then Labour Party chief whip Arthur Henderson (1863–1935), the Scottish-born foundryman and trade unionist who wrote the constitution of the Labour Party with Sidney Webb. After replacing Labour's founder Keir Hardie, Henderson

is dead, and sooner or later you've got to cut the rope and let it go, though the illusion persists. When Corbyn became the leader, nearly 200,000* people joined, but, in the end, the grip that the establishment has on the Labour Party meant that, as I was saying earlier, they just lied about him and got him removed.

Where does that leave the left now?

There's a political vacuum there. The whole spirit of '45, Corbyn/McDonnell's very popular manifesto . . . it's just ignored.

I wondered if The Spirit of '45 *was intended to address the class war more explicitly than you'd done in some of your narrative films and TV dramas. Among the antagonists in those films are the gentleman pit owner John Prichard in* Days of Hope, *who, in a Harold Wilson-like sop, offers beer and sandwiches to the striking miners who come to his mansion, and Will Hemmings, the bullying managing director of the new railway company in* The Navigators, *who's eerily similar to Blair's spin doctor Alastair Campbell. However, in the films the representatives of capitalism and Conservatives are often faceless. What you often present instead are struggles – and, frequently, betrayals by union leaders and others – within the working class. In contrast,* The Spirit of

---

led the party from 1908 to 1910, and subsequently from 1914 to 1917 and from 1931 to 1932. When Prime Minister Herbert Asquith formed a wartime coalition government in 1915, Henderson was appointed president of the Board of Education, becoming the first Labour cabinet minister. The socialist politician Philip Snowden (1864–1937) was chancellor of the exchequer (the Labour Party's first) in 1924 and from 1929 to 1931.

* In an article headlined 'Revealed: How Jeremy Corbyn Has Reshaped the Labour Party', published in the *Guardian* on 13 January 2016, Ewen MacAskill reported: 'Between 7 May and 11 September, 116,753 joined and 5,393 left – 4,066 of whom cancelled their direct debit without informing the party why – and 1,327 resigning. Between Corbyn becoming leader on 12 September and Christmas Eve, 87,158 joined, with 8,567 leaving, of whom 4,692 cancelled their direct debit and 3,875 resigned. (The number of joiners and leavers did not match the total membership figure because the party allows a six-month grace period before cancelling membership.)'

'45 emphasizes, for example, that Churchill was an inveterate class warrior who, in warning that socialism would lead to totalitarianism, cited Friedrich Hayek's The Road to Serfdom *(1944), which also influenced Thatcher's free-market thinking.*

It's another form of dirty tricks to argue that if you vote for Labour, you will bring on totalitarianism. A particularly harsh example of it was Thatcher's ascension to the top of government. If we were to redo *The Spirit of '45*, it would just need a sharper analysis of what Thatcher's project was – the pursuit of ruling-class interests. The old saying we might use is: 'The ruling class can survive any crisis, provided the working class pays the price.' That's absolutely true of Thatcher's politics and what she embodied. It was endorsed by Blair, carried out by Cameron, and it will be by Starmer. It doesn't matter whether it's enacted by the old-style Tories like Cameron and Johnson, from Eton and Oxford, that old aristocratic or wealthy class, or right-wing social democrats who pursue the same basic programme, with maybe a slightly modified attitude to extreme poverty. It's the same in essence. They act on behalf of the same class. That's absolutely part of the story of *The Spirit of '45*, but I think it's implicit in pretty much every film we've done.

The first two-thirds of The Spirit of '45 *show a succession of nationalizations – the health system, transport, the railways, the docks, electricity – and the creation of the welfare state, with housing a priority. It's an ascent followed by a plunge, as you show Thatcher privatizing the nationalized industries in the 1980s. It's revealing that, as unemployment soared, the right-wing media latched onto and endorsed the calculated slights Thatcher and her speechwriters used to shame the jobless and other people on welfare benefits – 'moaning Minnies' and 'the nanny state' being the most frequently quoted.*

The media is an essential part of the state army. The BBC's got a particular role because it is the state broadcaster. They proclaim their independence: 'We are directly accountable to the people who pay their TV licence fees. The money doesn't go to the government – it's ours. We can speak truth to power.' And yet when you analyse their politics, it's very clear where they stand. They stand alongside politicians like Ken Clarke,* who's a more liberal conservative. He's the BBC's ideal, the acceptable face of the Tory party. The same band stretches to the right wing of the Labour Party. The BBC didn't like Blair's Iraq War, but once it was under way, of course, they supported it. You can see very clearly how the BBC manipulated the news on the miners' strike. Books have been written about that.

The BBC were central to promoting the smear against Corbyn. They promote the monarchy and the established Church, but anything that smacks of socialism they have no time for. They hate strikes: 'You're holding the country to ransom.' The destruction of the Labour Party wasn't a story to the BBC. That nearly 100,000 people left the party in 2021† was never mentioned, and the BBC has never held Starmer to account for it. He might be held to account occasionally for breaking the promises that he made to become leader, but the actions that he took afterwards [in purging the party's left wing] were not mentioned by the BBC.

The political vacuum is not mentioned. The Labour Party that nearly won the 2017 election is no longer part of any political discourse and none of the ideas are carried on, whereas Boris Johnson's only got to break wind and it's national news. While the BBC has no space for left-wing politics, it's obsessed with the right. They don't like the far right, but they love talking about it. They will not allow the left wing a presence. It's interesting how they will report on dissident right-wing Tories' support for the former home secretary Suella Braverman, but, to the BBC, left-wing Labour doesn't exist. The BBC is the gatekeeper of media opinion, and once they accept a line of political argument, then the right wing can drive it through and exaggerate and make hay with it. The BBC sanctioned the attack on Corbyn, and then the right wing just ran amok with it; so did the *Guardian*.

---

* Kenneth Clarke (b.1940) was a cabinet minister in the governments of Margaret Thatcher, John Major and David Cameron. He has been a member of the House of Lords since 2020.
† The Labour Party's financial statements (published by the Electoral Commission) for the year ended 31 December 2021 reported that total individual membership of the party had fallen from 523,332 to 432,213, a difference of 91,119.

And it comes from the top?

Two Tories run the BBC: the chair [Samir Shah] and the director general [Tim Davie]. That's it.

Going back to The Spirit of '45, *why did you shoot the new material in black and white?*

All the archive footage is black and white, and we didn't want to keep jumping between black and white and colour. I love black-and-white photography, and it just seemed more pleasing and more of a piece with the subject. We kept the whole thing black and white until right at the end, when the VE Day celebrations are in colour. The footage is really lovely, but I am tempted to have another go because the film just peters out. There's a real story to tell there, because the spirit of '45 infused Jeremy Corbyn and his movement, and it still does. We really pushed the door open in 2017, and the reaction of the ruling class was to stamp on it – and stamp on it with lies. They never confronted the arguments or said, 'No, the private health companies must stay part of the system,' or 'We shouldn't take water back into public ownership.' Their tactic is to smear people. That's why they attacked Benn as unstable. They attacked Arthur Scargill for having his mortgage paid by the Russians. Well, he didn't have a mortgage.* Doesn't matter – tell

---

* In Loach's Channel 4 documentary *The Arthur Legend* (1991), producer–reporter Lorraine Heggessey defended Scargill from allegations made by the *Daily Mirror* and ITV's *The Cook Report* that he had misused funds donated by Libya and the Soviet Union to support miners during the 1984–5 strike. Referring to Gavin Lightman QC's inquiry on behalf of the NUM, David Rolinson notes on BFI Screenonline: 'Building upon the Lightman inquiry's findings that the stories' key claims against Scargill were "entirely untrue", Heggessey disproves the existence of a damning mortgage, challenges witness testimony with forensics and interviews, queries witness payments, visits the Soviet Union to track allegedly missing money and questions the role of intelligence services. The reports' anger about alleged strike support from Libya is contextualized alongside the government's increased Libyan oil imports (trading with "the enemy without" to defeat "the enemy within").' See also Gavin Lightman, *The Lightman Report on the NUM* (Penguin, 1990); Arthur Scargill, *Response to the Lightman Inquiry*, pamphlet published by the Campaign to Defend Scargill and Heathfield (1990);

the story. They attacked Corbyn as a racist, but nothing could be further from the truth.

The Spirit of '45 echoes Days of Hope, *among your other TV dramas and films, in showing people mobilizing to fight for workers' rights and better conditions. In the absence of industry, where organization was strongest, and given that union membership has plummeted, is a determined working-class movement even possible?*

The mines have gone, so the miners' union has gone. The steelworkers' union wasn't a militant union, but it was big and had power that it never used properly. The car industry has gone – that had a big, powerful union. The Transport and General Workers' Union has largely gone. The docks have been casualized. The dockers' lockout during the Liverpool strike was pivotal – we did that little film about it, *The Flickering Flame* – in marking the end of their job security.

The development of the economic system, turning workers into insecure gig-economy workers, weakened the trade unions, but there has been a surge of union organization among railway workers, health workers and public service workers. That's where the strength of the unions appears to be now. The bakers' union is a good union that has organized strikes at McDonald's and other parts of the fast-food industry. Teachers have got a very strong, organized and principled union. The Fire Brigades Union is very strong. There's also a lot of strength in community organizations and in the climate change movement and organizations tackling homelessness and poverty, and it's on a scale we didn't have before. The old trade unions still have a role, but it's less.

One of the tasks of the left is to link the industrial struggle to the environmental one. The people who are pumping the poison into the atmosphere are the same ones who are reducing wages, making conditions of work worse, denying workers healthcare, sick pay and holiday pay. They turn labour on and off like a tap. There's no eight-to-five working day now. 'You work when we tell you to

---

Paul Routledge, *Scargill: The Unauthorised Biography* (HarperCollins, 1993); Roy Greenslade, 'Sorry Arthur', *Guardian*, 27 May 2002; Terry Pattinson, Frank Thorne and Ted Oliver, 'Roy Says We Were Taken in. We Were Not', *Guardian*, 3 June 2002.

work, and if we tell you it's fifty hours a week, it's fifty hours. If we tell you it's just twenty-five, it's twenty-five.'

Young people, including many who will soon vote for the first time, are environmentally conscientious and becoming increasingly angry about human rights abuses.*

I think there's a radical edge. The opposition has rebalanced itself, but the potential for struggle is still there. And I think that's why *The Spirit of '45* is now incomplete, because that spirit rose again, and we saw the response of the ruling class. Maybe if I can get myself together, we'll add some more and recut it.

What is the legacy of 1945 that Britain can most benefit from now?

Common ownership can be efficient. It shows that there can be good public services, responsible public utilities, a sound infrastructure and even industry itself, like the steel industry, without the profit motive. It can work in the public interest so that people are not getting ripped off, and that's a viable model. The idea that freedom equals the freedom to make profit is false. The free market equals the freedom to exploit. You can organize an economy without exploiting workers, because it was done. There are other lessons to be learned. It shouldn't be organized as it was organized in 1945. For example, the people who ran the coal industry had been managers for the owners, but you don't have to run it like a private business that happens to be owned by the public. There are better ways of organizing it. But the central point – that we can run the economy based on common ownership, not private profit – is the important one, I think.

---

* Demonstrated, subsequent to this interview, by the sustained student protests over the war in Gaza in the spring of 2024.

CHAPTER 14

The North-Eastern Trilogy

I, Daniel Blake, Sorry We Missed You, The Old Oak

The pauperizing of many working-class people during fifteen years of Tory misrule in the 2010s and early 2020s, which built on the deprivation inflicted by Margaret Thatcher and Tony Blair's policies, elicited from the Loach team three films set in the depressed north-eastern counties of Tyne and Wear and Durham. Though featuring occasional moments of humour – and notwithstanding the hopeful ending of *The Old Oak* (2023) – the concluding works of Loach's career in narrative cinema present some of its grimmest moments: a starving Katie Morgan (Hayley Squires) unable to restrain herself from opening a tin of beans and stuffing them into her mouth at a food bank in *I, Daniel Blake* (2016); delivery driver Ricky (Kris Hitchen), so mentally and physically exhausted by his delivery driver gig that he hits his misbehaving teenage son in *Sorry We Missed You* (2019); the publican TJ (Dave Turner), crushed on realizing that the communal meals he is hosting for his village's Syrian refugees and struggling locals cannot continue because racists among his customers have sabotaged the dining area in *The Old Oak* (2023).* For people of limited means, the otherwise wealthy Britain of the David Cameron–Rishi Sunak era is viciously unforgiving.

---

* The three regulars of the Old Oak pub who express racist attitudes and sabotage its electricity supply (with the help of TJ's disgruntled friend, Charlie) do not physically attack the Syrian refugees. However, the film, released in the UK on 29 September 2022, refers directly to the far-right public meetings that preceded the widespread violent anti-immigration protests and riots that took place in Britain between 30 July and 5 August 2024.

I, Daniel Blake, which, like *The Wind That Shakes the Barley*, won the Palme d'Or at Cannes, exposes how the British government's Department of Work and Pensions (DWP) weaponizes bureaucratic red tape, its automated telephone answering service and online questionnaires and forms to prevent the payment of benefits to claimants unfamiliar with modern technology. The film shows how the naturally optimistic Daniel (Dave Johns) is ground down by relentless obstruction and obfuscation, and how the system forces both him and his jobless friend Katie into increasingly humiliating situations. The kindness they show each other, and the discretion and empathy of the food bank workers, Daniel's neighbour China (Kema Sikazwe) and the one helpful Jobcentre worker, Ann (Kate Rutter), cannot withstand the power of state machinery that is impervious to individuals' health and welfare concerns and engineered to disallow and deny them their legal rights.

Against a black screen, the widowed fifty-nine-year-old Newcastle carpenter Daniel is first heard trying to establish his eligibility for employment support allowance in a phone call with an employee of an American company subcontracted by the DWP to handle claims. Prompted by an irrelevant question she asks him about the efficacy of his bowel movements, Daniel explains that he had a heart attack while working on a construction scaffold. Their exchange sets the scene for Daniel's fatal journey into a maze of bureaucracy calculated to deny unwell workers from benefiting from their National Insurance contributions. Daniel's repeated pointless visits to his local Jobcentre give the film a Sisyphean rhythm, while Loach and his editor Jonathan Morris's use of fades-to-black provides a scathing silent commentary on the inhumane treatment of this humble, gentle working man. As Daniel is forced into blind alley after blind alley, he recalls Franz Kafka's K hopelessly attempting to reach the Castle in the 1926 novel of that name.

After a nurse scans Daniel's heart, a doctor tells him that he must not return to work and that he might need fitting with a defibrillator. Between making further thankless calls to the DWP, Daniel collects wood from which to make ornaments and mobiles to pass the time as he sits on the phone. He sees a neighbour coax his dog to foul their common garden – a metaphorical echo, perhaps, of the disgusting system Daniel is mired in. At the end of a call lasting one hour and forty-eight minutes, he is told that, pending a final decision, an assessor has deemed him fit to work, punitively denying him the support allowance.

At his local Jobcentre, Daniel is told he can appeal the decision and apply for jobseeker's allowance online. Because he doesn't know how to use a computer, he will have to phone in again and say he is dyslexic. When he starts to feel faint, the sympathetic Jobcentre worker Ann makes him sit and brings him water. The agent interviewing Katie (Hayley Squires) calls a security guard to make her leave. A Londoner in her twenties, single mother Katie had arrived at the Jobcentre, accompanied by her children, Daisy (Briana Shann) and Dylan (Dylan McKiernan), without an appointment letter. When Daniel tries to help her sign on, he is thrown out with her.

Katie has only £12, so Daniel helps her buy groceries, and they go to her flat, where he fixes the cistern. She and the kids lived for two years in a homeless shelter. Since accommodating homeless people in London is expensive, she has been relocated to Newcastle, where she has no support system. Different men fathered her children, and Daisy is a mixed-race child; it is implied that the social services prejudicially shunted the family to the north-east, in the same way that the immigration authorities dump Syrian refugees there in *The Old Oak*.

After struggling with a library computer, Daniel returns to the Jobcentre, where Ann's supervisor rebukes her for trying to help him. China, a budding entrepreneur who has acquired a box of factory-surplus trainers he plans to sell on the street at below the retail cost, helps Daniel fill in his jobseeker's application form. Daniel decides to keep appealing his case to force a mandatory reconsideration of his claim for support allowance, but China warns him that the DWP will 'fuck you around' and 'make you as miserable as possible' to make him give up. Daniel spends another fifty-five minutes on the phone, only to learn that no decision has been made and no support benefit has been paid to him.

Daniel helps Katie fix up her flat and pays grandfatherly attention to Daisy and Dylan. Claiming she has already eaten, Katie gives Daniel her dinner. She conceals her despair from him and tries to get work as a cleaner. At the Jobcentre, an agent impatiently tells Daniel he must commit thirty-five hours a week to finding a job and provide evidence that he has done it. She orders him to attend a CV-writing workshop or face a sanction. The instructor explains that some employers will expect to see a video CV. Daniel starts looking for work.

Visiting a food bank with Daniel and her children, Katie is unable to restrain herself from eating on the spot and breaks down in shame. Shortly afterwards, a supermarket manager lets her off after she's caught shoplifting. Daniel, meanwhile, receives a call telling him he's fit for work and not entitled to support allowance. A Jobcentre agent tells him his handwritten CV is unacceptable and that he's likely to face a four-week sanction and the freezing of his unemployment benefits, though he might be eligible for a hardship allowance. She suggests he goes to a food bank. He sells his furniture but keeps his carpentry tools.

Daisy is mocked at school because her shoes have fallen apart. When Daniel is minding Katie's children, he figures out that their mother has started to work as a prostitute in a nearby brothel. He visits it and tearfully persuades her to leave. At the Jobcentre, Daniel explains to Ann that he has been shamed as a sick man forced to look for a job that he couldn't take even if it existed. He requests a date for his appeal; Ann warns him that his benefits will cease as he waits for his case to be heard, which could take weeks. On leaving the Jobcentre, Daniel sprays on its wall the words: 'I DANIEL BLAKE DEMAND MY APPEAL DATE BEFORE I STARVE AND CHANGE THE SHITE MUSIC ON THE PHONE'. He is arrested and given a caution for criminal damage. The weather turns cold; Daniel's health declines. Katie accompanies him to his appeal, where he collapses. He dies off-screen. His funeral is attended by China, Ann and Katie, who pays tribute to Daniel's kindness and says the state drove him to an early grave.

Sorry We Missed You denounces the gig economy – the neo-feudalistic twenty-first-century paid-assignment system that has eliminated workers' rights globally. The film targets companies' ruthless exploitation of 'independent service providers', who, deprived of the protections and structured working day afforded to traditional employees, are forced to work inhuman and erratically allocated shifts in order to survive. Though not without moments of gentle humour and family harmony, the film shows the damage the unregulated gig economy does to domestic life by increasing people's anxieties and exposing them to physical danger.

Labourer Ricky Turner (Kris Hitchen), who is a transplanted Mancunian, his wife Abby (Debbie Honeywood), their sixteen-year-old son Seb (Rhys Mcgowan) and tween daughter Liza Jane (Katie Proctor) live in a rented house in Gateshead. Ricky and Abby lost their opportunity to buy their own property thanks to the 2007–8 subprime mortgage crisis – specifically, the collapse of Newcastle's Northern Rock bank – and Ricky's loss of construction work. Despite mounting debts, and now in their early forties, they still aspire to owning a home. Living in rented accommodation has gnawed at their sense of stability, which is increasing, thanks to the generational conflict between Ricky and Seb, a gifted graffiti artist who provokes his dad by shoplifting spray cans and skipping school. Although Liza Jane is emotionally intelligent, she is troubled by the bickering at home.

In the opening scene, Ricky signs up to become an 'owner–driver franchisee', as opposed to an employee, for PDF (Parcels Delivered Fast), a courier firm serving a busy district of Newcastle for its multinational clients. Maloney (Ross Brewster), the burly supervisor who runs the loading and dispatch depot, 'onboards' the drivers and impresses on Ricky that he will be paid 'fees', not 'wages', and work 'with' the firm, not 'for' it. Ricky will have no job security and no paid vacation or sick leave. He must guarantee that his shift will be covered by another driver if he's absent, even in the event of an emergency, or else face punitive sanctions. He will also be liable for any losses unmet by the firm's insurance company. He must carry a computerized scanner that will enable the firm and its customers to track his movements; he will be fined for failing to meet the precise delivery times of the packages designated as 'precisors'. Since Ricky will earn more by delivering parcels – £1,200 in a six-day work week of fourteen-hour shifts – than Abby will from her draining work as a permanently on-call home caregiver, he decides that they should sell the family car she needs to reach her clients so he can buy a prohibitively costly van.

Some of the package deliveries are depicted humorously. His ungrateful clients include a belligerent Newcastle United fan (*The Old Oak*'s Dave Turner), who unsmilingly swaps jeers with Manchester United supporter Ricky. When Ricky leaves a package at an upper-middle-class residence, he is bitten on the behind by an unseen guard dog, which prompts Liza Jane – who's cheerfully accompanying Ricky on his Saturday shift – to leave the owner a cheeky note. Instead of turning a blind eye to the incident, the working-class turncoat Maloney, who toadies to the paying customers, bans his drivers from carrying passengers, depriving Ricky of the occasional pleasure of bringing Liza Jane to work.

Ricky is soon exhausted by his shifts, his temper frays, and he is unable to help Seb, who is acting out, in a way that the boy might respond to positively. Kept late at the depot one evening and unable to find a driver to cover him, Ricky fails to arrive at Seb's school in time for a meeting that might prevent him from being suspended for two weeks, following an incident in which a teacher was hurt. Further draconian treatment by Maloney and provocation by Seb cause Ricky to lose control and hit Seb. A comic scene shows Ricky riding a children's tricycle in his haste to apologize to Seb after he decamps to a mate's house. Seb rallies to Ricky's side after he is injured in a mugging and van robbery and tries to stop him risking his life by resuming his deliveries.

The scenes depicting Ricky's work troubles and the father–son struggle are balanced by those showing zero-hours contractor Abby's interactions with her mostly elderly, infirm clients and her female supervisor (a voice on a mobile phone), who instructs her which homes to report to on an ad hoc basis. A worker, wife, mother (and family peacemaker) of bottomless compassion, Abby works so late she is seldom home to see Liza Jane to bed. Stranded at a bus stop on one occasion, she complains to the supervisor that her most recent house call, which should have taken half an hour, has cost her because she won't be paid for the extra hour she spent cleaning up the client, who 'had shit all over her, under her nails; it was on the walls, all over me. I've got covered in scratches off her.' Rather than attend her next appointment and be paid for it, Abby stayed to clean up the first client properly, but she resents the supervisor's dismissal of this woman as 'difficult', asserting that she's 'vulnerable and needs more care'. The stench of a society in thrall to ruthless capitalist practices pervades the film. With no time to visit a public toilet while he's working, Ricky is forced to bring a bottle in which to relieve himself. After he uses it on one occasion, he is mugged by three men who rob his van and smash his scanner (which he'll have to pay for). One of them unscrews the bottle of urine and pours it on him. The scene echoes the incident in *The*

Navigators where Sheffield railway workers, who have been forced into unsafe, piecemeal agency work with no union protections, are splashed with human waste from a passing train. The message is that workers and their families are degraded by casualized employment and the gig economy.

Waiting in hospital with Ricky for his X-ray results, Abby grabs his mobile phone and reads the riot act to Maloney, who has foisted crippling charges on her beaten husband for the theft of two passports he was delivering and the smashing of his scanner by the muggers. *Sorry We Missed You* was partially inspired by the real-life case of Don Lane, a Dorset man with type 1 diabetes who was a courier for DPD, a company that delivers parcels for major high-street retailers. He once collapsed into a coma while driving his DPD van, but rather than face £150 fines (Ricky pays £100) for missing shifts or failing to cover them, he skipped appointments with specialists so he could work through the 2017 Christmas rush. He died, aged fifty-three, on 4 January 2018. At the first UK public screening of *Sorry We Missed You*, Robert Booth reported in the *Guardian*,* Lane's widow Ruth recounted how, while her husband was still working, she went to his depot's office and shouted at his manager: 'I said you are bloody killing him.' Her intervention came too late; it is unclear whether Abby's will be any more effective, the film ending moments after Ricky has barely avoided a road crash after falling asleep at the wheel.

All the family members in *Sorry We Missed You* are – or are in the process of being – enslaved by their mobile phones: Liza Jane takes selfies while making a meal for herself at home; Seb rages at Ricky when he confiscates his phone because, as Abby says, 'his life is on it'; Abby uses her phone to steer Liza Jane to bed, but, as Ricky is by his phone, she is controlled by hers via the NHS subcontractor who exploits her kindness by directing her from client to client. If Ricky didn't have to replace his scanner at a cost of £1,000, its destruction would benefit him, symbolically, but instead it tightens the noose around his neck. He had been perplexed during a doorstep exchange with a client who'd refused to give him his last name because of his Orwellian fear

---

* Robert Booth, '"You Give Don a Voice": Courier's Widow Praises Ken Loach Film', *Guardian*, 23 September 2019.

of 'Big Data . . . when people start hoovering up all our personal information'; amusing though it is, the scene comments on Ricky's digitally contrived entrapment.

A few uncomplicated moments of togetherness alleviate the Turners' stress before it gets out of hand: the enjoyment of a Saturday-night takeaway curry at home, followed by an unexpected outing in Ricky's van, celebrated by a singalong to a rap song on the radio, to bring Abby to the home of her favourite client, who is incontinent and cannot get up from her armchair. Abby, who is grieving for her mother three years after her death, has turned to this kind woman, Mollie, for maternal support, and they have previously looked at some of each other's treasured photos. Mollie is played by Heather Wood, who was born into a miners' family in the Durham village of Easington; she lost both her father and grandfather to the pits. During the miners' strike, Wood organized the free cafés to feed the strikers. Truth feeds fiction as Mollie shows Abby a photo of herself (of Wood, that is) in the Easington Colliery café as she learns that two busloads of pickets are about to arrive for a meal.* This unselfconscious meta moment harks back to a time when working people banded together to resist the fracturing of their communities. For the likes of Abby and Ricky, this past is a foreign country since, in the isolating world of the gig economy, there's no one else with whom to organize.

The Old Oak enfolds the British class war and the refugee crisis. Partially shot in Easington, the film is set in 2016, in a former Durham coal-mining village that has fallen into post-industrial decline and poverty, embittering many of the old pitmen and their struggling families. Some of the regulars who drink at the dilapidated eponymous pub, from which the doleful landlord TJ (Tommy Joe) Ballantyne (played by Dave Turner, a former firefighter and

---

* The same photo is among those on the walls of the room in TJ's pub in *The Old Oak*, where another woman played by Wood is among the villagers who eat alongside the Syrian refugees. It commemorates the last stand of working-class unity in Britain, before Margaret Thatcher's crushing of it precipitated the dismantling of the coal industry and a rapid decline in union membership. Loach and Laverty aim one of their sharpest digs at a racist Old Oak regular, Gary, by making him the son of a 'scab' – one of the strike-breaking miners who crossed the picket lines in 1984.

union official) scrapes a living, are aggrieved by the arrival of a busload of Syrian immigrants. TJ helps the community organizer Laura (played by Claire Rodgerson, an anti-racist activist based in nearby Sunderland) settle them into empty miners' cottages. An agency had purchased the properties on the cheap, greatly devaluing the locals' homes, as TJ's old schoolfriend Charlie (Trevor Fox), whose sick wife is wheelchair-bound, tearfully laments.

I, Daniel Blake began six weeks of principal photography in Newcastle upon Tyne and the surrounding area on 20 October 2015. Between October 2015 and September 2016, 4,162 Syrians were relocated to the UK under the Syrian Vulnerable Persons Resettlement scheme; 20,000 had been accepted by 2020. A third of them went to Scotland and a disproportionate number were settled in the north-east; nine-tenths of asylum seekers in the UK were living in the poorest two-fifths of the country. As of September 2021, 280 Syrians had been housed in County Durham.

A montage of black-and-white photos taken by twenty-five(-ish)-year-old refugee Yara (played by Ebla Mari, a Druze middle-class teacher from the Golan Heights) shows her arrival in the Durham village on a bus with her mother and younger siblings and other Syrians, mostly women and children. A drunk, Rocco (Neil Leiper), who is heard haranguing them on the soundtrack, appears in Yara's photos wearing the shirt of the Newcastle United football team (which, perhaps not coincidentally, is financed by Saudi Arabia's sovereign wealth fund, a prime example of 'sportswashing'). 'You shot my mate in Iraq,' bawls Rocco, for whom all 'fucking ragheads' are alike.

Though TJ urges Rocco to back down, he grabs, drops and breaks Yara's camera in a scuffle with her. She subsequently ventures into the Old Oak and asks TJ if he knows where she can get the camera fixed. Though TJ is nonplussed by the sight of Yara standing at his bar, the two soon strike up a low-key friendship. Inviting her into the room at the back of the pub, which TJ has kept closed for twenty years to save on insurance costs, he fetches a box of cameras and offers to trade two of them to pay for the repair of Yara's camera. TJ explains to Yara that the cameras belonged to his uncle, who took the photos mounted on the room's walls showing scenes from the 1984 strike. As a photographer who has taken pictures in a refugee camp, Yara is moved by images revealing the miners' collective strength and the pride of their womenfolk in being able to feed them on no wages. Above the one showing the packed food kitchen that Wood set up at Easington two weeks into the strike is the printed legend that becomes the film's rallying cry: 'When you eat together, you stick together.'

A character not without pathos, TJ has been divorced by his wife ('a good woman' whom he admits to having neglected) and cut off by his son, and he has only his little mongrel Marra for company. Yara fears for the survival of her father, who has remained behind in Syria, forced to stand in an overcrowded cell as a prisoner of Bashar al-Assad's police state. It is credible that, as a threatened alien, Yara should trust TJ as a kindly, protective older male. Their relationship echoes the father–daughter-like bond that develops between Daniel and Katie in *I, Daniel Blake*. Penniless, homeless, jobless Brits are as unwelcome in the capital and the wealthy Home Counties as asylum seekers.

Though some of the Old Oak's patrons, notably a couple of retired miners, feel sorry for the Syrians, Charlie, Gary (Jordan Louis) and the rancorous Vic (Chris McGlade) appeal to TJ to open his back room so they can hold a meeting there to protest the village being used as a dumping ground for refugees. TJ turns them down, having heard Vic's and Gary's racist slurs and another patron's warning that such a meeting would attract right-wing extremists. Paul Laverty's script reflected local realities. In 2016, far-right groups had exploited a twenty-six-year-old mother's online allegation that she had been raped by six Middle Eastern migrants by holding thirteen rallies in thirteen months in Sunderland. (The police investigation of the case found insufficient evidence to warrant a prosecution.) Before becoming an adviser to Laverty on *The Old Oak* and acting in it, Rodgerson and other activists had held workshops for disenfranchised young people drawn to right-wing politics, 'to help [them] disentangle their economic and political fears from their outward expressions of racism'. She had handed out flyers to some of them after screenings of *I, Daniel Blake* and *Sorry We Missed You*. 'In Sunderland, the summer I met Paul there had been seven far-right leaders visit our city,' Rodgerson told the *Big Issue* newspaper. When Laura and TJ deliver donated items (a mattress, clothes, a rug, a child's bike) to the refugees, TJ – conscious or not of how racism takes root – pauses to tell three local boys, peeved because their families aren't the recipients, that the Syrians have 'lost everything'.

In a story strand that seems tangential but demonstrates the causality and airtightness of Laverty's screenwriting, an undernourished white teenage girl, glimpsed earlier in the film, drops to the ground while taking part in the park races that Laura has organized to help unite the communities. Yara helps the girl walk to her home and looks in the kitchen to find her something to eat, but the cupboards are bare. The resolution of a misunderstanding with the girl's angry mother leads Yara to take photos at a ladies' hairdressing salon, where the chatter brings home to her the need for all the villagers to be fed. However, TJ refuses Laura and Yara's request that the three of them host communal meals in the back room, his anger stemming from his fear that feeding the Syrians there would alienate Charlie, Vic and Gary irrevocably, causing him to lose custom. It is unclear if they egged on the youths whose ferocious pit bull savaged Marra – her killing, heard but not seen, echoing that of Billy's kestrel in *Kes*. But the incident triggers TJ's decision to do up the back room and open it for the proposed meals. As he suspected it would, this move enrages the malcontents and their friend Eddy (Col Tait). Though no fighter, TJ hurls himself at Vic when he snidely speculates that TJ is 'shagging [Yara] in the fucking cellar'.

Loach has occasionally invested his realist TV dramas and films with moments of magical realism – football inspiring them in *The Golden Vision* and *Looking for Eric*. 'Magical' spaces (sites of change, accord or occurrences of fate) are rare in the films, though Jimmy Gralton's hall is one. In *The Old Oak*, three haunted or sacred spaces (but a single church) work on the characters in vital ways. One is the back room where the first communal meal goes ahead and is a great success. Another is the beach near where TJ's father was killed in an undersea mining shaft accident; it is also where, as TJ recalls via a flashback, the friendly stray Marra diverted him from drowning himself following the collapse of his marriage.

Then there is Durham Cathedral, which Yara and TJ visit to collect donations for the Syrians. Moved by the choral music though she is, Yara has a more complicated response to the numinous atmosphere than the epiphany that stirs transnational fellow feeling in the American soldier visiting Canterbury Cathedral in Michael Powell and Emeric Pressburger's *A Canterbury Tale* (1944). Reflecting on the Islamic State's destruction of a Palmyra temple that 'my children will never see', Yara questions the value of hope in the face of the West's inadequate response to the barbarous war that the Assad regime has been waging on the Syrian rebels since the Arab Spring, but she concludes she cannot live without it.

Hope is the revivifying currency of *The Old Oak*. TJ must summon it again after Charlie, Vic and their cronies sabotage the electrical system in the pub's back room, putting it out of use. Yara, too, after she learns her father has died. His death galvanizes the locals to turn out en masse in sympathy with Yara's family, the spirit of solidarity carrying over into the Durham Miners' Gala (held each July), where Yara and TJ, accompanied by friends like Laura and Yara's mother Fatima (Amna Al Ali), carry a specially made banner bearing an oak tree that symbolizes the unity of the surviving ex-miners and their families and the Syrians.

British critics on both the right and left who criticized *The Old Oak* for being sentimental, wish-fulfilling and implausible neglected to mention that so, too, are the majority of movies, and that the upbeat finale doesn't mitigate the looming closure of TJ's pub. Nor did those critics observe that Loach and Laverty injected far less humour into the north-eastern trilogy than their other British state-of-the-nation films – or pay heed to Loach's familiar recognition that, true to human nature, some working people are fated to betray their own. The saboteurs Vic, Gary and Eddy disappear from the film unpunished. Shamed by TJ for helping them, Charlie sheepishly wheels his wife towards the throng of villagers paying their respects to Yara's grieving family, but he knows that the harm he and his more bigoted friends have done is unconscionable. That is realism enough, and it's small wonder that Loach should want to end *The Old Oak* – and his extraordinary run of fiction films – with joyful shots of working-class Durham people and their new Syrian neighbours united under a banner proclaiming 'Strength, Resistance, Solidarity' in both English and Arabic.

GRAHAM FULLER: *Paul has said that his research for* I, Daniel Blake *revealed cases of people unable to get their unemployment and support benefits that were more grievous than Daniel's and Katie's in the film.*

KEN LOACH: It's a consistent way of working. You don't go for the most extreme case because the people who attack us – and they always do – can say, 'Well, you've just picked something that isn't typical.' But what happens to Daniel happens frequently. People are told they're fit for work when they're not, and the consequences can be disastrous. In the end, no one's held accountable. There was the case of Michael O'Sullivan, a sixty-year-old London builder who suffered from depression. He went through the work capability assessment and was told he was fit for work by the DWP. He got a job and was due to start work, but he committed suicide [on 23 September 2013]. It was clearly the pressure of being told to do something that he knew he couldn't do. The coroner said the DWP was to blame.* This is the department that imposes the punishments – financial sanctions – on people who are seen as scroungers, when they are potentially ill. His daughter, Anne-Marie, a brilliant young woman, has fought the work capability assessments for years. We've become friends and communicate every now and then. The DWP will not accept responsibility for what they've done, as a general rule. I've been to demonstrations outside the Jobcentres they run, and the battle to get them to admit that they were wrong has been extraordinary, because, of course, once they did, they'd have many hundreds of claims against them. They have to say it's not their fault when plainly it is and coroners have said it is. The families of the victims struggle and have to fight over and over again.

You've used the expression 'conscious cruelty' in relation to what Daniel and Katie go through in the film. Because it implies a degree of moral judgement, the idea that sanctions are imposed punitively is sinister.

---

* In the 'Circumstances of Death' section of the 'Regulation 28: Prevention of Future Deaths Report' submitted to the DWP on 13 January 2014, Senior Coroner M. E. Hassell of St Pancras Coroner's Court, London, stated: 'I found that the trigger for Mr O'Sullivan's suicide was his recent assessment by a DWP doctor as being fit for work.'

It is, because the people on benefits are receiving charity. Benefits used to be called 'social security', which was a better term because it refers not to a gift, but to the security that everyone is entitled to. When the government imposes financial sanctions, they know that the people whose money they are stopping have no resources. In most cases, they have no savings and don't have a bank account they can just draw from endlessly. Mostly, they don't have a family who can give them money. By and large, they are poor people. So, if you stop their benefits, what are they going to do? They will either not pay their rent or go hungry, because if they've got children, they'll feed them with what they've got. They've got to keep a roof over their heads and they've got to keep the electricity on to heat the kids' food. Look at the rise of food banks. Well over a million people can only eat now when people give them charity food* – and there's been an enormous increase in desperate poverty since we made *I, Daniel Blake*. The government knows all this and uses hunger as a weapon, which is why I think 'conscious cruelty' is an accurate phrase.

What, in your opinion, is the government's motive for withholding benefits? Is it to avoid paying the money?

No. I think the prime motive is discipline. The thinking is, 'You will take whatever job there is going, however badly you're exploited. Whatever crap wages you get, however appalling the conditions, you will work.' Paul found a quote from an eighteenth-century vicar which I carry in my diary. He said, 'Hunger will tame the fiercest animals, it will teach decency and civility, obedience and subjugation to the most brutish, the most obstinate, and the most perverse.'† The idea was that only hunger will drive the poor to

---

* In fact, in 2022–3, more than 2.99 million three-day emergency food parcels were distributed by food banks across the UK-wide Trussell Trust network. Its website, trusselltrust.org, reported that between 1 April 2023 and 31 March 2024, food banks distributed more than 3.1 million such parcels, an increase of 94 per cent over the previous five years.
† From *Dissertation on the Poor Laws* (1786), written by the Reverend Joseph Townsend (1739–1816), who opposed state provision of financial help for the able-bodied poor but advocated compulsory weekly paid memberships of the Friendly Societies to provide insurance

work, however much it would keep them in poverty and however bad and dangerous the work, to keep the threat of the workhouse at bay. The conditions in them were appalling, so you only went there as a last resort. Now, the sanctions fulfil the same role as that threat. It goes back to the Poor Law and the idea of the 'sturdy beggar'* being driven out of the village in Elizabethan times. 'Look at him, he can walk – why can't he work?' It's what George Bernard Shaw called 'middle-class morality'.†

Under a veneer of moral outrage, right-wing newspapers highlight cases of people abusing the benefits system to attack the system itself.

Yes, they show photographs of them on holiday in Spain. There might be one or two who do that. The Tory politicians then punish what they call 'scroungers' and 'skivers'. When he was chancellor of the exchequer, George Osborne talked about them hiding behind their closed blinds when all the decent people were going to work.‡ As if they had a choice. I'm sure some people do swing the lead, as we used to say, and take advantage, but the overwhelming majority of people who are sanctioned are desperate.

---

for sickness benefits, free medical treatment and burial costs, a scheme eventually adopted by the 1911 Health Insurance Act. Despite his harsh admonitions, Townsend was an enemy of poverty, not the poor. As a practising physician in his parish of Pewsey, Wiltshire, he ran a free medical service for paupers for over fifty years.
* In historical English law, a 'sturdy beggar' was someone who was fit and able to work, but begged for a living. The Statute of Cambridge 1388 differentiated between sturdy beggars and poor people who were disabled or elderly. The Act for Punishment of Sturdy Vagabonds and Beggars, passed by King Henry VIII in 1536, provided relief for the 'impotent poor' but compelled each 'valiant Beggar or sturdy Vagabond' to 'be kept in continual labour' or face an initial punishment of a whipping. Relief was funded by voluntary subscription and administered by the parish.
† In *Pygmalion* (1912).
‡ At the Conservative Party conference in Birmingham, on 8 October 2012, Osborne said: 'Where is the fairness, we ask, for the shift-worker, leaving home in the dark hours of the early morning, who looks up at the closed blinds of their next-door neighbour sleeping off a life on benefits?'

Though not in a Luddite way, I, Daniel Blake *contrasts Daniel's use of his carpentry skills to help Katie fix up her place with the obfuscating use of technology harnessed by the DWP to thwart people seeking benefits. There's something Kafkaesque about Daniel's plight as an ordinary man, nearly sixty, who doesn't know how to use a computer to fill in forms and is flummoxed by having to negotiate an automated phone system, which can demoralize even the hardiest and most tech-savvy. We all know what it's like being stuck on the phone talking to robots with patronizing voices for forty-five minutes.*

I've got great sympathy for this poor guy confronted by the computer screen, because I can't use computers at all. However many courses I try, they baffle me. My mind doesn't work in that way; it becomes paralysed. Technology is imposed unilaterally, and the government knows there will be people who can't use it. Again, it's a form of cruelty. The idea is not that the government is there to serve you; it's there to deny you the things that are the basic stuff of life. If you can't measure up and use a computer, too bad. You fail; you don't eat.

The NHS is introducing automated phone calls. Our local GP's practice went through a period when you could only renew your prescription if you did it online, and I couldn't do it. The woman behind the counter at my GP's surgery was very nice and would say, 'Oh, give it to me, I'll do it,' but she was breaking the rules. Now, they've finally had to say it doesn't work and have gone back to human connection. To behave like normal human beings, you have to make contact with other people. Technology not only can't do that, it destroys human situations. It's fracturing and fragmenting society. The prospect of AI is terrifying, and it's driven again by those who will control it. They are trapped in their own contradictions because they will have to sack half the workforce if they use it, yet the fewer and fewer people who are used to create services and goods, the more they will need those people as consumers. They'll be the sturdy beggars you've got to drive out of town because they're fit for work, but where is the work? Not everyone will have the talent to work these complex systems.

One of the Jobcentre workers, Ann, feels sorry for Daniel and tries to help him, and she later comes to his funeral. Was it important to show that not all DWP employees are uncaring?

Yes. The idea that Jobcentres are just full of hard-nosed people isn't true. Most people we found operating the system did it with a lot of reluctance. The ones who were there just needed the job, which is understandable. The people who acted in those scenes were ex-Jobcentre workers, many of whom had left because they just couldn't stand it. One experienced worker said that he'd never get a promotion because he was an active trade unionist. He was marked down and he left. Obviously, he objected to the way the whole system worked. Their union, the Public and Commercial Services Union – which is led by one of the best union leaders, Mark Serwotka* – helped us a lot with the research and was very supportive.

The story of the single mother, Katie, has elements of Cathy Come Home. *She and her two kids have been relocated from a homeless shelter in London to Newcastle, nearly 300 miles away, where she hasn't a single friend. The idea that they couldn't be affordably housed in London is absurd.*

There are many families in Katie's situation, living in villages like those where we filmed *The Old Oak*. The village in that film, which is imaginary, was shot in three villages in County Durham – Murton, Horden and Easington – that are closely connected and full of the old miners' houses, typically terraced. A huge number of them are empty. Councils in the more affluent areas of England, particularly in the south-east, that are paying housing benefits to people on low incomes or living in shelters find agencies who buy these houses when they're very cheap – you can buy one for £5,000 now. Then the councils try to persuade the people they're having to support to move to the cheaper area, and, of course, they try to offload people who have problems. So it's often the people with difficulties who have to move north. If you drive around the streets in these villages now, it's like the Wild West. A lot of the people who have moved there have problems with addictions. The people who have lived

---

* Serwotka was general secretary of the PCS from 2000 until his retirement in 2024. Fran Heathcote replaced him on 1 February of that year.

there all their lives would drink on a Saturday night, but they were coherent communities and didn't have so much drugs and crime. So the story of Katie in *I, Daniel Blake* has become amplified.

Is there work there for people sent from the south?

There's no work in the villages. That's why the houses are empty. There's work in Sunderland, but a lot of it is gig-economy work. There's very little transport to get to and from anywhere. What there is is intermittent and expensive. There's a railway line, but it only stops at one of the villages, and then you've got to walk to it. How are you going to get there? It's not down the end of the road, but a few miles away. People are not motivated to travel. You could find a way out if you're very clever, but if you were that clever, you wouldn't have been moved there in the first place. The villages are dumping grounds. When the Syrians are sent there, as we show in *The Old Oak*, it fits that pattern.

Daniel and Katie repay each other's kindnesses in I, Daniel Blake, *as do TJ and Yara in* The Old Oak. *Abby's kindness in* Sorry We Missed You *extends beyond her job as a professional carer. It's rare to see films in which kindness and generosity are valued so highly.*

I hadn't thought of that. How strange. I don't get to the cinema so much now, that's the problem.

What I mean is that the care and warmth strangers often show one another are considered antithetical to drama in much commercial cinema, or are just a source of sentimentality. Humour has also been an essential ingredient of your work, yet you mentioned the other day that there's less of it in the three north-eastern films than in your other work with Paul. Can you elaborate on that?

I think these are just harsher times. Whichever writers I work with – I've been with Paul for thirty years now, and before that Jim Allen and Barry Hines – many of the subjects have humour, because that's the nature of the stories we're telling. The situations are inherently or potentially funny and they make you smile. The way we work, it's always been, 'What's the story? Is it worth telling? What's the core of it? What are the essential scenes we've got

I, Daniel Blake: Briana Shann, Hayley Squires, Dave Johns and Dylan McKiernan.

to show? Are they worth showing?' We'd never say, 'God, we're telling a miserable story. We better put in a funny scene or a joke or two,' because they'd never work. Some scenes Paul has written were funny when I read them, but somehow when we shot them they weren't, so we cut them out. In the end, the only truth is the truth of the characters – the situation, the people around them, the way they speak. In *The Old Oak*, some of the people in the pub are quite funny that way. It's unconscious humour, but there's not a lot there.

I might be wrong, but I think a lot of the humour has gone out of life. In the gig economy, people are mainly working on their own, and you don't get the comedy there is on a building site, on the docks or on the railways. Wherever people work in gangs, they take the mickey out of the bloke in charge – the foreman or works manager – and each other. People are given nicknames, and there are always running gags. Now, there's very little collective organization, and so people are separated from each other. Humour comes from being together and having a laugh, sharing the harshness of the job, or whatever the conditions are, and seeing the funny side of it. You don't get that so much now.

Leaping ahead briefly to Sorry We Missed You, *there are a few funny moments involving Seb's graffiti crew, and also when Ricky takes his daughter, Liza Jane, on a delivery run. But then Ricky is forbidden by his boss from letting her accompany him.*

Despite the fact he's meant to be a free agent and his own boss, he isn't at all. Paul's scenes with Ricky and Liza Jane are very good. She talks to him about his job. 'Who's organizing this? Who's putting all these restrictions into your phone? Why are they doing it? Why don't they build in the fact that you need to go to the lavatory sometimes?' It's the innocent child asking simple questions about the gig-economy job that nobody else asks.

Returning to I, Daniel Blake, *Daniel feels a sense of injustice when he sees Katie being stonewalled in the Jobcentre, and perhaps he intuits she's as socially isolated as he is.*

Daniel is a widower, obviously. He and his wife weren't able to have children, so, yes, he's quite isolated. He's made a friend of his neighbour, the lad who's being a bit of an entrepreneur, and he makes fun of him – he's got a sense of humour. From his work days, he's got a sense of justice, so when he sees Katie being bullied in the Jobcentre, he speaks up for her. Then he helps her get home with the kids. So their circumstances bring them together. Because he's got no immediate family, Katie's someone he can help, and it gives a focus to his life. He uses his skills to help her repair the flat she's been given. It's very concrete help, just simple things. He doesn't have grandchildren, so seeing her kids fills a little void for him, and he tells Katie about his wife. Then, when he declines, she and the kids help him. I can't say that they're that close, but there's a kind of mutual respect. If someone has helped you, then you've got a soft spot for them. It's just recognizing the kindness in a world that can be brutal.

Heartbreakingly, Katie gives Daniel her dinner to thank him, pretending she's not hungry.

As much as anything, she's ashamed that she can't feed herself. She hasn't got enough food to go around. She and Daniel are each trying to maintain their pride, and at the same time lend a helping hand when they can. She's a feisty girl, Katie. She'll stand her ground, but she's in an impossible situation.

It's unfathomable that a mother should not have enough to eat in one of the world's wealthiest countries. Can you talk about the food bank scene?

Daniel's far too proud to think of using the food bank himself, but he sees that Katie's struggling to get food and, since there are kids involved, he takes her there. She's so desperate for food that she loses her self-control. Paul heard from a Glasgow food bank where the exact same thing happened: a young mother was so desperate for food that she opened a tin of whatever it was – I think it was beans – and just put some in her mouth. That seemed such an extraordinary image of the consequences of this conscious cruelty that we thought we should include it. I knew that for it to work, everyone had to be shocked by it. If I rehearsed it, the shock would have worn off, because we would have talked about it. Hayley [Squires] knew what she was going to do as Katie, but nobody else did. We set it up with two cameras and arranged the furniture in such a way that we could pan around the room and get a clear view of her when she's given the food.

There were little side aisles and a main table down the centre with a chair so that the woman who was taking Hayley around would see it and sit Hayley in it, which she did, fortunately. If she hadn't, Hayley, who knew the plan, would have made her way towards it. One camera was able to see Hayley when she moved to where she would get the tin, and then where she would sit down. A broad table was placed between that camera and Hayley so that no one could block the shot. The other camera was [trained] on the other people facing Hayley, either to bring them up to the right position or to be there for a two-shot. We planned this very simple choreography as best we could and hoped that the people would go to the right positions. It sort of worked.

All the people in the queue were familiar with the food bank. Most of them had used it and were happy to be in the queue. And the people running it ran either that bank or another one. One of them was the woman who took Hayley around. A small woman, lovely – the kindness, again, is extraordinary – she said, 'Let me help you with your shopping.' It was incredibly sensitive, the way she made sure to give dignity to this woman who can't feed her kids. You think, 'This is who we are as a people,' and yet the state that is supposed to represent us is the harshest it can be. Why is there this disconnect between the kindness of the women and men who run the food banks and the cruelty of the state, our elected representatives? The answer is that the state imposes an economic system that we've been told equals freedom, but it is, in fact, about inequality between those with economic power and those who sell their labour or suffer because they can't.

Katie feels abased again when she's forced to work as a prostitute so she can buy food. Were you able to keep this from Dave Johns, who plays Daniel, so that he'd be upset when he discovers it?

We filmed that as a surprise, when he finds out the address where she's working, but he knows what she's doing when he goes there to confront her and tells her she mustn't do it.

We see her anguish.

Yes, the humiliation of it. Paul did the research and discovered there's an increase in women turning to that.

One commentator criticized that sequence, arguing that having Daniel judge and act on Katie's decision to take up prostitution robs her of agency. But if prostitution is a valid choice for some women, in Katie's case it's clearly a choice made under extreme duress.*

The people who write those things are usually immune from having to make that choice. Again, it's middle-class morality, without an understanding of the depths of poverty. There's been a consistent strand in Paul's writing, from *My Name Is Joe* onwards: What choices do people have? Katie's choice may be horrible and disgusting, but at least she's got some independence. She can put food

---

* Kate Bradley, 'Ken Loach, Sex Work and Paternalism', published on the *Revolutionary Socialism in the 21st Century* website, 9 October 2019. www.rs21.org.uk.

on the table. She can organize the rest of her life and try to get out of her situation. It's a slippery slope, of course. Once you've done it [worked as a prostitute], it's hard to give it up because of the income. It's something I can't pontificate about, only record it as a fact. People do it, and you can understand why.

How was the experience of filming I, Daniel Blake *in the north-east?*

It's a very good place to work. One thing you look for is a rich culture of comedy and struggle that can inhabit the film and become a character in it. Liverpool has it. Manchester has it, to an extent. South Yorkshire has it. I'd never really worked at length in the north-east before, and I'd always felt it was a place where the language was strong. The Geordies have a beautiful dialect and a concise but eloquent way of speaking. So there are all the elements of an identifiable local culture that people are very proud of.

As a landscape, it's extraordinary. It crystallizes the economic struggle over the decades since Thatcher. Coal mining was big – that's gone. Shipbuilding was big – that's gone. Steel was big in context – that's gone. All the old industries have disappeared from an area that was almost totally dependent on them; it's a contained space, so it becomes immediately apparent when you're there what has happened. Some new industries have started up. There are some middle-class areas of Newcastle that are very pleasing. The centre of the city is stunning, but the poverty around it in other quarters is still intense. The mining villages – most were in County Durham, though there's some in Northumberland and elsewhere – have clearly been abandoned and left to rot. Some have actually been marked for no future development, but people still live in them. All signs of the pits have been removed, apart from the winding wheels.

One other thing: there are a lot of very talented people there. You find talented people everywhere, but they're very sharp in the north-east. They've been sharpened by the conflicts; a lot of their culture comes from the industrial struggle.

Sorry We Missed You, *the next film you made in the area, follows* Riff-Raff, The Flickering Flame *and* The Navigators *in that it shows how casual employment has become normalized. Ricky and*

Abby, the struggling couple in the film, aren't salaried employees but independent contractors who work gigs. How do you see the gig economy in historical context?

When you've lived a long time, you see the course of how work has been transformed, from the trade union struggles for basic rights – the eight-hour day, paid holidays, sick pay, a decent pension, and so on – right back to the 1945 post-war settlement, which created an infrastructure to support private business and a healthy, well-housed workforce to repair the damage of the war. We didn't have the workforce after the war, hence the *Windrush* generation and encouraging immigration. But big production was in the hands of private businesses and, towards the end of the 1970s, that created problems. So much had been won in the '40s, '50s and '60s, then in the '70s it all began to fall apart. Thatcher came to power determined to rescue British capitalism, reduce the power of the working class and make it easier to exploit them. She didn't use that language, obviously, but that was the point. In 1974, Heath had gone to the polls on the slogan 'Who Governs Britain?'* and lost. It was the same for Thatcher, basically – 'Who runs the country, the unions or your democratically elected government?' – but she won the 1979 election with a big majority.†

The gig economy has its roots in Thatcher's privatizing of public services and the utilities. Once she began her transformation of the economy, the whole consciousness was changed. Everything followed from there, including the worship of the entrepreneur who makes money out of other people's labour. Because capitalism is dynamic, not stable, small companies get taken over by big ones. It's endemic in the system that all the investment will go to the

---

* When Prime Minister Edward Heath addressed the nation on 7 February 1974, he said: 'Do you want a strong government which has clear authority for the future to take decisions which will be needed? Do you want Parliament and the elected government to continue to fight strenuously against inflation? Or do you want them to abandon the struggle against rising prices under pressure from one particularly powerful group of workers [the miners]?' The general election on 28 February resulted in a hung Parliament and Heath's resignation. On 4 March, Harold Wilson returned to power as leader of a Labour minority government.
† Held on 3 May 1979.

company making the most profits, and when the competition is between corporations, they compete on quality and costs. They reduce the costs of raw materials, but the big one is that they're under constant pressure to find different ways of decreasing the costs of labour to avoid being priced out of the market. So, if you employ people, you don't abide by trade union agreements but try to find a way of not paying holiday pay, sick pay or the minimum wage. You might be forced to pay a minimum hourly wage, but you're not guaranteeing any hours. Reducing people's hours renders the minimum wage meaningless.

The ending of the agreement the Liverpool dockers had for job security was massively significant. It wasn't that the trade unions were right and the employers were wrong. As we showed in *The Flickering Flame*, the issue at stake was the casualization of the workforce, which the dockers had fought for so long. *The Navigators* and *It's a Free World . . .* were very much about the same issue. *Which Side Are You On?*, our documentary about the miners' strike, was about the destruction of the communities we revisited in *The Old Oak*; in fact, Heather Wood, whom we'd filmed feeding the miners for free in Easington in 1984, acts in a scene in *The Old Oak* that we shot in the same village. So there's a process at work that's been on the go for approaching half a century. I did a broadcast with Heather and one of the Easington miners' leaders for the Labour Party in 2017. The miners' struggle has been her life, really.

These were all steps in the development of a casualized workforce that struggles for its basic rights. You've made the point that it's much harder to organize trade unions now that the industrial working class has fragmented. It's the epitome of the class struggle. I'm reminded every day of the ideas that we had in the 1960s. I joined the Labour Party and supported Harold Wilson in 1964, but soon the group I was in realized he wasn't going to change anything. And sure enough, he didn't. We connected to various anti-Stalinist left groups – the Trotskyist groups, of which there were three main ones in Britain. There was the old slogan, 'If you want to be a communist, go and live in Russia.' Well, no, because Stalin was an appallingly monstrous dictator who destroyed so much of the 1917 Revolution. Another slogan on the left was: 'Neither Washington nor Moscow.' From the different texts our group gave us and which we discussed, I learned the fundamental principles of the class struggle and class division and a view of history that made sense for the first time.

The whole process from Thatcher onwards endorses that analysis of the fundamental split in society between those who own, control, and – because of the system they operate in – exploit those who sell their labour, the workers themselves. The class conflict is not something that extremists talk about. It's actually an essential consequence of the economic system. As I've said, business cannot exist without making profits and competition, because the competition for market share means you have got to keep cutting the cost of labour. And because the workforce must, of course, try to defend and improve their wages and conditions, there's no way out of that conflict. That realization I had back in the '60s is, on every day that passes, visible and palpable in the news.

The polarization of the classes in terms of wealth, or the lack of it, recalls the 1930s. The fact that nearly everyone has a mobile phone now doesn't disguise the fact that 18 per cent of the British population live in absolute poverty, the same figure as in 1936.

The stakes get higher all the time. The food banks have gone up 50 per cent in a year. Mainly people are working, but they can't survive. A whole generation of younger people have no chance of buying a home.

The Sorry We Missed You *couple Abby and Ricky, who are in their early forties, never became homeowners because they lost their savings at Northern Rock* during the 2007–8 financial crisis. To try to save again, they're working gruelling gigs.*

They're trapped by the system. It's like being in a bog, isn't it? The more you try to take steps out of it, the further your feet sink in. Ricky's in exactly that situation. He's taken on this delivery job to pay off his debts, but he's bought the van to get the job, so he's further in debt.

---

* The Northern Rock bank and mortgage lender, based in Newcastle upon Tyne, failed owing to a liquidity crisis and was nationalized in February 2008.

Having sold the family car to help pay for the van, Ricky has made it difficult for Abby to carry out her duties as an on-call home healthcare worker. She can make her house calls only by using buses and walking.

Again, Paul's such a brilliant writer because he brings these contradictions together.

Abby and Ricky love their kids, Seb and Liza Jane, but they neglect them because of their long hours. Liza Jane, a pre-adolescent who's good at school and wise for her age, has become anxious due to missing her mother. Seb, who's in the rebellious teenager phase, skips school and shoplifts spray paint to do his public graffiti art with his friends. He's a talented artist and savvy social sceptic, though, who recognizes that people are manipulated by capitalism, which is why he sprays on advertising hoardings.

And he derides his dad because he's a victim of it, constantly chasing around. Seb is sixteen, so, of course, his dad is his worst enemy. Ricky tells him he's got to be good at school, but because he's always working, Seb says, 'Where are you? You could give me lessons.' Part of being a teenager is that you become separate by distancing yourself from your parents. For a boy, that means separating from his dad. Most people have been through that. You rebel, which is a natural thing. The poor girl in *Family Life* [1971] couldn't do that, which is why she didn't know who she was in the end. But, as you say, Seb's bright, and his father only begins to realize that towards the end, because being a teenager, Seb's secretive. When you're that age, you don't share what you've got. You're busy building your own personality, and you do it away from your parents. The privacy of teenagers is necessary because they're insecure, and to show something you've developed in your mind to someone else is risky because they could criticize it.

I was thinking about this last night after we'd spoken. We've quite rightly talked about the ideas in the films, but when you're making the films, you never talk about politics. It's not relevant to the actors in the films as they perform their parts. What you say is, 'What's the reality of what you're doing? How would you react in this situation? What's the right thing, and how do you feel about it?' Often you say nothing. If you've got the right people, they will

Sorry We Missed You: Debbie Honeywood, Katie Proctor, Rhys Mcgowan and Kris Hitchen.

react in the right way. Though the words they say are Paul's – and there's space, of course, for them to add bits – they have to own them and not be aware that someone else wrote them.

The politics is the submerged part of the iceberg. I don't want the actors to have an objective view of it. They're simply at ground level, living the struggle, trying to survive. You don't have to be political to do that. You may be political in effect, but not consciously. You're not articulating it, so it's really important that we don't talk about that. It's about finding the truth of the moment and, in the case of something like *Sorry We Missed You*, the truth of the family.

Seb is making a political protest by spraying graffiti on advertising boards, even if he doesn't know it's political.

He knows it's bollocks what the ads are saying, but that's as far as you want to go with it. Rhys,[*] who played him, didn't have

---

[*] Billed as Rhys Stone (his surname being his mother's maiden name) in *Sorry We Missed You*, the actor was subsequently billed as Rhys Mcgowan (his father's surname) in *The Old Oak*.

the easiest start to life, but he's a very nice, very talented young man. Katie Proctor, who played the little girl, was a joy. She said she wanted to be a doctor. I said, 'Why?' She said, 'Then I'll be Dr Proctor.' And she's a brilliant gymnast. Her emotions are so close to the surface, and she was an extraordinary talent at that point in her life. I'm sure she'll go on to do lots of good things – and not necessarily acting.

Debbie Honeywood brings warmth and compassion to Abby in Sorry We Missed You. *It was gratifying to see that you then cast her and Rhys in* The Old Oak.

Debbie was working in a school as a teaching assistant for kids who need special help. The character in *Sorry We Missed You* is very like her: a kind, caring woman, always looking after people. Paul and I found that the people who do caring work are often torn. They're being ripped off financially but can't walk away from the people who need them, and so, of course, they do more hours than they're paid for, and their own families can suffer.

There's a tender scene where Seb sadly parts from the girl in his graffiti crew, Roz. She leaves on a bus for Blackpool because she's been bullied for being different, she says. There's a hint of trouble at home, possibly abuse, and of a life spiralling out of control.

Who knows? We know there's a lot of bullying. She's a teenager. She's obviously not got a good home life. She just wants to get away, and she's got a connection. She has a sort of dream that things will be better there. She says there'll be more jobs, so she just gets on the bus and goes. Again, another talented little girl. They don't have it easy, kids.

You included that scene to show another side to Seb?

It seemed to be a grace note in the film, another little incident in his life. He isn't just an angry teenager. And he and the girl are just being true to who they are.

Because his nerves are frayed owing to the pressure, Ricky cracks at one point and clouts Seb, who goes to stay with his mate overnight.

There's a welcome dab of humour when Ricky grabs a child's tricycle and rides it in his haste to find and apologize to Seb. When Ricky gets mugged shortly afterwards, Seb immediately shows his dad he loves him. This is a close-knit family that will survive, as long as Ricky doesn't crash his van through exhaustion – but the film ends suggesting that's a real possibility.

You want to end it with a certain jeopardy because you know Ricky is dangerous now. Paul met a guy who'd carried on driving with a broken leg and was a danger to himself and everyone else on the road. Ricky is in the same danger, but he's trapped. That's the point of the story. People are trapped.

Kris Hitchen had a small role in The Navigators, *so it must have been pleasing to cast him as Ricky. He plays a husband and father whose pride is at stake because of the fear he'll fail his family. It's an emotionally demanding role.*

Kris is a good pro. He hadn't acted for a long time and had mainly been working as a plumber. Driving a van was what he did anyway [as part of his job]. It's important to find people who have the basic skills of the part so that there's never an issue. What you learn through work, Kris had all that, absolutely. And a good sense of humour, a lot of energy and all that optimism Ricky has at the beginning. He was very good to work with.

The other drivers in the film were all played by drivers. Ross Brewster, who played Maloney, the manager of the depot, had been a policeman. Another policeman we worked with up there, Stephen Clegg, played the Jobcentre manager in *I, Daniel Blake* and the police officer in *Sorry We Missed You*.

Rather than read the riot act to Seb after he's been caught shoplifting, he patiently explains to him that he's lucky to have a family that loves him.

Yes. He tells Seb about the chances he has to make a go of things – it's a lovely scene. [Brewster and Clegg] were good actors for the parts because the police have to have real strength in saying what they say, and they don't apologize for it. The interesting thing is that, within the terms of their employment, the police can take film

Sorry We Missed You: Liza Jane (Katie Proctor) joins her dad Ricky (Kris Hitchen) on a delivery round.

work and play policemen and policewomen, but people in the DWP cannot play people who work in a Jobcentre. Whereas the police authorities are confident about the police's role and their workforce, the people who run the Jobcentres must assume a film would present them badly and don't want their employees colluding in that. The Jobcentre parts were actually quite difficult to cast. Apart from the two in speaking roles, they were ex-Jobcentre workers who came in to audition for us.

Maloney is not simply Ricky's adversary or the film's heavy, is he? As a gig-economy boss, he's a sign of the times.

The key thing with Maloney is that he has to explain that he's got the opportunity to expand the package delivery business by winning a lot of corporate contracts, and he sets out the rules of the game that Ricky has to follow as a driver. Some critics just saw Maloney as the bad guy, but to see the logic of his position – fulfilling his role according to the task he's being given – was very important. He's absorbed the propaganda and tells Ricky that he's his own boss, an entrepreneur, a knight of the road – whatever it is.

He tells Ricky, 'You're not working for us, you're working with us.'

Exactly, and Ricky buys it. But Maloney's very clipped, very strong, and he doesn't take any nonsense. Any driver who can't fulfil their contract will suffer the consequences. As I was saying earlier, it's the logic of employment for the employer to make money by competing with people who are pulling the same tricks.

The film shows in microcosm how the transformation of work to serve capitalists at the workers' expense imposes an archaic set of strictures on people that can't help but create misery and conflict. The Industrial Revolution created a form of slave labour where people worked sixty to ninety hours a week in factories, with fines and physical punishments for minor offences. The machinery was dangerous and the working conditions horrendous. Perhaps it catastrophizes the gig economy to say it echoes such an inhumane system, but there are parallels.

I think that's true. When the Industrial Revolution began, people went from the countryside into the factories in the cities, and the terms and conditions were very exploitative. As a result, workers banded together to fight for their rights, and a lot of people, such as the Tolpuddle Martyrs, suffered for it. Out of that came the growth of the big trade unions and their long struggles, back and forth, some of which they won and some of which they lost, but gradually they established basic rights, and the spirit of '45 played a part in that by bringing the idea of common ownership into the structure of society.

I carry around with me a quote from my original Labour Party [membership] card that's worth repeating. The party was set up by the trade unions and, in Clause IV, it stated its key aim was 'To secure for the workers by hand or by brain the full fruits of their industry and the most equitable distribution thereof that may be possible upon the basis of the common ownership of the means of production, distribution and exchange, and the best obtainable system of popular administration and control of each industry or service.' The idea that people get the full fruits of their industry is incompatible with the system they're working under, because if the employers have got to make a profit, the profit is surplus value.* In other words, the workers don't get the full fruits of their labour. So their struggle for trade union rights – which led to a real challenge in the minds of some, in that you could only achieve the full fruits of your industry by changing the basis of the economic system – was lost. And that has been the great problem we've had.

Whenever Labour have won the general election, the party that has chosen to represent the interests of labour in that inevitable conflict has represented the interests of the other side – the interests of capital. It's been a huge political failure. Ideally, the votes for the Labour Party should come from the vast majority of the common people demanding their rights, but the leadership of the party we've put in power says, 'Sorry, we're actually working for the other side.' It's not something you suddenly see from a distance, but it's happening day by day now with Starmer, who has said he's going to be more Blairite than Blair. This constant presentation of the leaders of the Labour Party being, in fact, the alternative leadership for capital is the essence of what's happened. And, as we were saying earlier, as capitalism develops, the power is no longer with the local factory owner, it's with international corporations that own businesses across every field of industry. Whether they're invested in media, production, services or whatever, many of them are bigger than individual states. And because they're under constant pressure to reduce the power of labour, because their main competitors will be doing it, that's made matters worse and will continue to do so.

The other problem is climate change. When politicians are still talking about growth, corporations will not concede that they have to stop using more resources and cut down on transport. The more they do that, the more they poison the atmosphere. It's the only way they can see the world, and it's a trap. It's as if they're in charge of a runaway train that's going to run off the rails and can't get

---

* Karl Marx explained: 'Capitalist production is not merely the production of commodities, it is essentially the production of surplus-value. The labourer produces, not for himself, but for capital. It no longer suffices, therefore, that he should simply produce. He must produce surplus-value. That labourer alone is productive, who produces surplus-value for the capitalist, and thus works for the self-expansion of capital.' *Das Kapital*, Vol. 1 (1867), Part V, Chapter 16: 'Absolute and Relative Surplus Value'.

hold of the controls – and don't want to. Paul and I talk a lot about the climate emergency, which is so intense. The cause of it is so transparent, and everybody across the world can see it, but no one can stop it.

How can films make a difference?

It's a long, slow process and a battle, but you try to build consciousness. So then the question is: How does consciousness develop? The classic answer is, you learn through a struggle, through actually confronting the issues of where you get your daily bread, of work and of how you meet your financial needs. The process of being part of the struggle means you learn the reality of how society is structured. The miners' strike was a huge learning curve for a lot of people, and many came to politics through it. But then the memory of these struggles fades.

What, then, sets the tone politically in the national psyche?

The propaganda comes from the big consensus broadcasters. Political correspondents like Andrew Marr and Nick Robinson are the key ones; Jeremy Paxman used to be. They do history-of-England-type summaries, and the general attitude to Thatcherism is: 'It was a terrible process, and she destroyed a lot of communities, but we are liberals, you know, and our heart bleeds for them. People lost their jobs, factories were shut, there was massive depression and poverty, but it had to be done, it was a cruel necessity.' Of course, when you look back, Thatcherism was a disaster on every front. It not only destroyed people's lives, but contributed to climate change, which is destroying the planet. I can't see how together we can husband the world's resources now.

Do you feel that the opponents of capitalism now have enough teeth to stem the tide?

I don't know. The old saying is – and I think Sam Watts in *The Spirit of '45* says it – 'If workers knew the strength they had, they could change the world.' We had a few lines expressing that in *The Old Oak*, but we cut them out because it seemed like Paul was saying it rather than the characters.

One of the problems is that the mass media hates films or plays or books or stories in which people share their strength. Everyone's got to be a victim. 'Oh, it's a terrible story. Have a charity pass the hat around.' It's a pass-the-hat-around society. That's why they will never tell the proper story of the miners' strike. Anything that indicates organized strength is the enemy, because that suggests, 'Yes, we can do things. We can bring about change.'

Daniel spray-paints his name and a desperate protest demanding his benefits appeal date on the wall of the Jobcentre in I, Daniel Blake, *and Seb's graffiti scorns advertising's illusory panaceas in* Sorry We Missed You, *but they're lone voices in the dark, aren't they?*

Yes. *Land and Freedom, Bread and Roses* and *The Wind That Shakes the Barley*, for example, are about organized power and resistance, but often a documentary can speak more clearly than a fiction film [about collective action]. To make good work, you can't impose a consciousness on the characters that they wouldn't have; it becomes false when you speak through characters. You have to cut out words that would clarify things. When you make films about strikes or industrial struggles or civil wars, you realize people do learn through their struggles. That's when they do speak – and they speak really clearly. I've met so many political working-class men and women who speak with the directness that you don't get in economists, academics who wrap everything in long sentences or professional politicians, who are used to not speaking clearly because they don't want to give hostages to fortune. People actually engaged in confronting their employer in an industrial struggle speak with absolute clarity.

The people do, too, in the debates in Land and Freedom, The Wind That Shakes the Barley *and* Jimmy's Hall.

They are passionate in those debates because the issues have got massive consequences for them. That day or tomorrow.

Like The Navigators, I, Daniel Blake, Sorry We Missed You *and* The Old Oak *have a near docudrama quality reminiscent of some of your early films, but there's an extra anxiety in the way people walk and how they talk to each other – a renewed urgency.*

That was a conscious choice for the last few films because obviously I knew I was getting towards the end of what I can do. Working with Robbie Ryan was a factor in that. He and Barry Ackroyd are both brilliant cameramen, but they have different strengths. I had the feeling that I wanted to work in a clear, simple, economic way, shorn of frills, to say things in very plain language, while at the same time not diminishing the nuances of the relationships or the complexity of people's positions, like the man running the delivery depot. The hope each time was to create, if we could, a film where those complexities and nuances are protected and there are no exaggerations. The films should be aesthetically pleasing, but clear and pared down. We tried to find a lucidity and a limpid quality in them; in the clarity you try to tell the story.

With Barry's camerawork, he would find images as he moved from one person to the other, in the same way that your eye moves. If he'd filmed that bunch in the pub in *The Old Oak*, he would maybe have panned from the back of the head of the person speaking to find their full face. And once they've been interrupted, he'd find someone else, maybe starting again with the back of their head. Robbie shot those scenes by going from frame to frame. It has the same sense of spontaneity and observation, but the shots were just simpler.

What's aesthetically pleasing about these films is their lack of artifice or self-conscious pictorialism. The beauty is in the rawness or austerity.

'Austerity' is the word I was looking for. There's a beautiful poem by Brecht that I keep in my diary and quote sometimes: 'And I always thought: the very simplest words / Must be enough. When I say what things are like / Everyone's heart must be torn to shreds. / That you'll go down if you don't stand up for yourself / Surely you see that.'* It's not a very poetic translation from the German, but there it is – the simplest of words must suffice. This is an instinct also.

---

* 'And I Always Thought' ('Und ich dachte immer') (c.1956), translated by Michael Hamburger, in Bertolt Brecht, *Poems, 1913–1956* (Eyre Methuen, 1976), p. 452.

Does that also apply to how you use music in the films?

The biggest dilemmas in film-making are often about the music. I've always worked with George Fenton, and gradually over the years we've cut down on the amount of music we've used. In both *I, Daniel Blake* and *Sorry We Missed You*, the music emerges only at the end, whereas in *Land and Freedom* it's a stronger presence: if it's not as constant as in most films, it carries you through much of the story. George is always concerned to do the right thing for the film. He couldn't be less pretentious or less attached to the idea of all his music being included, but on *The Old Oak* I started off thinking we could include more than usual. George wrote some beautiful stuff, though we ended up using very little, and not as much as we wanted to. That's the danger. I felt bad, as if I was letting him down. On a personal level, it's really difficult, because he's a lovely man and we're great friends. But equally, the music can lessen the rawness of a film. Music should just indicate something's important, or else make it more generalized. If you're saying something very specific on a small scale, the music can say this is a big issue. There might be just two people in the scene, but the music can suggest there's a breadth to what you're saying.

Is it harder to make difficult decisions – such as omitting part or all of someone's contribution – at different times during the film-making process?

When you're in the middle of post-production, by which time you're very familiar with the film, your judgement can go. At the beginning, your judgement's pretty sharp. You were able to say, 'No, we don't need this scene. We can go from X to Y. That's the shape we can make it.' Towards the end, when you've done all that and you know the film inside out, your instinct about it is weaker because you know what's coming. It becomes so much harder to judge, really.

Over the years, have you and your editor Jonathan Morris adhered to a key principle of editing?

The key thing is keeping the principle of the observer, so you cut when your eyes would move. The old, traditional film-editing rule was: 'Cut before they speak.' In fact, I sat alongside one editor once who said, 'Cut a few frames before they speak, because then you keep the audience on their toes.' But I think the reverse is true. The audience has a thought process. If it was sitting in the room with the characters, it would look across to the person who's going to make the next intervention or the person who is maybe challenged. When you hear something that makes you shift your look, that's the point at which you cut. Barry Ackroyd's camera movement is always cued by something. Barry doesn't know – and the camera doesn't know – where to go, until something happens in the room or at a meeting or whatever. But if you were there, you would look. So it's a human thought, not an editor's in respect of what people are thinking, that dictates where you cut. If you are talking and I interrupt you, the camera doesn't know I'm going to interrupt you until it hears the interruption, and then that's where the cut is.

So a cut mustn't second-guess the characters in the midst of a conversation?

Right. It's just a general principle that emerged. Jonathan and I never talk about it, but that's the rationale.

You don't use dissolves much.

Haven't used one for ages. Watch out – there might be one in *The Old Oak*, but there's a reason for it, which might be apparent. No, we hardly ever use dissolves. We've started to use fades a little more recently, just to allow things to linger in your mind before the next thing comes in. It's to do with being more measured as well. If you do a scene that you've pared to the bone and cut immediately to something else, it might not register, so you want a moment's reflection in the audience before you move on.

To create a pause, a second where the viewer thinks, 'What have I just seen?' or has an emotional response to it?

Yes. Again, you've got to be careful the viewer doesn't start to fidget. You have to earn the pause.

After completing I, Daniel Blake *and* Sorry We Missed You, *did you feel you had unfinished business in the Newcastle–Durham area?*

I think that's true. I always had a lingering thought that those two pointed to a third film, if we could find it, but it was a big mountain to climb.

What was the main idea behind The Old Oak?

The punishment through the withholding of social security [in *I, Daniel Blake*] and the consequence of how work has been transformed with the gig economy [in *Sorry We Missed You*] are complementary. In different ways, both are portraits of exploitation. They relate because the punishment in one forces people to endure the punishment in the other, because they have to work, and gig-economy jobs are the only option. Both films have got very harsh outcomes, so we thought it would be good to tell a story in which – without minimizing the harshness of life – some human connections are made, something we can build on. Finding a story to say that without being falsely optimistic was quite tricky. But it did seem to be the final brick in the pyramid, as it were.

Did you encounter Syrian refugees in the north-east when you were filming I, Daniel Blake *and* Sorry We Missed You?

We were aware there were refugees there, but we didn't seek them out because we were working on those other projects. I think it was as we were filming *Sorry We Missed You* that Paul became particularly conscious of them. One of the starting points was his friendship with the [Gateshead] vicar John Barron and his wife, Val, a community organizer, who were very active in supporting the Syrian refugees. They had helped them right at the beginning, when the local authorities had had little warning [of the refugees' arrival] and were caught on the hop. The scene at the beginning of the film where the refugees get a hostile reception as they arrive on a bus in the village was based on John and Val's experience of seeing an incident like that. What we show is pretty bad, but it was probably a little bit worse in reality.

The Old Oak is set in the summer of 2016. The Brexit vote was held on 23 June of that year. Were you and Paul prompted by the belief that Brexit had brought xenophobia and racism to the surface? Or was there evidence of some people in the north-east expressing resentment that Syrian refugees had arrived?

It was very much in the air. We met people who said, 'This is unfair,' and there were a lot of reports [of discontent]. We knew Claire Rodgerson,* who plays the community organizer Laura in the film and works combating the far right and the spread of racism among young people. Tommy Robinson† held meetings there. The crowds weren't entirely hostile to him, and he obviously felt there was some fruitful ground for him.

I think a lot of the people who voted for Brexit were not racists but just felt the system was broken. They were in trouble, and nothing was working for them. They refused to give the government an endorsement when they wanted it – and not just the government, but the political establishment, which very much includes the Labour Party. In the north-east, people felt the local authorities had done very little for them, whether there was a Tory government or a Labour one. The pit villages are a case in point. They were abandoned by the Tories, Blair's Labour government and the Labour local authorities.

The north-east has a tradition of supporting refugees. The Durham Miners' Association stood with Jewish and Spanish refugees during the 1930s.

Yes, that was pointed out to us by some of the older County Durham mining people, particularly one or two of the older wives, and David Temple,‡ an ex-miner I know who's a historian there. They're very

---

* In an article written by Adrian Lobb for the *Big Issue*, 25 September 2023, Rodgerson is quoted as saying: 'In Sunderland, the summer I met Paul [Laverty] there had been seven far-right leaders visit our city. I was working trying to help young people disentangle their economic and political fears from their outward expressions of racism. I was also part of an anti-racist collective in Sunderland called Sunderland Unites.'
† Robinson (born Stephen Christopher Yaxley in 1982) is a far-right, anti-Islam campaigner.
‡ Temple is the author of *The Collieries of Durham Vol. 1* and *Vol. 2*

proud of that tradition and conscious of the obligation history owes them for welcoming the refugees. We thought of including it in the film, but we'd have had to drag a little speech into the story, which always smacks of 'We're telling the audience something they ought to know,' rather than it being part of the emotional exchanges or arguments of real people. In this case, maybe we erred too much on the side of not telling people [about that continuity].

The Home Office has an out-of-sight, out-of-mind policy with respect to asylum seekers. It's estimated that the north-east has taken three times as many refugees per 10,000 people as London and the south-east combined. The policy seems to be 'send them away from the capital and forget about them', just as Katie and her kids are relocated from London to Newcastle in I, Daniel Blake.

I suspect it's a cynical policy. Obviously, we're not privy to the discussions that go on about these things, but that's the only way it makes sense. There's cheap accommodation for refugees in the north-east, and it's not an area where people of influence will complain. From the government's point of view, it's the obvious place to send them. And the people who do complain about refugees will be put down as racists, Brexiteers and Little Englanders, as opposed to sophisticated people from the south-east.

The film's main character, T. J. Ballantyne, the Old Oak's publican, played by Dave Turner, is a lonely, depressed, middle-aged man who hasn't allowed his losses and sufferings to compromise his principles or his capacity for compassion. How does TJ's past inform the story?

As a kid, he worked in the mines with another character in the film, his friend Charlie. TJ had done various jobs since the pit closed and now runs the local pub. He was militant during the [1984] strike and worked hard for the community, as there was so much to do to try to keep people together. And like a lot of people over the years,

---

(both 1994), *Durham Miners' Millennium Book* (2000), *Above and Below the Limestone: The Pits and People of Easington District* (2001) and *The Big Meeting: A History of the Durham Miners' Gala* (2011), all published by TUPS Books.

I think he's lost hope and is just getting through the day. The pub's falling apart because he's got no money. The old regulars come in with the same old bile and backchat. Then the Syrians arrive, and they have more problems, which the village can't sustain. The film is about how TJ responds to this.

Early on, the pub locals, all from old mining families, complain about the devaluation of their terraced houses, which are being bought cheaply by a Cypriot company. Charlie, whose wife is ill, breaks down because his house, once valued at £50,000, is now worth about £8,000. He and a few of his fellow drinkers channel their distress into anger at the Syrian refugees who are being placed in the empty cottages.

At that point, the Syrians have just arrived, but the locals haven't really met them yet. There's general unease about them that obviously takes the villagers in different directions. As the scene develops and Yara comes into the pub for the first time, it sets the reality of the story. What we tried to show in the pub is all gradations of response. One of the drinkers won't join in the criticism of the refugees. One little woman there just sees the problems with the village – with the school, with the queues for the doctors, and so on. She sees that the infrastructure is already failing and fears it will fail even more when the refugees have moved in, because there will be more demands on it, which is a reasonable concern. So some of them begin by feeling hostility towards the refugees, but most end up feeling compassion for them, in the way people often do. The instinctive responses they have at the end of the film are not a thought-out position. When the villagers learn that Yara's father has been killed, they say, 'Someone's lost a father, someone's lost a husband. I want to be with them, I want to support them.'

There are gradations, too, among the ones who try to make life intolerable for the refugees. There's Eddy, the one who is the most articulate; Vic, who veers towards racism; and Gary, who's got a sharp wit and echoes what Vic says. They're not the hardcore types who would support fascism, probably. Rather than say that, we wanted to say, 'Here they are. From the beginning of the film, they just want to get rid of foreigners,' and I think we see that their attitudes are rather broad and predictable. All we wanted to do is show the process and the soil from where racism can spring.

Was the pub in the film based on a real one?

No, it's just a pub, and it's called the Old Oak for obvious reasons – 'hearts of oak', the ships built of oak that defeated the Spanish Armada, all that. The oak tree was used as a place for justice in the Middle Ages. People held gatherings beneath the oak tree, as a symbol, for centuries.

Was it always intended that the film would begin with the montage of photos taken by Yara as she arrives in a village on a bus with the other refugees, or was it something you added later?

The idea came after Paul had written the script. He always writes a lot, which is brilliant because it gives a very rounded picture of what the story is and who the people are. I was trying to find an economical way of introducing the idea that Yara is a photographer. Initially, I thought [the montage] would make a good title scene, but actually when we were doing it we realized it wouldn't work with the titles because we'd have had to put translations of the dialogue there. We wanted to go to live action quite quickly and saw it would be a real tangle. Paul didn't want to put titles over the camera being taken by the guy [Rocco] in the Newcastle United shirt who harangues the Syrians, because it's too important an action. So it didn't turn into the title sequence, but it did seem a concise way of introducing the idea of Yara being a photographer.

Why did you choose to make her a photographer?

Paul makes the point in the script that it filters her raw experience of the horror she's seen in Syria: the bombings, the destruction of communities, people being wounded, mutilated, and dying. That must be overwhelming. The process of recording it means you select the images you want to be memorable. They are the medium between you and the harshest direct experience. She draws a philosophy from it: 'I can only survive if I can see some hope in it somewhere.'

The Old Oak: T. J. Ballantyne (Dave Turner), outside his ailing pub in County Durham.

The long-closed back room in the pub becomes contested territory. First, TJ refuses to let Charlie and his mates hold a meeting there to build opposition to the refugees. Then, at the suggestion of Yara and Laura, TJ has the room refurbished for the serving of meals to the refugees and impoverished locals as a single community. In fact, Yara's admiration of the photos of the miners' strike, taken by TJ's uncle and mounted on the walls of the room, prefigure its regeneration as a unifying space, so that it's no longer a dusty shrine to the past.

It rediscovers its role. During the strike, the miners and their families and supporters would have come together in places that are no longer there, like the miners' welfare clubs, which were huge spaces, and there'd be hundreds of people sitting down. They've all gone, so in the film this is the only space the villagers have got, and it seats fifty rather than two or three hundred people. But, yes, it rediscovers its purpose, that's for sure.

The room has an echo of Jimmy Gralton's Pearse–Connolly Hall.

I was aware of that and tried not to have the same shots. I didn't mention it to anyone in case it gave them pause. I was thinking, 'Christ, another big dusty room with cobwebs. Open the blinds, the light floods in . . .' So it was a tricky one, but fortunately the concentration was on the photos on the wall, not on the room itself.

As in I, Daniel Blake, *in* The Old Oak *an older white male helps a young woman in difficulties simply out of compassion, perhaps from a fatherly impulse – not because he has a sexual agenda, as Vic spitefully suggests. Like simple acts of kindness, the idea that a man could befriend a woman disinterestedly is unusual in films now.*

Films get drawn to the lurid, don't they? I can understand why – it's box office – but it's demeaning and diminishing. That friendships between men and women have to be coloured or manipulated in that way is just a cliché of commercial film-making. As in the story, in the making of the film Ebla Mari [who plays Yara] and Dave Turner became really good friends. What you see in the film is how they actually worked together. They just chatted away. And Dave's got a daughter who's older than Ebla, and they were good pals. Ebla was pals with everyone, really.

Tell me about working with Dave Turner.

It was much simpler than Dave often makes it sound. As you know, we do these short improvisations when we're considering people for the roles. They're nothing to do with the film but are little scenes that draw on the same kinds of emotions that they have to share in the film – a break-up of a relationship, a moment of jealousy, scenes that have real emotions that everyone can imagine. From the very simple ones to really quite complex ones, Dave was always spot on.

I usually do these improvisations sitting across a table from the other person. It's just an exchange between two or three people at the most. I observe the eye contact that they make, how they use language, to see whether I believe in what they're doing. When we get towards the end, Kahleen [Crawford, casting director] videos it on the phone. You see who the person is and what they communicate, and you form a judgement about whether the audience will respond to them, how truthful they are, whether they will touch you, whether they've got some natural timing and rhythm, whether they will be credible as the character. If we can reveal the person themselves, then that will also reveal the character in the film. Dave did everything we hoped for.

Dave is a Newcastle United supporter and plays one in Sorry We Missed You – *the client who gives Ricky a mouthful because he's wearing a Manchester United shirt. They cite results from their teams' 1990s rivalry to one-up each other. Dave's character in that scene is much more aggressive than TJ.*

I don't know [*laughs*] – if Dave put TJ in that situation, he'd probably react the same way because that's how Dave reacts. Yet when Ebla and Laura bring food to TJ to comfort him after his dog's been killed, Dave handles it with such delicacy. Just the little things he does that he's unaware of are spot on – the way he's embarrassed to eat, the respect he shows them, the way he shakes his head, putting on a brave face. There's no way you could direct someone by asking him to do any of those things, because it would unbalance what he's already doing and be totally false. This is who he is, and he just responds to the situation. I think a lot more people can do it than one can imagine, because there's such a mystique built up around acting that I think is really a sham. But, equally, it's quite special to find people with such sensitivity.

The killing of Marra, TJ's dog, reminded me of the killing of Kes. The teenage boys whose dog attacked Marra didn't intend it to happen, but the incident suggests that, unlike Billy Casper, they've got nowhere positive to channel their energies and probably limited hopes for the future.

I guess they wouldn't see it like that. They enjoy their dog and its presence. They enjoy trying to keep it in order, matching their strength against the dog's strength. It's all very youthful, macho stuff, isn't it? You know, 'I'm a real lad with a bit of strength, and I've got a dog that shows that and a thick strap I can whack it with if it doesn't behave.' Asserting themselves in ways that are antisocial, like having a bloody big dog, is a substitute for doing constructive things that lads like that ought to be doing. So, in reality, I think you're right. Theirs will be lives of intermittent casual work and financial insecurity, lived in a backward culture that we know only too well. Obviously, drugs are available. The consequences are various addictions and broken families.

Working on The Old Oak *with Claire Rodgerson and actual Syrian refugees, as well as people born in the Durham area, you must have had a sense that the solidarity the film celebrates was also present in the making of it, a living example of what can be achieved.*

I don't think of it in those grand terms. You just find people you can link up with who will help you put the film on the screen, but in practice that certainly happened in the making of *The Old Oak*, and there are now very good links, particularly between the women in Easington and the Syrian women. Heather and others have been instrumental in that by arranging gatherings, feasts of Syrian food and evenings together, which has been really positive.

What's difficult – well, it's more to do with decisions rather than difficulties – is a question that relates to both *The Old Oak* and *Route Irish*, where there are situations of people who have experienced the destruction of their towns and villages and homes, mutilations, children killed, husbands killed, terror that leaves scars we can't begin to imagine. On *The Old Oak*, the question was very specific. We worked with a very powerful, strong woman, Hasna Al Hassoun, one of three sisters from Syria living in Durham, who'd suffered the most appalling tragedy. A bombing in her street* had killed her husband and their two children and left her with no legs. When you hear that about someone, you think, 'How can they possibly recover?'

You see her in the film. We did a scene in which Yara talks to her and comes back and tells TJ what her situation is and her story. Then they went on to talk about the photographs in the pub, but the magnitude of Hasna's tragedy is so great that we just said, 'Why are we bothering with the photographs?' We almost felt there was an obligation to scrap what we were going to do and just have Hasna tell her story, so we made her a character and gave her a speech and put it in, then Yara and TJ walk on in silence. But, mistakenly or not, we cut the speech because it unbalanced the film. I think Hasna found it quite distressing. I have nightmares about this

---

* In Homs, western Syria, in 2012.

because, obviously, if people on a film are sharing their lives, you have an obligation to protect them. I made the mistake of shooting the speech in the first place and not judging that it might be difficult to include it. For the audience to have the memory of that tragedy in their heads and then suddenly be asked to be interested in a bunch of old photographs on a wall . . . it just wasn't a good sequence of thoughts. But I feel that in cutting out Hasna's story we let her down. It's really one of the most difficult decisions we've made.

The racists – Vic, Eddy and Gary – sabotage the electricity in the back room so it's unsafe and unusable. They're helped by Charlie, which is a terrible betrayal of his and TJ's friendship. When TJ realizes that he won't be able to continue hosting the communal meals, and that he might have to close the pub, he's so dejected it looks like he's going to throw in the towel. I wondered if that reflected pessimism on your and Paul's part?

I think it's about understanding pessimism. You know, you get up every morning and look out the window, and you see that thousands of [ruling-]class forces are against us. But what TJ says thank you for – before the Durham Miners' Gala – is that Yara has had the confidence to stick with hope, because she's seen the neighbours come out to share her and her family's grief after they learn her father has been killed. The local people don't turn their backs on the refugees. Though some idiots have destroyed the communal eating project, and TJ and Yara and the others will have to find a way to revive it, nevertheless, in a moment of real seriousness, people do come out of their homes and show which side they're on. That's the purposeful moment, and the miners' parade that follows it is, in a way, an expression of their support for the Syrians.

Do you think the friendships between the villagers and the Syrians will endure?

They may, they may not. It depends on if the villagers will continue them, and how well the Syrian families integrate. It depends on what happens to their kids and if they keep the community going. But it's certainly there now.

The Old Oak: solidarity at the Miners' Gala – Ebla Mari, Dave Turner and Hasna Al Hassoun (in wheelchair).

For everyone's benefit, the government needs to pump some money into the north-east to regenerate the villages and towns, create jobs and support the families.

Yes, it needs public investment, and that's one thing that, ideologically, neither the Tories nor the new Labour Party will provide. As far as they're concerned, the market will provide. But we've got forty years' experience of the market not providing.

Finally on The Old Oak, *whatever future there is or isn't for the pub and the communal meals, TJ and Ebla's march with their silk banner, painted in the style of the old colliery banners, offers hope for solidarity. If this does end up being your last fiction film, does that feel like a suitable conclusion?*

It could be worse. It's quite a good experience, getting up there and marching with the gang and sharing their strength. That always cheers you up. It's not too bad an ending to go out marching behind a brass band.

CHAPTER 15

Rebecca O'Brien

Interview with Loach's producer
partner at Sixteen Films

GRAHAM FULLER: *I understand that your mother was instrumental in helping theatre companies in Scotland. That sounds like it was a blueprint for your career as a film producer.*

REBECCA O'BRIEN: I grew up with a big family in a big home, Kerfield House, in Peebles, a small town about twenty-five miles south of Edinburgh. My mum was manic depressive, but also a very inspirational creative entrepreneur. She was a good organizer who did things like arrange a garden fete with knobs on that turned out to be an incredible fundraiser for the Freedom from Hunger campaign in 1963. We opened the entire grounds of the house for this event, the likes of which had not been seen there before. Rather than a 'Guess the Weight of the Cake' stall, we had 'Guess the Weight of the Elephant', because my uncle bought an elephant at Harrods. They said, 'You can't have one elephant – you have to have a herd,' but they gave him a cheque for a hundred quid for the cause, which was quite a lot at the time and got publicity.

My father eventually ran away and the family split apart, but my mother always tried to find ways to make a going concern of the places where we lived. She was an artist, and we got involved in the arts world in Edinburgh, where I went to school. A key person there was Richard 'Ricky' Demarco [born 1930], who was one of the co-founders [in 1963] of the Traverse Theatre and had a gallery in the city for many years. He introduced many interesting artists to Edinburgh and was very involved in the fringe side of the festival. Artists like Joseph Beuys came to Edinburgh because of Ricky, and he ran events where all sorts of theatre companies would turn up, and we would get involved. In 1976, Tadeusz Kantor's Polish theatre company Cricot 2 came to Edinburgh at the last minute and there was nowhere for them to stay, so my mum said they could come and stay in Peebles.

We got local B&B places involved, and the whole troupe arrived in their bus. Cricot 2's production of Kantor's *The Dead Class* was performed at the Edinburgh College of Art. It was an amazing show and it was huge – the hit of the festival. I was eighteen at the time, and that show was seminal in making me understand that 'event life' is better than normal, staid life. At the same time, I was getting involved with the Edinburgh Film Festival, which Lynda Myles was running at the time. I asked her two years running if I could come and help her out. Then, the third year – the landlord of my university accommodation had paid me to get out because he wanted the flat back – I wrote to Lynda and said, 'I'm actually coming to work for you because I can pay my way' [*laughs*]. I worked on the film programme for her the whole summer, saw lots of films and learned so much from Lynda. After I left university, I worked for David Gothard at Riverside Studios, in London, while going back to work at the Edinburgh Film Festival for two more years.

After Edinburgh, Cricot 2 had gone on to Riverside [in 1977], and it opened up as an arts centre shortly after that. It was another extraordinary place to be. I first worked there as a volunteer, and then in programming. We brought in all sorts of interesting theatre events from all over the world. I worked there for two years, but theatre wasn't right for me, so I left to do a one-week film-making course at a company called Crosswind Films. And that was it – that was my epiphany.

What was so special about Crosswind?

It was just a tiny, ambitious outfit, but the guy who ran it, Steve Bernstein, was very entrepreneurial and had decided to start teaching. He had a camera and lighting equipment, and it was an opportunity to get my hands on it and learn the basics – and it was very basic – of film production. I can load a camera and operate a Nagra sound machine, but I discovered I wasn't going to become an expert on that side of film-making. I'm good at organizing – at getting people together and understanding all the different departments.

Doing production made sense to me, and I knew there'd be a job out there for me. Crosswind employed me to work for them for a few months, and then Peter Wollen and Laura Mulvey, whom I'd met at Edinburgh and got to know socially, asked me if I would come to work with them on the low-budget film they were making for the BFI.

The film was Crystal Gazing *(1982)?*

Yes. It wasn't their best film, though it's an interesting conceit. It's a series of tableaux of theatrical scenes set in different locations around Ladbroke Grove, where I still live. I ended up being the production manager, and set up the different locations for the shoot. From there, I worked my way up in production by working as a location manager on films such as My Beautiful Laundrette [1985] and other projects, and also as a production manager.

I just got lucky, and part of that was getting in on the Film4 wave when that started. I got involved with that through Riverside Studios, when I was helping get the cinema off the ground there. One of the things I did that was quite important was running a week of television films. Interesting directors were making very good feature-length films for television, and we did a season of them, including The Imitation Game [1980], written by Ian McEwan, a couple of things that Stephen Frears had directed and some of Ken Loach and Jim Allen's dramas. Since the unions wouldn't allow them to be shown in cinemas to a paying audience, I set up discussions with people like Jim and the director John Mackenzie, and that's what the audience paid to see, though we showed the films as well. David Rose and other people who were involved in setting up Film4 came along and said it was an interesting [exhibition] model. That was really the first thing that I set up myself.

How did you meet Hanif Kureishi at Riverside?

The artistic director, David Gothard, was running the programme. Hanif was basically his assistant, but David said that he should be writing, so he pushed him downstairs into the bookshop to write, and I took over his job. While I was there, we did a season of readings of plays by young minority ethnic writers, including Hanif's first project, The Mother Country [1980]. Getting to know

Hanif was, of course, how I ended up working on *My Beautiful Laundrette*. When I interviewed with Stephen Frears, he said, 'You know, Hanif, right? And you know our designer and you just know everybody, so you've got the job.'

You also worked on the kids' television show Everybody Here *(1982–3). How did that come about?*

That was after *Crystal Gazing*. Barry Hanson and his wife Susanna Capon had a TV company, and Susanna was producing a multicultural kids' magazine programme that the children's writer and poet Michael Rosen had devised. This was commission number three at Channel 4, so it was really early days. My job was production assistant, which meant getting the thing made. It was an incredible apprenticeship. I did two years, making probably two hundred short films. We had about seven little stories each week: bits of drama, bits of storytelling and games. We filmed all over Britain, including Belfast, and worked with real kids, so it was very Loachian in that respect. It was intended as an antidote to *Blue Peter*.* Michael was brilliant and fully engaged in understanding kids. He played this character called Dr Smartypants, and we filmed in my flat. The show was a very obvious Channel 4 commission, but it was great fun. I think we did thirty episodes, all shot on film on location. And I'm still doing films on location [*laughs*].

What did it teach you specifically about production?

Production is a difficult thing to teach because it's about people skills, it's about diplomacy, it's about knowing bits of legal stuff. You've got to contract everybody on the film. You've got to organize the props. You've got to get people to places. And you can only do all that on the job. I was definitely influenced by my mother, who was a very modern and unusual woman. She brought out my curiosity about the arts with all the exhibitions and plays we went to and the fearlessness that comes from having a very disturbed family background [*laughs*]. You just roll up your sleeves and make things happen.

---

* The BBC's children's magazine programme that has been running since 1958.

As a film producer, you have to get people to part with money. What's the key to that?

You've got to have the courage of your convictions – a very strong belief in what you are proposing and what you are getting people to do. You have to convince them that what you're doing is a great idea. If you are genuinely committed to what you're doing, you can end up working on some very good things. I learned so much about that through working with David at Riverside, then through the ideas that Michael Rosen was running around doing. I was lucky to be around a lot of dynamic creative people.

Watching movies with Lynda was an important experience, too, because suddenly she'd have to go off and make a phone call to the States. I'd be stuck watching a film by myself, and afterwards I'd have to give her my opinion of it. That's how you learn. It was also a very good time to be at the Edinburgh Film Festival because there weren't so many festivals then, and we did challenging programmes, including the first feminist film events, and structuralism and semiology events. There was a lot of talking, but I was more about the doing. I was less interested in the intellectual side of things than in getting things made. I loved the movies from going to the cinema at an early age, and I loved the art of film and knew that was something I'd want to be involved in.

Working with Ken Loach, Jim Allen and Paul Laverty, you've presumably supported the political ideas behind the films. Can you tell me about your own political education and discovering which side you were on?

Because of my mother's illness, she was in and out of hospital. What was interesting was that when she became ill, people disappeared. I come from quite a posh background, and there was certainly no support from the better-off members of the family. That possibly had a socialization effect on me, because I thought, 'That's not very kind, is it?'

Then, when I became a student at Bedford College, on day one I joined the student magazine. I ended up being the editor for a couple of years, because at that point I thought I wanted to be a journalist, so I was on the students' union executive. This was the late 1970s, and I was politically educated very quickly because, although I didn't fully understand politics, I met other journalists who were politically inclined. The Edinburgh Festival politicized me, too. Through Lynda's circle, for instance, I met Neal Ascherson and other interesting journalists working in Scotland at the time.

The other thing that happened when I was at university that was a sort of political act was the emergence of punk. Because I was on the union exec, I was involved in organizing the concerts, which meant meeting all the bands. So there have been many areas where I was in the right place at the right time. It was different to how Ken had his political awakening by meeting certain people at the BBC; for me, it was more about the tornado I was in the middle of. In terms of the arts, I learned a lot from the political works that international theatre companies brought to Riverside Studios.

A lot of Channel 4's early-1980s programming was anti-Thatcher. Film4 financed a number of tough, urgent little films that gave a voice to youth and immigrant communities.

I remember one of the first things Channel 4 did was to have a disabled person sitting at the front desk. I think that spirit got lost in the 1990s and 2000s, when independent films became the thing to do and money took over. The studios muscled in, and the more political cinema was suppressed.

Through your own experiences, can you trace how the landscape for production changed in the period before you started working with Ken?

In the 1980s, you could make a low-budget independent film with almost 100 per cent of the money from Film4 or BBC Films. They would cost £1.2 million, £1.5 million, something like that. But after Working Title had a couple of huge hits, it was capitalized. Polygram came in and started financing them, then they started making bigger films; in fact, I co-produced the Rowan Atkinson film *Bean* for them in 1995. There was also a realization that the talent that had been spawned and developed working on these little films could go on to work on more competitive, commercial films. So that became a thing.

In terms of my own trajectory, the first film I produced was Peter Wollen's *Friendship's Death* in 1987. It was funded completely by the BFI. Peter asked me to do it because of our friendship. I had line-produced and production-managed before, so it was a wonderful opportunity to put together a little film with Peter and a good team. It was a little gem that's stood the test of time. I then began working with Sarah Radclyffe and Tim Bevan at Working Title. They needed someone else to work with them who had already produced a film, and they knew me because I'd worked on *Laundrette* and Stephen and Hanif's *Sammy and Rosie Get Laid* [1987]. They asked me to produce an Irish TV series called *Echoes* [1988], based on a big fat Maeve Binchy beach novel. It apparently made me Working Title's Irish expert. Sarah was developing a film called *Fools of Fortune*, which they wanted Ken to direct, and they put me together with him because they thought, 'Rebecca knows how to work in Ireland.' So off we went, and, of course, I immediately hit it off with Ken. I was a huge Ken fan anyway, because I loved his films from the 1960s and '70s. I'd seen *Cathy Come Home* when I was little, and *Kes*, of course. I remember watching *Days of Hope* when I was at boarding school in London for two years, and what knocked me out about it was how real and believable the characters were. I thought, 'How on earth do you do that? How was that made?' Watching it had a powerful impact on me as a teenager.

We were about four weeks away from shooting *Fools of Fortune* when Ken and Working Title had a terrible fallout because he couldn't see eye to eye with the writer. Ken was trying to turn what was ostensibly a romantic novel into a film like *The Wind That Shakes the Barley*. I think he was right to try to politicize it, but it was a bridge too far for Working Title and the writer. We got sacked, basically. Ken said to me, 'I've got this other script, *In the Heel of the Hunt*,' which was Jim Allen's original title for *Hidden Agenda*. 'Would you be interested in trying to get the money for it?' I said, 'Ken, look, I've never raised money for a film. I can "production" it, but I can't raise the money.' So we sort of put a pin in a map of Soho and came up with somebody to be an executive producer for us, and that was Eric Fellner. With Eric's help – though actually it was me who found the money, weirdly, through serendipity – we were able to get *Hidden Agenda* off the ground. It took us two and a half years. There was resistance to it because of the content. We went to Film4, we went to Granada. We went right to the top of different companies. The film executives all wanted to do it, but when it came to the organization bosses, they said, 'No, no, no, it's a hot potato. We can't do it.' We thought the project was doomed, but by chance this clever young Irish woman who'd been doing research for us was at a cocktail party with horse-racey people in Dublin over Christmas, and got chatting to a guy there. She told him she was working on a political thriller that Ken Loach was going to direct. And he said, 'Oh, I've produced political thrillers.' It turned out he was John Daly, who ran Hemdale Communications. She recounted this story to me and said he would be interested in financing it. So I got hold of Eric and told him to try Hemdale, which agreed to pay all the production costs. I think Eric had to put his house in hock, but he was married to a wealthy woman at the time, so somehow he managed to make it all right.

It was a fraught production, wasn't it, a baptism of fire for you?

Hemdale was great, though it was a very difficult film to make because of the Troubles. We wanted to film it all in Belfast, but the completion guarantors wouldn't let us. They wanted us to shoot most of it in England before going to shoot stuff in Belfast, but, of

Rebecca O'Brien and Ken Loach during the filming of *Sorry We Missed You*.

course, Ken always shoots his films in sequence. As you know, one of the main characters [human rights lawyer Paul Sullivan, played by Brad Dourif] gets killed in the first act. So what we did was run two schedules. We told the completion guarantor that we were going to do some rehearsals and camera tests in Belfast, and that the actors would need to come with us to find out what it's like. We ended up spending two weeks in Belfast and did a week's shooting there before we even started the film, so we were already a week ahead of schedule before we started principal photography [*laughs*]. Then we shot most of the main scenes in London and the south-east, but we went back to Belfast at the end and reshot certain scenes.

The day before we finished shooting, the first assistant director rang me in the Europa Hotel, saying, 'Come down. There's a guy from the RUC here who wants to have a word with you and Ken.' I thought, 'Oh, yeah, he's winding us up because it's the last day.' In fact, there were two guys from the RUC waiting for us in the lobby, and they'd had a drink. They took Ken and me up to this little room in the hotel and said, 'We are not happy about the fact that you've been filming with a low loader on the road without proper permission.' That was just a pretext, because they started laying into us about making a film inspired by the Stalker Affair* and said, 'The sooner you get out of Belfast, the better for you.' It was very heavy, and afterwards I was shaking like a jelly. Then, on the last day of filming, there seemed to be a helicopter above us all the time. It was terrifying, and I was so happy to get out, but it was also exciting that we managed to shoot this film in this time and place, when we hadn't even raised the money for it yet. I remember we shot the Orange Parade pretending that we were a news crew and got one of our characters to weave in and out of the marchers; nobody noticed that we were using a 35mm movie camera. This was a real eye-opener for me. The Orange parade was actually the first thing Ken and I shot together; it's amazing that the last thing we shot together was another parade, the Durham Miners' Gala, in *The Old Oak*.

Ivor Stanbrook MP, in his wisdom, described Hidden Agenda *as 'the IRA entry at Cannes'. Did that make you realize that the films you produced for Ken would constantly provoke attacks by the right?*

* See p. 93.

It's obviously so. I've actually always embraced that sort of stuff. For instance, the press conference at Cannes, when the film critic Alexander Walker stood up, red-faced in a furious rage, and denounced *Hidden Agenda*, was nothing but good publicity. The international journalists there could not understand why he should be so enraged by the film, but Alex was from the Belfast area and he felt it was directly attacking his people. Yes, those are political attacks, but they also air and publicize the issues. I was amazed that the same thing happened with *The Wind That Shakes the Barley* sixteen years later. I could not believe that Michael Gove and others would attack this film that was based on historical truth.

What I found so interesting about *Hidden Agenda* was the fact that every issue we raised in that film was proved to be true over the following years. We'd done our research well. One of the things that I always liked about working with Ken was the fact that it was paramount to get the research right. Even after the writers had written the scripts, we would follow up by having a researcher on the film, making sure that it stood up to examination and everything was verified, because we would always be challenged.

Another valuable thing about working with Ken has been the opportunity to speak truth to power by attacking institutions that are so self-important. Being able to stick two fingers up to them is important. All that has given me a great sense of pride. I'm not overtly political myself in an ideological way; it's not my bag. The only time I've been a member of a political party was when Jeremy Corbyn was in charge of the Labour Party, and I left as soon as he was sacked. I'm more of a socially political person, I would say, but working with Ken fitted me very well. As a producer, one is always the first audience for a film, and you've got to become convinced by the story that's being told. The veracity of it has to work with me first, so I can give the first second opinion, as it were. As the first audience, I will challenge it if it doesn't add up.

Because of the responsibilities involved, do you have to be knowledgeable about jurisprudence?

To a certain extent. When I first started working with Ken at Parallax, [producer] Sally Hibbin introduced us to Stephen Grosz, who became our film lawyer. His practice at Bindmans was a very useful resource for us because they're human rights specialists. Contracting a film, which you have to do as a producer, is a big, complex legal process, and it's got bigger and more complex as time has gone on; a film I'm working on now has about a hundred and fifty contracts. I've learned the legal and financing sides of the job gradually through experience, and sometimes I think I might as well be a lawyer. In my entire career with Ken, nobody has taken either of us to court, which stands to reason because the due diligence is always done and the films are accurate. There's a certain routine you go through with film legals anyway, but Paul's research is impeccable. He reads everything, and we collect all the details. I've always had to feel confident that the research is right so that we can go forward with a film.

Ken and Jim Allen each told me that when they were conceiving a film, they would get together and talk about the issues they wanted to address, then Jim would write the script, and they'd meet again to discuss any changes. At what point did you come into the process?

On both the films that I did with Jim – *Hidden Agenda* and *Land and Freedom* – Ken had already developed the ideas and the script with Jim, so I came in at a slightly later stage. *Land and Freedom*, for instance, was a project called *The May Days* that, I think, David Puttnam had commissioned back in the mid-1980s. It was more about a printing press and had the bare bones of what became *Land and Freedom*. When I read the original screenplay, I realized that there was no way we could make the film that Jim had written because it involved the enormous uprising in Barcelona in 1937. Ken suggested to Jim that it become more the story of a POUM militia that takes place in the countryside, which made it much more doable. One of Ken's skills is to persuade people that you can make a project smaller but still tell the story you want – less is more. He did the same with Paul on *The Wind That Shakes the Barley*. Ken's kind of dramaturgy, as you know, is to focus on a small group of people and tell a big story that way.

One thing about Ken that's not always noticed by people is his understanding of dramatic structure and how to tell a story economically. That comes out of his knowledge of theatre and him learning about theatrical structures at an early age. He has taught every writer that he's worked with how to tell a story so that it has the right beats and the right story arcs. What Ken loved about Jim was that he could write great scenes and really good dialogue, but he wasn't very good at joining the dots. Ken is very good at joining the dots, so his process would be about sitting down with Jim or Paul and finding a way of joining one to the other and making the story flow. Paul wasn't an expert at that at first, though with Ken's suggestions he's become really good over the years. We've also worked with script editors, particularly Roger Smith, to help with dramatic structure.

In Paul's case, he'll go and do research for six months, then sit down and build some sort of document that would have some ideas, some scenes, some characters and what happens to them. He would write beautiful things like that, then have a meeting with Ken where they would discuss what is the right project to do. That's when I'd start to be an audience and communicate whether it would be a film I would go to see or not. Then Jim or Paul would go off to write a draft [of their individual scripts], and Ken would spend a day or two with them and perhaps ask them to write another draft, which I would also read. I would probably have only a few things to say to them. Paul would then do a tidy-up in another draft, having had more input from Ken. Really, my input is minimal. I might just say, 'I'm not sure about that character,' or 'That's a bit long-winded,' but very little, because they know what they're doing. Maybe what I've brought to Ken and Paul's work particularly is giving them an open place where they can do the work that they want to do, rather than coming in and saying, for example, 'You've got to have a film star.' It's more, 'Let's make the film that you want to make, and then I will support you in the best way I can. And if there are hazards along the way, let's talk about it.' It's always been a conversation, never a situation where anybody gets bossed around. As an experienced production person, though, I'm very involved in deciding where a film is set. I always said to Ken that I thought the Newcastle area would be an interesting as well as a nice and easy place to make a film in, so I think that he and I, between us, came up with the idea of shooting *I, Daniel Blake* and the next two films there. I studied geography at university, and when we go on a recce I'm very involved in choosing which locations we should use. My involvement is very much about the where and the how.

On the issue of whether to have a star in a film or not, do you think your sensibility is different to that of producers who will always want big names because their priority is making a box-office hit?

Well, it's a decision, isn't it? I've known all along that we'll have a certain amount of money that we can raise for a Ken Loach film, which is up to about four or five million quid. If we can make the film for that, then we don't need to have stars. And Ken is the star, anyway, because he is the person who's known, and we've got a market for his films all over the world. In the case of *The Wind That Shakes the Barley*, it was very serendipitous that Cillian Murphy came from Cork [*laughs*], and also, of course, that he's a brilliant actor. He was the right person to be Damien in that film.

Actually, none of the people who have gone on to be stars in our films were stars at the time we made them. I remember persuading Sara Geater, who was at Channel 4 Films at the time, to let Peter Mullan off the editing period on his own film, *Orphans* [1998], so that we could work with him on *My Name Is Joe*. I said to her, 'Look, Peter's been cast in this film that's been written for him and that Ken's going to direct. If he's in it, it'll go to Cannes, and he might even win best actor, which will do your film, *Orphans*, the world of good,' and that's exactly what happened. I could see from Paul's script that Joe would be a really powerful role for somebody like Peter, who is a brilliant actor but wasn't well known yet. Over the years, I guess without thinking about it, we've built up that ability to turn actors into stars, or at least give them a leg up. Look at *Hidden Agenda* with Frances McDormand and Brian Cox. They caught on like the flu [*laughs*]! Still, I think Ken has shown over the years that the films work much better on the whole if they don't have A-list actors in them – because audiences tend to think about an actor, not the character – so we've stuck to that.

How did Sixteen Films come into being?

Sally Hibbin was a member of Parallax Pictures, which was a film-making co-operative, and she had developed *Riff-Raff* with Ken more or less at the same time as we were making *Hidden Agenda*, and they shot it the following year. Sally had invited Ken to be part of Parallax, which he did join. The directors Les Blair and Phil Davis and the producer Sarah Curtis had joined the company, too. Because Ken wanted to keep working with me, he'd got me some work as a production manager on a documentary that we did after I'd had my son. I was also developing what became *Land and Freedom*. He wanted me to be part of Parallax, so I joined them. That meant there were three directors and three producers. For three or four years, it was quite busy, with all of us working. I worked as a location scout on *Ladybird, Ladybird* with Sally, and she started developing what became *Carla's Song* with Ken and Paul, and between *Ladybird* and *Carla's Song*, Ken and I made *Land and Freedom*. Sally was an executive producer on it and helped me get the co-production off the ground. As Parallax continued, Sally worked with Phil, and Sarah worked with Les, and then everybody started going their separate ways. After *Carla's Song*, Ken decided he just wanted to work with me rather than anybody else, and we started developing *My Name Is Joe*. Then we made *Bread and Roses* and *The Navigators* and started working on *Sweet Sixteen*. By 2001, Sally was doing a film every so often, but Ken and I felt we were holding up the edifice and, between ourselves, thought we should have our own partnership rather than pay more than needed for a company that was basically mainly us. So we had a summit meeting with the Parallax people and, in 2001, decided to leave and form our own company, which is Sixteen Films, named after *Sweet Sixteen*.

By the beginning of 2002, it was up and running, and it was such a relief to have our own company, just to be able to get on with our work and not have to deal with the politics of what was ostensibly a film-makers' co-operative. The idea of it was good, but these things often don't work when people go off and do their own things. You can keep it going only for a certain length of time, so Ken and I were very happy to sidle off and do our own thing.

As Paul became part of the film-making team, did the three of you immediately develop the pattern of working that would become your modus operandi, or did it evolve over the first few films you did?

It more or less started straight away. *My Name Is Joe* was the first one that the three of us did, and it felt completely natural that it should be that way. It wasn't even spoken of – it was obviously the way to go forward. By the time we did *Sweet Sixteen*, our way of working was set.*

How does your producer's eye and experience ease the path of pre-production? I'm thinking specifically of Bread and Roses, *because it was filmed in America, and I imagine that must have felt like a risk.*

It was terrifying, because we were making a film about unions with the most difficult unions that exist. They're guilds in America – like SAG [Screen Actors Guild] and the WGA [Writers Guild of America]. It was quite difficult because we thought we were going to get some US funding, but we never did. It was an entirely European film set and shot in Los Angeles, which was bizarre, yet we needed to make it under union rules. So I went to IATSE [International Alliance of Theatrical Stage Employees], which is the US equivalent of the UK's BECTU [Broadcasting, Entertainment, Communications and Theatre Union], and explained that we were doing a low-budget film. They were OK, but SAG needed to understand that we wanted to work with actual workers in our film, particularly the office cleaners.

My approach is always to face something head-on and tackle it before it becomes an issue. So I showed SAG's people the land reform debate in *Land and Freedom* and challenged them afterwards to tell me who was an actor and who wasn't. I explained to them, 'We don't want actors who are currently working as waiters and waitresses to be in the film; we want to cast people who are real cleaners and know what the stakes are – and they'll probably be migrant workers. And you're welcome to come along and invite them to join the union while we're filming.' And they said, 'Fair enough,' and that's what they did – and, actually, they were great.

One of the things we found difficult, though, was the drivers. With the films we make, we're used to travelling around in minibuses. It's very important for us that nobody gets a private car and

---

* Full-length features produced or co-produced by Sixteen Films that were not directed by Ken Loach include: *Summer* (2008), *Oranges and Sunshine* (2010), *Warbook* (2015), *Versus: The Life and Films of Ken Loach* (2016), *City of Tiny Lights* (2017), *You Were Never Really Here* (2018), *Harvest* (2024) and *On Falling* (2024).

driver and all the rest of it. But because of the Teamsters' rules, we had more drivers than anything else, and it really drove us up the wall. Also, our line producer just couldn't get her head around the way we were working. It was difficult, and we didn't enjoy it much because we were working in a system that didn't function well for us. But the nice thing was that we were able to work with the people that we wanted and get it made in that way. It was a bit of a problem for us, having to have some actors who were serious SAG people and expected certain treatment. But certainly the more senior ones knew about Ken. And I recall somebody saying that some very interesting actors came along for the auditions. Apparently, David Schwimmer and Keanu Reeves turned up because they knew who Ken was – in fact, that's how we cast Adrien Brody, though he didn't know who they were. Ken and Paul went to Mexico to cast Pilar Padilla.

Though you said you didn't know how to raise money at the time of Hidden Agenda, *you've since become very successful at financing Sixteen Films' work by putting together European co-productions. Do you think British film institutions could have been more supportive over the years?*

No, I don't think they could have. Anyway, we've almost always had some funding from the UK Film Council,* the BFI, early on Film4 and latterly BBC Films. The BBC supported *I, Daniel Blake*, *Sorry We Missed You* and *The Old Oak*, and the BFI supported *I, Daniel Blake*, too. Interestingly, I asked Film4 if they would support it, and they said, sadly, they couldn't because they'd just done [the 2014 TV documentary series] *Benefits Street*. That was outrageous, because we thought they were going to come aboard, but then BBC Films did, straight away. So we've had good support from the public funders over the last twenty years. On *The Wind That Shakes the Barley*, the Film Council rescued us at the last minute with a goodly amount after a bank didn't come through. *Route Irish* was one we didn't get British institutional funding for, but one way or another we've muddled through with our patchwork

---

* Established in 2000, the UKFC was abolished in 2011. Its funding and much of its world were absorbed by the BFI.

of co-productions. Support from the French has always been very important; they always want to put our films in cinemas. Why Not Productions asked us to make the film with Eric Cantona that became *Looking for Eric* [2009] – which was an irresistible opportunity – and I've been doing proper French co-productions with them ever since. Why Not have been incredible supporters.

When you are working on films with people who have been through difficult and sometimes appalling situations, like the Syrian refugees in The Old Oak, *or people who've been exposed to hardships in Scotland or the north-east, or wherever it might be, do you, as the producer, play a part in establishing an atmosphere in which they feel safe?*

I think that's essential. It's not always perfect. The particular functions of making a film and all that entails don't necessarily [generate] a caring situation, so it's quite a difficult thing to manage, but it's very important to be aware of the fact that you are working with vulnerable people – and that they need aftercare, as well. We've certainly had that with quite a few of the young Scottish actors that we've worked with. For instance, Paul is still in touch with Paul Brannigan from *The Angels' Share*, who's had a very up-and-down life and career. I find I've probably had to do more in terms of support for the non-actors who have been leads in our films. Dave Turner from *The Old Oak* has been fantastic. He's been very easy because he's such a natural, but I'm in touch with him probably more than I would be with a professional actor. I was in touch with Dave Johns after doing *I, Daniel Blake*, and then Debbie [Honeywood], Kris [Hitchen] and Rhys [Mcgowan] from *Sorry We Missed You*. This is important for people for whom acting isn't their normal experience. A lot of reassurance is required. And, largely, they don't have agents, so they will communicate with me once the rest of the team has disappeared. You never actually finish a film because you're always in touch with people you've worked with.

What are your feelings about the long journey you've taken with Ken and Paul in terms of holding up a mirror to society, and perhaps hoping that the films can benefit people's lives?

Sadly, I don't think you can change the world with a film. It would be nice if you could. But you can start a conversation, and that's what we would have hoped to have done. I've always been proudest of the moments when the films have actually taken on cultural ownership. *The Wind That Shakes the Barley* spawned a debate about the issues in the Dáil. *I, Daniel Blake* had an incredible response because it couldn't have come out at a better time. Mhairi Black did a whole speech based around it in Parliament; Jeremy Corbyn challenged Theresa May with it, so it became part of the zeitgeist, and when a film becomes part of the national conversation, it can have an impact on it. It's not just about now; all three of the north-eastern films, for instance, tackled crucial issues of our times and became a record of them, so they will be a very valuable historical resource for people in the future. From a personal point of view, it's extraordinary to have been part of helping to get them off the ground.

CHAPTER 16

Paul Laverty

Interview with Loach's long-time screenwriter

GRAHAM FULLER: *You were born in Calcutta (now Kolkata), right?*

PAUL LAVERTY: Yes. It was an accident. My dad was from Motherwell and my mum was from County Limerick, in Ireland. She came over to Scotland to work with her uncle, who was a priest in Glasgow, and met my father there. My father's father was a shoemaker, and his mother was from a mining family, but because of the Church my father and his siblings got a better education than was normal, so he became an accountant and got a job when he and my mother went to Calcutta. It was the 1950s, they were quite naïve, and, to be honest, I think they wanted to get away from interfering families and go on an adventure. Unfortunately, after I was born there, my father got tuberculosis and nearly died, so they came back to Scotland when I was nine months old. I've tried to get to India three different times and haven't made it, but I'll get there yet. I just heard an amazing documentary* on Radio 4 about the famine in Bengal in 1943. People were dying on the streets of Calcutta. I was born there in 1957, but I never heard a single thing about it growing up. It's unbelievable how a famine that killed over three million was ignored and written out of history. It just shows you how some narratives take shape and others don't.

Why did you switch from studying for the priesthood to law?

I grew up in a little village called Wigtown [in Dumfries and Galloway], where there was one Catholic classroom inside the

---

* *Three Million: The Bengal Famine* (2024), presented by Kavita Puri, produced by Ant Adeane.

Protestant school, and the Protestant children and the Catholic children had different playgrounds and playtimes. Our teacher, Mrs Mills, had to teach from primary one to primary seven inside that one classroom, so she was under tremendous pressure – and how it told. As a result, me and my brother Andy failed the eleven-plus.* Andy was quite brilliant, but I wasn't so smart [*laughs*]. Of course, if you failed it, you were sent off to do non-academic subjects like woodwork and metalwork. That might have given me a good career – who knows? – but my parents said, 'If you go to a seminary, you'll be able to sit your O-grades and your Highers.'† My cousin had been to [St Vincent's College], a seminary in Langbank [Renfrewshire], and then to Blairs [College, near Aberdeen], a seminary for diocesan priests in Scotland. I was persuaded it would be a good idea and went with my brothers at the age of twelve to Langbank and then to Aberdeen – it was fucking freezing up there, by the way – to become priests. In those days, if you thought there was going to be a good football team and you'd get a good football strip, you'd think, 'Ah, maybe it's not a bad idea,' but in retrospect it was a totally surreal life. It was indoctrination. You're taught by priests, many of them working-class Catholics with Irish backgrounds from Glasgow. That's where I got my Glasgow accent from. Most were decent men who had been indoctrinated years earlier, though we discovered after, inevitably, that two had been paedophiles.

Eighty per cent of my friends were from Glasgow – from Maryhill, from Toryglen, from Partick – and we'd go to see Celtic matches during the holidays, so I had a whole map of Glasgow in my mind. Apart from holidays, I never came home again. I was sent to [the Pontifical Gregorian University in] Rome to get a more academic background. There were students from all round the world, but, strangely again, I felt cut off. We did a philosophy degree there

---

* The standardized examination, once given to all students in British schools in the final year of primary school, to determine admission to grammar schools or non-selective comprehensive schools for secondary education.
† O-grades (which have been discontinued) and Highers are qualifications of the Scottish secondary education system, roughly equivalent to the O-level and A-level qualifications conferred under the General Certificate of Education system in the rest of the UK.

taught by Jesuits, but that was even more indoctrination. We even did part of a course studying Marxism, in order to undermine Marxism. Some of it was great fun, and being in Rome was an eye-opener, but intellectually it became more and more claustrophobic, then unbearable by the time I was twenty.

You left after two years?

I was given an ultimatum. The rector summoned me and said, 'We've had a meeting, and we're giving you one week to change your personality.' I burst out laughing, which didn't help. Even for the 1970s, that was comic. Anyway, that was the end of that. I got kicked out, and it was a relief to go. Looking back, I often wonder if, from the age of twelve to twenty, it was great preparation for writing, because it gave me the curiosity to look beyond a world carved up to be black and white – answers stuffed down our throats, so much time daydreaming in the deep boredom of hours supposedly spent in prayer. Did I really live through all that nonsense? Bonkers. But having said that, I still do find wonder in great places of worship. I thought of it when I wrote the scene in Durham Cathedral in *The Old Oak*. When I left the seminary, I felt like I was like a whippet leaving the box on a racetrack. I went on to do a law degree in Glasgow, which wasn't exactly exhilarating, but quite an easy task because I was so used to studying. The apprenticeship was vital, because it was with a criminal and civil court practice, which was a real eye-opener to the rawness of life. We received women coming in from the street who'd been battered by their husbands, child custody cases, a lot of criminal cases. I'll always treasure that experience: the world of work, how to navigate bosses and fellow lawyers and staff and, of course, the myriad people who came through the door – a surprise every day. I met a very good young lawyer there, Kenny MacAskill, who later became the cabinet secretary for justice [2007–14] in the SNP [Scottish National Party]. Kenny had great energy and cared about life beyond the law. He still does.

We worked like dogs and were mostly left to our own devices and became more political, engaging in welfare law, housing, homelessness, sometimes raising actions in court that we knew might not win but would cause havoc or up the ante to help people. We helped workers who were occupying a factory, and even set a precedent, suing the DWP for a lost giro cheque. It was a modest sum but affected thousands up and down the country. That was all very exciting, but during that period I became more and more interested in politics generally. I was involved, too, with what was going on in Nicaragua. I suppose the revolution there [1979–90] was our generation's equivalent of the Spanish Civil War. As you know, we saw the Sandinistas overthrow the Somoza dictatorship, and then the United States tearing the country apart in the most systematic fashion.

I always wanted to learn another language, always wanted to travel – I think it was because I'd been wrapped up in the seminary for so long. So, after doing a year's practice in law, I said, 'What the hell?' and went out to Nicaragua. I wasn't any use to anybody because I couldn't speak Spanish, so I tried to learn it on the street, volunteered to pick coffee and met people. When I came home, I got involved with a modest but very effective solidarity group called Scottish Medical Aid to Nicaragua, mostly doctors and nurses, that worked with trade unions and churches, trying to tell the truth and build public opinion about what was happening in Nicaragua. Every time there's a war, there's always a battle about human rights.

The next time I went out to Nicaragua, I went with Kate Hughes, the nurse and midwife whom I was married to at the time. Financed by the group I just mentioned, Kate did brilliant work in the isolated island of Ometepe, teaching traditional midwives way out in the countryside. I learned so much from Kate's empathetic way of teaching, and it made me realize, too, how a revolution can stretch out to the most humble and change lives for ever. I treasure those memories and the people we met.

I worked for a human rights organization for two years. What was good about that was that I got a bird's-eye view of the destruction and saw how sophisticated it was. I saw how the United States co-ordinated their policies with the IMF and the World Bank, cutting off loans to the Nicaraguans. I saw how the CIA blew up the port at Corinto, how they orchestrated propaganda campaigns, how they set up bogus parallel organizations within Nicaragua, from trade unions to so-called human rights organizations, how they trained the Contras – the counter-revolutionaries, some of whom I spoke to during a truce – how they attacked civilians and used terror as a tactic to murder and torture people for ten years, to intimidate them from working in state schools, health centres and much besides. I saw how the economic embargo meant that there were no spare parts for buses. I saw how all the machines didn't work and saw all the blackouts – all done to make life absolutely miserable and to break down the infrastructure, which they then tried to blame on the local government. It was a systematic, intelligent, precise, incredibly violent attempt to tear this country of only three million people apart. I was a witness to that, and it was a real eye-opener to how power and realpolitik operated. So much creativity, intelligence and resources, to cause so much horror. I saw it all play out in front of my eyes on a daily basis. I will never forget the face of a father who described how his daughter was tortured by the Contras, but it was all connected up – a speech from Reagan and then Bush Sr, followed up by violent attacks, one seamless fabric of cruelty.

Oxfam came up with a great answer to the question of why the American government wanted to destroy Nicaragua: 'Because it was the threat of a good example.'* The Sandinista Revolution wasn't a deep revolution in many ways, and it didn't have the international support to survive the onslaught. But there was a significant change of power. They taught their people to read and write, which was very important. They wiped out polio. There was some land reform. They were actually more Catholic than Marxist [*laughs*], but still, they stepped out of line and the CIA was absolutely determined to crush them. That was a profound lesson for life for me. Just look at the scale of destruction around the world as the United States has striven to impose its interests.

In a strange way, I don't think I could have written *The Wind That Shakes the Barley* in the same way if I hadn't been to Nicaragua and met all those people in Central America damaged by the war, and Ken shared this, too, and was really keen to show that war should not be glorified. There is dialogue in the film that is very important to me, when Damien [Cillian Murphy] has been ordered to execute the landlord [Roger Allam] and his [Damien's] young friend Chris [John Crean], who has been found to be a traitor. Damien says

---

* *Nicaragua: The Threat of a Good Example?* is the title of the 1985 Dianna Melrose book published by Oxfam GB.

to his friend Dan [Liam Cunningham], 'I studied anatomy for five years, and now I am going to shoot an old man in the head . . . I've known Chris since he was a child . . . What kind of Ireland are we fighting for, Dan? I hope to Christ it's worth it.' After the executions, he tells his girlfriend, 'I've crossed a line, Sinéad . . . and I can't go back.' When you see the cost of war, that breaks your heart. There's a lack of imagination about how the pain and misery and suffering continues from one generation to the next. This is what still kills me about Fallujah. In Iraq, to this day children are still being born with massive defects [from the pulverized uranium shell tips on weapons], long after George [W.] Bush and Tony Blair – and his cabinet, who took that awful decision – have retired to tend their roses. Obviously, we made *Route Irish* in response to what happened in Iraq. You do fear what's going to happen after the war in Gaza, when there will be an army of orphans, and all the trauma and despair and hatred and anger that will come from that. You reap what you sow.

What was your specific job in Nicaragua?

I had to speak to journalists and delegations arriving in Managua for fact-finding missions. I also met with trade unionists, politicians, artists, actors, singers. It was a joy to meet with Pete Seeger. Kris Kristofferson came down; so did Ed Koch, the mayor of New York. We would try to give our take on what was happening. They'd see the United States-backed human rights organizations, then they would see the organization I worked with, which – to be open about it – received goodwill from the Nicaragua government, but most of the finance, as I recall, came from bona fide NGOs in Europe, which meant there were no secrets about how they were financed. The whole human rights question became massively politicized.

I'd also go out into the countryside where Contra attacks had taken place to have a better idea of what was going on with human rights abuses, and after two and a half years of that I became sick of writing human rights reports and speaking to the delegations. In my innocence, I said, 'I'm going to write a film about this,' but I didn't have a Scooby [clue] about how to go about it. I suppose I just saw film as a substitute for politics, because so much about war is narrative. I ended up spending three years in Central America. I went up to El Salvador and Guatemala and saw how brutal the death squads were in those countries. El Salvador in those days was particularly dangerous. Looking back, I was very lucky. A journalist I had been travelling with at one point was murdered by paramilitaries on a trip he asked me to join him on, but fortunately I changed my plans.

Meanwhile, in Nicaragua, I had met a lovely film-maker and actor, David Hayman.

He later played the drug lord, McGowan, in My Name Is Joe.

Right. David was a brilliant actor on stage and in film, and he was trying to direct a film in El Salvador. He told me how hard it would be to get one made, but even listening to someone talk about it was inspirational. Why not have a bash?

How did you first approach Ken Loach with your idea for Carla's Song?

After coming back home, I was still determined to make a film, but I knew nothing about it. So I bought a lot of books to try to figure out what a treatment was, and then I started watching more films. I'd heard about Ken, and I loved the sensibility of *Riff-Raff*. It had really human characters, but you could sense the politics underneath, and it had a tone that I identified with. It doesn't take long to find out there are not many political film-makers, but I wrote to dozens of directors, and, of course, most of them didn't answer. The ones who did said, 'Nicaragua's a war zone. There's no actors and no film industry there, so it's impossible.' But I'd written to Ken as well, and one day I was doing the dishes and got this call. He said, 'It's Ken here' – very modest, of course – 'and if you're ever down in London, let's meet up for a cup of tea.'

Did you write a treatment?

Yes, but I've never written one since. Thank Christ. It seems all back to front to me; it's a strange beast, declaratory, stating what the story will be and what you want to achieve. A script changes so much from the initial intention.

What work were you doing at the time?

I was doing lots of solidarity work as an activist, going to churches, trade unions and schools, carrying all these slides with me, which I would show. Dozens of meetings in dingy halls around the country. There was a great initiative at the time called the Enterprise Allowance Scheme. It would give you the same money you'd get if you were on the dole, but you had to set up an enterprise [*laughs*]. I said I wanted to be a writer, but, of course, they didn't accept that. The *Glasgow Herald* then published a review of a play by Donal O'Kelly, an Irish mate and a wonderful writer I'd met in Nicaragua, and in my view the reviewer misunderstood the play. I wrote a letter to the *Herald* in response, and it was published. The actual critic was very gracious and wrote to me, asking if I wanted to start reviewing plays. I didn't take it up as I was up to my eyes in activist stuff and trying to write, but his kind offer did save my bacon with the Enterprise Allowance Scheme when I sent them a copy of his letter. Although they didn't think my plan to write screenplays was feasible, they did accept the possibility I could be a critic. That gave me time, which was precious, and I felt very fortunate to get the chance. It's a funny old game. I owe that kind critic a drink!

Ken Loach and Paul Laverty during the filming of *Sorry We Missed You*.

Maggie Thatcher had just deregulated the buses, and I was able to get from Glasgow to London for a fiver. I met Ken, and he read the treatment I'd written and said it was interesting. He was fascinated by what I'd seen in Nicaragua, and we connected politically and had fun. It didn't matter to him that I'd never written a screenplay. He said, 'I can't speak Spanish, and there's a war going on out there, so it's a very long shot, but why don't you have a bash at writing a few scenes?'

I went back up to Glasgow and started writing, and the whole first half of *Carla's Song* just popped out. I've never done drugs in my life, but I imagine the feeling I got from writing it must be what it's like when you're high. Instead of writing an essay, a thesis, a human rights report or a treatment, I got to pick characters, make them speak and listen to them. I imagined the interactions, all the dialogue. Exhilarating. Fortunately, that sense of excitement still hasn't left me. So I sent Ken these scenes, and I think he was more surprised than I was. He must have recognized there was some life to it, because he said, 'We'll try to get you a commission.' I'd lived on $150 a month in Nicaragua and had been totally skint for years, so this was very welcome. It took some time, but on the basis of these scenes, I managed to get a commission to write the screenplay, which I'd been continuing with. But from meeting Ken to getting *Carla's Song* made took five years, because he'd been working on *Land and Freedom* for much longer, and *Raining Stones* and *Ladybird, Ladybird* were both ahead of it, so I had to take my turn.

There was one other lovely thing about the second time I met Ken. I said I'd pop down to London to see him again, if he wanted to talk some more, but he said, 'No, I always follow the writer. I did it with Barry Hines and Jim Allen, so I'll come up to Glasgow to meet you.' I felt embarrassed, because he was this famous director, but he came up to Glasgow, and we spent a few days talking and working on the screenplay. You couldn't imagine anyone being more supportive of writers. He always says the writing is the most creative part of making a film because you're facing a blank page. And, despite the stamp he puts on the films, he says he doesn't write.

I think Ken has always given people confidence. I always feel he's like a football manager who's very canny about who he picks for the team; in Ken's case, it's about who's right for all aspects of making a film. He never asks someone to do something they can't do, because they would become miserable. And I've never felt him on my shoulder. He's always said, 'Just follow your instincts,' and I think that's been the secret of our relationship. He's a director and I'm a writer, but we meet in the middle as film-makers and through our loyalty to the project. He's never asked me to write what I couldn't write or don't want to write.

Has he ever baulked at anything you've written?

I soon learned he didn't like night scenes! With some scenes, he'd say, 'Well, I don't know how to direct that.' I'd say, 'Right. Out with it. We'll find another solution.' I don't think we've ever had a creative fight in all these years, because neither of us thinks we're the Pope, with special access to the truth. We've just tried to figure it all out and make it work – and I suppose we understand each other's sensibility. The key was to be our own toughest critics.

Whenever Ken and Kahleen Crawford were doing the casting for a film, I would join them. Sometimes they'd do improvisations with the people they were meeting, and sometimes I would join in. Watching and listening to the people who come into those casting sessions helps you define the characters you've written. Ken has always said, 'The casting is about, "How do we best find flesh and blood for the character as imagined in the screenplay?"' There's lots of choices within that, and I learned so much from going through that joyful process with him. Afterwards, we'd talk about how the person might have touched us. Sometimes we would have different opinions on it, but we would make the big decisions together, which was wonderful. Of course, it was always his final choice to make, and I'd always be supportive of it.

How did you get the Fulbright award that enabled you to study screenwriting at the University of Southern California (USC)?

My screenplay for *Carla's Song* was put forward for it, though not by me. My life has been a series of accidents; I've never planned too far ahead. I should thank John Cleese for what happened. He set up a scholarship fund for screenwriters with the Fulbright Commission, after he sued a newspaper, as I recall. For several years, the committee would pick one new writer from Britain to go to study screenwriting in the United States. I was invited to go for what turned out to be a totally surreal interview. Cleese was on the interview committee with this rather old, reactionary character, who told me, 'They'll never let you into the country after what you've done in Nicaragua.' This seemed to put Cleese on my side, and I got the place. Cleese could not have been more supportive; he was a genuine enthusiast of the art of screenwriting. I would have been much happier in New York, but I knew I wanted to go and perhaps find a Latino story in LA. I could speak Spanish and thought it would be a roar [laugh] in Los Angeles, so I went out to USC. It was harder to get into [its School of Cinematic Arts] than Harvard Law School, to be honest, but it was supremely boring. I thought it'd be full of young people and vibrant ideas. I knew it would be Hollywood-ish in some way, but it was tedious beyond words, apart from a brilliant old Czech guy there called Frank Daniel [1926–96]. Every Thursday, he would show us one of his favourite films. We'd sit there and watch *The Apartment* [1960], or something like that, and he would do a running commentary on it. He was so sharp and bright. I learned a lot from him.

When I watch your and Ken's films, I'm never aware of the conventional three-act structure in your scripts. If you use it, it's always invisible.

I hope it's invisible, but I think structure's everything. A story will not hold if it hasn't got a strong backbone. Structure is symbiotic with the character, the premise and staying on story. At USC, they had all sorts of courses, but, to be honest, I didn't go to many of them. I think my legal background was more helpful, because when you tell a story or write a script, you're actually making a case for all the characters. Structure is absolutely vital to that. Obviously, I'm talking about traditional storytelling. You could do a nice abstract story, or something that's offbeat or random that can make you think in a different way, but in the type of stories that I've done with Ken, I've worked hard on the structure and getting the character right, because you have to believe in their circumstances. And if you don't get the premise and the forward momentum of the story right, you'll run out of steam, and the story will fall apart in your hands.

Staying on story is one of the hardest things to do, because you can so easily write something that leads you up a blind alley. It might be interesting in itself, it might be a good scene, but does it serve the story? Another difficult task is to try to get the story into two hours of film. With *The Wind That Shakes the Barley*, there was so much studying I had to do before I wrote a single word. It was a massive challenge just to get my head around all the history, and [there were] so many developments and all these different voices to get in. At one point, I suggested to Ken and Roger Smith* that maybe we should do two films, one on the War of Independence and one on the Civil War. I could see their eyes light up with the idea, but, on reflection, we realized we were going to get only one crack at it.

The reason for doing so much research was because I knew the film was going to be massively contested, and that everything was going to be torn apart, that they would really go for us if there were any mistakes. I must mention here the wonderful support and friendship of the historian Donal Ó Drisceoil, who always had our back, on both *Barley* and *Jimmy's Hall*. It was the same with *I, Daniel Blake* – you might disagree with the politics, but there was nothing that they could get us on factually. We also made a big choice at the beginning of *Barley* to have fictional characters, but to be absolutely truthful to the times. I was very keen on this, and Ken was up for it when I spoke to him about it.

I thought some characters were based on real people. As I mentioned to Ken, Damien Kearney's portrayal of Finbar has something of Ernie O'Malley's look and demeanour, judging by photos of him and his writing.

There might be some superficial similarities, but I wasn't thinking of Ernie O'Malley when I wrote Finbar. I don't know how the flying-column leader Tom Barry was, but Finbar is probably closer to him because he did the same job. During the research period, I read many history books, went to museums and spoke to the children and grandchildren of men in the flying columns. Key was

---

* Loach's story editor since *Wear a Very Big Hat* (1965), made for the BBC's *The Wednesday Play* anthology series.

walking through the countryside and visiting the sites of ambushes. It was February and March, wet and freezing. I learned something vital: youthful strength and vitality had to be at the heart of it. Youth, too, can see life more in black and white, less tempered by experience. I tried to find someone who had actually been in a flying column, but I didn't have any luck. It stunned us when this older man turned up at the premiere in Cork with his granddaughter. I remember they came on a bus from the west. It was a marvellous conversation. He was tough as nails and understated, but his eyesight wasn't good and he nearly choked on a cocktail stick with some olives at the reception after. Thankfully, his granddaughter saved the day. Imagine surviving all that, and then . . . Jaysus, it gave me a cold shiver.

From the research and talking to people, I learned that many families were divided during the Civil War, with catastrophic results. How could that not make an impression? I was also told by several people that the medical faculty in Cork University was very Republican at the time. That's where the idea of Damien [O'Donovan] being a doctor came from.

After all the research, and before writing the script, I wrote imaginary mini-biographies for all the characters, even the smaller parts. The son of a farmer and a farm labourer are worlds apart. We had so many characters, but I hope there is a sense of their lives and differences beyond what we had time to show in the film; I hope there is a rich subtext. For example, we know that Steady Boy [Aidan O'Hare], another member of the flying column, had served in the British Army. That's vital to understanding him when he walks off and refuses to fight in the Civil War. Or when we know that the character Dan was a witness to the Dublin Lockout in 1913 and remembers the brutality of William Martin Murphy, a right-wing employer. Republicanism has many shades!

It might surprise, but the key to imagining the screenplay was the old woman, Peggy [Mary O'Riordan], who is menaced on her farm by the Black and Tans. At an early stage of the research, I went to the little museum in Clonakilty,* in County Cork. I'll never forget it. It was just one room, unmanned. There were ancient photographs there, including one of this grandmother

---

* The West Cork Regional Museum.

figure whose family had experienced the Great Hunger [1845–52]. She was kicked off her land three times in the course of her life. This woman really caught my imagination and became a building block for the other characters and the opening of the film. What would it be like to be evicted for the third time? Then I wondered what her daughter would be like, and then her daughter in turn. I imagined the fictional character Sinéad [Orla Fitzgerald] had a grandmother like the old woman in the photo. I imagined Sinéad had a brother [Micheál, played by Laurence Barry], who is beaten to death for giving his name in Gaelic to the Black and Tans at the beginning of the film.* Where would he get the balls and the madness to speak to the British Army and challenge them so? I imagined that came from that old woman, his grandmother, who had been evicted three times, and the stories of past brutality were in the young man's blood. I had no more information about that old woman, other than her stubborn face as she was evicted in that old photo. I can still feel the hairs on the back of my neck rise, because that grandmother was the line and the connection that really helped me imagine what the story turned out to be. After the Auxiliaries burn down the old woman's farmhouse in the film, she says, 'I'm not leaving. I'll just go to the chicken coop.' In wars of resistance, women are so often written out of history, when, in fact, they are often the backbone.

Another small but important part is Mrs Rafferty (Clare Dineen), who's sued in the Dáil court by the merchant, Sweeney [Kieran Aherne], for the ludicrously exorbitant interest on the loan he's made to her. That prompts Damien and Dan to put their case for a socialist Ireland, to stop the businessmen and landlords exploiting poor people like her.

We had to find dramatic moments like that, which hint at a much bigger picture, scenes that had conflict and a bit of fun, that opened up the whole question: Are these guys going to be in charge? It's like the whole thing that [James] Connolly said: 'What's the point

---

* Article III of the Statute of Kilkenny (1367), enacted by the wealthy Hiberno-Norman landowners of the Irish Parliament, proscribed the speaking of Gaelic by English colonists in Ireland and by the native Irish when conversing with them.

of hoisting the green flag over Dublin Castle? What kind of Ireland is it going to be?"* Every single scene had to serve a purpose, and that was the biggest challenge in *Barley*: how to squeeze the War of Independence and the Civil War, with rich characters, not just paper stereotypes, into one film. It was a battle, but a great joy to attempt.

The Wind That Shakes the Barley is imbued with Connolly's spirit; Jimmy's Hall (2014), too. Damien's friend Dan and Jimmy Gralton [Barry Ward] walk in his shoes.

You know, he was born in Edinburgh. One of my sons plays in a band, and the venue they often perform in is near Connolly's birthplace. There is an insignificant little plaque on the wall there that doesn't do the great man justice. It's in a dingy, dark corner under a bridge in what was then known as Little Ireland. If ever I win the football pools, there is a huge wall opposite, and that would be the place to create a dynamic mural to commemorate this brilliant man's achievements, from his organizing in the States to the forming of the Citizen Army in Ireland. I know how the mural would end: his wife, Lillie, saying goodbye to him the night before he was executed. Her last words were: 'Your beautiful life, James, your beautiful life.'

At USC, you must have come across all the standard screenwriting guides and books. Some screenwriting gurus swear by Aristotle's Poetics *(c.335 BCE), for example.*

I remember reading about it. I think it's probably another framework in a different vocabulary about making a story move forward.

---

* Connolly's actual words were: 'If you remove the English army tomorrow and hoist the green flag over Dublin Castle, unless you set about the organization of the Socialist Republic your efforts would be in vain. England would still rule you. She would rule you through her capitalists, through her landlords, through her financiers, through the whole array of commercial and individualist institutions she has planted in this country and watered with the tears of our mothers and the blood of our martyrs. England would still rule you to your ruin, even while your lips offered hypocritical homage at the shrine of that Freedom whose cause you had betrayed.'

It doesn't help me, really, but I can see why people use it. You can break down a script in many ways. As a principle, I think the more pressure you put on characters – as in real life – the more that will reveal who they are, unless your character is like James Bond, who never changes. In the type of stories that we do, you've got to put them under the cosh to see what they're made of. The more difficult the choices are, the more painful they are, and the more revealing they are. But those choices have to be true to the time and place. I think that's an ancient principle, too, because writers have always done that in different ways. If those choices don't become apparent in a script as the main character tries to figure out what to do, I think the story's dead. When a character is just drifting through scenes, that's when you literally lose the plot. You can tell that's happened when the audience drifts off, too. You can smell it in the cinema when the vital connection is broken. And the opposite is true. I remember seeing [Michael Haneke's] *Caché* [2005] – a brilliant film – in a cinema, and you could feel the tension in the room. You're on story, and you're gripped. If you can do that, I think it's a very attractive way of telling a story. Some people try to make a story more reflective or add some distance – that Brechtian idea – but, for me, the most seductive part of the film experience is when you're in it, when you're in those people's shoes, and you don't realize time is passing.

You often crank up pressure on your characters by making them choose between two awful options. Casim is faced with breaking Roisin's heart or his father's. Joe has to do the drug run, or else McGowan will order his boys to break Liam's leg. Damien has to execute Chris, or else the flying-column volunteers won't be able to trust each other and discipline will collapse.

That's what life does to us, again and again and again. You can climb the greasy pole if you bow to the powerful, but if you slip off it, you'll be crushed. Our choices reveal who we are. What I loved about the Justice for Janitors women I met in LA, out of which we made *Bread and Roses*, was that they faced an existential choice: whether to [accept their lot] or challenge their employers and risk being sent back to Guatemala or El Salvador. Then they would have years of misery trying to get back to the States again, risking their lives with coyotes.* In their daily lives in LA, because of the pressures of work and not being in a trade union, they hardly saw their children and, more important, didn't have any healthcare insurance for themselves or their families. What a fucking choice – fight for your rights and change the life of your family, or lose and be deported. You understand why people are bought off and betray others. I think that's the stuff of drama, and why the choice of what story you want to tell and the premise and the characters around that are absolutely critical. If you don't get that right, you'll end up with a bland film.

That, to me, is the secret of telling a good story. It's a quirky thing, because it's part gut instinct, part intellect and part luck. If you don't get the main character right and understand who they are, I don't think you'll want to go on a journey with them. I'll never forget sitting down to write *My Name Is Joe*. I wrote that first scene in the AA meeting, and I heard Joe in my head say, 'Thank fuck I'm *not* an alcoholic.' And then I thought, 'Wow, what's going to happen here? This guy is going to take me on an adventure, and I can't wait.' I remember sitting down to write *Sweet Sixteen* and going, 'God, this kid! I want this to go like a train.' It's about the choices he has to make all the way through. I think that if you feel like that when you're writing, then there's a chance that the story might work for everybody else who's got to work on it. That was the great thing about handing over the first version of a screenplay to Ken. It was always very exciting and nervy . . . Fortunately, our passions seemed to have bobbed along in tandem.

One of the hallmarks of the films is that people within a community, an organization or a family end up betraying it or committing an act of sabotage, because they're under threat and are scared. These are always people whose well-being has been compromised, or who believe it will be if they disobey the person or thoughts that are pressuring them, like Chris in The Wind That Shakes the Barley *and Pinball in* Sweet Sixteen. *Even little Liza Jane in* Sorry We Missed You *– she hides the keys to her dad's van because the pressure of his delivery gig is causing family fights.*

---

* People smugglers.

Those characters are the ones that attract me as a writer, because their contradictions emerge as you're doing it. Rosa, for example, who goes absolutely crazy in that brutal scene between the sisters near the end of *Bread and Roses* [when she tells Maya that she's been forced to work as a prostitute since she was seventeen]. Before writing it, I went down to the *maquila* factories* along the US–Mexico border. I talked to trade unionists there who were being pursued and threatened with murder, and I went to the areas where young women are brought into prostitution. I met nuns there and other people who worked with them [the prostitutes]. If I hadn't seen all that, I couldn't have written Rosa. That's where she came from; she wasn't copied from anybody I met but was informed by that reality. All these young women come to work in these massive factories and are dumped in the middle of nowhere. They're alienated, they're left on their own and they're very vulnerable. Many of them drift into prostitution, because it's the only way to survive and get money to send home. When you see that, you see the contradictions. So I understood Rosa. She said, 'I only believe in that' – she means her own hand – because she doesn't trust anyone. I had great sympathy for her. I really, really loved that woman; she was the most exciting person to write and very truthful.

Not for the first time in Ken's career, I, Daniel Blake *exposed brutal truths about the British welfare system. How did you unearth them?*

Lots of digging around, as ever. Ken and I had been to a lot of food banks, and so we wanted to get our heads around all the complexities of the welfare system. We heard stories from those working on the front line. We could have told a story about somebody who was disabled, somebody who's got mental health difficulties, perhaps a young person, but Daniel Blake came into my mind after I'd steeped myself in the research. After all the journalistic work, you have to have the confidence to write a piece that will be robust.

---

* A *maquila*, or *maquiladora*, is an internationally owned factory, located in Mexico, near the US border, where cheap labour is exploited to manufacture products that are exported back to the owner company's country at lower tariffs than those from other countries. The highest concentrations of these factories are in Baja California and Chihuahua.

What was absolutely key was that I found these whistleblowers inside the DWP – they were lovely people – who showed me the lies from management. Government ministers were saying to us that there was no target for sanctions [for stopping, suspending or reducing welfare benefits], but sanctions had gone up by millions. I managed to make contact with this one whistleblower in the DWP who was a mine of information. He showed me a letter that he and all his fellow workers in his office had received from their area manager. From memory, it had the names of around thirty-five workers. The letter pointed out that only the top four or so had carried out enough sanctions that month, and if they didn't carry out more, they would be put on something called a 'PIP' – a personal improvement plan, to use the full Orwellian term. Later, I met another DWP worker who had lost his job after refusing to raise the number of sanctions in accordance with the new instructions.

I thought of all the stories I'd heard from people who went through it and all the bullshit that bastard Damian Green* gave us about not setting targets for sanctions. Lies! Getting sanctioned torments people. They get no money, so they and their families are condemned to hunger. You have more rights with a parking ticket. And then the penny dropped, especially after speaking to the whistleblower inside the DWP. I realized this wasn't a bureaucratic fuck-up, but a systematic cruelty to frighten and humiliate people. And then I felt in my bones, 'Right, now I can go for it and share with Ken, "Look at this. Look at these people. This is what's happening. This is the big picture."' I think that building a screenplay is about understanding the deep connections. You begin to see the pattern. Why do they humiliate people like that? Because people who are humiliated are frightened. They won't join a trade union. They'll keep their heads down. Sanctioning is a way of controlling them and keeping them in place. It fits so much of how society operates. There was that 'pulled-down blinds' comment by George Osborne.† Rishi Sunak started it up again with his speech [in April 2024] about 'sick-note culture'. It suits the Tories to be hard on the poor because it's typical bait for the usual suspects, from the hard right in the Commons to their cheerleaders in the press.

* Secretary of state for work and pensions (2016–17).
† See footnote, p. 325.

You told me in an interview we did in 2016 that, in your research, you found instances of sanctioned people who had been worse off than Daniel or Katie.

Much worse. People collapsing and dying from heart attacks after they'd been told they were fit for work. I remember a doctor I met here in Edinburgh who told me about one of his patients, who was dying of cancer. He collapsed in his house and bloodied his face, the poor sod. His neighbours called the ambulance, but he refused to get into it because he was signing on the next day and was scared that he was going to get a sanction and be left with nothing.

I met another old man who had been sanctioned for three years. [His Jobcentre] said he had to go to do a specific task. He was an ex-electrical engineer, and he said, 'I could teach young people, I could do all sorts of stuff, but I'm not jumping through hoops doing that shite.' So he lived off tins of spaghetti hoops for three years in a cold flat in Wishaw, near Motherwell, where my dad used to live. I tried to keep in contact with him because the temperature was dropping. I was scared he was going to freeze to death, but that gives you anger and fuel when you come to write. You can read all the books that you want – and that's very important – and speak to all the academics you want to get the big picture, but you've just got to go round and smell how things are. I remember their eyes. When you've met people who are feeding their children with biscuits, who are humiliated and frightened, you don't copy it from the street, but it gives you the energy and the confidence to write the piece.

I'm curious about what you think of academic commentary on the films. It's been suggested, for example, that My Name Is Joe *and* The Angels' Share *are discourses on urban versus rural life in Scotland. Such theories must help film students expand their thinking, but what worries me about them is that they separate the films from the basic needs of the people the films are about.*

My favourite one was when someone called Joe's act of cutting up celery for a salad 'a middle-class signifier'. You've got to smile. In regard to *The Angels' Share*, many people who live in places like Glasgow and Edinburgh have never been to the countryside, and that's implicit in the film. Some of them have never even been to a park. So when they do go to the country, it's a very different experience for them. There's also this corny stereotype of Scotland that it's hard not to poke fun at. That's why Rhino wears his kilt back to front, though I wasn't trying to undermine people who wear kilts or live in the countryside.

When you're writing, you do things by instinct when it's truthful to the character. I've always tried to work that way, because if you try to set up a character as a great big symbol or cypher, you're going to be in trouble. It just isn't going to be truthful to the premise. People say we live in an '*I, Daniel Blake* society' now. It's strange when a piece of fiction enters the public discourse like that, but maybe Daniel Blake works because, even though he's a fictional character, he is truthful to his world and truthful to what was going on and still is going on, unfortunately.

Some reviews of The Old Oak *said that its optimistic ending was a wish fulfilment, a fantasy of unity, with TJ, Laura, Yara and some of the other Syrians joyfully marching in the Durham Miners' Gala. Yet, in practical terms, TJ will not only have to stop hosting the communal meals, but it looks as if he'll have to close the pub for good.*

From the beginning, Ken and I have always examined the notion of where people find hope and how they nourish each other. If you tag a happy ending onto a film, but you don't earn it, the whole thing falls apart. I wasn't very sure at first if the story that we were telling in *The Old Oak* would earn the Durham Miners' Gala at the end; you always have to be faithful to the premise of the story. Obviously, the previous two films, *I, Daniel Blake* and *Sorry We Missed You*, were tragedies in their own ways, and I'm glad we made them. Daniel Blake and Ricky in *Sorry We Missed You* are decent, apolitical men. TJ is very different to them. He knows about the miners' strike and is steeped in that tradition. Like many people I've met, he had been ground down by life, a bit like Steve Evets's character in *Looking for Eric*. He was isolated, worn down, humiliated, and was on the point of suicide. But you have to believe, by the end of the film, that he's found hope. He's made a deep connection with Yara and Laura, and that's enabled him to find the better part of himself again. You're in his shoes when he sees the community coming together and the sheer goodwill of the people that makes the Syrian mother [Fatima] cry as they come to her [after learning her husband has died]. That strikes a profound chord with TJ.

Where does he go from there? It's a good question, but I think him finding friends, and what that sets in motion, transcends what happens to the pub. The idea is that he's made friends for life. If we had made that story up out of nothing, it would have been a lie. But I did find people like that in these communities, salt-of-the-earth types, an inspiration to me, who had the intelligence, the creativity, the imagination and the empathy to put themselves in the shoes of the Syrians, or to put themselves in the shoes of the local people and understand where their anger was and try to disentangle it all. These are real people, not fictional characters. They were cooking and eating together, and people are still making those friendships. It takes a lot of graft, but they give of themselves and are nourished by each other, and that's where hope comes from. I can see it happening again with activists in Gaza, where many people who didn't know each other well are coming together for a common purpose.

When I interviewed Ken about The Old Oak *and asked him about the longevity of your partnership, I remember he joked, 'We're like Morecambe and Wise.' But no other long-running, British-based writer–director partnership has been so driven to interrogate and condemn injustice, inequality and oppression in depth, on an international scale. It must have been hard when Ken said* The Old Oak *would be his last film.*

It's kind of you to say that, and I notice you say 'driven'. You put your finger on it. It's a mad old job making films, and I realize now that for a creative partnership to work there has to be some very deep connection, quite apart from the fact we have different jobs to do. You have to be fired up, feel compelled; maybe get mad and laugh at the same kinds of things. It's beyond sharing the same political inclinations – that makes it too shallow – but there has to be some deep sympathy between us about how we see the world, feel it, beyond the rational, or react to it. We are both endlessly curious about how power operates in our lives: who has it, who hasn't, and how it all affects how we live, and even how it will affect the lives of people in the future. Each story is a great big puzzle to try to untangle, and it's addictive, because each film has been a struggle to understand what's going on around us. Stories can help us understand our lives. No wonder [storytelling] was going on around the flickering fires of ancient caves, long before celluloid.

Ken has been saying since *Looking for Eric* that this might be his last film. But this time it is true. It was a monumental effort to make *The Old Oak* in the time of Covid. Ken had his eighty-sixth birthday during the shoot. I'm convinced it was his political will that got him through it, a fierce energy in that tiny frame. Not to say courage, a very attractive quality, which he has shown throughout his life, way beyond films. When you mention partnership, I must mention our magnificent producer, Rebecca O'Brien. Would Ken have had the second half to his career without her? I wouldn't have had my part, that's for sure; she has allowed us to get on with the research, the writing and then the making of the films without all the desperate hassle so many go through. So partnership, yes, but it takes three to tango.

It's shocking, but time does creep up on us and runs out. But I see the glass as half full, not half empty. What luck I have had to share this life adventure, not just film, with such a brilliant friend, his family and our film family, with whom we have spent so much time. Jammie bastards we are!

CHAPTER 17

Conclusion

GRAHAM FULLER: *I can't recall you speaking directly about cinema specifically as an artist's medium, presumably because you've been focused on what the films say through the stories they tell.*

KEN LOACH: I have spoken about it a few times. One of the comments about *The Old Oak* that would have made me angry if I were prone to anger – instead, it was water off a duck's back because I have no respect for the person who said it – was that I have no respect for the aesthetics of film-making and that I'm only interested in getting a message across. Well, nothing could be further from the truth. The lights, the lens, the perspective of sound, the human positioning of the camera – which means there's a lot of shots you wouldn't think of doing because they would break the sense the audience has of being an observer – all that is carefully considered. The camera is as close as someone would be if they were known to the participants, but the audience understands that they're not an intrusive presence, which is why I hate intrusive close-ups. It's about not only having a sense of respect for the characters, but also caring for them. I would find it difficult to do films about people I didn't care for. You have to have a human response to people, and that means understanding that the people who are hostile to TJ in *The Old Oak*, for example, are not head-banging racists at all. They've got real concerns, but those concerns turn into something else. The aesthetics of the film-making work to enable that understanding in the audience.

As we see with Charlie. It's important not to overlook the fact that the film shows the sorrowful course his life has taken. His wife is ill, his house has been devalued, and because he's disgruntled, he yields to the temptation to help the saboteurs of the pub's communal meals. I was struck by the way Trevor Fox shows Charlie's mortification, when TJ confronts him about his betrayal. Though afterwards Charlie remorsefully joins the other villagers in mourning Fatima's husband – Yara's father – there's a furtiveness about the way he wheels his wife's wheelchair at the edge of the crowd.

I think it's shame. He almost doesn't want to be noticed, because he says to his daughter, 'You go' [to Fatima and Yara's house], but he doesn't go in himself because that would be too much of a climbdown somehow. He isn't ready for reconciliation, but he has to acknowledge Fatima's grief to help restore his pride and self-respect, to recover from the shame he feels for what he's done. He and TJ would get together at a later time, if they could. We thought very carefully about the fact that he would just be there on the periphery. If somebody saw him, that's fine. And if nobody did, that's fine, too. I'm pleased you noticed this. Trevor Fox is a fine actor, and his instinct for this moment was just perfect.

Charlie's made a start at least, a gesture towards solidarity.

Yes, it's a start. He's more comfortable with himself at the end than when TJ confronts him at the moment when he feels his shame most keenly. To create a true sense of things like this demands a certain set of aesthetics in the way the story is presented. It's about how people speak, how you capture their body language, how you read what their life has been, right through to the pores of their skin. Are their knuckles swollen? Is their skin coarse or free of the marks that manual labour gives you? Film sees all these things. Most films ignore them, but I think they're essential to the physical presence of the people in the images. It goes along with their emotional depth and the truth of their interactions, how they listen and respond with a genuine sense of spontaneity because something is happening for the first time.

How we use music is crucial. I might think we have a good scene, but then the violin comes in, and that can have a great effect, but it can also be destructive. I often think, 'Just keep quiet there. We don't need it because the scene is already telling us everything.' Our composer, George Fenton, is vital to the process because of his instincts and sense of what is and isn't needed. A lot of critics don't see that all these decisions affect the aesthetics of what is on the screen and what the audience hears.

It's now April 2024. You've said that The Old Oak *will be your last film. Do you have thoughts about how you might engage politically in the future?*

It's very ad hoc. I've met so many people over the years in campaigns and in different trade unions and organizations, many local activists, that there's no shortage of invitations – which is very kind of people – for me to make some kind of contribution. I am very lucky because that could be a full-time job. It means you can say, 'These are the big issues for now, so I'll spend more time dealing with them.'

It would also be good to put something down on paper, even if it were just a pamphlet, a few basic thoughts on the work that we've tried to do, the mistakes we've learned from and the ideas we've tried to express while working with friends and other people in a series of relationships that support the whole – a group of people with one voice. It's rooted not in film techniques, but in a view of the world. That is the springboard of what we do. It doesn't come from watching films and thinking, 'I like that. How can we do that?' It comes from – or I hope it comes from [*laughs*] – a view of the world that leads you to historical–political perspectives.

We've addressed in passing how your films embody a Marxist critique of how capitalism exploits working people. Is that a precept that you ever discussed with your writers and producers, in terms of representing it in the films, or did you usually start with the struggles people are going through, and what they can do to help themselves?

I think we've always started with the particular struggles that caught our eye and seem significant because they indicate the wider principles. Some struggles may seem so peripheral that they don't go to the heart of the essential conflict. I think the struggles that have attracted us are the ones that shine the light on the roots of society. But I think that's understood. We – originally, Tony Garnett and me, and then Barry Hines, Jim Allen, and Paul and Rebecca, obviously – would never say that to each other. We'd just say, 'Have you seen this? Have you seen that?' That's the heart of it. You don't need to spell out what the connection is to that essential conflict. It's a given in our endless conversations that we've had over many years. The key thing then is to tell a story where, without hammering it out in boring detail or long speeches, people will go away and reflect on the wider questions, without thinking, 'Oh, God, that's the same message I've heard before.' It's not so much about messages as it is about the human cost. It's about how we experience these struggles, how we experience exploitation, oppression, poverty, whatever. There's an old quote that often comes to mind that was spoken by a priest, Hélder Câmara:* 'When I give food to the poor, they call me a saint. When I ask why they are poor, they call me a communist.' That encapsulates something very clear. Another way of putting it is summed up in a line Paul wrote in *The Old Oak*: 'This is solidarity, not charity.' The idea is that you share because you share that common denominator of class interest, rather than one side being rich and having more than the other side through being the beneficiary of exploitation. Out of their kindness, TJ and the others give something to the Syrians and other people in the village, without being aware that what they're giving is theirs because of the exploitation of those to whom they are giving – though that's rather a cumbersome way of putting it.

A final question, Ken: as far as you're concerned, the struggle goes on?

Yes [*laughs*]! Once you're hooked, you're hooked, aren't you? There's no way out. I think it would be a betrayal if you just walked away. You're limited by what you can do, the older you get. Occasionally sticking your head above the parapet and chipping in is maybe all you can do as time passes. I don't know – we'll see. You keep your hopes up.

---

* Câmara (1909–99) was a Catholic prelate, communist, human rights activist and leading proponent of liberation theology. He was archbishop of Olinda and Recife (1964–85) during the Brazilian military dictatorship.

Filmography

(as director, unless stated)

TELEVISION

1964
Catherine
A BBC Television production for the *Teletale* series
BBC, 24 January
Producer: James MacTaggart
Script: Roger Smith
Production designer: Robert Fuest
Music: Dennis Wilson
Cast: Geoffrey Whitehead (narrator), Kika Markham (Catherine), Peter Hoy (car salesman), Gilbert Wynne (Jack), Tony Garnett (Richard), David Bedard (Dave), Tony Selby (singer), David Hart (first youth), Peter Blythe (second youth), John Downey (third youth), Patricia Leverton (girl in coffee bar)
30 minutes. Black and white

Z Cars episode 'Profit by Their Example'
A BBC Television production
BBC, 12 February
Producer: David E. Rose
Script: John Hopkins
Script editor: Robert Barr
Production designer: Frederick Knapman
Cameraman: David Prosser
Editor: Christopher La Fontaine
Cast: James Ellis (PC Lynch), Colin Welland (PC Graham), Frank Windsor (Detective Sergeant Watt), Michael Forrest (PC Hicks), Robert Keegan (Sergeant Blackitt), Kate Allitt (Pamela Earnshaw), John Harvey (Arthur Monks), David Morrell (Geoff Payne), Richard Wilding (Jim Egan), Peter Goss (Harry O'Neill), Jessica Dunning (Sally Monks), Julia

Jones (Mrs Egan), Malcolm Patton (Michael Heseltine), Fred Ferris (Mr Heseltine), Robert Flynn (Donald McQueen)
50 minutes. Black and white

Z Cars episode 'A Straight Deal'
A BBC Television production
BBC, 11 March
Producer: David E. Rose
Script/script editor: Robert Barr
Production designer: Stanley Morris
Cameraman: David Prosser
Editor: Christopher La Fontaine
Cast: James Ellis (PC Lynch), Colin Welland (PC Graham), Stratford Johns (Detective Chief Inspector Barlow), Frank Windsor (Detective Sergeant Watt), Robert Keegan (Sergeant Blackitt), Kate Allitt (Pamela Earnshaw), Allison Bayley (Ma Tansfield), Patrick Westwood (Josh Tansfield), Norman Wynne (George Hoyle), Jean Patten (Mrs Hoyle), Larry Burns (Jim Ryan), George Layton (Jack Simpson), John Dearth (Jackie Small), John Lowe (Joe Emmett), Jack Cunningham (PC Patterson), Henry Moxon (Mr Bampton), Tanya Trude (Emmett's girlfriend)
50 minutes. Black and white

Z Cars episode 'The Whole Truth'
A BBC Television production
BBC1, 8 April
Producers: David E. Rose, Ken Loach
Script/script editor: Robert Barr
Production designer: Donald Brewer
Cast: James Ellis (PC Lynch), Colin Welland (PC Graham), Stratford Johns (Detective Chief Inspector Barlow), Frank Windsor (Detective Sergeant Watt), Michael Forrest (PC Hicks), Robert Keegan (Sergeant Blackitt), Brian Blessed (PC Smith), Joseph Brady (PC Weir), Brian Rawlinson (Daniel 'Punchy' Palmer), Judy Parfitt (Mrs Palmer), Michael Goldie (Ted Martin), Alan Foss (Charles Clements), John McKelvey (Jim Appleton), Edward Kelsey, Fred Haggerty (Wilson brothers), Rex Robinson (scrapyard owner), Paul Barnes, Syd Deller, Steve Potters (policemen), Doreen Ubels (policewoman), Darrell Richard, Roy Senton (scrap dealers)
50 minutes. Black and white

Diary of a Young Man
Survival (episode 1), Marriage (episode 3), Life, or a Girl Called Fred (episode 5)

A BBC Television production
BBC1, 8 August (episode 1), 22 August (episode 3), 5 September (episode 5)
Producer: James MacTaggart
Script: Troy Kennedy Martin, John McGrath
Story editor: Roger Smith
Production designer: John Cooper (episodes 1 & 3), Peter Seddon (episode 5)
Cameraman: John McGlashan
Editor: Christopher La Fontaine
Stills: Derek Nice
Music: Stanley Myers
Cast: Victor Henry (Joe), Richard Moore (Ginger), Nerys Hughes (Rose)
Episode 1: Sally Mates (girl at laundry), Frank Williams (interviewer), Will Stampe (Uncle Arthur), Glynn Edwards (police constable), Barry Lineham (police sergeant)
Episode 3: Harry Towb (first worker), Alister Williamson (second worker), George Tovey (third worker), Peter Blythe (National Insurance man), Wally Patch (Big Jim), Roy Godfrey (Mr Silver), Leslie Dwyer (Mr Gold), Ann Mitchell (Eileen), Frank Williams (registrar), Glynn Edwards (police constable), Will Stampe (Uncle Arthur), Frank Williams (Mr Wilcox), Jane Freeman (nurse)
Episode 5: Jean Marsh (Fred), John Warner (Truscott), Roy Godfrey (Mr Silver), Leslie Dwyer (Mr Gold), Carl Duering (psychiatrist), Frank Williams (biologist), Nora O'Rawe (housekeeper), David Blake Kelly (priest), Glynn Edwards (police constable), George Little (chief beatnik), Donald McCollum (philosopher), Noel Howlett (Lord Chief Justice), Robin Parkinson (store detective), Wally Patch (Chelsea pensioner), David Crane (man in street), Joseph Wise (colonel), William Hurndell (Irish clerk), Arthur Lawrence (vegetarian), David Baxter (student), Lisa White (girl), Gina Cola (Italian), Frank Littlewood (general), Bruce Wightman (man), Robert Lee (Buddhist), Danvers Walker (Arthur)
45 minutes each episode. Black and white

1965
Tap on the Shoulder
A BBC Television production for the *Wednesday Play* series
BBC1, 6 January
Producer: James MacTaggart
Script: James O'Connor
Story editor: Roger Smith
Production designer: Eileen Diss
Cameramen: John McGlashan, Ken Westbury
Editor: Geoffrey Botterill

Music: Stanley Myers
Cast: Lee Montague (Archibald Cooper), Richard Shaw (Ronnie), Judith Smith (Hazel), Griffith Davies (Terry), George Tovey (Patsy), Tony Selby (Tim), Edwin Brown (George), Mark Elwes (pub customer), John Henderson (Clegg), Tom Bowman (Charlie), Rose Hill (Emma Cooper), Charles Rea (policeman), Noel Johnson (chief constable), Michael Mulcaster (major domo), Walter Horsbrugh (bishop), Lucy Griffiths (bishop's wife), Sarah Hayter (deb), Michael Goldie (inner security guard), John Blythe (first security guard), Tony Caunter (second security guard), Michael Collins (police sergeant), John Waite (Detective Sergeant Nash), Carmen Dene (first girl), Christine Rodgers (second girl), Harry Tracey (waiter)
70 minutes. Black and white

Wear a Very Big Hat
A BBC Television production for the *Wednesday Play* series
BBC1, 17 February
Producer: James MacTaggart
Script: Eric Coltart
Story editor: Roger Smith
Production designer: Peter Kindred
Cameraman: Stanley Speel
Editor: Norman Carr
Music: Stanley Myers
Cast: Neville Smith (Johnny Johnson), Sheila Fearn (Ann Johnson), William Holmes (Snapper Melia), Johnny Clive (Billy Moffatt), Nola York (shop assistant), Malcolm Taylor (Stan), Alan Lake (Harry Atkins), Royston Tickner (pub landlord), William Gaunt (Peter), James Hall (Colin), Margery Campi (girl), Ken Jones (Dyke), David Jackson (Joey), John Swindells (pub customer), Tomi Yap, Cecil Ching (waiters), Jack Cunningham (first Irishman), Dermot MacDowell (second Irishman)
75 minutes. Black and white

Three Clear Sundays
A BBC Television production for the *Wednesday Play* series
BBC1, 7 April
Producer: James MacTaggart
Script: James O'Connor
Story editor: Roger Smith
Editor: Pam Bosworth
Story editor: Roger Smith
Lyrics: Nemone Lethbridge
Cameraman: Tony Imi
Lyrics: Nemone Lethbridge

Cast: Tony Selby (Danny Lee), Dickie Owen (Big Al), Will Stampe (Porky), John Blythe (Jimmy the Gent), Finuala O'Shannon (Rosa), George Sewell (Johnny May), Rita Webb (Britannia Lee), Glynn Edwards (Prison Officer Johnson), Kim Peacock (prison governor), Len Russell, Leslie Bates, Dave Griffiths, Yemi Ajibade (in the pub), Bernard Shine (policeman 'One-a-day'), Wally Patch, Ken Wayne (two prisoners in Black Maria), Howell Evans (Prison Officer Morgan), Alan Cooper, Fred Rawlins, David J. Grahame (prisoners), Eric Mason (Millin, an orderly), George Webb (Jim Ritchie, a prisoner), Alec Ross (Nick Carney, a prisoner), Brian Weske (Lou), Griffith Davies (Joss), Glynn Williams (Abel), Michael Goldie (gaoler), David Crane (Winters, a prisoner), Harry Littlewood (Cook, a prisoner), Ken Jones (Robbo Robertson), Edwin Brown (chief prison officer), Iain Anders, Desmond Cullum Jones, Bob Lane, Leslie Shannon (gaolers), Leonard Webb (Cock-Eye), Allan Selwyn, Ralph Katterns, Andrea Lawrence (gamblers), George Tovey (Little George), Kenneth Colley (Nick), Dermot MacDowell (Father Cavanagh), David Baxter (Tony Hobbs, a prisoner), Henry Webb (Sam Goldstein), Hayden Jones (Silent Sam), Jack Cunningham (Nobby Rogers), Ron Welling (prison orderly), Anthony Blackshaw (Prison Officer Rice), Anthony Woodruff (Dr Crosby), Reg Lever (a juror), Jack Melford (a judge), Haydn Jones (clerk of the court), David Crane (counsel), James Appleby (Prison Officer Fred), Howard Goorney (Albert Ketch), Ben Howard (Charlie, his assistant), Winnie Donovan (street singer), Harry Price (harmonica player)
75 minutes. Black and white

Up the Junction
A BBC Television production for the *Wednesday Play* series
BBC1, 3 November
Producer: James MacTaggart
Script: Nell Dunn, based on her novel
Story editor: Tony Garnett
Production designer: Eileen Diss
Cameraman: Tony Imi
Editor: Roy Watts
Title music: Paul Jones, arranged by Mike Vickers
Songs sung by Russ Parker, played by Winifred Helliwell, Marie Cleve
Cast: Carol White (Sylvie), Geraldine Sherman (Rube), Vickery Turner (Eileen), Tony Selby (Dave), Michael Standing (Terry), Ray Barron (Ron), Rita Webb (Mrs Hardy), Hilda Barry (Old May), Jessie Robins (Fat Li!), George Sewell (Barny), Ann Lancaster (Winnie), Rose Howlett (Rube's mother), Frank Jarvis (Rube's brother), Ronald Clark (Sylvie's husband), Gilly Fraser (Annie)
72 minutes. Black and white

The End of Arthur's Marriage
A BBC Television production for the *Wednesday Play* series
BBC1, 17 November
Producer: James MacTaggart
Script: Christopher Logue, Stanley Myers
Production designer: Robert MacGowan
Cameramen: Brian Probyn, Johnny Ray
Editor: Stan Hawkes
Music: Stanley Myers
Title music: Paul Jones, arranged by Mike Vickers
Songs sung by: Christine Holmes, Long John Baldry, Samantha Jones, Rita Williams
Cast: Charles Lamb (Dad), Winifred Dennis (Mum), Janie Booth (Mavis), Ken Jones (Arthur), Maureen Ampleford (Emmy), Neville Smith (He), Tracy Rogers (She), Joanna Dunham (Mrs Thurloe), Edward de Souza (Mr Thurloe), Robert Dougall (newsreader)
70 minutes. Black and white

The Coming Out Party
A BBC Television production for the *Wednesday Play* series
BBC1, 22 December
Producer/story editor: Tony Garnett
Script: James O'Connor
Production designer: Michael Wield
Cameraman: Alan Jonas
Editor: Michael Johns
Music: Stanley Myers
Title music: Paul Jones, arranged by Mike Vickers
Lyrics: Nemone Lethbridge
Cast: Toni Palmer (Rosie), George Sewell (Ricketts), Dennis Golding (Scimpy), Jayne Muir (Sister Bridget), Wally Patch (Grandpa), Hilda Barry (Grandma), Will Stampe (scrap merchant), Carol White (The Princess), Julie May (Wendy), Rita Webb (Floss), Andrea Lawrence (Sandra), Ted Peel (Harry)
65 minutes. Black and white

1966
Cathy Come Home
A BBC Television production for the *Wednesday Play* series
BBC1, 16 November
Producer: Tony Garnett
Script: Jeremy Sandford, Ken Loach
Production designer: Sally Hulke
Cameraman: Tony Imi

Editor: Roy Watts
Sound: Malcolm Campbell
Music: Paul Jones
Cast: Carol White (Cathy), Ray Brooks (Reg), Wally Patch (Grandad), Winifred Dennis (Mrs Ward), Adrienne Frame (Eileen), Emmett Hennessy (Johnny), Ronald Pember (Mr Jones), Liz McKenzie (Mrs Jones), Anne Ayres (Pauline Jones), Geoffrey Palmer (property agent), Gabrielle Hamilton (welfare officer), Phyllis Hickson (Mrs Alley), Frank Veasey (Mr Hodge)
75 minutes. Black and white

1967
In Two Minds
A BBC Television production for the *Wednesday Play* series
BBC1, 1 March
Producer: Tony Garnett
Script: David Mercer
Production designer: John Hurst
Cameraman: Tony Imi
Editor: Roy Watts
Sound: Geoff Tookey
Cast: Anna Cropper (Kate Winter), Brian Phelan (interviewing doctor), George A. Cooper (Mr Winter), Adrienne Frame (hairdresser), Helen Booth (Mrs Winter), Peter Ellis (Jake), Christine Hargreaves (Mary Winter), George Innes (Paul Morris), Anne Hardcastle (doctor), Eileen Colgan (sister), Edwin Brown (mental welfare officer), Bill Hays, Vickery Turner (at the rehearsal room), Yvonne Quenet, Neville Smith, Malcolm Taylor (at the pub), Julie May (nurse), Patrick Barr (consultant)
75 minutes. Black and white

1968
The Golden Vision
A BBC Television production for the *Wednesday Play* series
BBC1, 17 April
Producer: Tony Garnett
Script: Neville Smith, Gordon Honeycombe
Production designer: Malcolm Middleton
Cameraman: Tony Imi
Sound: Derek Lawrence
Editor: Roy Watts
Cast: Ken Jones (Joe Harrigan), Billy Dean (John Coyne), Neville Smith (Vince Coyne), Joey Kaye (Brian Croft), Johnny Gee (Syd Paisley), Flora Manger (Annie Coyne), Angela Small (Celia Horrigan), Patricia Bush

(Muriel Coyne), Vera Gillan (Sylvia Croft), Carol Williams (Carol Croft), Anne O'Sullivan (Doreen Coyne)
75 minutes. Black and white

1969
The Big Flame
A BBC Television production for the *Wednesday Play* series
BBC1, 19 February
Producer: Tony Garnett
Script: Jim Allen
Production designer: Geoff Patterson
Cameraman: John McGlashan
Editor: Roy Watts
Sound: Ron Hooper
Cast: Godfrey Quigley (Jack Regan), Norman Rossington (Danny Fowler), Ken Jones (Freddie Grierson), Peter Kerrigan (Peter Connor), Daniel Stephens (Joe Ryan), Tommy Summers (Alec Murphy), Meredith Edwards (Logan), Michael Forrest (Garfield), John Riley (Bruno), Harold Kinsella (Andy Fowler), Joan Flood (Liz Fowler), Terence Flood (son of Fowler), Ron Davies (Steve Fowler), Roland MacLeod (Mr Weldon), Gerald Young (judge), Philip Ross (inspector), Griffith Davies (O'Neill)
85 minutes. Black and white

In Black and White
A Save the Children Fund production by Kestrel Films for LWT
Producer: Tony Garnett
Script: Ken Loach
Narrator: Alan Dobie
50 minutes. Colour
Not transmitted

1971
The Rank and File
A BBC Television production for the *Play for Today* series
BBC1, 20 May
Producer: Graeme McDonald
Script: Jim Allen
Script editor: Ann Scott
Production designer: Roger Andrews
Cameraman: Charles Stewart
Editor: Roy Watts
Sound: Eoin McCann, Mike Billings
Costumes: Pam Doolan
Cast: Peter Kerrigan (Eddie), Billy Dean (Billy), Bert King (Bert), Tommy

Summers (Les), Neville Smith (Jerry), Mike Hayden (Mike), Johnny Gee (Johnny), Joan Flood (Joan), Jimmy Coleman (Jimmy), Ernie Mack (Bill Hagan), Michael Forrest (Holtby), Charlie Barlow (Charlie), Bernard Atha (personnel officer)
75 minutes. Black and white

After a Lifetime
A Kestrel Films production for LWT
ITV, 18 July
Producer: Tony Garnett
Script: Neville Smith
Production designer: Andrew Drummond
Cameraman: Chris Menges
Editor: Ray Helm
Sound: Frederick Sharp
Music: John Cameron
Cast: Edie Brooks (May), Neville Smith (young Billy), Jimmy Coleman (Aloysius), Peter Kerrigan (Uncle John), Bill Dean (Uncle Sid), Johnny Gee (Frank), Sammy Sharples (Uncle Gus), Joey Kaye (Mike), Joan Flood (Cissie), Mike Hayden (Father MacNally), Bert King (undertaker), Rosalind Elliott (Maureen), Len Annett (Joe Horrigon), Ernie Mack (insurance agent), Pat Gillon (Mr Pimlett), Laidlaw Dailing (doctor), Penelope Higginbottom (Auntie Millie), Helen Quinn (Florrie)
75 minutes. Colour

1973
A Misfortune
A BBC Television production for the *Full House* series
BBC2, 13 January
Script: Ken Loach, based on the short story by Anton Chekhov
Editor: Jeremy Thomas
Cast: Lucy Fleming, Ben Kingsley, Peter Eyre, Xenia Deberner, Vyvan Ekkel, John Langford
38 minutes. Colour

1975
Days of Hope
A BBC Television production, in association with Polytel
Part 1: *1916: Joining Up*, BBC1, 11 September
Part 2: *1921*, BBC1, 18 September
Part 3: *1924*, BBC1, 25 September
Part 4: *1926: General Strike*, 2 October
Producer: Tony Garnett
Script: Jim Allen

Production designer: Martin Johnson
Cameramen: Tony Pierce-Roberts, John Else
Editor: Roger Walsh
Costumes: Sally Nieper
Music: Marc Wilkinson
Cast: Paul Copley (Ben Matthews), Nikolas Simmonds (Philip Hargreaves), Pamela Brighton (Sarah Hargreaves)

Part 1: Helen Beck (Martha Matthews), Cliff Kershaw (Tom Matthews), Peter Russell (soldier on leave), Fred Feast (police sergeant), Bernard Atha (vicar), Norman Tyrrell (George Lansbury), Olga Graham (woman at NCF meeting), John Rolls (magistrate), Ted Carroll (old soldier), Charles Cork (army captain), Margaret Heery (woman in NCF office), Robert Booth (vicar in NCF office), Peter Armitage, Ian East (conscientious objectors), Dominic Allan (major in France), Robin Scobey (adjutant in France), Ian Munro (sergeant in France), David Neville (army captain in Ireland), Martin Skinner, Dougie Brown, Jimmie Coleman, Hal Nolan (soldiers in Ireland), Triona O'Donnell (girl), John Metcalf (boy)

Part 2: Gary Roberts (Joel Barnett), Jean Spence (May Barnett), Christine Anderson (Jenny Barnett), Robert Bradley, Gillian Hall (children), Alun Armstrong (Billy Shepherd), Hughie Turner (Tom Crisp), Ernie Mack (Bassett), Tommy Buller (coal merchant), Edward Underdown (John Pritchard), Margaretta Scott (Mrs Pritchard), Edward Sivell, Max Stewart (police sergeants), Edwin Brown (pit manager), Barry Stokes (army officer), Freddie Clemson (army sergeant), Joey Kaye (lorry driver)

Part 3: Brian Hawksley (prison chaplain), Bert King (prison warder), Patrick Barr (Mr Harrington), Peter Kerrigan (Communist Party member), Melvin Thomas (Ernest Bevin), Eric French, George Howard (shop stewards), Stephen Rea (reporter), Gary Roberts (Joel Barnett), Alun Armstrong (Shep), Hughie Turner (Tom), John Phillips (Josiah Wedgwood), Richard Marner (Suslov), Sarah Paget, Ned Cohen (Sarah's children)

Part 4: Russell Waters (J. H. Thomas), Neil Seiler (Arthur Pugh), Brian Harrison (Alfred Purcell), Dai C. Davies (A. J. Cook), George Wilkinson (Herbert Smith), Richard Butler (Walter Citrine), Melvin Thomas (Ernest Bevin), John Young (Ramsay MacDonald), Brian Hayes (Stanley Baldwin), Emrys James (Thomas Jones), Noel Coleman (Sir Arthur Steel-Maitland), Alan Judd (Lord Birkenhead), Philip Lennard (Joynson-Hicks), Leo Britt (Churchill), Derek Farr (Lord Wimborne), Joan Henley (Lady Wimborne), Hilary Wontner (Lord Reading), Joan Haythorne (Mrs Snowden), David Markham (Sir Herbert Samuel), Jeremy Child (Selwyn Davies), Bernard Padfield (Sir Abe Bailey), Anthony Nash (Sir Horace Wilson), Brian Phelan (solicitor), Peter Kerrigan (Peter), Anthea Meadows

(Elsie), Sarah Paget, Ned Cohen (Sarah's children), George Tovey, James Marcus (building workers), Laurie Asprey, Robert Cawdron, Martin Matthews (reporters), Stuart Hibberd (newsreader)
Part 1, 95 minutes; part 2, 100 minutes; part 3, 80 minutes; part 4, 135 minutes. Colour

1977
The Price of Coal
A BBC Television production for the *Play for Today* series
Part 1: *Meet the People: A Film for the Silver Jubilee*, BBC1, 29 March
Part 2: *Back to Reality*, BBC1, 5 April
Producer: Tony Garnett
Script: Barry Hines
Production designer: Martin Collins
Photography: Brian Tufano
Editor: Roger Waugh
Sound: Andrew Boulton
Costumes: Roger Reece
Cast: Bobby Knutt (Sid Storey), Rita May (Kathy Storey), Paul Chappell (Tony Storey), Jayne Waddington (Janet Storey), Haydn Conway (Mark Storey), Jackie Shinn (Mr Forbes), Duggie Brown (Geoff Carter), Bert Oxley (Phil Beatson), Ted Beyer (Harry), Hughie Turner (Bob Richards), Tommy Edwards (Alf Meakin), Anne Firth (Sheila), Robbie Platts (Mr Atkinson), Stan Richards (Albert), Philip Firth (Ronnie), Michael Hinchcliffe (Jimmy)

Part 1: Vicky Dale (Edna), Danny James (bank man), Edward Underdown (Sir Gordon Horrocks), Tony Graham (painter), Peter Russell (telephonist), Johnnie Allan, Peter Martin (Bomb Squad)

Part 2: Max Smith (NUM official), Les Hickin (Eric), Peter Black (Pete), Wilfred Grove (deputy), Gary Roberts (George Kay), Jean Spence (Mrs Kay), Mary Wray (Mrs Dobson), Ron Delta (Mr Dobson), Christie Gee (Mrs King), Olga Grahame (Salvation Army lady), Paul Bryan (Mr Oates), Henry Moxon (Eric Johnson, MP)
Part 1, 75 minutes; part 2, 95 minutes. Colour

1980
A Question of Leadership
An ATV Network production
ATV, 13 August 1981 (postponed from 5 August 1980)
Producer: Ken Loach
Cameramen: Chris Menges, John Davey
Editor: Roger James
Sound: Andrew Boulton
50 minutes. Colour

The Gamekeeper
An ATV Network production
ITV, 16 December
Script: Barry Hines, based on his novel
Production designers: Martin Johnson, Graham Tew
Cameramen: Chris Menges, Charles Stewart
Editor: Roger James
Sound: Andrew Boulton, Peter Rann
Costumes: Maxine Henry
Cast: Phil Askham (George Purse), Rita May (Mary), Andrew Grubb (John), Peter Steels (Ian), Michael Hinchcliffe (Bob), Philip Firth (Frank), Les Hickin (Jack), Jackie Shinn (landlord), Paul Brian (butcher), Ted Beyer (Alf), Chick Barratt (Henry), Willoughby Gray (duke), Mark Elwes (Lord Dronfield), Gary Roberts (poacher)
84 minutes. Colour

Auditions
An ATV Network production
ITV, 23 December
Producer: Ken Loach
Cameraman: Chris Menges
Editor: Jonathan Morris
Sound: Bob Bentley
With: Penni Dunlop, Karen Williams, Janet Cooper
60 minutes. Black and white

1983
The Red and the Blue: Impressions of Two Political Conferences – Autumn 1982
A Central Television production
Channel 4, 1 October
Producer: Roger James
Cameraman: Chris Menges
Editor: Jonathan Morris
Sound: Judy Freeman
90 minutes. Colour

Questions of Leadership
A Central Television production
Executive producer: Roger James
Producer: Ken Loach
Cameraman: James Dibling
Editor: Jonathan Morris
4 episodes, 50 minutes each. Colour
Not transmitted

1985
Which Side Are You On?
An LWT production for *The South Bank Show*
Channel 4, 9 January (postponed from November 1984)
Executive producer: Melvyn Bragg
Producer: Ken Loach
Cameramen: Chris Menges, Ken Morse, James Dibling
Editor: Jonathan Morris
Sound: Judy Freeman, Terry Hardy
Songs and poems: written by miners and their families

We Should Have Won: The End of the Battle, But Not of the War
A Diverse production for the *Diverse Reports* series
Channel 4, 27 March
Producer: Alex Graham
Director: Philip Clark
Editor: Ken Loach
Researcher: Roy Ackerman
27 minutes. Colour

1989
Time to Go
A BBC Television Community Programmes Unit production for the *Split Screen* series
BBC2, 9 May
Producer: Gavin Dutton
Research: Tony Mulholland
Cameraman: Barry Ackroyd
Editor: Jonathan Morris
Sound: Michael Lax
15 minutes. Colour

The View from the Woodpile
A Central Television production for the *Eleventh Hour* series
Channel 4, 12 June
Executive producer: Roger James
Producer: Ken Loach
Research: Sheila Ford
Cameramen: Barry Ackroyd, Robin Probyn
Editors: Paul Jackson, Mike Burch
Sound: Steve Philips, Derrick Thompson, Robin Ward
Music: Simon Lanzon, Chumbawamba
Cast: Jimmi Dunn, Paul Harp, Steve Page, Caroline White, Roy 'Beastie' Stokes, Simon Lanzon
52 minutes. Colour

1991
The Arthur Legend
Clark Productions for the *Dispatches* series
Channel 4, 22 May
Producer and reporter: Lorraine Heggessey
Production manager: Rebecca O'Brien
Research: Ian Pollard
Cameramen: Barry Ackroyd, Stephen Standen
Editor: Jonathan Morris
Sound: Simon Okin
40 minutes. Colour

1996
The Flickering Flame: A Story of Contemporary Morality
UK/France; produced by Parallax Pictures/AMIP/BBC/La Sept ARTE for the *Modern Times* series
BBC2, 18 December 1996
Executive producers: Stephen Lambert, Thierry Garrel
Producers: Rebecca O'Brien, Xavier Carniaux
Assistant producer: Claire Powell
Production manager: Georgina Isherwood
Cameramen: Roger Chapman, Barry Ackroyd
Editor: Tony Pound
Sound: David Keene, Chris Tussler
Music: George Fenton
Narrator: Brian Cox
50 minutes. Colour

1997
McLibel: Two Worlds Collide
UK; Spanner Films
Producer/director: Franny Armstrong
Assistant producer: Sharon Davey
Re-enactments director (uncredited): Ken Loach
Cinematography: Franny Armstrong, Peter Armstrong, Neve Cunningham, Mick Duffield
Editor: Gregers Sall
Sound: Brian Healy, Ian MacPherson
Cast: Helen Steel, Dave Morris, Veronika Hyke, Mike Love, T. Colin Campbell, Jeremy Corbyn, Sue Dibb, Lynne Franks, Dan Gallin, Stephen Gardner, Geoffrey Giuliano, Keir Starmer, Shelby Yastrow (voice); re-enactment actors: Bruce Alexander, Pip Donaghy, Ian Flintoff, Oliver Ford Davies, Richard Hope, Fred Pearson, Malcolm Tierney
53 minutes. Colour

1998
Another City: A week in the life of Bath's football club
A Parallax Pictures Production for HTV
HTV, 23 April
Producer: Rebecca O'Brien
Research: Julia Faulkner
Cameramen: Steven Sanden, Nick Jardine
Editors: Jonathan Morris, Anthony Morris
Sound: Fraser Barber, Steve Haynes
26 minutes. Colour

FEATURE FILMS AND OTHERS

1967
Poor Cow
UK; Vic Films
Producer: Joseph Janni
Script: Ken Loach, Nell Dunn, based on Dunn's novel
Production designer: Bernard Sarron
Cinematography: Brian Probyn
Editor: Roy Watts
Sound: Kevin Sutton, Gerry Humphreys
Music: Donovan
Music director: John Cameron
Songs: 'Be Not Too Hard' by Donovan and Christopher Logue; 'Colours', 'Poor Love' by Donovan
Cast: Carol White (Joy), Terence Stamp (Dave), John Bindon (Tom), Kate Williams (Beryl), Queenie Watts (Aunt Em), Geraldine Sherman (Trixie), James Beckett, Bill Murray (Tom's mates), Ellis Dale (solicitor), Gerald Young (judge), Gladys Dawson (Bet), Ron Pember (Petal), Malcolm McDowell (Billy), Winnie Holman (woman in park), Rose Hillier (customer in hairdresser's), George Tovey, Will Stampe, Bernard Stone, John Halstead (photographers), Peter Claughton (driving examiner), Julie May (woman in Sheppey), Philip Ross (Shelley), Martin King (prison warder), Muriel Hunte (woman at prison), James Thornhill (prisoner), Mo Dwyer (prisoner's wife), Terry Duggan (second prisoner)
101 minutes. Colour

1969
Kes
UK; Kestrel Films/Woodfall Films
Producer: Tony Garnett

Script: Ken Loach, Barry Hines, Tony Garnett, based on Hines's novel *A Kestrel for a Knave*
Production designer: William McCrow
Cinematography: Chris Menges
Editor: Roy Watts
Sound: Peter Pierce, Tony Jackson
Music: John Cameron
Cast: David Bradley (Billy Casper), Lynne Perrie (Mrs Casper), Freddie Fletcher (Jud), Colin Welland (Mr Farthing), Brian Glover (Mr Sugden), Bob Bowes (Mr Gryce), Robert Naylor (MacDowall), Trevor Hesketh (Mr Crossley), Geoffrey Banks (maths teacher), Eric Bolderson (farmer), Joey Kaye (pub entertainer), Zoe Sutherland (librarian), Joe Miller (friend of Mrs Casper), David Glover (Tibbutt), Bernard Atha (youth employment officer), Stephen Crossland, George Speed, Frank Norton (boys), Martin Harley (younger boy), Duggie Brown (milkman), Billy Dean (fish and chip man)
113 minutes. Colour

1971
Talk About Work
UK; Ronald H. Riley Associates for the Central Office of Information and the Central Youth Employment in association with the Department of Employment
Producer: Michael Barden
Script: Ken Loach
Cinematography: Chris Menges
Editor: Alan Price
Sound: Fred Sharp
15 minutes. Black and white
Rejected by the Central Office of Information and never shown

Family Life
UK; Kestrel Films/Anglo EMI
Executive producer: Bobby Blues
Producer: Tony Garnett
Associate producer: Irving Teitelbaum
Script: David Mercer, based on his TV play *In Two Minds*
Production designer: William McCrow
Cinematography: Charles Stewart
Editor: Roy Watts
Sound: Peter Elliott, Frederick Sharp, Gerry Humphries
Music: Marc Williamson
Cast: Sandy Ratcliff (Janice Baildon), Bill Dean (Mr Baildon), Grace Cave (Mrs Baildon), Malcolm Tierney (Tim), Hilary Martyn (Barbara Baildon), Michael Riddall (Dr Donaldson), Alan MacNaughton (Mr Carswell),

Johnny Gee (gardener)
108 minutes. Colour
US title: *Wednesday's Child*

1979
Black Jack
UK; Kestrel Films in association with the National Film Finance Corporation
Executive producer: Bobby Blues
Producer: Tony Garnett
Script: Ken Loach, based on the novel by Leon Garfield
Production designer: Martin Johnson
Cinematography: Chris Menges
Editor: William Shapter
Sound: Andrew Boulton
Music: Bob Pegg
Cast: Stephen Hirst (Bartholomew 'Tolly' Pickering), Louise Cooper (Belle Carter), Jean Franval (Black Jack), Phil Askham (hangman), Pat Wallis (Mrs Gorgandy), John Young (Dr Hunter), William Moore (Mr Carter), Doreen Mantle (Mrs Carter), Russell Waters (Dr Jones), Brian Hawksley (Parson Hall), Packie Byrne (Dr Carmody), Joyce Smith (Mrs Carmody), Andrew Bennett (Hatch), Malcolm Dixon, Mike Edmonds, David Rappaport, Tiny Ross (Tom Thumb's Army), Arthur Davies (Mr Hannah), Jackie Shinn (Arbuthnot), Cilla May (Mrs Hannah), Dave Daniels, Michael Hinchcliffe (footmen), Mary Wray (Mrs Arbuthnot), Les Hickin (Jed), Brian Lewis (Jethro), Patti Nicholls (Mrs Mitchell), Ted Beyer (innkeeper), Gary Roberts (sexton), Hughie Turner (porter)
110 minutes. Colour

1981
Looks and Smiles
UK; Black Lion Films/Kestrel Films/MK2 Productions for Central Television
Producer: Irving Teitelbaum
Associate producer: Raymond Day
Script: Barry Hines
Production designer: Martin Johnson
Cinematography: Chris Menges
Editor: Steve Singleton
Sound: Andrew Boulton
Music: Marc Wilkinson, Richard and the Taxmen
Cast: Graham Green (Mick Walsh), Carolyn Nicholson (Karen Lodge), Tony Pitts (Alan Wright), Roy Haywood (Phil Adams), Phil Askham (Mr Walsh), Pam Darrel (Mrs Walsh), Tracey Goodlad (Julie), Patti Nicholls

(Mrs Wright), Cilla Mason (Mrs Lodge), Les Hickin (George), Arthur Davies (Mr Lodge), Deirdre Costello (Jenny), Jackie Shinn (gatekeeper), Christine Francis (careers officer), Rita May (receptionist), Ernest Johns (army major), Marie Mason (mother in shoe shop), Paul Tuke (training officer)
104 minutes. Colour

1986
Fatherland
UK/France/West Germany; Kestrel II Films/Film Four International/MK2/ZDF/Clasart Film
Executive producer: Irving Teitelbaum
Producer: Raymond Day
Associate producers: Ingrid Windisch, Catherine Lapoujade
Script: Trevor Griffiths
Production designer: Martin Johnson
Cinematography: Chris Menges
Editor: Jonathan Morris
Sound: Karl Laabs, Kevin Brazier
Music: Béla Bartók, Benjamin Britten
Songs: 'Guilty' written and performed by Randy Newman; 'Old Star'
Cast: Gerulf Pannach (Klaus Drittemann), Fabienne Babe (Emma de Baen), Cristine Rose (Lucy), Sigfrit Steiner (James Dryden), Robert Dietl (East German lawyer), Heike Schrotter (Marita), Stephan Samuel (Max), Thomas Ohlke (Young Drittemann), Patrick Gillert (Thomas), Heinz Diesing (Jürgen Kirsch), Eva Krutina (Rosa), Hans Peter Hallwachs (Rainer Schiff), Ronald Simoneit (Uwe), Marlowe Shute (American official), Jim Raketa (Braun), Bernard Bloch (journalist), Winfried Tromp (Herr Hennig)
110 minutes. Colour
US title: *Singing the Blues in Red*

1990
Hidden Agenda
UK; Initial Film and TV Productions in association with Hemdale
Executive producers: John Daly, Derek Gibson
Producer: Eric Fellner
Co-producer: Rebecca O'Brien
Script: Jim Allen
Production designer: Martin Johnson
Cinematography: Clive Tickner
Editor: Jonathan Morris
Sound: Simon Okin
Music: Stewart Copeland

Songs: 'Joe McDonnell' written by Brian Warfield and performed by Ron Kavana and Terry Woods; 'Young Ned of the Hill' written and performed by Ron Kavana and Terry Woods
Cast: Frances McDormand (Ingrid Jessner), Brian Cox (Kerrigan), Brad Dourif (Paul Sullivan), Mai Zetterling (Moa), Maurice Roeves (Harris), Robert Patterson (Ian Logan), Bernard Bloch (Henri), George Staines (tall man), Michelle Fairley (Teresa Doyle), Brian McCann (Molloy), Des McAleer (Sergeant Kennedy), Mandy McIlwaine (RUC policewoman), Ivan Little (television journalist), Llew Gardner (television announcer), Patrick Kavanagh (Alec Nevin) John McDonnell (Labour MP), Kate Smith (news reporter), Victoria D'Angelo (journalist), John Benfield (Maxwell), John Keegan (Detective Sergeant Hughes), Jim Norton (Brodie), Jack McElhinney (Jack Cunningham), Maureen Bell (Mrs Molloy), Stephen Bridgen (army major), Kym Dyson (Carol), Oliver Maguire (Superintendent Fraser), Jim McAllister (Liam Philbin), Ron Kavana, Terry Woods (musicians), Bernard Archer (Sir Robert Neil), Gerry Fearon (taxi driver)
108 minutes. Colour

1991
Riff-Raff
UK; A Parallax Pictures Production for Channel 4
Producer: Sally Hibbin
Script: Bill Jesse
Production designer: Martin Johnson
Cinematography: Barry Ackroyd
Editor: Jonathan Morris
Sound: Bob Withey
Music: Stewart Copeland
Songs: 'Always on My Mind' by Wayne Carson, Johnny Christopher, Mark James; 'With a Little Help from My Friends' by John Lennon, Paul McCartney; 'I'm So Excited' by T. Lawrence, A. Pointer, J. Pointer, R. Pointer; 'Good Morning' by Nacio Herbe Brown, Arthur Freed; 'Won't You Charleston with Me?' by Sandy Wilson; 'Spread a Little Happiness' by Gordon Sumner, Vivian Ellis; 'Everytime I Say Goodbye' by Cole Porter; 'The Sun Has Got His Hat On' by Noel Gay
Cast: Robert Carlyle (Stevie), Emer McCourt (Susan), Jimmy Coleman (Shem), George Moss (Mo), Ricky Tomlinson (Larry), David Finch (Kevin), Richard Belgrave (Kojo), Ade Sapara (Fiaman), Derek Young (Desmonde), Bill Moores (Smurph), Luke Kelly (Ken Jones), Garrie J. Lammin (Mick), Willie Ross (Gus Siddon), Dean Perry (Wilf), Dylan O'Mahoney, Brian Coyle, Stuart Peveril (youths), Terry Bird (van driver), Jimmy Batten (man buying kango), Tracy Brabin, Debra Gillett, Benjamin Lush, Jayne MacKenzie, Johanne Murdock (singers), David

Adler (director), David Taegar (producer), Dominic Barlow (pianist), Terry Duggan (boss in office), Angela Morant (estate agent), Lila Cherif, Joumana Gil, Zohra El Harrack (clients), Peter Mullan (Jake), John Kazek (Robert), Anne Marie Timoney (Fiona), Maureen Carr (Ellen), James MacDonald (funeral director), Vicky Murdock (medical secretary), Mike Haydon (security guard), Martin Clapson, Tex Comer, Les Davidson, Jimmy Jewell, Len Stonebridge (pub band)
95 minutes. Colour

1993
Raining Stones
UK; A Parallax Pictures Production for Channel 4
Producer: Sally Hibbin
Script: Jim Allen
Script supervisor: Susanna Lenton
Production designer: Martin Johnson
Cinematography: Barry Ackroyd
Editor: Jonathan Morris
Sound: Ray Beckett
Music: Stewart Copeland
Songs: 'Something Good' by Kate Bush and Utah Saints, performed by Utah Saints; 'Nasty' by Mark French, Bradley Carter, performed by Sy-Kick; 'Lock Up' by and performed by Zero B
Cast: Bruce Jones (Bob Williams), Julie Brown (Anne Williams), Gemma Phoenix (Coleen Williams), Ricky Tomlinson (Tommy), Tom Hickey (Father Barry), Mike Fallon (Jimmy), Ronnie Ravey (butcher), Lee Brennan (Irishman), Karen Henthorn (young mother), Christine Abbott (May), Geraldine Ward (Tracey), William Ash (Joe), Matthew Clucas (Sean), Anna Jaskolka (shop assistant), Jonathan James (Tansey), Anthony Bodell (Ted), Bob Mullane (Ted's mate), Jack Marsden (Mike), Jimmy Coleman (Dixie), George Moss (Dean), Jackie Richmond (club steward), Tony Little (Cliff), Derek Alleyn (factory boss)
91 minutes. Colour

1994
Ladybird, Ladybird
UK; A Parallax Pictures Production for Film Four International
Producer: Sally Hibbin
Script: Rona Munro
Script supervisor: Susanna Lenton
Production designer: Martin Johnson
Cinematography: Barry Ackroyd
Editor: Jonathan Morris
Sound: Ray Beckett

Music: George Fenton, Mauricio Venegas
Songs: 'Candles' by Domitila Cane'k; 'Delilah' by Les Reed, Barry Mason; 'I Like It' by Mitch Murray; 'Whole Lotta Shakin' Goin' On' by Curlee Williams; 'Ain't Nothin' Goin' On But the Rent' by Gwen Guthrie; 'I Never Promised You a Rose Garden' by Joe Smith; 'The Rose' by Amanda McBroom; 'Up Where We Belong' by Jack Nitzsche, Will Jennings, Buffy Sainte-Marie; 'La Felicidad' by Palito Ortega
Cast: Crissy Rock (Maggie), Vladimir Vega (Jorge), Sandie Lavelle (Mairead), Mauricio Venegas (Adrian), Ray Winstone (Simon), Clare Perkins (Jill), Jason Stracey (Sean), Luke Brown (Mickey), Lily Farrell (Serena), Scottie Moore (Maggie's father), Linda Ross (Maggie's mother), Kim Hartley (Maggie, aged five), Jimmy Batten (karaoke compere), Sue Sawyer (foster mother), Pamela Hunt (Mrs Higgs), Alan Gold (neighbour), James Bannon (fast food manager), Christine Ellerbeck (Moira Denning)
101 minutes. Colour

1995
A Contemporary Case for Common Ownership
UK; Defend Clause Four Campaign
22 minutes. Colour
Alternative title: *Clause IV: The Movie*

Land and Freedom
UK/Spain/Germany; Parallax Pictures/Messidor Films/Road Movies Dritte Produktionen
Executive producers: Sally Hibbin, Gerardo Herrero, Ulrich Felsberg
Producer: Rebecca O'Brien
Associate producer: Marta Esteban
Script: Jim Allen
Script editor: Roger Smith
Script supervisor: Susanna Lenton
Production designer: Martin Johnson
Cinematography: Barry Ackroyd
Editor: Jonathan Morris
Sound: Ray Beckett
Music: George Fenton
Songs/music extracts: 'A las Barricadas' by Valeriano Orobón Fernández, Józef Pławiński (tune 'Whirlwinds of Danger'); 'La Internacional' by Christianus Geyter Petrus; 'A las Mujeres', 'Ramonda' by Mabel Wayne, Wolfe Gilbert; 'Si Me Quieres Escribir' by Juan Ignacio Cuadrado Bueno
Cast: Ian Hart (David Carr), Rosana Pastor (Blanca), Icíar Bollaín (Maite), Tom Gilroy (Gene Lawrence), Marc Martínez (Vidal), Frédéric

Pierrot (Bernard), Andres Aladrén, Sergi Calleja, Raffaele Cantatore, Pascal Demolon, Paul Laverty, Josep Magem, Eoin McCarthy, Jürgen Müller, Roca, Emili Samper (militia), Suzanne Maddock (Kim), Mandy Walsh (Dot), Angela Clarke (Kitty), Rafael Díaz (barracks officer), Felicio Pellicer (Nationalist officer), Ricard Arilla (priest), Jordi Dauder (Salas), Pep Molina (Pepe), Enriqueta Ferré (concierge), Asunción Royo (old woman), Francese Orella (Casado), Phil O'Brien, Dave Seddon (ambulance men), Neus Agulló, Pepe Cortés (Bianca's parents)
110 minutes. Colour

1996
Carla's Song
UK/Germany/Spain; Parallax Pictures/Channel 4 Films/Road Movies Dritte Produktionen/Tornasol Films SA
Producer: Sally Hibbin
Co-producers: Ulrich Felsberg, Gerardo Herrero
Script: Paul Laverty
Script supervisor: Susanna Lenton
Production designer: Martin Johnson
Art director: Llorenc Miquel
Cinematography: Barry Ackroyd
Editor: Jonathan Morris
Sound: Ray Beckett
Music: George Fenton
Cast: Robert Carlyle (George), Oyanka Cabezas (Carla), Scott Glenn (Bradley), Subash Sing Pall (Victor), Stewart Preston (McGurk), Gary Lewis (Sammy), Margaret McAdam (George's mother), Pamela Turner (Eileen), Louise Goodall (Maureen), Salvador Espinoza (Rafael), Richard Loza (Antonio), Norma Rivera (Norma), José Meneses (Harry), Rosa Amelia López (Carla's mother)
125 minutes. Colour

1998
My Name Is Joe
UK/Germany/Spain/France; Parallax Pictures/Channel Four Films/Road Films/Vierte Produktionen/Tornasol Films S.A./La Sept ARTE
Executive producer: Ulrich Felsberg
Producer: Rebecca O'Brien
Line producer: Peter Gallagher
Script: Paul Laverty
Script supervisor: Susanna Lenton
Production designer: Martin Johnson
Cinematographer: Barry Ackroyd
Editor: Jonathan Morris

Sound: Ray Beckett
Music: George Fenton
Songs: 'Down the Dustpipe' by Carl Groszmann, performed by Status Quo; 'Stinger' by the NFMO; 'Hi Ho Silver Lining' by Scott English, Larry Weiss, performed by Jeff Beck; 'In the Summertime' by Ray Dorset, performed by Mungo Jerry; 'Stand by Your Man' by Tammy Wynette, Billy Sherrill, performed by Tammy Wynette; 'Spirit in the Sky' written and performed by Norman Greenbaum; Ludwig van Beethoven: *Violin Concerto in D major*, op. 61, Marcia Crayford (violin) George Fenton (conductor)
Cast: Peter Mullan (Joe), Louise Goodall (Sarah), Gary Lewis (Shanks), Lorraine McIntosh (Maggie), David McKay (Liam), Annemarie Kennedy (Sabine), Scott Hannah (Scott), David Peacock (Hooligan), Gordon McMurray (Scrag), James McHendry (Perfume), Paul Clark (Zulu), Stephen McCole (Mojo), Simon Macallum (Robbo), Paul Gillan (Davy), Stephen Docherty (Doc), Paul Doonan (Tattie), Cary Carbin (Sepp Maier), David Hayman (McGowan), Martin McCardie (Alf), James McNeish (Shuggy), Kevin Kelly (Jake), Brian Timoney (Scooter), David Hough (referee), Sandy West (DSS investigator), John Comerford (DSS supervisor), Carol Pyper Rafferty (Rhona), Elaine M. Ellis (second receptionist), Stewart Ennis (Doctor Boyle), Andy Townsley (husband), Ann Marie Lafferty (wife), Bill Murdoch (postman), Kate Black (kiosk attendant), Rab Affleck (lorry driver), Archie Clark, Tom Dingwall, Amanda Godfrey, Jimmy Hanlon, Eddie McIntyre, Fr Joe Mills, John Smith, Dorothy Jane Stewart, Rab Wilson. With the participation of the Drumchapel Unemployed Workers, Rutherglen and the Wynnes, and The Wanderers Unemployed Centre football teams.
105 minutes. Colour

2000
Bread and Roses
UK/Germany/Spain; British Screen/BSkyB/Cineart/Filmcooperative Zürich/Parallax Pictures/BM Distribution/Alta Films/BAC Films/Road Movies Filmproduktion/Tornasol Films
Executive producer: Ulrich Felsberg
Producer: Rebecca O'Brien
Script: Paul Laverty
Script editor: Roger Smith
Script supervisor: Susanna Lenton
Production designer: Martin Johnson
Art director: Tucker Doherty
Cinematography: Barry Ackroyd
Editor: Jonathan Morris
Sound: Ray Beckett
Music: George Fenton

Costume designer: Michele Miche
Casting directors: Richard Hicks, Rosalinda Morales, Ronnie Yeskel
Cast: Pilar Padilla (Maya), Adrien Brody (Sam Shapiro), Elpidia Carrillo (Rosa), Jack McGee (Bert), George Lopez (Perez), Monica Rivas (Simone), Frank Davila (Luis), Lillian Hurst (Anna), Mayron Payes (Ben), Maria Orellano (Berta), Elena Antonenko (Maria), Olga Gorelik (Olga), Melody Garrett (Cynthia), Gigi Jackman (Dolores), Beverley Reynolds (Ella), Eloy Méndez (Juan), Jesus Perez (Oscar), Alonso Chavez (Ruben), Estela Maeda (Teresa), José Jiménez (Freddy), Sherman Augustus (Ernest), Julia Orea, Javier Torres (Coyote), Roscio Saenz (Emma), Blake Clark (Mr Griffin), Pepe Serna (restaurateur), Tony Rizzoli (personnel manager), Tom Gilroy (director of campaigns), Neal Baer (doctor), David Steinberg (lawyer), Ted Baer (lawyer), Gail Thomas (corporate lawyer), Terry Anzur (TV reporter), Greg Montgomery (supervising policeman), Clement Blake (gas station attendant), Tom Bailey (truck driver), Richard Bravo (INS officer), Robert Stachowiak (INS officer), Gary Fredo (police sergeant), Miguel Angel Varela Fimbres (teenage demonstrator), Vanessa Angel, William Atherton, Lara Belmont, Cooper Campbell, Benicio del Toro, Ogded Fehr, Stuart Gordon, Rick Otto, Chris Penn, Ron Perlman, Tim Roth, Robin Tunney, Samuel West, Stephanie Zimbalist (party guests)
110 minutes. Colour

2001
The Navigators
UK/Germany/Spain; Alta Films/Parallax Pictures/Road Movies Filmproduktion/Tornasol Films/WDR-Arte
Producer: Rebecca O'Brien
Co-producers: Michael André, Ulrich Felsberg
Line producer: Peter Gallagher
Script: Rob Dawber
Script editors: Barry Hines, Roger Smith
Production designer: Martin Johnson
Art director: Fergus Clegg
Cinematography: Barry Ackroyd, Mike Eley
Editor: Jonathan Morris
Sound: Ray Beckett
Music: George Fenton
Costume designer: Theresa Hughes
Cast: Dean Andrews (John), Thomas Craig (Mick), Joe Duttine (Paul), Steve Huison (Jim), Venn Tracey (Gerry), Andy Swallow (Len), Sean Glenn (Harpic), Charlie Brown (Jack), Juliet Bates (Fiona), John Aston (Bill Walters), Graham Heptinstall (Owen), Angela Forrest (Tracy), Clare McSwain (Lisa), Megan Topham (Chloe), Abigail Pearson (Eve),

Charlotte Hukin (Rose), Jamie Widowson (Michael), Andy Oldham (PICOP), Nigel Harrison (Will Hemmings), Charles Armstrong (John Wilson), Charlie Wathen (chip shop owner), John Roy (installation man), Kevin Carroll, Tim Cooper, Max Lemon, Tony Nyland (company reps), Gerry McMahon, Tony Maskell (Essex builders), Mike Wattam (supervisor), Sue Robbie (video narrator), Sue Thompson, Betty Noble (voices of interviewers), Paul André, Neil Baggot, Ian Best, Stuart Brierley, Kevin Broadhead, Matt Brown, Wayne Clark, Jason Croot, Glyn Davis, John Earl, Ken Ellis, Graham Heath, Kris Hitchen, Philip Johns, Pete Martin, Gary Maycock, Paul Morris, Steven Mowatt, Austin Wagstaff, Peter Wardlow (other workers), Jonathan Bridge (man asleep at union meeting), Joe Gradwell (dancer in pub)
96 minutes. Colour

2002
Sweet Sixteen
UK/Germany/Spain; Sixteen Films/Scottish Screen/BBC Films/Road Movies Filmproduktion/Tornasol Films/Alta Films
Producer: Rebecca O'Brien
Co-producers: Michael André, Ulrich Felsberg, Gerardo Herrero
Line producer: Peter Gallagher
Script: Paul Laverty
Script editor: Roger Smith
Script supervisor: Susanna Lenton
Production designer: Martin Johnson
Art director: Fergus Clegg
Cinematography: Barry Ackroyd
Editor: Jonathan Morris
Sound: Ray Beckett
Music: George Fenton
Additional songs and music: 'The Arrival of the Queen of the Night' from *The Magic Flute* by Wolfgang Amadeus Mozart, performed by Failoni Kamerazenekar and Helen Kwon; 'I'll Stand by You', written by Tom Kelly, Billy Steinberg, Chrissie Hynde, performed by The Pretenders; 'Burn in Hell', written by Otten/Skog/Tell/Torstensen, performed by Clawfinger; 'Dogman', written by Tristan Hervo, performed by Wide Open Cage; 'Bushes', written by Markus Nikolai, Theo Krieger, Clair Dietrich, performed by Markus Nikolai; 'Ain't No Love (Ain't No Use)', written by Melanie Williams, Jimi Goodwin, Jez Williams, Andy Williams, performed by Sub Sub featuring Melanie Williams; 'Let Me Entertain You', written by Robbie Williams, Guy Chambers, performed by Robbie Williams; 'You Stole the Sun from My Heart', written by James Dean Bradfield, Nicky Wire, Sean Moore, performed by Manic Street Preachers; 'I Go to Sleep', written and composed by Ray Davies, performed by The Pretenders

Costume designer: Carole K. Millar
Cast: Martin Compston (Liam), William Ruane (Pinball), Annmarie Fulton (Chantelle), Michelle Abercromby (Suzanne), Michelle Coulter (Jean), Gary McCormack (Stan), Tommy McKee (Rab), Calum McAlees (Calum), Robert Rennie (Scullion), Martin McCardie (Tony Douglas), Robert Harrison, George McNeilage, Rikki Traynor (Tony's gang members), Jon Morrison (Douglas), Junior Walker (Night-time), Gary Maitland (Side-kick), Scott Dymond (Davi-Vampire), Mark Dallas, Stephen McGivern, Robert Muir (pizza boys), Matt Costello (motorbike policeman), Sandy Hewitt (truck driver), Lily Smart (barmaid), Bruce Sturrock (caravan site manager), William Cassidy, Robert McFadyen, Stephen Purdon (muggers), Tony Collins (cold pizza man), Marie Shankley (woman on stairs), Tam McKinley (pub landlord), Barry Cameron (clubber), Rene Costa (busker), Mercy (three-legged dog)
106 minutes. Colour

11'09"01 – September 11
UK/France/Egypt/Japan/Mexico/USA/Iran; Catherine Dussart Productions/Comme des Cinémas
Artistic producer: Alain Brigand
Eleven short films, each 11 minutes, nine seconds and one frame
Total running time: 135 minutes
Directors: Samira Makhmalbaf ('Iran'), Claude Lelouch ('France'), Youssef Chahine ('Egypt'), Danis Tanović ('Bosnia-Herzegovina'), Idriissa Ouédraogo ('Burkina Faso'), Ken Loach ('United Kingdom'), Alejandro González Iñárritu ('Mexico'), Amos Gitai ('Israel'), Mira Nair ('India'), Sean Penn ('USA'), Shōhei Imamura ('Japan')
Credits for 'United Kingdom' only:
Producer: Rebecca O'Brien
Script: Paul Laverty
Cinematography: Peter Hellmich, Jorge Müller Silva
Editor: Jonathan Morris
Sound: Kevin Brazier
Songs: Vladimir Vega
Cast: Vladimir Vega
Colour with black-and-white archival footage

2004
Ae Fond Kiss/A Fond Kiss/Just a Kiss
UK/Belgium/Germany/Italy/Spain; Sixteen Films/Bianca Film/Cinéart/Glasgow Film Office/Matador Pictures/Scottish Screen/Tornasol Films
Executive producers: Ulrich Felsberg, Paul Ward
Co-executive producer: Nigel Thomas
Producer: Rebecca O'Brien

Line producer: Peter Gallagher
Script: Paul Laverty
Script editor: Roger Smith
Script supervisor: Susanna Lenton
Production designer: Martin Johnson
Art directors: Ursula Cleary, Fergus Clegg
Cinematography: Barry Ackroyd
Editor: Jonathan Morris
Sound: Ray Beckett
Music: George Fenton
Songs: 'Rahaye Rahaye', written by Harjinder Singh Bopari, Balwinder Safri, performed by the Safri Boys; 'Chit Kanda', written and performed by H. S. Talwar; 'Intimacy', written by Ketil Bjørnstad, performed by Ketil Bjørnstad, Eivind Aarset, Nora Taksdal, Kjetel Bjerkestrand; 'Mali Twist', written and performed by Boubacar Traoré; 'The Viaduct (On the Right Banke of the River Mix)' by Stephen McRobbie, Katrina Mitchell; 'Tracy (Playing with the Young Team Remix)', written and performed by Mogwai; 'Djam Leelii', composed by Baaba Maal, performed by Baaba Maal, Mansour Seck; 'Strange Fruit', written by Lewis Allan, performed by Billie Holiday; 'A Man's a Man for A' That' and 'Ae Fond Kiss' by Robert Burns; 'Ah, Vous Dirai-Je, Maman (K265)', composed by Wolfgang Amadeus Mozart
Costume designer: Carole K. Millar
Casting director: Kahleen Crawford
Cast: Atta Yaqub (Casim Khan), Eva Birthistle (Roisin Hanlon), Ahmad Riaz (Tariq Khan), Shamshad Akhtar (Sadia Khan), Shabana Akhtar Bakhsh (Tahara Khan), Ghizala Avan (Rukhsana Khan), David McKay (Wee Roddie), Raymond Mearns (Big Roddie), Gary Lewis (Danny), Shy Ramzan (Hammid), Emma Friel (Annie), Karen Fraser (Elsie), John Yule (headmaster), Ruth McGhie (Mary Nolan), David Wallace (Father David), Dougie Wallace (janitor), Jacqueline Bett (Jacqueline), Pasha Bocarie (Amar), Foqia Hayee (Amar's mother), Abdul Hayee (Amar's father), Sunna Mirza (Jasmine), Balquees Hassan (Jasmine's mother), Gerard Kelly (parish priest), Isabel Johnston (housekeeper), Tommy McKee (dog walker), Laura McMonagle (Rukhsana's friend), Rik Makarem (dancer), Kevin Quinn (Danny)
104 minutes. Colour

2005
Tickets
Italy/UK; Sixteen Films/Fandango/Medusa Film
Executive producer: Paul Trijbits
Producers: Rebecca O'Brien, Carlo Cresto-Dina, Babak Karimi, Domenico Procacci

Directors: Abbas Kiarostami, Ken Loach, Ermanno Olmi
Art director: Alessandro Vannucci
Music: George Fenton
Casting directors: Gent Minga, Laura Muccino, Annamaria Sambucco
Total running time: 109 minutes. Colour
Credits for Loach segment only:
Script: Paul Laverty
Cinematography: Chris Menges
Editor: Jonathan Morris
Sound: Ray Beckett
Costume designer: Carole K. Millar
Cast: Martin Compston (Jamesy), Gary Maitland (Spaceman), William Ruane (Frank), Kladji Qorrajj (Albanian family boy), Blerta Cahani (Albanian family girl), Aishe Gjuriqi (Albanian family mother), Sanije Dedja (Albanian family grandmother), Kledi Salaj (Albanian family baby), Edmond Budina (Albanian family father), Barry Cameron (Scottish tourist)

McLibel
UK
Cinema-release version of *McLibel: Two Worlds Collide* (1997; see p. 418)
Additional credits:
Executive producer: Peter Armstrong
Assistant producers: Dan Davey, Lizzie Gillett
Editor: David G. Hill (with Gregers Sall)
Music: Chris Brierley, Johny Brown, Luminous Frenzy, Guy Jackson, Band of Holy Joy, The Playthings, Alfie Thomas
Cast: Morgan Spurlock, Eric Schlosser, Howard Lyman, Anita Anand, Peter Armstrong, Chris Brierley, Rhona Cameron, Chris Haagens (voice-overs)
85 minutes. Colour

2006
The Wind That Shakes the Barley
Ireland/UK/Italy/Germany/France/Spain/Switzerland; Sixteen Films/Screen Ireland/Tornasol Films/UK Film Council/BIM Distribuzione/TV3 Ireland/Matador Pictures/Cinéart
Executive producers: Ulrich Felsberg, Ed Guiney, Andrew Lowe, Nigel Thomas, Paul Trijbits, Mark Woods
Producer: Rebecca O'Brien
Co-producers: Gerardo Herrero, Redmond Morris
Assistant producer: Camilla Bray
Script: Paul Laverty
Script editor: Roger Smith
Script supervisor: Susanna Lenton

Production designer: Fergus Clegg
Art directors: Michael Higgins, Mark Lowry
Cinematography: Barry Ackroyd
Editor: Jonathan Morris
Sound: Ray Beckett
Music: George Fenton
Songs: 'The Wind That Shakes the Barley', traditional, words by Robert Dwyer-Joyce; 'Amhráin Na bhFiann', traditional, words by Peader Kearney, Patrick Heeney; 'Oró! Sé Do Bheatha 'Bhaile', traditional, words by Padraic Pearse; 'The Doon Reel', traditional, arranged by the performers
Costume designer: Eimer Ní Mhaoldomhnaigh
Casting director: Oonagh Kearney
Additional casting: Kahleen Crawford, Chuck Douglas
Cast: Cillian Murphy (Damien O'Donovan), Pádraic Delaney (Teddy O'Donovan), Liam Cunningham (Dan), Orla Fitzgerald (Sinéad Ni Shúilleabháin), Mary O'Riordan (Peggy), Mary Murphy (Bernadette), Laurence Barry (Micheál Ó Súilleabháin), Roger Allam (Sir John Hamilton), Damien Kearney (Finbar), Frank Bourke (Leo), Myles Horgan (Rory), Martin Lucey (Congo), Aidan O'Hare (Steady Boy), John Crean (Chris Reilly), Shane Casey (Kevin), Máirtín de Cógáin (Sean), Keith Dunphy (Terence), Kieran Hegarty (Francis), Gerard Kearney (Donacha), Shane Nott (Ned), Kevin O'Brien (Tim), Mark Wakeling (British lieutenant), William Ruane (Johnny Gogan), Anthony Byrne (British interrogator), Fiona Lawton (Lily), Kieran Aherne (Sweeney), Clare Dineen (Mrs Rafferty), Noel O'Donovan (station guard), Peter O'Mahoney (stoker), Danny Riordan, Peg Crowley (elderly couple), Tomas OhEalaithe (boy on bike), Peggy Lynch (singer at wake), Barry Bourke, Seamus Moynihan (policemen), Sean McGinley (Father Denis), Frank O'Sullivan, Diarmuid Ó'Dálaigh (men in pub), Corina Gough (woman in search), Sabrina Barry (Julia), Siobhán McSweeney (other Julia), Nora Lynch (mother of sick child), Diarmuid Ní Mheachair (sick child), Denis Conway (priest), Neil Brand (newsreel piano accompanist), Gary McCarthy, Tim O'Mahon, Graham Browne, Owen Buckley, Aidan Fitzpatrick, Vince Hannington, Denis Kelleher, Colin McClery, Finbar O'Mahon, John Quinlan, Karl Dawson (IRA volunteers), Tom Charnock (British soldier at cottage), Alan Ready (British sergeant at station), Anthony Mark Streeter, William Armstrong, Christopher Bown, Mark Bryce, Alex Dee, Jonny Holmes, Allan Huntley, Bill Hurst, Daniel Kington, Jamie Lomas, Anthony Martin, Owen McQuade, Richard Oldham, Colin Parry, Scott Peden, Bernie Sweeney, Derek Taylor, Neil Alan Taylor, Gregor Wood (British soldiers), Barry L. Looney, Connie O'Connail, Aine O'Connor, Francis O'Connor, Peadr O'Riada (ceilidh band), Fergus Burke (theatre attendee), Richard Burke (soldier)
127 minutes. Colour

2007
To Each His Own Cinema
France; Elzevir Films
Producer: Gilles Jacob
Total running time: 119 minutes
Directors: Ken Loach and thirty-five others
Credits for Loach segment, 'Happy Ending', only:
UK; Sixteen Films
Producer: Rebecca O'Brien
Script: Paul Laverty
Production design: Fergus Clegg
Cinematographer: Nigel Willoughby
Sound: Ray Beckett
Cast: Bradley Walsh, Joe Siffleet
3 minutes. Colour

It's a Free World . . .
UK/Italy/Germany/Spain/Poland; Sixteen Films, in association with Channel 4 Television/Tornasol Films
Executive producers: Ulrich Felsberg, Lena Kozlova
Producers: Rebecca O'Brien, Ken Loach, Liza Marshall, Kathryn Williams, Valerie Phil
Co-producers: R. J. Buks, Piotr Reisch
Line producer: Tim Cole
Script: Paul Laverty
Script editor: Roger Smith
Production designer: Fergus Clegg
Art director: Peter James
Cinematography: Nigel Willoughby
Editor: Jonathan Morris
Sound: Ray Beckett
Music: George Fenton
Costume designer: Carole K. Millar
Casting director: Kahleen Crawford
Cast: Kierston Wareing (Angie), Juliet Ellis (Rose), Lesław Żurek (Karol), Joe Siffleet (Jamie), Colin Coughlin (Jeff), Maggie Russell (Cathy), Raymond Mearns (Andy), Davoud Rastgou (Mahmoud), Mahin Aminnia (Mahin, Mamoud's wife), Shadeh Kavousian, Sheeva Kavousian (Shadeh and Sheeva, Mahmoud and Mahin's daughters), Frank Gilhooley (Derek), David Doyle (Tony), Eddie Webber, Johnny Palmiero (company directors), Faruk Pruti (angry worker Emir), Jackie Robinson-Brown (headmistress), Miro Somers (attacker), Neal Barry, Mick Connolly, Sian Wheldon (youth-offending care team), Małgorzata Zawadzka (Polish translator), Marina Chykalovets, Chisana Gayves (Ukrainian translators),

Steve Lorrigan (police sergeant), Nadine Marshall (Diane), Serge Soric (Toni), Branko Tomović (Milan), Radoslaw Kaim (Jan), Carlos Morales (factory worker)
96 minutes. Colour

2009
Looking for Eric
UK/France/Italy/Belgium/Spain; Sixteen Films/Why Not Productions/Canto Bros. Productions/Icon Films/Goodfellas S.L.
Executive producers: Pascal Caucheteux, Vincent Maraval, Eric Cantona
Producer: Rebecca O'Brien
Co-producer: Mariela Besuievsky, Gerardo Herrera
Line producer: Tim Cole
Script: Paul Laverty
Script editor: Roger Smith
Script supervisor: Susanna Lenton
Production designer: Fergus Clegg
Art director: Julie Ann Horan
Cinematography: Barry Ackroyd
Editor: Jonathan Morris
Sound: Ray Beckett
Music: George Fenton
Costume designer: Sarah Ryan
Casting director: Kahleen Crawford
Cast: Steve Evets (Eric Bishop), Eric Cantona (*lui-même* – Eric Cantona), Stephanie Bishop (Lily), Lucy-Jo Hudson (Sam), Gerard Kearns (Ryan), Stefan Gumbs (Jess), John Henshaw (Meatballs), Justin Moorhouse (Spleen), Des Sharples (Jack), Smug Roberts (Smug), Johnny Travis (Travis), Greg Cook (Monk), Mick Ferry (Judge), Matthew McNulty (young Eric), Laura Ainsworth (young Lily), Max Beesley Sr (Eric's father), Kelly Bowland (Ryan's girlfriend), Julie Brown (nurse), Steve Marsh (Zac), Cleveland Campbell (Buzz), Ryan Pope (Fenner), Omar Abdul, Adam Beresford, Ciaran Clancy, Steve Cook, Sheila Diamond, Marvin Gilbert, Ben Jackson, Wendy Kennedy, Trevor Dwyer-Lynch, Jake Manning, Tom Meredith, Eddie Riley, Conor Saunders, Venn Tracey, Guy Wills (the Emperors of Rhythm), Cole Williams, Dylan Williams (Daisy)
116 minutes. Colour

2010
Route Irish
UK/France/Belgium/Italy/Spain; Sixteen Films/Why Not Productions/Wild Bunch/Alta Producción/Canal+/Canto Bros. Productions/CinéCinéma/Cinéart/Diaphana Distribution/France 2 Cinéma/France Télévisions/Inver Invest/Les Film du Fleuve/MEDIA Program Development Fund/Magasin

Duck Liège/Modal Installation/North West Vision/Sofica UGC 1/
Tax Shelter du Gouvernement Féderal Belge/Tornasol Films/Urania
Pictures S.r.l.
Executive producers: Pascal Caucheteux, Vincent Maraval
Producer: Rebecca O'Brien
Co-producer: Conchita Airoldi
Supervising producer: Linda Mutawi (Jordan)
Line producer: Tim Cole
Script: Paul Laverty
Script editor: Roger Smith
Script supervisor: Susanna Lenton
Production designer: Fergus Clegg
Cinematography: Chris Menges
Editor: Jonathan Morris
Sound: Ray Beckett
Music: George Fenton
Songs: 'Rocks', written by Bobby Gillespie, Robert Young, Andrew Innes, performed by Primal Scream; 'Baghdad', written by Ilham al Madfai, lyrics by Nizar Qabbani, performed by Talib Rasool
Casting directors: Kahleen Crawford (UK); Lara Atalia, Raya Hamdan, Basil Karim (Jordan)
Cast: Mark Womack (Fergus), Andrea Lowe (Rachel), John Bishop (Frankie), Geoff Bell (Alex Walker), Jack Fortune (Haynes), Talib Rasool (Harim), Craig Lundberg (Craig), Trevor Williams (Nelson), Russell Anderson (Tommy), Jamie Michie (Jamie), Bradley Thompson (young Fergus), Daniel Foy (young Frankie), Najwa Nimri (Marisol), Maggie Southers (Frankie's mother), R. David (David), Tony Schumacher (Andy), Gary Cargill (undertaker), Donna Elso (Peggy), Stephen Lord (Steve), James Locke (Jay), Tayf Basil (Yousef), Ranj Hawra (Ranj), Martin Webster (Iraq archival footage), Hind Kamil (mother), Paul J. Dove, Robert Rae-Lewis (ferry passengers), Connor Harrison (funeral attendant), Tess (three-legged dog)
109 minutes. Colour

2012
The Angels' Share
Executive producers: Pascal Caucheteux, Vincent Maraval
Producer: Rebecca O'Brien
Line producer: Peter Gallagher
Script: Paul Laverty
Script editor: Roger Smith
Script supervisor: Susanna Lenton
Production designer: Fergus Clegg
Art director: Zoe Wright

Cinematography: Robbie Ryan
Editor: Jonathan Morris
Sound: Ray Beckett
Music: George Fenton
Songs: 'Some Chords', written and performed by Deadmau5; 'I'm Gonna Be (500 Miles)', written by Charlie Reid, Craig Reid, performed by The Proclaimers
Costume designer: Carole K. Millar
Casting director: Kahleen Crawford
Cast: Paul Brannigan (Robbie), John Henshaw (Harry), Gary Maitland (Albert), Jasmin Riggins (Mo), William Ruane (Rhino), Roger Allam (Thaddeus), Siobhan Reilly (Leonie), Gilbert Martin (Matt), Scott Kyle (Clancy), Neil Leiper (Sniper), Daniel Portman (Sniper's pal), James Casey (Dougie), Caz Dunlop (Caz), Charles MacLean (Rory McAllister), David Goodall (Angus Dobie), Scott Diamond (Willy), Joy McAvoy (Mairi), Roderick Cowie (Anthony), Alison Mcginnes (Anthony's mother), Andy McLaren (Anthony's father), Kelly Scott (Anthony's sister), Lynsey Lawrie (Anthony's girlfriend), Lynsey-Anne Moffat (Grace), Paul Donnelly (Jamie), Robert McHarg (moderator), Stewart Preston (sheriff), Vincent Friell (procurator fiscal), Kristin Murray, Nick Farr, Charles Jamieson (defence lawyers), Barrie Hunter (police inspector), Jim Sweeney, Russell Anderson (policemen), Lorne MacFadyen (Matthew/PC), Dai Tabuchi (Kaneyama), Kasumi Kitano (Hitomi Takenata), Chooye Baye (Tai Pan), Bruce Addison (auctioneer), Paul Birchard (North American bidder), Gordon Ryde (Australian bidder), Robert J. Goodwin (man at auction), Jimmy Chisholm, John P. Arnold (volunteer tasters), David Graham, Fernando Velasquez (park delinquents), Christopher James Healy (Calvin), Ford Kiernan (stationmaster's voice), Zac Reilly (baby Luke)
101 minutes. Colour

2013
The Spirit of '45
UK; Sixteen Films/Fly Film/British Film Institute/Film4/Channel 4
Executive producers: Katherine Butler, Lizzie Francke, Anna Higgs, Anna Miralis
Producers: Rebecca O'Brien, Kate Ogborn, Lisa Marie Russo
Script: Ken Loach
Script editor: Roger Smith
Film archivist: Jim Anderson
Research: Izzy Chapman
Music: George Fenton
Cinematography: Stephen Standen
Editor: Jonathan Morris
Sound: Paul Parsons, Kevin Brazier, Ian Tapp

Colourist: Gareth Spensley
Cast: Dr Julian Tudor Hart, Dai Walters, Ray Davies (South Wales); Tony Mulhearn, Doreen McNally, John Farrell, Eileen Thompson, Sam Watts, Tony Nelson, Terry Teague (Liverpool); Karen Reissmann, Dena Murphy, Margaret Battin (Manchester); Dot Gibson, Deborah Garvie, June Hautot, Tony Benn, Raphie de Santos, Alan Thornett, Anthony Richardson, Harry Keen, Jacky Davis, Jonathan Tomlinson, Ray Thorne, Alex Gordon (London); Bill Ronksley, Ray Jackson, David Hopper, Stan Pearce, Inky Thomson, Simon Midgley, Adrian Dilworth (Sheffield); Kate Hardie, Jamie Michie, Tansy Hoskins, Trevor Fox, Mark Womack (voices)
94 minutes. Colour, with black-and-white archival footage

2014
Jimmy's Hall
UK/Ireland/France; Sixteen Films/Element Pictures/Why Not Productions/Film4/Wild Bunch
Executive producers: Pascal Caucheteux, Ed Guiney, Andrew Lowe, Vincent Maraval, Grégoire Sorlat
Producer: Rebecca O'Brien
Script: Paul Laverty, inspired by Donal O'Kelly's play *Jimmy Gralton's Dancehall*
Script editor: Roger Smith
Script supervisor: Susanna Lenton
Production designer: Fergus Clegg
Art director: Stephen Daly
Cinematography: Robbie Ryan
Editor: Jonathan Morris
Sound: Ray Beckett
Music: George Fenton, Riopy
Songs: 'Sugar Foot Strut', written by Harry Myers, Billie Pierce, Charles Schwab, Georges Matis, performed by Louis Armstrong and His Savoy Ballroom Five; 'Goose Pimples', composed by Jo Trent, Fletcher Henderson, performed by Bix Beiderbecke and His Gang; 'I'm Lonesome, Sweetheart', written by Joseph Oliver, Davidson C. Nelson, performed by Joe Oliver and His Orchestra; 'Weeping Willow Blues', written by Paul Carter, performed by Bessie Smith; 'Bridie Morley's', arranged and performed by Gearoid Devane, Stephen Doherty, Thomas Doherty, Sarah Egan, Fiachra Guihen, Cónan Marren, Liam O'Connor, Fiachra O'Maolagáin; 'Stack of Barley', arranged and performed by Gregory Daly, Colm Gannon, Gerry Harrington, Ben Lennon, Brian McGrath, Shane Meehan; 'The Moving Bog'/'The Sailor on the Rock'/'Bank of Ireland'/'The Taproom', arranged and performed by Harry Bradley, John Carty, Mary Corcoran, Charlie Harris, Mossie Martin, Seamus

O'Donnell, Seamie O'Dowd, Jesse Smith; 'That's a Plenty', written by Lew Pollack, Ray Gilbert; 'Boogie Woogie', written by Davidson C. Nelson, Joseph Oliver, arranged and performed by Jimmy Higgins Sr, Frank Kilkelly, Stephen Kohlmann, Eddie Lee, Seamie O'Dowd, Kieran Quinn, Cathal Roche, Ciaran Wilde; 'Siúil a' Ghrá', attributed to Thomas Moore

Costume designer: Eimer Ní Mhaoldomhnaigh
Casting director: Kahleen Crawford
Cast: Barry Ward (Jimmy Gralton), Jim Norton (Father Sheridan), Simone Kirby (Oonagh), Andrew Scott (Father Seamus), Francis Magee (Mossie), Aileen Henry (Alice), Aisling Franciosi (Marie O'Keefe), Brían F. O'Byrne (Commander O'Keefe), Rebecca O'Mara (Mrs O'Keefe), Stella McGirl (Stella), Karl Geary (Seán), Sorcha Fox (Molly), Martin Lucey (Dessie), Mikel Murfi (Tommy), Shane O'Brien (Finn), Denise Gough (Tess), Seán T. Ó Meallaigh (journalist), Conor McDermottroe (Doherty), John Cronogue (Séamus Clarke), Seamus Hughes (Ruairí), Michael Sheridan (Fintan), Diane Parkes (Mossie's wife), Donal O'Kelly, Padraig Fallon, Chris MacManus (Roscommon IRA), Johnny O'Dowd (steward), Anna Crossley (young dancer), Róisín Judge (young violinist), John McCarrick (mayor), Hugh Gallagher (senior guard), Colm Gormley, John Colleary, Shane Cullen, Joe Lafferty, Tom Colsh, Shane Cronogue (guards), Dorothea Jones (Marie's friend), Dorothy Jones (dancer), Niko El Santo Zavero (gaoler), Sean Fox
109 minutes. Colour

2016
I, Daniel Blake
UK/France/Belgium; Sixteen Films/Why Not Productions/Les Films du Fleuve/Wild Bunch/BBC Films/BFI
Executive producers: Pascale Caucheteux, Vincent Maraval, Grégoire Sorlat, Tania Antonioli, Delphine Thomson, Rosa Attab, Pauline Bénard, Benjamin Toussaint, Carole Baraton, Emmanuelle Castro, Jacqui Barr, Zoe Brown, Christine Langan, Ruth Sanders, Livy Sandler, Michael Wood, Joe Oppenheimer, Clare Coulter, Will Evans, Emma Kayee, Fiona Morham, Sofia Neves, Ben Roberts
Producer: Rebecca O'Brien
Associate producer: Philip Logie
Line producer: Eimhear McMahon
Script: Paul Laverty
Script editor: Roger Smith
Production designers: Fergus Clegg, Linda Wilson
Cinematography: Robbie Ryan
Editor: Jonathan Morris
Sound: Ray Beckett

Music: George Fenton
Additional music: 'Sailing By', composed by Ronald Binge, performed by the Alan Perry/William Gardner Orchestra, conducted by Ronald Binge
Costumes: Vivienne Race, Nisha Williams
Casting director: Kahleen Crawford
Cast: Dave Johns (Daniel Blake), Hayley Squires (Katie Morgan), Briana Shann (Daisy Morgan), Dylan McKiernan (Dylan Morgan), Kate Rutter (Ann), Sharon Percy (Sheila), Kema Sikazwe (China), Magpie Richens (Piper), Amanda Payne, Natalie Ann Jamieson (employment support allowance assessors), Chris McGlade, Shaun Prendergast, Gavin Webster (men at sawmill), Sammy T. Dobson (specialist nurse), Mickey Hutton (neighbour with dog), Colin Coombs (postman), David Murray (benefit enquiry line advisor), Stephen Clegg (Jobcentre floor manager), Andy Kidd (Jobcentre guard), Dan Li (Stan Li), Jane Birch (librarian), Kimberley Blair Smith, Junior Atilassi (students), John Sumner (CV instructor), Dave Turner (Harry Edwards), Jackie Robinson, Kathleen Germain, Christine Wood, Rob Kirtley (food bank workers), Micky McGregor (supermarket guard Ivan), Neil Stuart Morton (supermarket manager), Roy McCartney (decision-maker), Stephen Halliday (furniture dealer), Julie Nicholson (businesswoman), Viktoria Kay (woman in house), Malcolm Shields (Scotsman), Bryn Jones, Helen Dixon (police officers), Gary Jacques (senior police officer), Mick Laffey (welfare rights officer), Harriet Ghost (appeal receptionist), Mark Burns (jobseeker), James Hepworth (shopper), Patricia Roberts, Yvonne Maher, Susan Robinson, Mike Milligan, Laura Jane Barnes-Martin, Brian Scurr (bit parts)
100 minutes. Colour

In Conversation with Jeremy Corbyn
UK
Producer/writer: Ken Loach
Cast: Jeremy Corbyn, David Kirkham
60 minutes. Colour

2019
Sorry We Missed You
UK/France/Belgium; Sixteen Films/BBC Films/Les Films du Fleuve/Why Not Productions/Wild Bunch/Casa Kafka Pictures
Executive producers: Pascale Caucheteux, Vincent Maraval, Grégoire Sorlat
Producer: Rebecca O'Brien
Assistant producer: Jack Thomas-O'Brien
Line producer: Eimhear McMahon
Script: Paul Laverty
Script editor: Roger Smith

Script supervisor: Susanna Lenten
Production designer: Fergus Clegg
Art director: Julie Ann Horan
Cinematography: Robbie Ryan
Editor: Jonathan Morris
Sound: Ray Beckett
Music: George Fenton
Song: 'Know How', written by Matt Dike, Isaac Hayes, John Wylie King, Michael Simpson, Marvin Young, performed by Young MC (Marvin Young)
Costume designer: Jo Slater
Casting director: Kahleen Crawford
Cast: Kris Hitchen (Ricky Turner), Debbie Honeywood (Abby Turner), Rhys Mcgowan (Seb Turner), Katie Proctor (Liza Jane Turner), Ross Brewster (Maloney), Charlie Richmond (Henry), Julian Ions (Freddie), Sheila Dunkerley (Rosie), Maxie Peters (Robert), Christopher John-Slater (Ben), Heather Wood (Mollie), Albert Dumba (Harpoon), Natalia Stonebanks (Roz), Jordan Collard (Dodge), Dave Turner (Magpie), Stephen Clegg (policeman), Darren Lee Jones (council worker), Nikki Marshall (traffic warden), Mike Milligan (man with drip), Grace Brown (Snapchat friend), Steve Hogg (neighbour), Mary Shearer (woman at door), Christine Beck (woman at bus stop), Micky McGregor (man who won't show ID), Gavin Webster (janitor), Alex Houston, Jordan Sawyer, Russell Jones (attackers), Vicky Hall (corridor nurse), Andy Kidd, Lee Hall, Carol Anderton, Carol Littlefair, Tim McGuire, John Torrance, Anthony Cummings, Alfie Dobson, Anthony Hogg, Mark Birch, Linda E. Greenwood (drivers), Paul Woodhead, Randolph Paul, Rob Kirtley, Jack Hamilton, Andrea Johnson (packers), Anita Starker, Harriet Ghost (office staff), Jack Berry (footballer), Mark Burns (homeless man), Brad Hopper (concerned builder), Michael Hunter (construction worker), Simran Kaur (patient), Norman Sansom (depot assistant)
100 minutes. Colour

2023
The Old Oak
UK/France/Belgium; Sixteen Films/Why Not Productions/Les Films du Fleuve/BBC Films
Executive producers: Pascal Caucheteux, Vincent Maraval, Grégoire Sorlat
Producer: Rebecca O'Brien
Associate producers: Philippe Logie, Jack Thomas-O'Brien
Line producer: Eimhear McMahon
Script: Paul Laverty
Script editor: Roger Smith
Production designer: Fergus Clegg
Art directors: Lili Lea Abraham, Byron Broadbent (prep.)

Cinematography: Robbie Ryan
Editor: Jonathan Morris
Sound: Ray Beckett
Music: George Fenton
Additional music: 'O nata lux', composed by Thomas Tallis, and 'Agnus Dei', composed by William Byrd, both performed by the Durham Cathedral Choir; 'The New Colonial March', composed by Robert Browne Hall, performed by bands of the Durham Miners' Gala; tunes for oud composed by Saied Silbak
Costume designer: Jo Slater
Casting director: Kahleen Crawford
Cast: Dave Turner (T. J. Ballantyne), Ebla Mari (Yara), Claire Rodgerson (Laura), Trevor Fox (Charlie), Chris McGlade (Vic), Col Tait (Eddy), Jordan Louis (Gary), Chrissie Robinson (Erica), Chris Gotts (Jaffa Cake), Jen Patterson (Maggie), Arthur Oxley (Archie), Joe Armstrong (Joe), Andy Dawson (Micky), Maxie Peters (Tommy), Amna Al Ali (Fatima), Yazan Al Shteiwi (Bashir), Diyaa Al Khalid (Salim), Rahaf H (Nadia), Neil Leiper (Rocco), Micky McGregor (estate agent), Rhys Mcgowan, Reuben Bainbridge, Jack Staples (Chopper's owners), Ruby Bratton (Linda), Michelle Belle (Molly), Alex White (Max), Debbie Honeywood (Tania), Mandy Foster, Joanne Hague, Debbie Cook (hairdressers), Chris Braxton (Sadie; voice), Jake Jarratt (Tony), Ali Mohamed (Syrian boy in video), Rob Kirtley (older neighbour), Lloyd Mullings (Garry's pal), Laura Lee Daly (Rosie), Heather Wood (meal guest), Rosa Crowley-Bennett, Bobby Beldrum (union supporters), Andrea Johnson (Amy), Diala, Iman Awad Hamdan, Abigail Lawson (bit parts), Lola (Marra, TJ's dog), Sasha (three-legged dog)
113 minutes. Colour

Bibliography

BOOKS IN ENGLISH

Allen, Jim, *Perdition: A Play in Two Acts* (Ithaca Press, 1987).
Archibald, David, *Tracking Loach: Politics, Practices, Production* (Edinburgh University Press, 2023).
—— *The War That Won't Die: The Spanish Civil War in Cinema* (Manchester University Press, 2012).
Campbell, Fergus, *Land and Revolution: Nationalist Politics in the West of Ireland 1891–1921* (Oxford University Press, 2005).
Cardullo, Bert, *Loach and Leigh, Ltd.: The Cinema of Social Conscience* (Cambridge Scholars Publishing, 2010).
Connolly, James, *Collected Works, Vols 1 and 2* (New Books, 1987).
Ferriter, Fiarmaid, *Between Two Hells: The Irish Civil War* (Profile Books, 2021).
Forrest, David, and Vice, Sue, *Barry Hines: Kes, Threads and Beyond* (Manchester University Press, 2017).
Forrest, David, *Kes* (BFI Film Classics, British Film Institute/Bloomsbury, 2024).
Hayward, Anthony, *Which Side Are You On?: Ken Loach and His Films* (Bloomsbury, 2004).
Hill, John, *Ken Loach: The Politics of Film and Television* (BFI; Palgrave Macmillan, 2011).
Kynaston, David, *Austerity Britain 1945–51* (Bloomsbury, 2008).
Lacey, Stephen, *Tony Garnett* (Manchester University Press, 2012).
Laverty, Paul, *The Angels' Share* (Route, 2012).
—— *Bread and Roses* (Screenpress Books, 2000).
—— *Carla's Song* (Faber, 1997).
—— *I, Daniel Blake* (Route, 2016).
—— *Jimmy's Hall* (Route, 2014).
—— *Looking for Eric* (Route, 2009).
—— *My Name Is Joe* (Screenpress Books, 1998).

—— *The Old Oak* (Route, 2023).
—— *Route Irish* (Route, 2011).
—— *Sorry We Missed You* (Route, 2019).
—— *Sweet Sixteen* (Screenpress Books, 2003).
—— *The Wind That Shakes the Barley* (Galley Head Press, 2006).
Laybourn, Keith, *The Rise of Socialism in Britain* (Sutton, 1997).
Leigh, Jacob, *The Cinema of Ken Loach: Art in the Service of the People* (Directors' Cuts, Wallflower Press, 2002).
McKnight, George (ed.), *Agent of Challenge and Defiance: The Films of Ken Loach* (Praeger, 1997).
Murray, Jonathan, *The New Scottish Cinema* (I. B. Taurus, 2015).
O'Malley, Ernie, *On Another Man's Wound: A Personal History of Ireland's War of Independence* (Rich & Cowan, 1936; Roberts Rinehart, 2001).
Ó Súilleabháin, Cormac, *Leitrim's Republican Story 1900–2000* (Cumann Cabhrach Liatroma, 2014).
Ransom, Bernard, *Connolly's Marxism* (Pluto Press, 1980).
Shubik, Irene, *Play for Today: The Evolution of Television Drama* (Davis Poynter, 1975; revised 2001).
Sinfield, Alan, *Literature, Politics and Culture in Postwar Britain* (University of California Press, 1989).
Sked, Alan, and Cook, Chris, *Post-War Britain* (Penguin, 1979).
Tulloch, John, *Television Drama: Agency, Audience and Myth* (Routledge, 1990).
Winstanley, Asa, *Weaponising Anti-Semitism: How the Israel Lobby Brought Down Jeremy Corbyn* (OR Books, 2023).

BOOKS IN OTHER LANGUAGES

Bollaín, Icíar, *Ken Loach. Un Observador Solidario* (Aguilar, 1996; Spanish).
Brusco, Carlos García, *Ken Loach* (Ediciones JC, 1996; Spanish).
De Giusto, Luciana, *Ken Loach* (Ediciones Mensajero, S.A, 2013; Spanish).
Fedeli, Sveva, *Ken Loach* (Mediateca Regionale Toscana, 1992; Italian).
Lillge, Claudia (ed.), *Ken Loach* (Edition Text + Kritik, 2018; German).
Loach, Ken, and Barat, Florent (trans.), *Défier le récit des puissants* (Rue Echiquier, 2024; French).
Loach, Ken, and Louis, Édouard, *Dialogue sur l'art et la politique* (PUF, 2021; French).
Öztürk, Serdar, *Ken Loach: Filmlerinde Mücadelenin Arkeolojisi* (Ütopya Yayinevi, 2020; Turkish).
Rousselet, Francis, *Ken Loach, un rebelle* (Éditions du Cerf, 2002; French).

Thomas, Erika, *Le cinéma de Ken Loach: Misères de l'identité professionnelle* (L'Harmattan, 2005; French).
—— *Ken Loach: un regard cinématographique sur l'aliénation familiale* (L'Harmattan, 2006; French).
—— *Ken Loach: Cinéma et société* (L'Harmattan, 2009; French).
Yalur, Tolga, *Ken Loach Soylesileri* (Agora Kitapligi, 2015; Turkish).
Yun, Jong Uk, *Die Spielfilme von Ken Loach: Perspektive eines realistischen Kinos* (Büchner Verlag, 2010; German).

SELECTED ARTICLES IN ENGLISH

Archibald, David, 'Correcting Historical Lies: An Interview with Ken Loach and Paul Laverty' (on *The Wind That Shakes the Barley*), *Cineaste*, vol. 32, no. 2, spring 2007.
Bond, Paul, 'A Fitting Tribute to a Man of Principle: *Perdition* by Jim Allen Premiered at the Gate Theatre, London', World Socialist website, wsws.org, 12 July 1999.
Bream, Paul, 'Spreading Wings at Kestrel', *Films and Filming*, vol. 18, no. 6, 1972.
Chambers, Jamie, 'On the Side of the Angels? Ken Loach, *The Angels' Share*, and the Pursuit of New Forms of Politically Engaged Cinema', *International Journal of Scottish Theatre and Screen*, University of Edinburgh, vol. 7, no. 1, January 2014.
Chick, Kristine, 'Crossing Enemy Lines in Ken Loach's *Ae Fond Kiss/Just a Kiss*: Representing Muslims and New Ethnicities in the Shadow of 9/11', *Angles: Open Edition Journals*, October 2020.
Christie, Ian, 'A Film for a Spanish Republic' (on *The Wind That Shakes the Barley*), *Sight and Sound*, vol. 5, no. 10, October 1995.
Cizek, Ozal, 'The Transformation of Ken Loach's Cinema Through the Concept of Job Insecurity: An Evaluation of *The Navigators*, *Bread and Roses* and *It's a Free World . . .*', in *Essays on Economics & International Relations*, *Global Studies*, vol. 11, IJOPEC Publication Limited, October 2023.
Clarke, Romy, 'From Text to Performance: Interpretation or Tradition? Trevor Griffiths' *Fatherland* as Directed by Ken Loach', *Language and Literature: International Journal of Stylistics*, vol. 8, no. 2, 1999.
Conroy Scott, Kevin, 'Paul Laverty: *Sweet Sixteen*', in *Screenwriters Masterclass: Screenwriters Talk About Their Greatest Movies* (Faber, 2005).
Crowdus, Gary, *The Wind That Shakes the Barley* review, *Cineaste*, vol. 32, no. 2, spring 2007.
Davies, Luke, 'Precarious Living in the Films of Ken Loach', in *Living with Strangers: Bedsits and Boarding Houses in Modern English Life*, Chiara Briganti and Kathy Mezei (eds) (Routledge, 2018).

English, James F., 'Local Focus, Global Frame: Ken Loach and the Cinema of Depression', in *Fires Were Started: British Cinema and Thatcherism*, Lester D. Friedman (ed.) (Wallflower Press, 2006).

Ferriter, Diarmaid, 'James Gralton', in *Dictionary of Irish Biography*, www.dib.ie/biography/gralton-james-a3569 (Royal Irish Academy, 2009).

Fuller, Graham, 'In This Corner, a Leftist, Riling the Right Again' (on *The Wind That Shakes the Barley*), *New York Times*, 4 March 2007.

—— '*Kes*: Winged Hope', criterion.com, 18 April 2011.

—— 'Beneath the Kilt, a Modern Scotland' (on *The Angels' Share*), *New York Times*, 5 April 2013.

—— 'The Cut and Thrust: The Power of Political Debate in the Films of Ken Loach', *Cineaste*, vol. 40, no. 4, fall 2015.

Grant, Nick, 'Keeping It Real: The Brutal Art of Ken Loach', *International Socialism: A Quarterly View of Socialist Theory*, issue 160, 2018.

Hacker, Jonathan and Price, David, 'Essay on Ken Loach', in *Take Ten: Contemporary British Film Directors* (Clarendon Press, 1991).

Hattenstone, Simon, 'Ken Loach: If You're Not Angry, What Kind of Person Are You?' (on *I, Daniel Blake*), *Guardian*, 15 October 2016.

Hill, John, 'Bonnie Scotland, Eh? Scottish Cinema, the Working Class and the Films of Ken Loach', in *Scottish Cinema Now*, Jonathan Murray, Fidelma Farley and Rod Stoneman (eds) (Cambridge Scholars Publishing, 2009).

Jackson, Kevin, 'The Parallax View of the Cinema', *Independent*, 25 February 1994.

James, Nick, 'Hope Has a Political Context' (on *The Old Oak*), *Sight and Sound*, vol. 33, no. 8, October 2023.

Johnston, Sheila, 'How to Make a Drama Out of a Crisis' (on *The Navigators*), *Guardian*, 17 November 2001.

Kao, Wei H., 'Irish Pride and Disgrace in Recent Films: Ken Loach and Paul Greengrass on *The Wind That Shakes the Barley* and *Omagh*', *Studies: An Irish Quarterly Review: Views of Ireland*, autumn 2008.

Kennedy Martin, Troy, 'Nats Go Home: First Statement of a New Television Drama', *Encore*, March–April 1964.

Kerr, Paul, 'The Complete Ken Loach', *Stills*, May–June 1986.

Levin, G. Roy, 'Tony Garnett and Kenneth Loach', in *Documentary Explanations: 15 Interviews with Filmmakers* (Doubleday, 1971).

Loach, Ken, 'A Question of Censorship' (on *Questions of Leadership*), *Tribune*, vol. 47, no. 47, 23 November 1983.

—— 'Writers' Rights and a Kangaroo Court' (on *Perdition*), *Guardian*, 18 February 1987.

—— 'Run Fast to Stay Standing: A Political Assessment of 1993', *Guardian*, 31 December 1993.

MacArthur, Colin, '*Days of Hope*', *Screen*, vol. 16, no. 4, 1975/6.

Macnab, Geoffrey, '*Ladybird, Ladybird*: The Director', *Sight and Sound*, vol. 4, no. 11, November 1994.
Madden, Paul, 'Jim Allen', in *British Television Drama*, George Brandt (ed.) (Cambridge University Press, 2018).
Monbiot, George, 'Occupations Brutalise' (on *The Wind That Shakes the Barley*), *Guardian*, 6 June 2006.
Morris, E. 'How Privatisation Became a Train Wreck', *Access Magazine*, no. 28, spring 2006.
Ó Drisceoil, Donal, 'Framing the Irish Revolution: Ken Loach's *The Wind That Shakes the Barley*', *Radical History Review*, no. 104, 2009.
Petley, Julian, 'An Interview With Ken Loach', *Framework*, no. 18, 1982.
—— 'Ken Loach – Politics, Protest, and the Past', *Monthly Film Bulletin* (London), March 1987.
Porton, Richard, 'The Revolution Betrayed: An Interview With Ken Loach' (on *Land and Freedom*), *Cineaste*, vol. 22, no. 1, winter 1996.
Porton, Richard, and Ryan, Susan, 'The Politics of Everyday Life: An Interview With Ken Loach', *Cineaste*, vol. 21, no. 1, winter 1998.
Quart, Leonard, 'A Fidelity to the Real: An Interview with Ken Loach and Tony Garnett', *Cineaste*, vol. 10, no. 4, fall 1980.
Remport, Eglantina, 'Dancing for Freedom in Ken Loach's *Jimmy's Hall*', *The AnaChronisT* (Budapest), vol. 21, no. 1; *The Reel Eye*, 15 July 2023.
Rickards, Carolyn, 'An Ordinary Spectacle: Critical Responses to Fantasy and Whimsy in *Looking for Eric* and *The Angels' Share*', *Journal of British Cinema and Television*, September 2018.
Sandford, Jeremy, '*Cathy Come Home*', in *The New Documentary in Action: A Casebook in Film Making*, Alan Rosenthal (ed.) (University of California Press, 1971).
Saynor, James, 'Imagined Communities' (on Tony Garnett), *Sight and Sound*, vol. 3, no. 12, December 1993.
Smith, Gavin, 'Voice in the Dark' (on *Fatherland*), *Film Comment*, vol. 24, no. 1, March–April 1988.
—— 'Sympathetic Images', *Film Comment*, vol. 30, no. 2, March–April 1994.

A Note on the Editor

Graham Fuller is an editorial associate at *Cineaste* magazine and film editor at *The Arts Desk*. He has edited the film sections of seven other publications and written on film and television for *Sight and Sound*, *Film Comment*, the *New York Times*, the *Los Angeles Times*, the *Guardian*, the *Observer*, the *Financial Times*, *The Times*, the *Independent*, *Art Forum*, *Art in America*, *Artnet*, *Village Voice*, *Vanity Fair*, *Rolling Stone* and the Criterion Collection. He conceived and edited Faber & Faber's (Dennis) *Potter on Potter* and contributed to Faber's screenplay series and *Projections*. He is a member of the New York Film Critics Circle.

Index

Page numbers in *italics* refer to photographs. Page numbers followed by 'n' refer to notes on the same page.
KL = Ken Loach.

3 Clear Sundays (TV drama), 22
11'09"01 – September 11 (film), xvii, 144, 200–3, 213–15

ABC TV, 1, 6
Ackroyd, Barry: cinematography for *Bread and Roses* (film), 197, 199, 207, 213; cinematography for *Raining Stones* (film), 139; cinematography for *Riff-Raff* (film), 139; style of filming, 90, 139–40, 197, 346, 348
Adie, Kate, 135
Ae Fond Kiss (film), 151–5, *153*, 172–8, 176, 279
After a Lifetime (TV drama), 14n, 30–1, *30*
Aherne, Kieran, 218, 391
Ainsworth, Lily, 281
Aitkenhead, Decca, 87
Akhtar, Shamshad, 152
Al Ali, Amna, 322
Allam, Roger, 149, 217, 382
Allen, Jim, *102*; life, 31n, 93, 258–9; *Perdition* (play), 31n, 72, 84–6, 136–7, 137n; political views, 12, 55, 57, 93, 211, 244; on three-act structure, 187; other TV work, 14n, 31n
  COLLABORATION WITH KL (SCRIPTS): listed works, 31n; *The Big Flame* (TV drama), 31–2, 86; *Days of Hope* (TV drama), 38, 53–5, 216, 228; *Hidden Agenda* (film), 89, 93, 136, 138, 370; importance of collaboration, 11, 89, 228; *Land and Freedom* (film), 89, 112, 113, 114, 117, 236–7, 370; *Raining Stones* (film), 89, 104–7; *The Rank and File* (TV drama), 32
Allen, Woody, 283
Allende, Salvador, 201, 201n, 203, 214
Allison, Malcolm, 280, 292
Anderson, Russell, 274
Andrews, Dean, 252, 253, *260*
The Angels' Share (film), *184*, *193*; academic commentary on, 397; casting, 150–1, 182, 192; cinematography, 185, 190; filming, 190–1, 192; research and script (Paul Laverty), 144, 150, 151, 183, 186–7, 397–8; storyline and characters, 148–50, 151, 166, 183–4, 186–7, 190–1; other mentions, 144, 161
Another City: A Week in the Life of Bath's Football Club (documentary), 280, 282, 291–2
Antonenko, Elena, 198
The Apartment (film), 388
The Archers (radio serial), 141
Archibald, David, xiv, 144, 150, 185, 220
Armchair Theatre (TV series), 10
Armstrong, Franny, 295, 295n
The Arthur Legend (documentary), 308n
Ascherson, Neal, 365
Askham, Phil, 64, *65*
Assange, Julian, 169n, 234, 295
Aston, John, 252
Attlee, Clement, 297, 299, 300–1
ATV (Associated Television), 38, 64, 73, 75
Auditions (documentary), 35
Avan, Ghizala, 152

449

Bakhsh, Shabana Akhtar, 152, 279
Ball, John, 212, 212n
Barron, John and Val, 349
Barry, Hilda, 22
Barry, Kathleen, 199n
Barry, Laurence, 217, 391
Barry, Tom, xvi, 229–30
BBC (British Broadcasting Corporation): concerns about *The Rank and File*, 34; financing from, 365, 375; 'McCarthyist' blacklist, 63; partisanship, 306–8; recruits trainee TV directors, 1; reportage of Battle of Orgreave, 134–5; socialist creatives in, 10, 34; Sydney Newman as head of drama, 10, 34; *see also* Catherine; *Diary of a Young Man*; *Play for Today*; *Wednesday Plays*; *Z Cars*
Bean (film), 365
Beckett, Ray, 90n, 139, 140
Beckham, David and Victoria, 280n
Bell, Geoff, 257
Benn, Tony, 303–4, 308
Beuys, Joseph, 360
Bevan, Nye (Aneurin), 298, 302
Bevan, Tim, 366
Beveridge, William, 298
Bevin, Ernest, 300–1, 302
BFI (British Film Institute), 362, 366, 375, 375n
Biden, Joe, 186, 186n
The Big Flame (TV drama), xi, xii, xiii, 11, 14n, 24, 31–2, 86
Bindon, John, 42–3, 42
Birthistle, Eva, 151, 153, 176, 279
Bishop, John, 255
Bishop, Stephanie, 281
Black Jack (film), 14n, 38, 58, 60–3, 62, 64
Blair, Les, 372, 373
Blair, Tony, 36, 165, 168, 244, 265, 270, 300, 303, 306, 383
Blake, William, 240
Boack, Mhairi, 377
Bocarie, Pasha, 152
Book, Tony, 280, 292
Booth, Robert, 317, 317n
Boyle, Danny, 151
Bradley, David, 45, 49, 49, 278
Bradley, Kate, 332n
Bradley, Patrick, 230–1, 230n

Bragg, Melvyn, 34, 83
Brannigan, Paul, 148, 150–1, *184*, *193*, 376
Bread and Roses (film), 209; casting, 199, 204, 213, 375; cinematography, 197, 199; editing, 200; filming, 203–4, 206–7, 208, 213, 374–5; origins, 195–7, 205; research and script (Paul Laverty), 197, 199, 205–6, 393–4, 395; storyline and characters, xv, 195, 197–200, 206–7, 209, 212–13, 395; other mentions, 221, 267, 345, 373
Brecht, Bertolt, 5, 9, 346, 346n
Brewster, Ross, 315, 340–1
Brigand, Alain, 200
Brody, Adrien, 197, 209, 213
Brooks, Nick, 291
Brooks, Ray, 25
Brown, Charlie, 253
Bush, George W., 202, 202n, 273, 273n, 383
Butler, Smedley, 213–14, 213n–14n

Cabezas, Oyanka, 121, 122, 124
Caché (film), 393
Câmara, Hélder, 404, 404n
Cameron, David, 300, 306, 311
Campbell, Alistair, 305
Campbell, Fergus, 222–3, 223n
A Canterbury Tale (film), 322
Cantona, Eric: approaches KL, 278, 281, 283–4; KL on, 286; in *Looking for Eric* (film), 282–3, 286, *286*, 287, 288–90, *289*; other acting work, 287; *see also Looking for Eric* (film)
Capon, Susanna, 363
Carla's Song (film), 122, 124, 125; budget, 90n; casting, 121; filming, 120–1; music, 104; research and script (Paul Laverty), 91, 120, 121, 144, 384, 386; storyline and characters, 91–2, 121–5, 144; other mentions, xii, xiii, xvii, 221, 373
Carlyle, Robert, 98, 100, *102*, 124, 138
Carrillo, Elpidia, 197, 207
Carter-Ruck, Peter, 80
Catherine (TV drama), 1
Cathy Come Home (TV drama), 25; filming, 26–7; innovations in, 10–11; KL's reflections on, 25, 39, 42, 132; in public discourse, 27–8, 36; storyline

and characters, 26, 112; other mentions, xi, 91, 298, 327
Cave, Grace, 51–3, 51, 192
Central Television, 35, 80–1, 97
Channel 4: broadcasts *Which Side Are You On?*, 83, 135; Film4, 362, 365, 366–7, 375; financing from, 90, 97, 365; refuses to broadcast *Questions of Leadership*, 78–81; *see also Everybody Here*; *Fatherland*
Chapple, Frank, 73, 78
Chavez, Alonso, 198
Chell, David, xn
Chick, Kristine, 152n
Churchill, Winston, 298, 299, 301n
Clarke, Kenneth, 307, 307n
Cleese, John, 387–8
Clegg, Fergus, 139
Clegg, Stephen, 340–1
Coleman, Jimmy, 31, 98
Collins, Michael, 232; *Michael Collins* (film), 219
The Coming Out Party (TV drama), 22, 23
Compston, Martin, 146, 150, 164, 178, 181, 279
Conefrey, Father Peter, 241n
Connolly, Bernard, 78
Connolly, James, 225, 225n, 228–9, 230n, 231, 239, 391–2, 392n
Connolly, Linda, 220n
Cook, Peter, 5
Cooper, Louise, 62
Corbyn, Jeremy: anti-Semitism smear, 137, 168–70, 297, 307, 309; *In Conversation with Jeremy Corbyn* (documentary), 170; impact on Labour Party membership, 305n, 369; KL on, 137, 167–70, 205, 300, 301, 302–3, 304, 308, 309, 377; time as Labour Party leader, 137n, 297, 303n
Coronation Street (TV series), 31n
Coulter, Michelle, 147
Cowie, Roderick, 148
Cox, Brian, 93, 138, 239, 372
Craig, Thomas, 252, 260
Crawford, Kahleen, 355, 387
Crean, John, 217, 382
Cricot 2 (theatre company), 361
Crosswind Films, 361–2
Crystal Gazing (film), 362
Cunningham, Liam, 216, 231, 383

Cure, Ken, 73, 78
Curtis, Sarah, 372

Daly, John, 367
Daniel, Frank, 388
Davey, Sharon, 295n
Davies, Ray, 299
Davis, Phil, 372, 373
Davis, Uri, 136–7, 137n
Dawber, Rob: life and KL's obituary, 254–5, 258–9; script for *The Navigators* (film), 251, 252, 255, 258–9, 260, 261
Days of Hope (TV drama), 55, 59; casting, 56; cinematography, 58; KL assesses value of, 58; Rebecca O'Brien on, 366; reception, 57–8; storyline and characters, 38, 54–5, 57, 221, 222, 228, 305; other mentions, xi, xii, 77, 170, 216, 309
de Valera, Éamon, 222, 230n, 231n, 244, 248n
Dean, Bill, 30, 33, 52, 262, 281
Delaney, Pádraic, 217, 217, 238
Dell, Edmund, 79
Demarco, Richard 'Ricky', 360
Denton, Charles, 64
Devane, Richard, 240
Dewhurst, Keith, 20
Diary of a Young Man (TV drama), 1, 8, 9
Dineen, Clare, 218, 391
Dorney, John, xvi
Dourif, Brad, 368
Duffy, Terry, 78
Dunn, Nell: marriage, 26; and *Poor Cow*, 37, 39, 41; and *Up the Junction*, 10, 15, 17, 18, 21
Duttine, Joe, 252, 260
Duvall, Robert, 131
Dworkin, Andrea, 199n

Echoes (TV series), 366
Edwards, Ruth Dudley, 246–7n
Eichmann, Adolf, 136, 136n
11'09"01 – September 11 (film), xvii, 144, 200–3, 213–15
Elkins, Caroline, 234n
Elliott, Nick, 83–4
Ellis, Juliet, 255
The End of Arthur's Marriage (TV drama), 21–2

Everybody Here (TV series), 363
Evets, Steve, 281, 285, 288–90, 289

Family Life (film), 51; casting, 51–2; commercial failure, 37–8; filming, 52–3, 192; origins, 11, 28; storyline and characters, 50–1; other mentions, xi, xii, 91, 337
Fatherland (film), 38, 68–71, 69, 89, 90, 90n, 135–6
Fellner, Eric, 366–7
Fenton, George, 347, 402–3
Film4, 362, 365, 366–7, 375
Fitzgerald, Orla, 217, 236, 391
The Flickering Flame (documentary), xii, 86–7, 251, 309, 333, 335
Fools of Fortune (film), 366
Forgan, Liz, 79
Forman, Miloš, 44
Forrest, David, xiv
Fortune, Jack, 257
Foster, Roy, 222
Fox, Sorcha, 227
Fox, Trevor, 319
Franciosi, Aisling, 224
Franval, Jean, 61, 62
Frears, Stephen, 362, 363, 366
French, Philip, 202
Fuller, Graham: *New York Times* articles, 151n, 221
Fulton, Annmarie, 147, 281

The Gamekeeper (film), xi, 38, 56, 64, 65
Garfield, Leon, 61
Garnett, Tony: acting work, 1, 7, 14n; early years, 14n; interest in psychology, 28; investigation by security forces, 63; political views, 12, 14; turned down by BBC, 93; other TV work, 14n, 31n
  COLLABORATION WITH KL (STORY EDITOR AND PRODUCER): *Black Jack* (film), 61; *Cathy Come Home* (TV drama), 10–11, 26; *Kes* (film), 49, 49; listed works, 14n; parting of ways, 63; *The Price of Coal* (TV drama), 59; *In Two Minds* (TV drama), 28, 37–8; *Up the Junction* (TV drama), 15
Gascoine, Jill, 5, 6
Geary, Karl, 227
Geater, Sara, 372

Gilbert, Martin, 137
Gilchrist, David, 141–2
Glenn, Scott, 123–5, *125*
Glenn, Sean, 252, 262, 263
Glover, Brian, 30, 50, 278
Godard, Jean-Luc, 43, 44
Godfrey, Brian, 292
Gold, Jack, 31n
The Golden Vision (TV drama), xii, 11, 14n, 29, 254, 278, 281, 282, 288, 293
Golding, John, 73
Goodall, Louise, 127, 145, *160*
Goodman, Lord, 85
Gothard, David, 362, 364
Gove, Michael, 247–8, 247n
Gralton, James, 223, 223–4n, 228n, 239–40, 242; *see also Jimmy's Hall* (film)
Green, Damian, 396
Green, Graham, 67
Greenwood, Anthony, 27–8
Griffiths, Trevor: script for *Fatherland* (film), 38, 68–9, 135
Grosz, Stephen, 369–70
Gruenwald, Malchiel, 136n
Gumbs, Stefan, 281
Guthrie, Woody, 242

Hamilton, Lionel, 6, 7
Hancock, Sheila, 5, 6
Haneke, Michael, 393
Hanson, Barry, 363
Harper, Keith, 78
Harrison, Nigel, 252
Hassell, M. E., 323n
Al Hassoun, Hasna, 357–8, *359*
Hattenstone, Simon, 284n
Hayman, David, 145, 150, 384
Hays, Bill, 5
Hayward, David, xiv
Heath, Edward, 28, 210n, 334, 334n
Heffer, Simon, 247, 247n
Heggessey, Lorraine, 308n
Hemdale Communications, 93, 367
Henderson, Arthur, 304–5n
Henry, Aileen, 224
Henshaw, John, 149, 263, 281, 285, 287, 290
Hibbin, Sally, 89–90, 97, 107, 369, 373
Hidden Agenda (film), 93, 95; budget and financing, 90n, 93, 366–7; casting, 238, 239, 243; filming, 110, 138, 367–8;

KL's reflections on, 70, 138, 239, 276; origins, 92–3; Rebecca O'Brien on, 366–8, 370; Rebecca O'Brien's involvement, 97; reception, 89, 94, 96, 247n, 368–9; storyline and characters, 90, 93–4, 96; other mentions, xi, xvii, 38, 136, 216, 372
Hill, John, xiv, 222–3, 256, 256n
Hines, Barry, 37, 48–50, 59–60, 64, 66–8, 72–3
Hirst, Stephen, 62
Hitchen, Kris, 279, 311, 315, *338*, 340, 341, 376
Hodge, John, 151
Holroyd, Fred, 94
Honeywood, Debbie, 315, *338*, 339, 376
Horgan, Myles, 219
Hudson, Lucy-Jo, 281
Hughes, Kate, 381
Huison, Steve, 252, 260
Hukin, Charlotte, 254

I, Daniel Blake (film), 329; casting, 327, 331, 340; filming, 319, 331–2; financing, 375; music, 347; in public discourse, 398; reception, 312, 332, 332n, 377; research and script (Paul Laverty), 322–3, 389, 395–7; storyline and characters, 207, 311, 312–14, 326, 327, 330–1, 332, 355; other mentions, 161, 264, 320, 328, 345, 349
IBA (Independent Broadcasting Authority), 73, 78, 79, 80
Imi, Tony, 15
The Imitation Game (TV drama), 362
In Black and White (documentary), 74–5
In Conversation with Jeremy Corbyn (documentary), 170
In Two Minds (TV drama), xi, 11, 14n, 28, 50–1
Isaacs, Jeremy, 79, 80–1
Ithaca Press, 137n
It's a Free World . . . (film), 251, 255–6, 264–9, 266, 270, 335
ITV (Independent Television): Armchair Theatre, 10; *see also* ATV; LWT

Jacob, Gilles, 280
Janni, Joseph, 37, 43, 43n
Jerusalem & Peace Service, 137n
Jesse, Bill, 31n, 89, 97, 98, 99, 132, 138

Jimmy's Hall (film), 243, 249–50; casting, 242, 243; KL's reflections on, 250; 'magical' space in, 321; research and script (Paul Laverty), 226, 227, 239–40, 242, 244, 248, 389, 392; storyline and characters, xv, 223–8, 241, 242, 243–5, 248; other mentions, 173, 200, 222, 354–5, 392
Joffe, Roland, 31n
Johansen, Hans Jørgen, 169n
Johns, Dave, 262, 312, 329, 332, 376
Johnson, Boris, 303n, 306, 307
Johnson, Martin, 63, 63n, 90n, 139
Johnston, Sheila, 253n
Jolie, Angelina, 278
Jones, Elwyn, 20, 21
Jones, Ken, 30, 282, 288
Jordan, Neil, 219

Kantor, Tadeusz, 360–1
Kasztner, Rudolf, 136, 136n
Kearney, Damien, 218, 229
Kearns, Gerard, 281
Keay, Douglas, 194n
Kennedy, Annemarie, 145
Kerr, Paul, 11n
Kes (film), 45, 49; casting, 49; cinematography, 44–6; commercial success, 37; filming, 49–50; KL on working with Barry Hines, 49–50; KL's reflections on, 132; storyline and characters, 48, 50, 66, 187, 278, 356; other mentions, xi, xii, 30, 67, 100, 321
Kestrel Films, 37–8
Kiarostami, Abbas, 178–80
Kirby, Simone, 225n, 243, 249
Koch, Ed, 383
Kristofferson, Kris, 383
Kureishi, Hanif: *The Mother Country* (play), 362; script for *My Beautiful Laundrette* (film), 363; script for *Sammy and Rosie Get Laid* (film), 366
Kyle, Scott, 149

Ladybird, Ladybird (film), 109; budget, 90n; casting, 108, 214; filming, 108–10, 111; KL's reflections on, 108, 111, 132; origins, 107, 120, 160; Rebecca O'Brien works on, 373; reception, 91n; script (Rona Munro), 107–8; storyline and

characters, 91, 107–8, 112, 159–60; other mentions, xi, xii
Laing, R. D., 28, 28n
Land and Freedom (film), 115, 118; budget, 90n; casting, 374; filming, 110, 117, 119–20; framing sequences, 116; KL's reflections on, 132; music, 104, 347; origins, 112–13; Paul Laverty in, 235; script (Jim Allen), 113, 114, 117; storyline and characters, 91, 113–17, 235; other mentions, xi, xii, xiii, xvii, 24, 170, 221, 345, 373
Lane, Don, 317
Laverty, Paul, 385; interview with, 378–400

COLLABORATION WITH KL (RESEARCH AND FILM SCRIPTS): *11'09"01 – September 11*, 144, 201, 202, 214–15; *Ae Fond Kiss*, 152, 154, 155, 173, 174, 176; *The Angels' Share*, 144, 148, 150, 151, 183, 186–7, 397–8; *Bread and Roses*, 197, 199, 205–6, 393–4, 395; *Carla's Song*, 89, 91, 120, 121, 144, 384, 386; co-decision making, 188, 387; first contact and meetings, 384, 386; *Happy Ending*, 280; *I, Daniel Blake*, 322–3, 389, 395–7; input to casting, 387; *It's a Free World . . .*, 251, 255, 264, 268; *Jimmy's Hall*, 226, 227, 239–40, 242, 244, 248, 389, 392; *Looking for Eric*, 281, 283–4, 285–6; *My Name Is Joe*, 89, 92, 125, 144, 146, 158, 373, 394; *The Old Oak*, 320, 321, 322, 344, 350, 353, 380, 398–9, 404; *Route Irish*, 251, 255, 257, 271, 272–3, 275, 383; *Sorry We Missed You*, 337, 385; *Sweet Sixteen*, 144, 148, 163–4, 374; *Tickets*, 144, 179, 181, 279–80; *The Wind That Shakes the Barley*, 216, 221, 222n, 228–9, 233, 236–7, 370, 382–3, 389–92

LIFE AND OTHER WORK: activism, 385; appears in *Land and Freedom*, 235; becomes interested in film-making, 383–4; childhood and family, 378–9; discovers Paul Brannigan, 150; Enterprise Allowance Scheme funding, 385; friendship with John and Val Barron, 349; Fulbright scholarship to study screenwriting, 195–6, 387–8; human rights work in Nicaragua, 120, 205, 215, 381–2, 383–4; Irish family history, 229; legal training and practice in UK, 380–1; in Los Angeles, 195–7, 205, 393–4; marriage to Kate Hughes, 381; religious indoctrination, 379–80; in Rome, 379–80

VIEWS: on academic commentary on films, 397; on Aristotle's *Poetics*, 392–3; on Bengal famine, 378; on Catholic Church, 174; on Celtic, 181; on cost of war, 382, 383; on DWP's systematic cruelty, 396–7; on Iraq war, 270, 383; on James Connolly's achievements, 392; on Justice for Janitors campaign, 196–7; on KL's work and skills, 384, 386–7, 399–400; on 'quaint view' of Scotland, 151, 398; on right-wing press response to *The Wind That Shakes the Barley*, 221; on Sandinista revolution, Nicaragua, 381–2; on University of Southern California, 388; on women's roles in wars of resistance, 391; on writing treatments, 384

WRITING (IN GENERAL): attention to research and accuracy, 370, 371, 389–90; humour, 186–7, 322, 328–9; invisible structure, 388; keeping truthful to characters, xv, 148, 398; KL on, 125, 337, 353; subjecting characters to pressure and impossible choices, 393–4; writing methods, 188, 371

Lawton, Fiona, 218
Leigh, Carol, 199n
Leigh, Jacob, xiv
Leiper, Neil, 279, 319
Lenin, Vladimir, 241n, 304, 304n
Lenton, Susanna, 139
Levin, Bernard: on *Perdition*, 85
Lewis, Gary, 145, 176
Lightman, Gavin, 308n
Limehouse Declaration, 79–80
Littlewood, Joan, 22
Loach, Ken, 41, 51, 55, 65, 102, 181, 286, 367, 385

LIFE: birth, 1; car accident and son's death, 53, 53n; childhood and youth, 1, 2–3; early interests, 2, 3; family, 2,

3, 66; involvement with anti-Stalinist socialists, 335–6; involvement with Bath City football club, 280, 291, 292–4; Labour Party membership, 335, 342; National Service in RAF, 3–4; at Oxford University, 1, 4, 5; produces Labour Party broadcast, 335; understudy for *One Over the Eight*, 5–6; watches football with Eric Cantona, 284

COLLABORATIONS: Abbas Kiarostami, 178–80; Barry Ackroyd, 139–40, 197, 199, 207, 213, 346, 348; Barry Hines, 37, 48–50, 59–60, 64, 66–8, 72–3; Bill Jesse, 89, 97, 98, 99, 132, 138; Chris Menges see under Menges, Chris; David Gilchrist, 141–2; Donal Ó Drisceoil, 389; Eric Cantona, 278, 281, 283–4; Ermanno Olmi, 178–80; Fergus Clegg, 139; George Fenton, 347, 402–3; James O'Connor, 22, 23, 183; Jim Allen see under Allen, Jim; Jimmy Seabrook, 74–5; John McGrath, 9; Jonathan Morris, 199–200, 276, 312, 347–8; Kahleen Crawford, 355, 387; Martin Johnson, 63, 90n, 139; Neville Smith, 11, 29–31, 278, 288; Paul Laverty see under Laverty, Paul; Ray Beckett, 90n, 139, 140; Rebecca O'Brien see under O'Brien, Rebecca; Rob Dawber, 251, 252, 255, 258; Robbie Ryan, 185, 346; Roger Smith, 1, 14, 371, 389, 389n; Rona Munro, 89, 107; Sally Hibbin, 89–90, 97, 107, 369, 373; Susanna Lenton, 139; Tony Garnett see under Garnett, Tony; Trevor Griffiths, 38, 68–9, 135; Troy Kennedy Martin, 9

DIRECTING CAREER see also individual films; individual plays; individual TV series and episodes: assistant director with Northampton Repertory Theatre, 1, 6–7; attention to research and accuracy, 369, 370, 389; ATV work, 64; awards, 312; BBC debut (*Catherine*), 1; BBC trainee TV director, 1, 7; directing own works, 34, 38, 61–3; documentaries, 35, 38, 68, 72–3, 74–81, 82–4, 86–7, 170, 280; early TV work, 1, 7–9; falling out with Working Title over *Fools of Fortune*, 366; feature film budgets, 90n; financial issues, 43, 61, 63, 68, 366–7, 375–6; first film for Channel 4, 38; first foray into feature films, 37; first shoot on film, 22; founds Sixteen Films with Rebecca O'Brien, 373; four phases of, xi; hiatus after family tragedy, 53; influence on others, xiii; joins Parallax Pictures, 372–3; Kestrel Films establishment, 37; *The Old Oak* as last film, 399, 400, 403; political censorship, 72–3, 75, 78–81, 82, 83–6, 96, 133, 135, 137; quiet periods, 34, 35; reflections on successes, 131, 132, 271, 276; rejects offer of script from Robert Duvall, 131; rejuvenation in 1990s, 89–90; scholarship on, ixn, xiv; self-criticism, 8, 9, 39–40, 55, 58, 68–70, 111, 136, 138, 208, 213, 239, 242, 250, 271, 276–7, 292, 351, 357–9, 358; significance of contribution, x, xiii; theatre, 6–7, 72, 84–6; TV commercials, 92

DIRECTORIAL APPROACH, ARTISTIC/TECHNICAL MATTERS: 16mm film use, 139, 140, 258; avoiding caricatures and clichés, 56, 88; black-and-white photography, 308; boom use, 140; breaking BBC rules and conventions, 16; camera placement and lens choice, 26–7, 47–8, 139–40, 185–6, 331, 401; casting convincing people for roles, 20, 42, 51–2, 56, 130, 178, 204, 237–8, 337–8, 340–1, 356, 372, 387; casting taking precedence, 208–9; casting unconventional actors, 23, 30, 42, 51–2, 64, 108, 130, 145, 150, 151, 182, 204, 253, 262–3, 285, 327, 331, 339, 340–1, 374; cutting to music, 9, 10, 18; detail focus, 179–80; dissolves, 348; dream sequences, 29–30; economy and 'austerity', 101, 185, 346, 353, 370–1, 392; editing decisions, 347–8, 357–8; fact-fiction interplay, 11, 18, 26, 35, 91n, 96, 107, 160, 317, 318, 389; fades, 312, 348; first-person narration, 37; fragmentation, 15, 22,

23–4, 67–8, 116; framing sequences, 116; inappropriate soundtracks, 24; influences on, 37, 39, 43–4, 235, 346; landscape use, 48, 64; lighting, 23, 44–6, 58, 139; live studio work, 1, 9; location filming, 10–11, 15–16, 120–1, 126, 216, 258, 270, 271, 275–6, 319, 321, 327, 331–2, 333, 354–5, 359, 367–8; love-making scenes, 176; magical realism, 282, 288; 'magical' spaces, 321–2; 'modishness', 39–40; music, 104, 177–8, 347, 402–3; naturalism, xi–xii, 10, 11; non-naturalistic devices, 9; off-screen violence, xvi, 219–20, 258; political discourse use, 24–5, 54–5, 216, 218–19, 226, 227, 235–7, 345; refusal to post-synch, 42–3; scene blocking, 46; stills, 9; talking to camera, 1, 16–17, 22, 39; voice-overs, 1, 9

DIRECTORIAL APPROACH, WORKING WITH PEOPLE: auditioning, 6–7, 121, 238, 263, 287, 355–6, 387; avoiding being consciously political, 337–8; bypassing first assistant director, 141–2; concealing script from actors, 53, 97, 110, 190–1, 206–7, 288–90, 331, 332; filming in sequence, 239, 368; giving actors space and freedom, 45, 46, 47–8, 49–50, 99–100, 108, 130–1, 162, 338, 356; inclusivity, 130; love-making scenes, 176; number of takes, 46–7, 191–2; off-camera directing, 99–100, 108; protecting child actors, 111; unobtrusive proximity to actors during filming, 180, 190; using improvisation, 54, 97, 98, 110–11, 117, 253, 263; using lead-ins and run-ons, 141; waterboarding scene, 275; whole-team focus, 142–3, 203; working with 'grain' of actors, 242–3; working with less-experienced actors, 42, 52–3, 99–100, 143, 192; yawning penalty box on set, 142

RECEPTION AND REVIEWS, xiv–xv, xvii; *The Angels' Share* (film), 397; *Days of Hope* (TV drama), 57–8; *Hidden Agenda* (film), 89, 94, 96, 247n, 368–9; *I, Daniel Blake* (film), 312, 332, 332n, 377; *Ladybird, Ladybird* (film), 91n; *My Name Is Joe* (film), 397; *The Navigators* (film), 254; *The Old Oak* (film), 322, 398, 401; *The Wind That Shakes the Barley* (film), 219–21, 222–3, 229, 246–8, 246–7n, 312, 377

THEMES IN WORKS: absence of available good choices, 158–9, 163–4, 207, 252, 265, 332–3, 393–4; alcoholism and drug culture, 144–6, 147–8, 156, 158, 162, 163, 166; anti-immigration racism, 311, 311n, 318n, 320–1, 352–3, 358; British imperialism in Ireland, 216, 228–9; class betrayal, xi, 10, 11, 38, 76–7, 91, 117–19, 146, 209–10, 305, 316; class consciousness and dialectical struggle, 13; class exploitation, x–xi, xvi–xvii, 251, 252, 255, 260–2, 264–5, 267, 306, 314, 316–17, 333–4, 335, 349, 393–5, 403–4; class system, 64; comedy of everyday life, 263–4, 328–9; football, 278–81; hope, xii; kindness, 328, 330, 331–2, 355; love stories, 125–6, 151, 153–5, 175–6; masculine pride and fear of losing face, 166; mobile phone enslavement, 317–18; moral decisions, 182, 260–1; power and conflict, 32; prostitution, 207, 395; Scotland's 'kilts and sporrans' image, 151, 161, 183–4; Scotland's social breakdown, 144–5, 148, 150, 151, 156, 163; social morality tales, 90–1; socialist perspective, 220–2; solidarity, 119, 320, 322, 357, 359, 404; teamwork, 281, 282–3, 287; unemployment, 66–7, 145, 147, 163, 165; weaponized bureaucracy and 'conscious cruelty', 312, 323–5, 326, 331; working-class poverty, 311; working-class power, 212, 345

VIEWS: on 9/11 attacks and US government hypocrisy, 202, 213–14; on acting as suspension of disbelief, 190–1; on actors' vulnerability, 40–2; on aesthetics of film-making, 401, 402–3; on Anglo-Irish Treaty, 231–3; on anti-Stalinist socialism, 12–13; on *The Archers*, 141; on assimilation, 155, 173, 175; on asylum policy, 351; on Brexit protest voters, 350; on British behaviour during Irish Civil War, 220; on British exceptionalism, 269–70; on capitalization of Iraq War, 257, 270–1, 272; on casualized economy, 87–8, 98, 309–10, 335–6; on Catholic Church, 174, 240–1, 248; on civil wars, 229; on class conflict and exploitation, 170–1, 267–8, 269, 336; on climate emergency, 343–4; on comedy of everyday life, 264, 329; on comic timing, 263; on common ownership, 310; on 'conscious cruelty', 323–5, 331; on Conservative Party, 158; on David Cameron, 300, 306; on digital cameras, 141; on Éamon de Valera, 245; on Eric Cantona, 286; on film critics, 94–5; on 'film-makers' and teams, 189; on film music, 104; on filming/including love-making scenes, 176; on football club ownership, 290, 292–3, 294; on free-market economics, 129–30, 301; on gig economy, 171, 309, 329, 330, 334–5; on globalization, 88, 129; on 'good/bad guys', 186; on greed, 267–8; on homelessness, 27–8; on importance of history, 57; on importance of writers, 188, 189–90, 386; on individual vs societal responsibilities, 156–8; on industry and the economy, 33–4; on IRA and anti-colonial struggle, 245–6; on Jeremy Corbyn, 137, 167–70, 205, 300, 301, 302–3, 304, 305, 308, 309, 377; on Keir Starmer, 172, 244, 250, 265–6, 295–6, 300, 303, 306, 307, 343; on Labour Party, 12, 13, 36, 38, 167–8, 250, 303, 304–5, 307, 342–3, 359; on making mistakes, 143; on march of technology, 326; on Margaret Thatcher and Thatcherism, 74, 128, 129, 134, 156–7, 158, 165, 194, 215, 244, 261–2, 267, 300, 301, 306, 334–5, 344; on media partisanship, 134–5, 137, 167, 168, 171, 246–8, 269, 306–9, 325, 345; on Mike Lynch, 171–2; on need for social change, 166, 193–4, 302; on northeast communities and landscape, 327–8, 333, 350–1, 358–9; on older vs younger people, 126; on optimism/pessimism, 132, 155; on Palestine, 295–6; on 'poetry' and inevitability in pleasing film, 237; on political censorship, 81, 84, 85, 86, 137; on political correspondents, 344; on political prisoners, 234; on possible forms for TV dramas, 35–6; on power and conflict, 32–3; on pre-war attitudes to fascism, 170; on predictability of TV dramas, 23; on prostitution, 207, 332–3; on Rebecca O'Brien, 400; on the Romantics and modern loss of pastoral connection, 66; on Scotland's 'kilts and sporrans' image, 151, 161; on selfies, 169; on social and healthcare services, 160–1, 172, 323–4, 326, 327; on social democrats, 235; on societal consciousness, 265–6, 344; on team well-being, 142–3; on teenagers, 337, 339; on themes of politics on left vs right, 117–19; on three-act structure, 187–8; on Tony Benn, 303–4; on Tony Blair, 165, 244, 265, 270, 300, 306; on unemployment, 165, 185, 328; on unions and union leaders, 76–8, 134, 209–10; on well-read socialists, 210–12; on working-class drama (by others), 19; on working-class eloquence, 24, 236–7, 345; on working-class power, 212, 344–5; on working in US, 131, 203–5; on writers and script 'worship', 20–1

Lobb, Adrian, 350n
Logue, Christopher, 21
Looking for Eric (film), 278, 281–90, 286, 289, 294, 376
Looks and Smiles (film), xii, 38, 66–8, 67, 101, 280
Lopez, George, 197, 213
Losinka, Kate, 73
Louis, Jordan, 320
Lowe, Andrea, 257, 276
Lowe, Arthur, 263
Luckhurst, Tim, 220, 220n
The Lump (TV drama), 14n, 31n, 161n, 261

Lundberg, Craig, 272, 272n
LWT (London Weekend Television), 75, 83–4, 135

MacAskill, Ewen, 305n
MacAskill, Kenny, 380
McCormack, Gary, 147
McCourt, Emer, 98, *102*
McDonnell, John, 167, 168, 303, 305
McDormand, Frances, 93, 138, 238, 372
McEwan, Ian, 362
McGee, Jack, 197
McGlade, Chris, 320
Mcgowan, Rhys, 315, 338–9, 338n, *338*, 376
McGrath, John, 1, 9
McKay, David, 145
McKee, Tommy, 147
McKiernan, Dylan, 313, 329
McKnight, George, xin, 91n
MacLean, Charles, 192
McLibel: Two Worlds Collide (documentary), 295
McNulty, Matthew, 281
Madden, Paul, 75–6
Maeda, Estela, 197
Magee, Francis, 226, 249
Maitland, Gary, 149, 178, *181*, 182, *184*, 190, 279
Major, John, 253
Makhmalbaf, Samira, 201
Mari, Ebla, 279, 319, 355, *359*
Marr, Andrew, 344
Marsh, Steve, 282
Martin, Gilbert, 149
Martin, Troy Kennedy, 1, 9, 10
Marx, Karl, 343n
Matthews, Peter, 202
Maxwell, Robert, 80
May, Theresa, 377
Mear One (Kalen Ockerman), 169n
Mearns, Raymond, *176*
Melrose, Dianna, 382n
Menges, Chris, 65; cinematography for *If* (film), 44; cinematography for *Michael Collins* (film), 219; on KL, x
COLLABORATION WITH KL (CINEMATOGRAPHY/CAMERA WORK): *Fatherland* (film), 136; *The Gamekeeper* (film), 38; *Kes* (film), 37, 44–6; *Poor Cow* (film), 44; *Route Irish* (film), 258; *Which Side Are You On?* (documentary), 83
Menzel, Jiří, 44
Mercer, David, 11, 28
Mercer, Joe, 292
Michael Collins (film), 219
Miliband, Ralph, 304, 304n
Mirza, Sunna, 152
Mohammed, Khalid Sheikh, 273n
Moore, Dudley, 5
Moorhouse, Justin, 282, 287, 290
Morris, David, 295
Morris, Jonathan: editing principles, 347–8; edits *Bread and Roses* (film), 199–200; edits *I, Daniel Blake* (film), 312; edits *Route Irish* (film), 276
Morrison, Jon, 147
The Mother Country (play), 362
Mr. Hulot's Holiday (film), 180
Mullan, Peter, 126–7, 145, 150, *157*, 160, 162, 279, 372
Mulvey, Laura, 362
Munro, Rona, 89, 107
Murfi, Mikel, 226
Murphy, Cillian, 216, 217, 237–9, *238*, 372, 382
Murphy, Mary, 217
Murphy, Pete, 140
Murphy, William Martin, 230n
Murray, Jonathan, 173
My Beautiful Laundrette (film), 362, 363
My Name Is Joe (film), 126–7, *157*, 160; academic commentary on, 397; budget, 90n; casting, 145, 162, 372, 384; filming, 126, 162; reception, 397; script (Paul Laverty), 92, 125, 144, 146, 158, 373, 394; storyline and characters, 125–6, 145–6, 156, 158–9, 161, 162, 279, 282; other mentions, xii, 151, 373
Myles, Lynda, 361, 364, 365

National Film Finance Corporation, 38, 61
National Film Theatre (NFT), 82
The Navigators (film), 260; casting, 262–3, 340; cinematography, 140; filming, 255, 262; reception, 254; script (Rob Dawber), 251, 252, 255, 258–9, 260, 261; storyline and characters, 251–3, 254, 256–7, 259–61, 263–4, 305, 316–17; other mentions, 280, 333, 335, 373

Neave, Airey, 94, 94n
Newman, Sydney, 10
Nimri, Najwa, 257
Northampton Repertory Theatre, 1, 6–7
Norton, Jim, 224, 243

Ó Drisceoil, Donal, 222, 223, 223n, 389
O'Brien, Rebecca: early life, 360–1, 364–5; influences on, 363, 364, 365, 366; interview with, 360–77; mother, 360, 363, 364; political education, 364–5
  EARLY CAREER: at Crosswind Films, 361–2; at Edinburgh Film Festival, 361, 364, 365; as location manager, 362, 363; as production assistant, 363; as production manager, 362; at Riverside Studios, 361, 362–3, 364, 365
  COLLABORATION WITH KL: *Bread and Roses* (film), 374–5; co-founds Sixteen Films, 373; first and last shoots, 368; first meeting, 366; input to casting, 372; input to locations, 371; input to writing, 371; joins Parallax Pictures, 373; location scout for *Ladybird, Ladybird* (film), 373; Paul Laverty on, 400; produces *Another City: A Week in the Life of Bath's Football Club*, 280; produces *Bread and Roses*, 195, 204, 373; produces *Hidden Agenda* (film), 96–7, 138, 366–9, 370; produces *Land and Freedom* (film), 370, 373; produces *Looking for Eric* (film), 376; produces *My Name Is Joe* (film), 372, 373; produces *Sorry We Missed You* (film), 367; produces *Sweet Sixteen* (film), 374; produces *The Navigators* (film), 373; recommends Ray Beckett to KL, 139
  OTHER PRODUCING WORK: *Bean* (film), 365; *Echoes* (TV series), 366; *Friendship's Death* (film), 365–6
  VIEWS: on funding for films, 375–6; on impact of KL's films, 377; on KL's work and skills, 366, 369, 370–1; on political conviction, 369; on production processes, 363–4, 369–70, 374–5; on working with vulnerable people, 376
O'Byrne, Brian F., 224

O'Connor, James, 22, 23, 183
O'Donoghue, Father, 240
O'Dowd, Father, 240
O'Duffy, Eoin, 224–5n
O'Hare, Aidan, 390
O'Kelly, Donal, 239, 239n, 385
The Old Oak (film), 354, 359; casting, 318, 320, 335, 339, 355–6, 357; cinematography, 354–5; editing, 348, 357–8; filming, 327, 356; financing, 375; as KL's last film, 399, 400, 403; KL's reflections on, 358; 'magical' spaces in, 320–1; music, 347, 402–3; reception, 322, 398, 401; research and script (Paul Laverty), 320, 321, 322, 344, 350, 353, 380, 398–9, 404; storyline and characters, 279, 311, 311n, 318–22, 318n, 328, 329, 349, 351–4, 355, 356–7, 358, 359, 398–9, 401–2; other mentions, xv, 313, 345
Olmi, Ermanno, 178–80
O'Malley, Ernie, 230, 389
Ondříček, Miroslav, 44
One Over the Eight (revue), 5
Orellana, Maria, 198
O'Riordan, Mary, 217, 390
Orphans (film), 372
Osborne, George, 325, 325n, 396
Osborne, John, 5
O'Sullivan, Michael, 323
Ouédraogo, Idrissa, 201
Oxford University, 1, 4, 5

Padilla, Pilar, 197, 206–7, 209, 375
Pannach, Gerulf, 69
Parallax Pictures, 89–90, 97, 369, 372–3
Parry, Marc, 234n
Paxman, Jeremy, 344
Pearse, Patrick, 232, 232n
Percival, Lance, 5, 6
Perdition (play), 31n, 72, 84–6, 136–7; published by Ithaca Press, 137n
Perrie, Lynne, 262
Pilger, John, 87
Pinochet, Augusto, 201, 202, 213, 215
Play for Today (TV series): *The Price of Coal*, 14n, 38, 59–60, 60; *The Rank and File*, xi, xiii, 11, 31n, 32, 33, 34
Play It Again, Sam (film), 283
Poor Cow (film), xii, 37, 39–40, 41–2, 42–3, 207

POUM (Partido Obrero de Unificación Marxista), 114, *115*, 116, 117
The Price of Coal (TV drama), 14n, 38, 59–60, *60*
Proctor, Katie, 315, *338*, 339, *341*
Puttnam, David, 92–3, 370

A Question of Leadership (documentary), 72–3, 75–6
Questions of Leadership (documentaries), xi, 24, 72, 73, 75–7, 78–80, 82–3

Radclyffe, Sarah, 366
Raddatz, Martha, 273n
Raining Stones (film), xii, xiii, 31n, 89, 90–1, 90n, 104–7, *106*, 139–40
Ramzan, Shy, 152
The Rank and File (TV drama), xi, xiii, 11, 31n, 32, *33*, 34
Rasool, Talib, 257
Rastgou, Davoud, 256
Ratcliff, Sandy, *51*, 52
Reilly, Siobhan, 149
Riaz, Ahmad, 152, *176*
Riddall, Michael, 51
Riefenstahl, Leni, 220, 220n, 247
Riff-Raff (film), 102–3; budget and financing, 90n, 97; casting, 98, 263; cinematography, 139; filming, 100; KL's reflections on, 99, 132; Paul Laverty on, 384; script (Bill Jesse), 97, 138; storyline and characters, 90, 98–9, 138, 164–5; other mentions, xii, xiii, 15, 31n, 221, 251, 333
Riggins, Jasmin, 149, *184*
Ritman, Alex, 296n
Riverside Studios, London, 361, 362–3, 364, 365
Robinson, Derek 'Red Robbo', 73
Robinson, Nick, 344
Robinson, Tommy, 350, 350n
Rock, Crissy, 108–10, *109*, 262
Rodgerson, Claire, 319, 320, 350, 350n, 357
Rolinson, David, 308n
Rose, David, 362
Rosen, Michael, 363, 364
Ross, Willie, 263
Route Irish (film), 274; Cannes screening, 270; cinematography, 258; filming, 275–6; financing, 375; KL's reflections on, 271, 276–7; research and script (Paul Laverty), 251, 255, 257, 271, 272–3, 275, 383; storyline and characters, 255, 257–8, 271, 273–5, 276–7; other mentions, xvii, 203, 251, 383
Royal Court Theatre, 84–6
Ruane, William, 147, 149, 178, *181*, *182*, *184*, 218, 279
Rutter, Kate, 312
Ryan, Robbie, *185*, 346

St. James, Margo, 199n
Sammy and Rosie Get Laid (film), 366
Sandford, Jeremy, 26, 41
Sarler, Carol, 91n
Save the Children Fund, 74–5
Scargill, Arthur, 77, 210, 210n, 308, 308n
Scott, Andrew, 226, 248
Seabrook, Jeremy, 7, 74–5
Seeger, Pete, 383
Serwotka, Mark, 327
Sewell, George, 16–17, 22
Shakespeare, William: KL's enjoyment of, 2, 235; *Much Ado About Nothing* (allusion to), 266; *Richard II*, 269n
Shann, Briana, 313, 329
Shaw, George Bernard, 325
Sherman, Geraldine, *17*
The Siege of Manchester (play), 20
Sight and Sound (magazine), 95, 202
Sikazwe, Kema, 312
Silkin, Sam, 80
Sixteen Films, 278, 281, 373–4, 374n
Skidmore, Rob, 293
Skirton, Alan, 292
Smith, Neville: acting work, 29, 31, *33*; Everton fan, 281; script for *After a Lifetime* (TV drama), 30–1; script for *The Golden Vision* (TV drama), 11, 29–30, 278, 288
Smith, Roger: importance of collaboration with KL, 14, 371; script editor for *The Wind That Shakes the Barley* (film), 389; script for *Catherine*, 1; story editor for *Wear a Very Big Hat* (TV drama), 389n
Snowden, Philip, 304n, 305n
Sorry We Missed You (film), *338*, *341*, 367, 385; casting, 338–9, 340–1; cinematography, 140; filming, 349; financing, 375; first UK public

screening, 317; music, 347; origins, 317; storyline and characters, 171, 262, 279, 311, 314–18, 330, 333–4, 336–42, 349, 356; other mentions, xv, 161, 197, 251, 269, 320, 328, 345
South Bank Show (TV series), 82, 83–4
The Spirit of '45 (documentary), 170, 201, 297–300, 301, 303, 305–6, 308, 309, 310, 344
Squires, Hayley, 311, 313, 329, 331
Stafford-Clark, Max, 84, 85–6, 137
Stalker, John, 93n
Stamp, Terence, 41
Stanbrook, Ivor, 247n, 368
Starmer, Keir, 172, 244, 250, 265–6, 295–6, 300, 303, 303n, 306, 307, 343
Steel, Helen, 295
Stone, Oliver, 267n
Stone, Rhys *see* Mcgowan, Rhys
Streeting, Wes, 172
Sugar, Alan, 267
Sunak, Rishi, 311, 396
Sweet Sixteen (film), 144, 146–8, 163–4, 164, 165–6, 179, 184–5, 281, 282
Sylvester, Rachel, 267n

Tait, Col, 321
Tap on the Shoulder (TV drama), 183
Tati, Jacques, 180
Temple, David, 350, 350–1n
Thatcher, Margaret, and Thatcherism: economic policies, 74, 129, 145, 194, 253, 256, 300, 301, 334–5; election results, 38, 334; KL on, 74, 128, 129, 134, 156–7, 158, 165, 194, 215, 244, 261–2, 267, 300, 301, 306, 334–5, 344; 'no such thing as society', 194, 194n; supports Pinochet, 215; and trade unions, 134, 261–2, 318n
Thompson, Eileen, 299
Thomson, Alice, 267n
Thomson, Lord George, 79
Thornett, Alan, 211, 211n
3 Clear Sundays (TV drama), 22
Tickets (film), 144, 178–82, 181, 279–80
Tickner, Clive, 138
Time to Go (documentary), xi
To Each His Own Cinema (anthology film): *Happy Ending* (KL and Paul Laverty's contribution), 280
Todd, Helen MacGregor, 200n

Tomlinson, Ricky, 98, 100, *103*, 138, 164, 211, 263
Tookey, Chris, 220
Townsend, Joseph, 324–5n
Tracey, Venn, 252, 260
Trainspotting (film), 151
Tressell, Robert, 211, 211n
Trump, Donald, 186
Trussell Trust, 324n
Turner, Dave, 279, 311, 315, 318–19, *351*, *354*, 355–6, *359*, 376
Turner, Vickery, 17

UK Film Council, 375
Up the Junction (film), 21
Up the Junction (TV drama), xii, 10, 14n, 15–21, 17, 19, 98, 100

Vega, Vladimir, 108, 201, 201n, 202, 213, 214–15
The View from the Woodpile (documentary), 35

Walker, Alexander, 215, 369
Walker, Peter, 297n
Wall Street (film), 267n
Wallace, Colin, 94, 94n
Ward, Barry, 223–4, 226, 242–3, 249–50, 392
Wareing, Kierston, 255, 266, 270
Watts, Sam, 299, 300
Wear a Very Big Hat (TV drama), 389n
Webb, Rita, 22
Wednesday Plays (TV series), 1, 10, 17, 35–6; *The Big Flame*, xi, xii, xiii, 11, 14n, 24, 31–2, 86; *Cathy Come Home see Cathy Come Home*; *The Coming Out Party*, 22, 23; *The End of Arthur's Marriage*, 21–2; *The Golden Vision*, xii, 11, 14n, 29, 254, 278, 281, 282, 288, 293; *In Two Minds*, xi, 11, 14n, 28, 50–1; *The Lump*, 14n, 31n, 161n, 261; *Tap on the Shoulder*, 183; *3 Clear Sundays*, 22; *Up the Junction*, xii, 10, 14n, 15–21, 17, 19, 98, 100; *Wear a Very Big Hat*, 389n
Welland, Colin, 50, 278
West, Sandy, *157*
Which Side Are You On? (documentary), xiii, 82, 83–4, 135, 335
White, Carol: in *Cathy Come Home*, 25,

26, 42; in *The Coming Out Party*, 22; KL on, 40–2; in *Poor Cow*, 37, 39, 41–2; in *Up the Junction*, 17; other work, 40

Why Not Productions, 376

Williams, Kenneth, 5

Williams, Trevor, 257, 275

Wilson, Harold, 334n, 335

The Wind That Shakes the Barley (film), 217, 236, 238; casting, 237–9; filming, 216; financing, 375; origins, 239–40, 382; premiere in Cork, 390; in public discourse, 377; published screenplay, 222, 222n; reception, 219–21, 222–3, 229, 246–8, 246–7n, 312, 377; research and script (Paul Laverty), 216, 221, 222n, 228–9, 233, 236–7, 370, 382–3, 389–92; storyline and characters, xv–xvi, 216–19, 220–2, 223, 228, 229–31, 233–4, 235, 237, 239, 240; other mentions, xvii, 151, 170, 345

Winstone, Ray, 111

Wise, Herbert, 20

Wollen, Peter, 362, 365–6

Womack, Mark, 255, 274, 275, 276

Wood, Heather, 318, 335, 357

Working Title Films Limited, 365, 366

Yaqub, Atta, 152, 153, 176, 279

Z Cars (TV series), 1, 7–9, 20

ZDF (Zweites Deutsches Fernsehen), 71

Zubaydah, Abu, 273n

Żurek, Lesław, 256